PARTIES AND DEMOCRACY

GW00760418

PARTIES AND DEMOCRACY: PARTY STRUCTURE AND PARTY PERFORMANCE IN OLD AND NEW DEMOCRACIES

Edited by Richard Hofferbert

ISBN 0-631-209301

First published 1998

Blackwell Publishers
108 Cowley Road, Oxford, OX4 1JF, UK

and

250 Main Street, Malden, MA 02148, USA.

British Library Cataloguing in Publication Data applied for.

Library of Congress Data applied for.

Printed in Great Britain by Page Bros, Norwich

Printed on acid free paper

CONTENTS

Acknowledgements

It is an honour to have been asked to edit a special issue of *Political Studies*. I wish, first, to thank two institutions for valuable support during the time that this volume was being organised: The Netherlands Institute for Advanced Studies, which provided me a Resident Fellowship; and my home institution, The State University of New York at Binghamton, for a sabbatical leave. In addition, I am very grateful to my contributors for their promptness, erudition, and helpfulness throughout this project.

Introduction: Party Structure and Performance in New and Old Democracies

RICHARD I. HOFFERBERT

Preface: A Common Model

By the late 1990s it has become commonplace to assert that the decade has been historically unprecedented in the number of countries throwing off authoritarian regimes – more or less peacefully – and beginning the process of building democracies. Certainly in the eyes of those who were themselves key actors in this surge of political experimentation, the structure and performance of political parties has been viewed as among the most, if not *the* most, significant part of the road to democratic consolidation. Thus it was appropriate and timely for *Political Studies* to commission a volume addressing party structure and performance. Upon accepting that commission, I cast widely for a group of authors qualified and motivated to address the theme. In assembling such a group, I was concerned to include both long-established and widely-recognized experts as well as younger scholars, especially from some of the emerging democracies. In addition to a generational and geographic mix of authors, I sought also to bring into the volume a variety of methodological approaches, in particular a mix of in-depth narrative case studies of particular countries' experiences, on the one hand, and cross-national comparative analyses, on the other. One of the insights gained from this effort was to affirm that the democratic experiments of the 1990s are, without question, being extraordinarily well-documented, both within and across the emerging democracies. A generation of talented and well-prepared social scientists from within those new polities has been launched upon the stage of international scholarship. Further, scholars from the older as well as the newer democracies are chronicling the experiments of the latter and testing with these experiments theories developed from the more established systems, often with the effect of challenging key assumptions of and research based upon long-standing approaches.

The mandate given to the authors in this volume was deliberately and stubbornly ambiguous. Potential authors were asked to submit a short prospectus, outlining how they would deal with the topic 'party structure and performance'. No definitions or limits were given. Requests for further elaboration were not honoured, in order that the products could themselves be used as a test of the extent to which there is a widely shared theory of parties, at least insofar as a *theory* consists of a delimited and mutually relevant set of core questions, the significance of which is generally accepted. In effect, the volume has been assembled in response to a survey of experts, requested to respond at their leisure to a broad open-ended question.

What have been the results of that 'survey'? They clearly affirm that there is a rudimentary theory of political parties shared across geography and generations of scholars. The list of questions addressed – at least by this set of twelve scholars, themselves from seven countries, collectively dealing with the experiences of dozens of polities – is delimited, connected, and generally shared. Scholars from emerging democracies ask many of the same questions (often employing the same measurement tactics) addressed by students of more established systems. The authors are uniform in their conviction that the health of political parties is a useful metric for the health of a democracy. And, while individually focusing on different facets, they exhibit little disagreement about the essential structural features of parties worthy of examination or about what performance standards should be met if parties are doing their job within the broad parameters of a democratic system.

In other words, it makes sense to explore the *structure* and the *performance* of political parties as a key facet of the functioning of a democratic polity. Beyond citing this rather rudimentary agreement, it is also possible, with but a bit of license, to construct out of this set of essays a simple model for the analysis of party structure and performance.

A Model for Analysis of Party Structure and Performance

In its (perhaps overly) elemental form a model that would encompass the concerns of the authors in this volume looks rather like this:

History—Society—Economy
↓
Institutional—Constitutional Design
↓
Organizational Form and Leadership
↓
Party Performance

History – Society – Economy: Political analysts often succumb to one of two avoidable threats. The first threat is excessive *historicism*, in which events are viewed from such a long perspective that the likelihood of purposeful and effective human intervention into political events is all but excluded from concern. Thus, one is sometimes tempted to accept the fact that Russia is doomed to political purgatory because of the history of royal and then communist absolutism.[1] Some post-communist countries had a pre-war democratic episode with vigorous parties bearing the same titles and, perhaps, comparable basic ideology as their contemporary counterparts. These historic roots provide at least symbolic continuity to some of today's parties.[2] Countries so blessed (for example, Lithuania, the Czech Republic) seem, on the whole, to be doing rather better in developing effective parties and party systems than countries lacking such a heritage.

More recent historical circumstances, especially those surrounding the fall of the communist regimes, also condition the pace and form of the party structures that emerge through post-revolutionary years. Although most of the work represented in this volume must, of necessity, rely on little more than a

[1] A lesson *not* drawn by Grigorii Golosov in his analysis, later in this volume, of Russia's frustratingly slow progress toward institutionalization of a competitive party system.

[2] See essays by, respectively, David Olson, Algis Krupavicius, Gabor Toka, and Michel Klima. Contrast the role of historical parties in the countries they examine with the experiences of Russia, reported by Golosov, and Turkey, reported by Carkoglu.

half-decade experience, that experience yields some clear evidence of some general patterns of transformation in party systems in new democracies.

One aspect that must be examined is the form of the movement that brought down the old system. Poland and Czechoslovakia had a very different experience, with more or less heroic leadership of mass movements, than was the case in Hungary, moving more stepwise through *goulash communism*. Mass movements held together by common loathing of the old regime are almost doomed to fracture when opportunities for competition are put in place. Neither Solidarity nor Civic Forum any longer dominates political power in their respective countries. No matter how much admiration observers may hold for Solidarity's heroic role in the fall of communism, it is still reasonable to assume that it could not encompass all the likely interests within a competitive political system. In that sense, however laudable their role in bringing down authoritarianism, heroic movements are doomed to dissolve or, at least, to undergo a drastic metamorphosis if they are to play the game of competitive politics. History dictates such a fate.

Thus, one must understand the constraints imposed by the recent as well as the distant past upon current actors. However, excessive stress on the force of history may merely provide excuses for contemporary blunders, if not for fatalism. Yet politicians can be held responsible for the manner in which they carry and dispose of the weight of history.

The second avoidable threat, however, is *ahistoricism*, in which the past is treated as an error term in the equation used to diagnose current events. That is, the only differences that seem to matter are those between sets of contemporary experiences. Parties are what they are now. If they do not adequately aggregate interests and present the voters with coherent choices, or if they do not sufficiently structure and discipline the behaviour of parliamentarians so as to produce effective policies, it must be because the parties within the system are improperly organized and/or poorly led. Such historical blunders reinforce a tendency to overstate the room for manoeuvre of current actors.

One can observe several countries' political parties, for example, and conclude that the key to effective performance is professionalized organization within individual parties or that intelligent reform of the electoral system will minimize distortion of interest representation via specialized parties. To improve party performance, the ahistorical approach suggests, policy makers need merely choose to re-draft the organization charts of the parties and/or redesign the electoral laws. This puts too heavy a burden on the policy maker, or at least leaves the analyst looking a bit naive in the face of striking differences in the historical setting.

The authors in this volume succumb to neither of these threats. Rather, as a set and usually individually, their essays look for the important elements of history that sets the stage, and thus constrain options for constitutional designers and party leaders. The essays recognize that those who design and those who work within contemporary institutions have some latitude to work with the material provided by history.

Institutional Constitutional Design

To be sure, a good stage set does not guarantee a good performance. Neither does a primitive set preclude stunning acting. The social circumstances with which would-be politicians and decision makers must deal may, at any moment, appear given. Yet even something so seemingly fixed as the country's boundaries have been shown to be eminently manipulable. Thus the *velvet divorce* in Czechoslovakia or the pace and form of German unification were matters designed and chosen by political actors working with and creating options out of inherited circumstances. The frequent military interventions in Turkish politics, along with the juntas' banning and selective licensing of parties, have led, as Ali Carkoglu's essay notes, to low voter involvement and loyalty, party fragmentation, and parties dominated by sometimes capricious elites. None of these circumstances was historically inevitable. It seems superfluous to make such observations about sophisticated social science; yet key elements of the interaction between history and individual initiative are often overlooked in the search for causal closure.

High on the agenda of seemingly malleable factors that condition the course of party development are institutional and constitutional design. From Aristotle's *Politics* to the current British Labour party programme, it has been recognized that legal rules and forms adapt to historical and cultural circumstances. The rules are never neutral in their impact. But the search for an appropriate match between society and institutions is guided by the choices made by those people who write franchise requirements and the basic rules by which such entities as parties are moulded. Some of the political science discipline's most distinguished figures have attained and sustained their eminence by studying and writing about the match between a polity's cultural and economic composition, on the one hand, and the structure of party-influencing institutions, on the other.[3]

Nothing short of morally repugnant ethnic-cleansing will remove the Russian minorities from the Baltics or the Turkish-speakers from Bulgaria. These ethnic groups are there because of often sordid historical experiences – experiences that cannot simply be willed out of the record. However, those who design and operate the machinery of government choose among options about how to set up, for example, an election law that ensures inclusion or exclusion of such groups from the kind of effective party system and representation they might feel is legitimate. Institutional design, in other words, can be used to address human conditions produced by unchangeable history.

The decade of the 1990s has seen a virtual orgy of institutional design, enhanced through academic tourism by scholar-advisors from established democracies travelling to the emerging ones. David Olson's essay, which immediately follows these prefatory remarks, provides a useful directory to the institutional choices made in the years following the fall of communism. The variation in electoral laws (for example, proportional representation vs. majority or plurality, vote thresholds, single member vs. multi-member districts) and structures of parliament (for example, unicameral vs. bicameral) stand as a challenge to any historical, social, or economic deterministic explanation of institutional design choices in the emerging democracies. As Algis Krupavicius shows in his carefully constructed analysis of Lithuania's evolving party system, even such seemingly mundane decisions as the size of parliamentary factions recognized in internal organization or the structure of public versus private

---

[3] See, perhaps most notably: A. Lijphart, *Democracy in Plural Societies* (New Haven: Yale University Press, 1977).

finance of parties' election expenses appear to have consequences that are relatively foreseeable.

Institutional design does not inevitably produce the expected result, as seen in the examples of Lithuania and Turkey (via Krupavicius and Carkoglu, respectively). In general, there is no reason to doubt the likely effect of steps taken to limit party fragmentation, in particular a first-past-the-post election system or a substantial hurdle under proportional representation. However, such devices are far from mechanically efficient. An ironic situation is seen in the contrast of the quite fractionalised Lithuanian Senate, with single member districts, and the more orderly party composition of the lower house, elected with PR. In Turkey, despite the imposition of an uncommonly high minimum threshold for entry into parliament (10%, nationally), there are six significant parties represented. Institutions and rules, therefore, themselves constrain leaders, but internal organizational form and choices of leaders matter as well.

An uncertainty evident in the following essays is how to view party fragmentation and volatility. Clearly, one party is not enough for a real democracy. But how many are too many? Apparently, Italy may have had too many. Maybe the United States has too few. In a sense, however, the numbers game begs part of the question of the bias of forms and rules. In a mature party system, it would seem that the fewer the parties, the less likelihood that new entities could evolve and join the circle. Joseph Willey presents sound theoretical reasoning in support of the argument that new parties have a relatively easier time gaining status as regular combatants in systems with many rather than few members per parliamentary district, where a national PR list system is considered a single district with as many members as there are seats in parliament, contrasted to a single member district system, where the number per jurisdiction is one.

Likewise, federal rather than a unitary and parliamentary rather than presidential systems should ease the way for new parties. With a novel dataset, covering several decades and nearly a score of established democracies, and using a generous rule for what constitutes a new 'party', Willey's analysis supports the claim that new parties' chances are affected by district 'magnitude'. But the expected disadvantage from either unitary or presidential systems is not evident. As Olson's enumeration shows, none of the newer democracies has adopted an exclusively single-member-district system, opting, as it were, for ease of entry by novel partisan entities at the possible price of party system stability.

Organizational Form – Leadership

Success may have doomed Solidarity or Civic Forum to 'step down' from their historic forms if they were to survive in the crass business of day-to-day political struggle. Status as a heroic movement does not necessarily translate into a readiness to become just one more competitor in an open contest. Walensa himself has often displayed impatience with, if not disdain for, opposing groups. As Michal Klima's essay suggests, Havel chose a different course, in effect, yielding operative power for a symbolic role, thus staying somewhat above the fray while still tolerating the nitty-gritty facets of partisan politics. Boris Yeltsin surely had some political capital that could have been invested in party organization. But his stance has been more in line with that of de Gaulle a few decades earlier, eschewing the mundane business of building a party structure.

Golosov's review of the trials of party-building efforts in Russia underscores the highly personalistic nature of the succession of groupings that have provided what little structure there has been in the succession of parliamentary elections there. The fragility of personalistic politics shows up both in Russia and in Turkey in the form of an extraordinary (for a system with half a century's experience with inter-party competition) fragmentation and volatility, with minimum opportunity for voter loyalty or party responsibility. Most of the detail on the new democracies suggests that the germ from which both the patterning of leadership and the policy identity of the parties emerges is most commonly found in the parliamentary groups. And, again, the extent to which parliamentary leaders take seriously the business of building party organization is variable and important.

Early scholarship on political parties would have expected modern parties to experience quite the opposite of personalistic partisanship. Roberto Michels, early in the present century, saw even the broad-based socialist parties as inevitably falling under the control of a small, professional elite. In fact, as Rachel Gibson and Robert Harmel clearly show, quite the opposite has happened. Examining loci of control by party family type, these authors contrast control by the extra-parliamentary elite, with the parliamentary party group, and both against membership control. And it is the socialist parties that show the greatest degree of internal democracy, having quite effectively resisted the *iron law of oligarchy*. Further, there is no evidence in any of the parties that the parliamentary group is subservient to extra-parliamentary party elites, contrary to Michels' prediction. On the other hand, there is little evidence, in the emerging democracies that mass membership will be a principle defining characteristic of the parties. Rather, Olson argues that they will stabilize as *cadre-catchall* parties. He does not, however, see such a development as particularly limiting on the general democratic performance of the party systems.

Party Performance

The contributing authors have produced a relatively short list of *performance* indicators. Most of the specific performance features examined are at least implicit in Krupavicius's outline of the purposes of parties in a democratic polity:

> ... a major element of the post-communist democratization is a revival of parties and multi-party systems. This element is important not only as a structural part of political or institutional democracy, but also as a basic component of the polity through which citizens can express their alternative demands and preferences, that is, a role of the parties as intermediate structures in a democratic political system. The parties serve as the channels through which societal interests are articulated and aggregated. They serve also as the procedural and institutional instruments for creating a competitive political environment. Finally ..., it is clear that consolidation of democracy takes the form of more or less stable party government.

Thus the parties that make up a system, to get a high performance score, must serve as a means by which voters can choose between competing entities standing for alternative policy packages. To some, such may seem an excessively

rigid standard. Comparative research on party programmes and policy priorities, however, suggest that it is not an unrealistic standard.[4] The articulation
and aggregation of societal interests by parties matched to the historical
cleavages in western systems has been a central theme of parties research at least
since the 1967 publication of Seymour Martin Lipset and Stein Rokkan's classic
essay.[5]

The extent to which parties fulfil these functions, however, require a degree of
stability in the structure of electoral competition and parliamentary organization. Much of democratic control rests not only on voters' ability to make
meaningful electoral choices *predictive* of policy performance, but also on the
ability of voters to inflict *retrospective* electoral punishment for party failure.
When the cast of combatants from one election to the next is unpredictable,
neither the preview nor the retrospection of responsibility is possible. Nor can
political leaders engage in policy making activity with the confidence and
persuasiveness that comes from a loyal corps of supporters in parliament and
the electorate. The extreme in electoral instability is seen when the major
contenders are nearly entirely different, or at least differently labelled, from one
election to the next, as has been the case in post-communist Russia and in
Turkey following each of the three military interventions between 1960 and
1980. Similar instability appears in parliaments when large numbers of
members defect to a partisan group different from the one under whose standard they were elected. Again, Russia provides the extreme case, but one of
degree rather than kind in the new democracies.

What pattern of interests are or ought to be articulated by the parties?
Established theory, flowing from the example of Lipset and Rokkan, sees
parties standing for the competing sides of societal cleavages. Those cleavages,
in turn, have evolved over the centuries, from the church-state conflict of former
times to the worker-capital competition in industrialized democracies. The left-
right dimension has been seen as the policy reflection of this feature of modern
democracies. Carkoglu sees the light at the end of the Turkish tunnel being the
eventual alignment of party competition along this 'modern' dimension, with
confusion and instability continuing so long as older lines of political combat
remain highly salient.

However, that may be a prescription for shooting at a moving target.
Cleavage politics, as such, anchored in long-standing sociocultural differences,
may be declining relative to seemingly more fluid *value* groupings in modern
societies. If voters make their selections on the basis of current values rather
than their 'deeper' concerns, based either on cultural identity or on socio-
economic status and its attendant material interests, we may have grounds to
fear for the processes of democratic competition in the so-called *established*
democracies, not to mention the effect of such seemingly fickle anchorage of
partisanship in the struggling newer democratic experiments. Gabor Toka offers
a counterweight to such concern. He analyses the extent to which voter loyalty
in Poland, Hungary, the Czech Republic, and Slovakia varies as a function of

[4] I. Budge, R. I. Hofferbert, and H-D. Klingemann, *Parties, Policies, and Democracy* (Boulder CO, Westview, 1994).
    [5] S. M. Lipset and S. Rokkan, 'Cleavage Structure, Party Systems, and Voter Alignments: An Introduction,' in Lipset and Rokkan (eds), *Party Systems and Voter Alignments* (New York, Free, 1967).

whether or not the electors are 'cleavage', socio-economic 'structural', or 'value' voters. He finds that, in fact, value-voting tends to yield more enduring party loyalty than either of the seemingly more solidly anchored alternatives. He draws the inference from this finding that parties will serve the democratic development of their countries best if they project and stick to a clear set of ideological and policy priorities, thus providing value-oriented voters with a reason to stay loyal.

Both volatility and party system fragmentation have the attractiveness of measurability at the aggregate level, and thus these features show up in several of the essays in this volume. Granting the relevance of party system stability to meaningful voter choice and parliamentary responsibility, low volatility or fragmentation are not democratic goals in themselves.[6] If the basic democratic premise is accepted that the ultimate test of the system is the extent to which it conforms to the will of the people, then one cannot assess the performance of a party system without attention to how citizens themselves react under differing partisan conditions.

Christopher Anderson confronts the question directly with data on 20 countries, including both old and new democracies. First, he clarifies the relationship between electoral structures, party fragmentation, and inter-election volatility. The greater the proportionality of the electoral system, the higher the fragmentation, such cases as the Lithuanian Senate or the Turkish National Assembly to the contrary notwithstanding. However, the higher the proportionality, the lower the inter-election volatility. Voters in more proportional systems have more parties from which to choose, but once they choose, they tend to stick with their choice from election to election. Anderson's analyses suggest that when given a more precise choice among competitors, voters are more loyal to the one chosen. Further, using membership as another measure of party performance, the higher the proportionality, the higher the gross membership in parties.

Employing Eurobarometer data, Anderson gets even more basic by asking how electoral rules and party system performance (fragmentation and volatility) affect citizens' satisfaction with democracy? Interestingly, electoral rules have the more consistent and stronger impact on democracy satisfaction. The evidence suggests that satisfaction with the functioning of democracy is, in part, a matter of habituation, since the newer democracies almost all have considerably lower democracy satisfaction scores than do their older counterparts. In fact, overlap between the set of newer democracies and the older in terms of democracy satisfaction is minimal. Were not the Czech Republic's level of satisfaction slightly higher than Spain's, the two sets would be absolutely distinct. Had the developmental process somehow levelled out in the emerging democracies, this distinction would be a cause for serious concern for all of them, rather than for just those few, such as Russia, that seem stuck in an pre-party system phase. The continuing developmental process, however, is a major facet of each country's story.

---

[6] Note should be taken of the fact that Toka uses survey data to construct a measure of volatility at the level of the individual voter, whereas most other scholars rely on measures at the aggregate, system level.

Conclusion: Developmental Aspects of Party Systems in New Democracies

I have here highlighted some of the analyses of party performance reported by the authors in this volume. In so doing, I have risked misrepresentation of the developmental aspect of party systems, particularly in the new democracies. In the discussion of the of impact recent history, I did note the non-viability of the revolutionary movements as monopolists in the post-revolutionary phase. However, the post-revolutionary reformation of those is a common story, if with a different story line, in each of the emerging democracies. Krupavicius offers a taxonomy of five steps in the maturation of party systems that should extend well beyond his Lithuanian experience.

Not all elements in this sequence are described in equally rich detail by the authors of the country case histories in this volume. But the set, along with the cross-national analyses, support the usefulness of this or a similar schedule. A party system develops from initial entry into confrontation (phase 2) to its maturation at stages 4 and 5, as the parties take on more and more their essential role as mediating institutions – mediating between interest groups and policy making entities, between organizational elements of the political system, and between citizens and their governors. As this role becomes more effectively pursued it also be comes more subtle and less visible via readily available evidence. And scholars tracking and assessing the development of party systems will have to develop observational capacities commensurate with that subtlety. The essays in this volume provide an excellent model and guide from which to develop strategies of inquiry commensurate with the increasing complexity that accompanies the development and change in party structures and performance.

Party Formation and Party System Consolidation in the New Democracies of Central Europe

DAVID M. OLSON

Introduction

Political parties and the party systems of the new democracies of post-communist Central Europe are in the process of formation through a sequence of elections and parliamentary terms. The sequence theory of election-parliament cycles suggests that in new democracies the formation of political parties and the definition of relationships among the parties proceed through a series of elections and the ensuing terms of parliament.

During the current beginning stages of the 'first generation' of parties and of whole political systems, the main question concerns democratic consolidation. For political parties, the question is one of emerging stability: to what extent do political parties have a continuous existence? For party systems the question is a double one: to what extent is the system consolidating from many small parties to fewer larger ones, and how stable is the relationship among them? While party formation is usually considered an important component in the formation and stabilization of democratic systems, some observers have suggested an 'over-partycisation' phenomenon in at least some of the post-communist democracies.[1]

In this essay I review the formation, splits and recombinations among various groupings active in the electoral process I also consider the resulting shape and characteristics of party systems in the new democracies of Central Europe. While some references will be made to the Republics of the former USSR, the main attention of this paper is on Central Europe, and especially upon the Visegrad 4: Poland, Czech Republic, Slovakia, and Hungary.

These questions are examined from the perspective of the electoral-parliamentary sequence. The tentative findings are that, in the first half-decade of the post-communist transition the major tendency in *party organization* was to develop a small set of activists who made broad issue appeals, thus resembling more the American model of parties, while the patterns in *party system* more resembled those of multi-party western Europe.

The Electoral and Parliamentary Sequence

Internal characteristics of political parties and their external relations in a party system may be expected to change through a sequence of elections and

---

[1] T. Remington, 'Introduction: Parliamentary Elections and the Transition from Communism', in T. Remington (ed.), *Parliaments in Transition* (Boulder CO, Westview, 1994), Ch. 1. A. Agh, 'The Central European Party System: Stages of Emergence and Types of Parties', (Paper read at International Political Science Association, Berlin), 1994.

parliamentary terms, extending over a decade or more, in new democracies. The content of these changes, however, are not necessarily either clear or unidirectional.

The initial democratic election differs from the subsequent ones. The initial elections have featured broad, amorphous, umbrella, conglomerate social movements (e.g., Solidarity, Civic Forum), which, once in office, have splintered and recombined into numerous smaller groupings. The shape of the party system in the first half-decade of post-communist democracies has been more dependent upon coalescence within the initial democratic reform movement than upon splits within the surviving communist parties. The name 'Forum' was much more accurate than 'Solidarity'.[2]

Participants in a new democracy learn through 'system time', over a series of elections and parliamentary terms.[3] They experiment and learn, through repetition, how to campaign effectively for votes. They also learn how to combine with and against each other to form governments and to decide policy in the ensuing parliamentary terms of office. This learning, in turn, creates the conditions for the next election. If the market is an analogy for elections, the election campaign is market day, while parliament is the bourse.

The electoral-parliamentary sequence hypothesis is a statement of the logic of events as they unfolded in the new democracies of post-communist Central Europe. This sequence may vary considerably from democratization processes in Latin America and the Mediterranean regions, and from those concurrently of the Republics of the former USSR. The formative 'moment' in the post-communist democracies of Central Europe is experienced through a series of elections and parliamentary terms; the 'founding election' in Central Europe is likely to extend through time.

This extended moment also occurs under unprecedented conditions of political system transformation, under the social and economic conditions of post-communism.[4] It may very well be that, as we observe party system formation in Central Europe, we will have an opportunity to suggest new ways of examining the conditions of party formation in established democracies.

Fission and Fusion: The Organizational Gamble

Political parties as a form of organization are not one of the givens, but one of the contingencies, in the new democracies of Central Europe. Parties, electoral coalitions, electoral lists, fronts, movements, associations, even work collectives, are only some of the terms applied in elections and also in parliaments.[5] These

[2] J. Skala and C. Kunkel, 'Auf dem weg zu einem Konsolidierten Parteiensystem?', *Geschichte und Gesellschaft*, 18 (1992), 292–308.

[3] Z. Mansfeldova and H. Kitschelt, 'Elite Strategies in Building Party Alternatives: A Process Analysis of Bulgaria, the Czech Republic, Hungary and Poland', (Paper read at conference on Party Formation and Public Opinion in Eastern Europe, Duke University, 1995). R. Markowski, 'Ideological Dimensions in Eastern European Context', (Paper read at conference on Party Formation and Public Opinion in Eastern Europe, Duke University, 1995). K. Jasiewicz, 'Poland' *European Journal of Political Research*, 22 (1993), 489–504. T. Remington and S. Smith, 'The Development of Parliamentary Parties in Russia', (Paper read at Midwest Political Science Association, Chicago, 1995).

[4] P. Lewis, 'Civil society and the development of political parties in East-Central Europe', *Journal of Communist Studies*, 9,4 (1993), 5–20.

[5] M. Waller, 'Political actors and political roles in East-Central Europe', *Journal of Communist Studies*, 9,4 (1993).

different forms appear and disappear rapidly. If political parties in the western sense do develop over time, many of the current electoral formations may be designated as *proto-* or *pre*-parties.

Political formations in elections do not necessarily equate with parties or groupings in Parliament. Furthermore, parties in parliaments often lose members, and new parties are formed from among deputies between elections. To form a new party, or to join an existing one, is a calculated organizational gamble by party elites. These calculations mainly occur in parliament; the new parties of Central Europe are parliamentary-centred.[6]

The tasks confronting putative leaders and aspiring candidates include the discovery of allies and the definition of opponents. A related question unites organizational tactics with electoral strategy: to what extent will either a broad inclusive unity or a narrow but more targeted appeal lead to a larger share of votes in the next election?

The uncertain calculations of aspiring leaders produce behaviour reflected in such terms as 'couch parties', for their quick formation among a few people in an apartment, while the term 'party tourist' refers to parliamentary deputies who have belonged to several different parties within a single term of office.

The Changing Party Formations

The flux of party formation, splits, and recombinations appears to occur more in parliament than outside during a parliamentary term, but accelerates both in and outside of parliament as an election approaches. The greater frequency of elections in Poland and Slovakia, contrasted with Hungary and the Czech Republic, for example, both reflect and stimulate party flux. Elections are an action-forcing event.

Unstable party formations are a common phenomenon in the early developmental stages of democratic party systems. In relatively young democratic systems, as in Spain, the search for effective party organization continues into the present.[7] Even in the established democracy of Sweden, for example, the new parties that entered Parliament in the 1980s and 1990s were also unstable and subject to the loss of members.[8]

One important characteristic of party systems in the post-communist countries is that all parties are new; even those with historic roots. All are continuously searching for effective ways of organizing themselves internally and of presenting themselves externally. An apparent distinction between the Latin and Central European transitions is that the Latin parties had a far greater continuity than was possible in communist systems.[9]

[6] A. Agh, 'The experiences of the first democratic parliaments in east central Europe', *Communist and Post-Communist Studies*, 28,2 (1995), 203–14. E. Nalewajko, Partie polityczne w Polsci – geneza i instytucjonalizacja', in Jacek Wasilewski (ed.), Konsolidacja elit politycznych w Polsce 1991–1993, (Warsaw, Instytut Studiow Politycznych PAN, 1994).

[7] R. Gunther, 'Electoral laws, party systems, and elites: the case of Spain', *American Political Science Review*, 83,3 (September, 1989), 835–58.

[8] D. M. Olson and M. Hagevi, The Parliament of Sweden: Riksdagen', World Encyclopedia of Parliamenst and Legislatures, (Washington, D.C., CQ Press, 1998).

[9] S. Mainwaring and T. R. Scully, 'Introduction: Party Systems in Latin America', in Scott Mainwaring and Timothy R. Scully (eds), *Building Democratic Institutions: Party Systems in Latin America* (Stanford, Stanford University Press, 1995), ch. 1. J. Hartlyn and A. Valenzuela, 'Democracy in Latin America since 1930', in Leslie Bethell (ed.), *The Cambridge History of Latin America*, vol. VI (Cambridge, Cambridge University Press, 1994), pp. 99–162.

In Hungary and the Czech Republic, two of the more stable political systems of Central Europe, parties have recombined in parliament between elections. In the Czech Republic (Table 1), eight political parties were elected in 1992 to the Chamber of Deputies. After that time, three parties split, one lost members, while only one gained members, and the number of independent deputies increased.[10] Preparatory to the 1996 elections, one small government party was absorbed into another; the Chamber of Deputies elected in 1996 had fewer parties than its predecessor.

During the Hungarian Parliament in the 1990–94 term, two new parties were formed as splits of existing ones, three parties lost members, while two gained slightly, and an independent grouping grew considerably. While in the Czech Republic party shifting and fragmentation occurred mainly among the opposition parties, the changes in Hungary occurred in both governing and opposition parties. A total of 14% of the members changed parties in the Hungarian Parliament, with two members changing twice.[11]

Party fragmentation can lead directly to a change of governments, as in Slovakia, within a parliamentary term (Table 2). The previous governing coalition lost its majority to a new government led by the dissenting members from the previous one.[12] The re-elected former government reacted to its previous experience by successfully moving to expel its one deputy from parliament who, following the 1994 election, had resigned from the governing Movement for a Democratic Slovakia (HZDS). That party used its government majority in parliament and on the relevant committees to remove its newest dissident in late 1996, not only from the party, but from Parliament itself.[13]

These within-term parliamentary party shifts are found in most of the newer parliaments such as, for example, Slovenia.[14] They are similar to the splits and recombinations witnessed earlier in the first two terms of the Polish Sejm, 1989–93[15] and later in the Duma of the Russian

[10] J. Reschova and J. Syllova, 'The Legislature of the Czech Republic', in David M. Olson and Philip Norton (eds), *New Parliaments of Central and Eastern Europe* (London, Cass, 1996).
[11] E. Oltay, Hungary: Csurka Launches 'National Movement', Radio Free Europe/Radio Liberty (RFE/RL), Research Report (26 March 1993), 25–31. L. Szarvas, Personnel and Structural Changes in the First Hungarian Parliament', in Attila Agh and Sandor Kurtan (eds), *Democratization and Europeanization in Hungary: The First Parliament, 1990–1994* (Budapest, Hungarian Centre for Democracy Studies, 1995). A. Agh, 'The First Democratic Parliament in Hungary (1990–94)', in David M. Olson and Philip Norton (eds), *New Parliaments of Central and Eastern Europe* (London, Cass, 1996).
[12] Sharon S. Fisher, 'New Slovak Government Formed after Meciar's Fall', RFE/RL Research Report (1 April 1994), 7–13. M. Zemko, 'Political Parties and the Election System in Slovakia', in Sona Szomolanyi and Grigorij Meseznikov (eds), *Slovakia Parliamentary Elections 1991* (Bratislava, Slovak Political Science Association, 1995), 40–55.
[13] A. Siskova, 'Slovakia's Christian Democratic Movement at a Crossroad', *OMRI Analytical Brief*, No. 413 (23 October 1996).
[14] S. Kranjc, 'Politicne Stranke in Parlament: Parlamentarne Frakcije (Skupine, Klubi)', in Drago Zajc (ed.), *Slovenski Parlament v Procesu Politicne Modernizacije* (Ljubljana, Univerza v Ljubljani, 1993).
[15] S. Gebethner, 'Political Parties in Poland (1989–1993)', in Gerd Meyer (ed.), *Die politischen Kulturen Ostmitteleuropas im Umbruch* (Tuebingen, Francke Verlag, 1993), pp. 311–38. S. Gebethner and K. Jasiewicz, 'Poland', European Journal of Political Research, 24 (December 1994), 519–35. D. M. Olson, 'Political Parties and Party Systems in Regime Transformation: Inner Transition in the New Democracies of Central Europe', in William Crotty (ed.), *The American Review of Politics; Special Issue: Political Parties in a Changing Age*, 14 (Winter 1993), 619–58.

TABLE 1. Party Votes and Seats and Party Changes Czech Chamber of Deputies by Party Alliances, 1992–1996

Party/Grouping	1992 Election			End of Term 1996		1996 Election		
	Votes (%)	Seats N	Seats (%)	Seats N	Seats (%)	Votes (%)	Seats N	Seats (%)
Government:								
Civic Democrat Pty (ODS-KDS)	29.73	76	38.00	72	36.00	29.62	68	34.00
Christian Dem Un (KDU-CSL)	6.28	15	7.50	24	12.00	8.08	18	9.00
Civic Dem Alliance (ODA)	5.93	14	7.00	16	8.00	6.36	13	6.50
Subtotal		105	52.50	112	56.00		99	
Opposition:								
Left Bloc (LB)	14.05	35	17.50	23	11.50		0	0.00
Communist Party (KSCM)				10	5.00	10.33	22	11.00
Czech Social Dem (CSSD)	6.53	16	8.00	22	11.00	28.44	61	30.50
Republican Assocn (RPR-RSC)	5.98	14	7.00	5	2.50	8.01	18	9.00
Liberal Social Un (LSU)	6.52	16	8.00	0			0	0.00
Lib National Soc (LSNS)				0				
Civic Natl Movmt (ONH)				6	3.00			
Morav/Silesn Movmt (HSD)	5.87	14	7.00	0			0	0.00
Cz/Mor Cent Pty (CMSS)				0				
Cz/Mor Cent Un (CMUS)				15	7.50			
Independents				7	3.50		0	
Subtotal		95	47.50	88	44.00		101	
Subtotal	80.89					90.84		
All others	19.11					9.16		
Republic Total	100.00	200	100.00	200	100.00	100.00	200	100.00

Notes: Includes only parties above 5% threshold for each election, plus party splits in parliament.
Sources: 1992: CSTK, 'Volby 92', June 7, 1992; Federal Election Commission, '1992 Report Disk'; and 1996: CTK, 'Volby 96' (internet).

TABLE 2. Party Votes and Seats and Party Changes Slovakian National Council by Party Alliance, 1992–1994

Party/Alliance	1992 Election Vote (%)	Seats N	Seats (%)	Feb 1994 Seats N	Mar 1994 Seats N	Seats (%)	Oct 1994 Votes (%)	Seats N	Seats (%)
Pro HZDS	Gov't				Oppos.		Gov't		
Movmt Democr Slov (HZDS)	37.26	74	49.33	57	57	38.00	34.96	61	40.67
Alliance of Democrats				8					
Democratic Union				8					
Slov Natl Pty (SNS)	7.93	15	10.00	8	8	5.33	5.40	9	6.00
Natl Dem Pty (DS)				6					
Assoc Workers Slov (ZRS)							7.34	13	8.67
Subtotal	45.19	89	59.33	87	65	43.33	47.70	83	55.33
Anti HZDS	Oppos.				Gov't		Oppos.		
Democr Left (SDL) Common Choice	14.70	29	19.33	28	28	18.67	10.41	18	12.00
Chris Democr Movmt (KDH)	8.88	18	12.00	18	18	12.00	10.08	17	11.33
Coexistence (EWSS)	7.42	14	9.33	14	14	9.33	10.18	17	11.33
Democr Union (DU)					8	5.33	8.57	15	10.00
Alliance of Demos					8	5.33			
Natl Democr Pty					6	4.00			
Independent				3	3	2.00			
Subtotal	31.00	61	40.66	63	85	56.66	39.24	67	44.66
Subt above threshold	76.19						86.94		
Democratic Party (DS)							3.42		
All others							9.64		
Subt below threshold	23.81						13.06		
Total	100.00	150	99.99	150	150	99.99	100.00	150	99.99

Note: Includes parties over 5% electoral threshold, and in 1994, one parliamentary group below threshold. The entry 'all others' includes all other parties under 5%, 1994.

Sources: 1992: CSTK, 'Volby 92' 7 June 1992; Federal Election Commission, '1992 Report Disk'; and 1994: Seats = RFE/RL Daily Report, 6 October 1994, #190; Votes = TASR, *Daily News Monitor*, 2 October 1994.

Federation.[16] The rate of defections by parliamentary deputies from one party to another has been in the 30%–20% range.[17]

Parties excluded from parliament by electoral losses, as well as those remaining in parliament but with reduced seats, have special reason to consider either internal change or the formation of broader coalitions. In both Poland and Slovakia, for example, previous governing parties and their leaders have been defeated.[18] Though in agreement on many issues, as different parties they continued in a multi-party PR system to run as rivals, more against one another than against the victorious parties. The dominant characteristic of these parties has been their fragmentation.

Their post-defeat response has been to combine in new political parties in an attempt to build leadership and unity among themselves. In Poland, the Democratic Union and the Liberal Democratic Congress formed the Freedom Union which later suffered both defections and expulsions.[19] Another attempt to unite post-reform parties in Poland is the Solidarity Electoral Action (AWS) coalition, created a year in advance of parliamentary elections to provide a united slate of candidates.[20] Its coalitional strategy succeeded in gaining over 40% of the parliamentary seats in the 1997 elections, becoming the single largest party in Parliament.

In Slovakia, similarly, the National Democratic Party merged with the Democratic Union; they had offered a joint electoral coalition in the previous year's election.[21] A variety of 'leftist' party groups in Slovakia, including the reformed Communists and Social Democrats, also discussed a 'forum' structure to coordinate among themselves,[22] while others, including the Christian Democratic Union formed a 'Blue Alliance', a full year in advance of the next regularly scheduled parliamentary elections.[23]

The organizational initiative among losing parties to join together, is an attempt to learn through electoral trial and error. In both Poland and Slovakia the same parties had inconclusively discussed pre-election coalitions or at least cooperation. Following electoral defeat, and experiencing their reduced status in parliament, they then experimented with new organizational formations. It is an open question, however, whether merger broadens or narrows the electoral appeal of the previously separate party groups.

---

[16] Remington, 'Introduction: Parliamentary Elections and the Transition from Communism', ch. 1. Jeffrey W. Hahn (ed), *Democratization in Russia: The Development of Legislative Institutions* (Armonk NY, Sharpe, 1996).

[17] D. Zajc, 'Functions and Powers of the Committees in the New Parliaments: Comparison between the East Central and West Central European Countries', (Paper presented to International Conference on The Changing Roles of Parliamentary Committees', Budapest, Hungary, June 20–22, 1996).

[18] P. Lewis, 'Political Institutionalisation and Party Development in Post-Communist Poland', *Europe-Asia Studies*, 46,5 (1994), 779–99. F. Millard, 'The Polish Parliamentary Election of September 1993', *Communist and Post-communist Studies*, 27,3 (September 1994), 295–314. Zemko, 'Political Parties and the Election System in Slovakia', 40–55.

[19] Radio Free Europe/Radio Liberty (RFE/RL), *Daily Report* (8 July 1994, email transmission). Open Media Research Institute (OMRI), *Daily Digest* (9 January 1997, email transmission).

[20] B. Pasek, 'Looking Towards Poland's 1997 Parliamentary Elections', *OMRI Analytical Brief*, No. 392 (1996).

[21] Open Media Research Institute (OMRI), *Daily Digest* (27 March 1995, email transmission).

[22] Open Media Research Institute (OMRI), *Daily Digest* (27 April 1995, email transmission).

[23] *Carolina* (Charles University News email, 27 November 1996).

These many shifts in party affiliations and group formation both within and outside of parliament are indicators of nascent party organizations. Especially in the early elections, neither potential parties nor candidates have a complete understanding of themselves, much less of each other. In the first election, all new groups were under time pressure to place candidate names on their ballots. The new party groupings did not have enough 'partisans and supporters, and in many cases the party candidates were not even sure of their own parties' policies'.[24] At the beginning, no one could be sure of either policies, personnel, leadership, or structure. These uncertainties continue.

Party Unity under Threat

The fusion phenomenon is closely linked to fission: many of the new parties of newly democratized systems are internally diverse and divided. As those internal divisions achieve some degree of membership and continuity, they become crystallized as factions. Though the term 'faction' has a diverse and contradictory usage, at least in English,[25] the term will be used here to designate subgroups within political parties.

Those political groups wishing to emphasize their diverse composition and abstract issue orientation tend to call themselves 'movements', rather than some more limited term such as 'party'.[26] One response to the omnipresent possibility of internal factionalism is to emphasize the necessity and superiority of its opposite – unity and agreement. The latter emphasis has characterized the conglomerate and umbrella regime-change social movements which have led the anti-communist changes toward a democratic political system.

Polish Solidarity, Czech Civic Forum, Slovakian Public Against Violence, the several Baltic Fatherland movements, the Romanian National Salvation Front, and the Bulgarian Union of Democratic Forces, all illustrate the broad, amorphous and diverse 'rainbow coalition' character of these regime change social movements. Achievement of their overarching goal – removal of Communist government – thereby destroyed the basis for their internal unity. Continuance of the broad fronts in Bulgaria and Romania is an indication that the party formation process in those two countries differs from the other countries of Central Europe.

In parliament, the initial response of the movement deputies to growing internal diversity was to permit the organization and functioning of sub-groups within their parliamentary party structure. Quickly, however, those factions became their own free-standing parliamentary party clubs, which then ran candidates against one another in ensuing parliamentary elections.

The latent factionalism within the post-communist parties became more visible after 1991–92, as they formed the new governments, than while they were in the discredited minority. Organizationally, they are among the oldest surviving parties in the new democracies. Their intensive internal disputes leading up to the collapse of communist rule, in which the reformers prevailed over the

[24] Szarvas, 'Personnel and Structural Changes in the First Hungarian Parliament', 203.

[25] P. Lewis, Party Factionalism and Democratization in Poland', (Paper presented to ECPR Workshop, Madrid, 1994).

[26] Olson, 'Political Parties and Party Systems in Regime Transformation: Inner Transition in the New Democracies of Central Europe', 619–58.

hard liners, cleared away a whole spectrum of political views and personalities from their internal decision-making, at least in Central Europe.[27]

But then they faced new factional divisions. The Polish reformed Communists, SLD, included deputies affiliated with OPZZ, the non-Solidarity pro-Communist labour group. Reminiscent of earlier factional formation within Solidarity, the OPZZ deputies in early 1994 formed a new parliamentary club, Defense of Workers' Interests. They publicly considered an effort to control the main reform Communist parliamentary club, the SLD.[28] Similar factions and splits are visible in many of the post-communist parties of the region.[29]

The potential pervasiveness of factionalism in all parties is illustrated in the post-1996 Czech Chamber of Deputies. Of the interviewed members, a full 60% indicated that there were subgroups within their parliamentary party. Of that 60%, a full two thirds also said they themselves were members of such factional groupings; they amounted to 40% of the total sample.[30]

If some groupings appear internally divided and uncoordinated, about which participants complain, other parties exhibit more unity and internal command, which produces opposite complaints. The Czech Civic Democratic Party, for example, is strongly led by the Prime Minister, Vaclav Klaus. The Foreign Minister in the same government and vice chairman of the same party, suggested shortly after the 1996 elections that the party would benefit from an increased degree of pluralism. That tentative suggestion was promptly rejected by the party leader.[31]

Electoral Coalitions: Hanging together Separately

Electoral coalitions are devices to cope with the details of electoral laws and to manage the strains between broad unity and separate identity. They also illustrate the ambiguities of the term *political party*.

The 1994 Slovakian parliamentary election illustrates some of the variable practices and unpredictable outcomes. While 18 electoral lists were offered to the voters, those lists included candidates from 31 different parties and electoral labels. Three of the 18 electoral lists were coalitions containing a total of 9 parties. Of the 18 electoral lists, seven were elected to parliament; while the seven have formed parliamentary parties consistent with their electoral

[27] K. Janowski, 'From Monopoly to Death Throes: The PZPR in the Process of Political Transformation', in George Sanford (ed.), *Democratization in Poland, 1988–90* (New York, St Martin's Press, 1992), 162–176. E. Oltay, 'Hungarian Socialists Prepare for Comeback', RFE/RL Research Report, (1 March 1994), 21–26.

[28] Lewis, 'Party Factionalism and Democratization in Poland', 8–9. M. Kramer, 'Polish workers and the post-communist transition, 1989–1993', *Communist and Post-Communist Studies*, 28, (1995), 71–114.

[29] J. T. Ishiyama, 'Communist parties in transition: structures, leaders and processes of democratization in Eastern Europe', *Comparative Politics*, 27,2 (January 1995), 147–66. A. Mahr and J. Nagle, 'Resurrection of the successor parties and democratization in East-Central Europe', *Communist and Post-Communist Studies*, 28, 4 (1995), 393–409.

[30] P. Kopecky, 'The Organization and Behaviour of Political Parties in the Czech Parliament from Transformative Towards Arena Type of Legislatures', in Paul Lewis (ed.), *Party Structure and Organization in East-Central Europe* (Aldershot, Edward Elgar, 1996).

[31] J. Pehe, 'Calls for pluralism in the strongest Czech Party', *OMRI Analytical Brief*, No. 263 (8 August 1996).

coalitions, those parliamentary parties actually contain deputies from 16 different political groupings.[32]

One of the ironies of the 1994 Slovakian elections is that the parties which did not join a coalition, as well as those which did, were both punished at the polls. The pro-market and pro-Europeanization parties narrowly failed to win any seats; had they combined in an electoral coalition, and had they together obtained all the votes which they had gained separately, their candidates would have been elected.

On the other hand, the reformed post-communist Party of the Democratic Left (SLD) in Slovakia, did form a coalition with other smaller parties, called Common Choice, and lost votes relative to its 1992 vote. One direct consequence of the coalition was the emergence of a new left party, the Association of Slovakian Workers (ZSR), which took votes away from the SLD and its new coalition.[33] The Common Choice electoral coalition of 1994 was apparently plagued by doubts and mutual distrust among party activists, illustrating that the appearance of organizational unity from above can bring the reality of human disunity from below.

Coalitions tend toward instability; they threaten to fly apart. In Bulgaria, for example, the 17 member groups belonging to the Union of Democratic Forces, a coalition dating from 1991, signed a revised cooperation agreement in 1994. The largest member party, however, refused to sign. The coalition had twice previously disintegrated. The revised agreement defined the decision-making bodies of the coalition, and threatened exclusion of members who did not adhere to those decisions.[34] In anticipation of the next parliamentary elections, the UDF Chairman proposed in 1996 that the Union should become a single political party, to avoid the continuing 'strong battles between personalities, groups and parties'. The internal divisions include disputes over policy as well as the distribution of potential government portfolios. The suggested alternate course of action was to consider party formation after, and if, the existing Union should win the next elections.[35]

External Units of Parties

Factionalism, splits, and recombinations appear mainly among parliamentary deputies. Other participants in national level politics – defeated parties in parliamentary elections, or aspirants for the presidential office – also appear as main players in the party drama. The office of President in Poland itself, quite apart from the actions of its occupant, have occasioned major splits within the Solidarity movement.[36] The external party includes the national convention, a

---

[32] Zemko, 'Political Parties and the Election System in Slovakia'.

[33] P. Juza, 'The Formation of the Coalition "Common Choice" and its Election Results', in Sona Szomolanyi and Grigorij Meseznikov (eds), *Slovakia Parliamentary Elections 1994* (Bratislava, Slovak Political Science Association, 1995), 220–34.

[34] Radio Free Europe/Radio Liberty (RFE/RL), Daily Report (11 September 1994, email transmission).

[35] M. Koinova, 'Will Bulgaria's Union of Democratic Forces become a party?', *OMRI Analytical Brief* (Internet, 4 December 1996).

[36] K. Jasiewicz, 'The Enfranchised, the Re-enfranchised and the Self-disenfranchised: The Politics of Electoral Reforms in Post-communist Poland', Paper read at American Political Science Association, San Francisco, 1996.

continuing executive board, the headquarters staff, and regional and local bodies.

National conventions of political parties are usually held annually.[37] An external convention was instrumental in the breakup of the regime change movement, the Civic Forum, in the Czech Republic in early 1991, leading to the formation of what has become that Republic's largest and governing Civic Democratic Party (ODS). A series of conventions quickly led to the formation of other parties, with similar events occurring also in Slovakia. These conventions outside parliament marked the end of the regime change movements in Czechoslovakia.[38]

Examples of national conventions of political parties in late 1996 include the Turkish Movement for Rights and Freedom in Bulgaria, Civic Democratic Party in the Czech Republic, the Coalition Party in Croatia, and the Alliance of Free Democrats in Hungary. Convention sizes, judged by the number of votes cast on contested issues, ranges from several hundred to over 1000 delegates.[39]

The national executive committees or governing councils of the parties are occasionally called upon for difficult decisions. The executive board of the Democratic Party Saimnieks of Latvia, for example, voted 56-2 to expel one of its party members, the incumbent Finance Minister.[40] In Poland, the National Council of the Freedom Union dismissed a leading member from the party's Presidium, while the Union of Labor also dismissed a member of its Presidium; both expulsions were in response to presidential elections and in anticipation of coming parliamentary elections.[41]

Special conventions and bodies at the national level can be convened as required to cope with crises of either leadership or electoral strategy. A 'plenary meeting', for example was held in the Bulgarian Socialist Party, consisting of a joint session between the Supreme Council and the party's parliamentary party members. The divided results (87–69 on support of the incumbent Prime Minister) led to the decision to hold an 'extraordinary' party congress to consider their internal divisions further.[42]

National level headquarters are another potential source of party structure and leadership. This organizational level has been reported active and important in the Czech Republic for some parties: the leaders of the Czech parties ran for election to the Federal Assembly in 1992. When that body was abolished upon the dissolution of the Federation, party leaders either entered the government of the new Republic or entered the headquarters of the opposition parties.[43] The usual solution to parliamentary-headquarters disputes, the personal union of leadership, was not possible following the 1992 elections.

[37] M. Grabowska, 'Social Cleavages and Political Spectrum in Post-Communist Poland', Paper presented at V World Congress for Central and East European Studies, Warsaw, Poland, 1995.

[38] J. Pehe, 'Czechoslovakia: The Realignment of Political Forces', RFE/RL Report on Eastern Europe (24 May 1991), 1–5.

[39] Open Media Research Institute (OMRI), *Daily Digest* (1 September–31 December 1996, email transmission).

[40] Open Media Research Institute (OMRI), *Daily Digest* (16 September 1996, email transmission).

[41] Open Media Research Institute (OMRI), *Daily Digest* (4 December 1996, email transmission).

[42] S. Krause, 'A tough week for Bulgaria's socialists', *OMRI Analytical Brief*, No. 473 (18 November 1996).

[43] Kopecky, 'The Organization and Behaviour of Political Parties in the Czech Parliament from Transformative Towards Arena Type of Legislatures'.

Interviews with parliamentary deputies in both Poland and Hungary suggest latent tensions between the central party office and their own party units. By party statutes, the central office and executive committee are superior to the parliamentary units. In practice, however, 48% of the Hungarian deputies were also members of their respective parties' national executive committee, while 65% of the Polish sample of deputies held similar overlapping memberships.[44]

In some instances, splits within parliamentary parties have produced a parliamentary-headquarters split. In Hungary's Smallholders' Party, for example, the majority within the parliamentary party split from the formal party group. The national chair of the party was within the parliamentary party's minority. Each tried to expel the other and to form the 'real' party caucus.[45]

Related evidence about party organization comes from local elections. In most newly democratized countries of Central Europe, the national level parties nominate candidates for local elections, but are electorally successful mainly in the large cities. Most elected municipal councilors are independent. Even when local groups affiliated with national parties do participate in municipal elections, they develop local coalitions which ignore the current coalitional patterns at the national level.[46] The mix of personality, local traditions, and party affiliation, in local elections vary idiosyncratically.

Persons identified as active in party leadership in local and provincial levels (e.g., voivodships in Poland) in four countries tended to occupy positions either in elected local councils or in regional party offices.[47] The closely collaborative relationship, at least at the local level, between parliamentary deputies and local party activists is illustrated by the practice of locating parliamentary constituency offices in the facilities of the local parties.

In the Czech Republic, only the post-Communist party was reported to have a membership in excess of 100,000; all others are considerably less.[48] A different but higher sets of membership numbers, however, have also been reported in the Czech Republic.[49] In Poland, only the Peasant Party was reported to have a membership of 200,000; the next highest, the post-communist Social

---

[44] A. van der Meer-Krok-Paszkowska and M. van den Muyzenberg, 'Orientation to the State? Parliamentary Parties in Hungary and Poland and their Relations with Party in Central Office', Paper presented to international conference, The New Democratic Parliaments: The First Years, Ljubljana, Slovenia, 1996.

[45] Szarvas, 'Personnel and Structural Changes in the First Hungarian Parliament', 204.

[46] A. Kroupa and T. Kostelecky, 'Party Organization and Structure at National Level and Local Level in the Czech Republic Since 1989', Paper read at workshop, Party Structure and Organization in East-Central Europe', Warsaw, Poland, 1994. M. Illner, 'Continuity and discontinuity: political change in a Czech village after 1989', Czech Sociological Review, 28 (Special Issue, 1994), 79–91. H. Balderheim and M. Illner, 'Local Democracy in East-Central Europe', Paper read at International Political Science Association, Berlin, 1994.

[47] Markowski, 'Ideological Dimensions in Eastern European Context'. G. Toka, 'The Programmatic Structuring of Party Competition: Bulgaria, the Czech Republic, Hungary, and Poland in Spring 1994', Paper read at conference on Party Formation and Public Opinion in Eastern Europe', Duke University, 1995. H. Kitschelt, 'Patterns of Competition in East Central European Party Systems', Paper read at Annual Meeting of American Political Science Association, Chicago, 31 August–3 September 1995.

[48] Reschova and Syllova, 'The Legislature of the Czech Republic'.

[49] Kroupa and Kostelecky, 'Party Organization and Structure at National Level and Local Level in the Czech Republic Since 1989'. P. Kopecky, 'Factionalism in parliamentary parties in the Czech Republic: a concept and some empirical findings', Democratization, 2,1 (Spring 1995).

Democracy, reported a membership of 65,000.[50] Several respondents have indicated that the organizational strength of the Peasant Party in Poland rests on a network of rural organizations, especially volunteer fire departments, while that of the Communists in the Czech Republic rests in the remains of worker party organization in the larger factories. In neither party, nor in any of the others, is there a sizeable grassroots network of active citizens.

With the exception of these specific references to rural groups and factory worker units, the formation of voluntary citizen organizations (as non-governmental organizations and interest groups), does not result in connections to political parties. The active encouragement by the Government of the formation of labour and employer groups capable of entering into social agreements with the state on the tripartite pattern of Austria, has directly stimulated the formation of both sets of private economic organizations. They explicitly, however, disavow any connection to political parties, at least in the Czech Republic and Poland.[51]

In the new democracies of Central Europe, people tend to withdraw from organizational affiliations. In 1990, organization membership in Poland was largely confined to professionals: almost 35% belonged to labour unions. By socio-occupational category, the higher proportion reporting membership in political parties were professionals (2.2%) and small businessmen (5.8%), with the national average at 1.8%.[52] At parliamentary campaign meetings, it has been observed that the few party activists and candidates present outnumbered the even fewer voters.[53] The 'common reaction' to release from communist rule and required memberships has been 'withdrawal and alienation'.[54] The predominant public orientation to political parties throughout the region is rejection, not trust or positive 'identification' with any party.[55] A new middle class may be active as entrepreneurs, but not as participatory citizens in either parties or interest groups.[56]

[50] P. Lewis, 'Political institutionalisation and party development in post-communist Poland', *Europe-Asia Studies*, 46,5 (1994), p. 787.

[51] Z. Mansfeldova, 'Social Partnership in the Czech Republic', Paper read at V World Congress for Central and East Europe Studies, Warsaw, Poland, 1995. J. Hausner and W. Morawski, 'Tripartism in Poland', Paper read at conference, Tripartisan in Central and Eastern Europe, Budapest, 1994. Kopekcy, Factionalism in Parliamentary Parties in the Czech Republic: A Concept and Some Empirical Findings'. D. M. Olson, Democratization and Political Participation: the Experience of the Czech Republic', in Bruce Parrott and Karin Dawisha, eds., *Democratic Consolidation in Central Europe*, (Cambridge, Cambridge University Press, 1997).

[52] W. Zaborowski, 'Social Structure and Political Participation', in Wladyslaw W. Adamski (ed.), *Societal Conflict and Systemtic Change: The Case of Poland 1980–1992* (Warsaw, IFIS Publishers, 1992), 57–67.

[53] D. M. Olson, 'Dissolution of the state: political parties and the 1992 election in Czecho-slovakia', *Communist and Post-Communist Studies*, 26,3 (September 1993), 301–14.

[54] W. Zaborowski, Social Structure and Political Participation', 67. A. Miszalska, On Political Alienation of Poles', in Jadwiga Koralewicz, ed., Party System – Political Behavior – Social Consciousness', *Sisyphus*,1 (IX) (1995), 141–60.

[55] F. Plasser and P. A. Ulram, 'Politische Systemunterstuetzung und Institutionenvertrauen in den OZE-Staaten', *Oesterreichische Zeischrift fuer Politikwissenschaft*, No. 4 (1994), 365–80. R. Rose, *What is Europe?* (New York, HarperCollins, 1996), 147–155. W. Wesolowski, 'Formation of Political Parties in Post-communist Poland', in Jadwiga Koralewicz (ed.), Party System – Political Behavior – Social Consciousness, *Sisyphus* 1 (IX) (1995), 9–32.

[56] M. Grabowska, 'Social Cleavages and Political Spectrum in Post-communist Poland', Paper presented at V World Congress for Central and East European Studies, Warsaw, 1995.

Types of Party Organization

By and large, parties in the new democracies are 'cadre' parties of a few active leaders, most of whom are found in or around parliament and presidential offices. Joined to a cadre structure is a broad diffuse electoral appeal in a 'catch-all' pattern.[57]

Cadre-Catchall

The cadre parties of the new democracies need not have the same organizational features as did those identified by Duverger (1954, pp. 63–4) or Weber (1946, pp. 101–5) in an earlier era in Western Europe. In the new democracies, the aspiring leaders of new electoral organizations function in an environment in which democracy is a known and preferred condition. A century ago in Western Europe, the leaders of cadre parties were in danger from the new and unknown conditions of democracy; now they are seeking to take advantage of those conditions. Current leaders can attempt to use for their own purposes, rather than resist, mass politics.

For the innovating leaders of new parties in new democracies, the cadre is more their model than is the mass party of western Europe. They have not inherited a mass organization, on which they must expend time and energy to support and to mobilize. Neither, with the instruments of mass communication, do they need to create such an inefficient and clumsy human organization for electoral purposes.[58] Central European party builders exist in an era of 'counter organizational tendencies'.[59] The aspiring leaders of the new parties of Central Europe need not recapitulate the development sequences of Western Europe, but rather can leapfrog directly into a mass communications video age.

For new putative leaders, and for new aspiring candidates, votes are what they need. Votes are more important than voters; either is more important than members.[60] A ballot, properly marked, is more important on election day than a membership card fully paid during the year.

The widespread practice of state financial support for parties and election campaigns is far more important than member dues. The minimum vote required for state financial subsidy for election costs is usually lower than the seat threshold. In both Slovakia and the Czech Republic, for example, the subsidy threshold is 3%, while the seat threshold is 5%. In Poland, a subsidy is paid on the basis of the number of candidates elected.[61] In addition, the provision of constituency offices to parliamentary members is an important support to parties at regional and local levels.

---

[57] O. Kirchheimer, 'The Transformation of the Western European Party Systems', in Joseph LaPalombara and Myron Weiner (eds), *Political Parties and Political Development* (Princeton NJ, Princeton University, 1966), 177–200.

[58] D. Perkins, 'Some Causes and Consequences of Party Formation in Western and Eastern Europe', Paper read at Southern Political Science Association, Atlanta, 1994. P. Kopecky, 'Factionalism in parliamentary parties in the Czech Republic: a concept and some empirical findings', *Democratization*, 2,1 (Spring 1995).

[59] L. D. Epstein, *Political Parties in Western Democracies* (New York, Praeger, 1967).

[60] S. E. Scarrow, 'The "paradox of enrollment": assessing the costs and benefits of party membership', *European Journal of Political Research*, 25 (January 1994), 41–60.

[61] Millard, 'The Polish Parliamentary Election of September 1993'. Van der Meer-Krok-Paszkowska and van den Muyzenberg, 'Orientation to the State? Parliamentary Parties in Hungary and Poland and their Relations with Party in Central Office'.

Furthermore, the vague slogans of the catch-all party are well adapted to the initial post-communist reform movements: instead of appealing to segments of the electorate, whether as 'classes' or 'interests', the regime change movements appealed to abstract but powerful feelings of national well being and patriotic morality. The emerging party type, the *cadre catch-all party*, like the regime change movement, fits the Eastern European tradition of the 'ruling party'; when the ruling parties have changed, the activists of the old have switched and continue participation in the new.[62]

The New and the Old

In electoral appeal tactics, if not also in party organization, there is a growing distinction between *historical* and the newer *post-transitional* parties. The historic parties, which have survived in spite of a half-century of war and dictatorship, have retained a known electorate and an expected structured relationship between voter and leader. Examples include the ethnic parties, as well as those with a religious orientation and those based upon economic segments.[63] The former, the ethnic and religious, tend to be part of the anti-communist reform wave, while the latter ones, based upon economic segments, include both the reform communists and, at least in Poland, the agricultural party.

The newer parties, by contrast, appeal to a floating electorate, and have neither a pre-existing electorate nor organization. These parties are the post-reform parties, whose leadership is located in parliament, and whose participants tend to the activist and cadre category. They incline strongly to the vague appeals of the catch-all party.

Several of the historic parties were included in the Popular Fronts of the Communist regime, indicating their importance to political stability. They have survived the transition. While they might have been discredited by their involvement with the Communist system, their tangible resources, such as buildings and newspapers, became usefully engaged in making the democratic transition possible.

Another characteristic of the older parties is that they are mainly not in competition with one another. That is, usually only one party in any one country appeals to an electoral segment. The three Hungarian parties of Slovakia are an exception, while the one Hungarian party of Romania illustrates the more common practice.

This distinction is more relevant for Central Europe and also for the Baltic States, than for the Republics of the former USSR. For them, there are few historic survivals on which to construct new parties. Virtually all parties are built on the remnants of the Communist Party and upon the socio-economic structure developed in that system for well over two generations. Not only are there no alternative historical bases on which to construct political parties, but the modern phenomenon of party, as a form of organization engaged in a competitive electoral relationship, seems a new and unstable idea. The status of

[62] Agh, 'The Central European Party System: Stages of Emergence and Types of Parties', 9.

[63] R. Rose, *What is Europe?*, 163. Kopecky, 'Factionalism in Parliamentary Parties in the Czech Republic: A Concept and Some Empirical Findings'.

political party, as a basic form of organization, is more uncertain in the Soviet survival Republics than in Central Europe.

Ethnic parties are the clearest exception to the vague and mass appeal option of the cadre party.[64] While we know little of their internal organization, there are difficult relations among their leaders, as illustrated by the three Hungarian parties in Slovakia.[65] They have perhaps the most clearly defined and most loyal electorate of any type of party in this region.[66] Their counterparts, the nationalistic parties, attempt to become for the dominant ethnic identity, what the ethnic parties are for their minority groups – the expression of social solidarity.[67]

The historic-based parties face an electoral dilemma: to broaden their appeal or to intensify their existing base of support. The post-communist parties seem to have resolved this question with greater success (at least as measured by votes) than have others. The Christian Democratic Party of Slovakia, for example, faced this question in the form of a leadership challenge: the challenger, who urged a broadening of the party to the 'wider masses', was defeated by the incumbent who has long personified the principled objectives of the party.[68]

Taken as whole structures, the political parties of the new democracies, especially the new parties, are more cadre than mass, more general than specific in their target audiences, and more concerned with votes than with members. Their efforts either to combine into larger coalitions, or to split into more specific groups, as well as their links to social organizations, seem more a matter of elite and leadership strategy and experiment than of membership decision.

Electoral and Party Systems

It is by no means clear that new party systems of the new democracies of Central Europe will resemble Western Europe in either number of parties or issue alignments. Following a discussion of electoral systems and their unique features in the new democracies, we will consider several different measures of party system characteristics.

Electoral Systems

The choices, and trials and errors, of party and electoral group leaders occur with the rules of any one election, which they themselves help formulate. Multi-party systems have survived in every one of the new democracies irrespective of the specific election system. While most countries use proportional representa-

[64] S. Roper, 'The Romanian political party system and the catch-all party phenomenon', *East European Quarterly*, 28,4 (January 1995), 519–32. J. Bugajski, 'Ethnic Politics in Eastern Europe: a Guide to Nationality Policies', in *Organizations and Parties* (Armonk NY, Sharpe, 1994).

[65] D. Malova, 'The Development of Hungarian Political Parties during the Three Election Cycles (1990–1994) in Slovakia', in Sona Szomolanyi and Grigorij Meseznikov (eds), *Slovakia Parliamentary Elections 1994* (Bratislava, Slovak Political Science Association, 1995), 200–34.

[66] A. Reisch, 'Hungarian Coalition Succeeds in Czechoslovak Election', RFE/RL Report on Eastern Europe, 1,26 (June 26, 1992), 20–22. D. Kostova, 'Political Action in Bulgaria: Challenges and Risks in the Parliamentary Elections'.

[67] T. S. Szayna, 'Ultra-nationalism in central Europe', *Orbis*, 37,4 (Fall 1993), 527–50. M. Shafir, 'Growing Political Extremism in Romania', RFE/RL Research Report, 2,14 (2 April 1993), 18–25.

[68] Siskova, 'Slovakia's Christian Democratic Movement at a Crossroad'.

tion in multi-member districts, with a threshold requirement, others continue a single member district system with a majority vote and even a majority turnout requirement. Still others use varieties of mixed systems on the German model.[69] In both Poland and the Czech Republic, the two chambers of parliaments use different election systems. Directly elected presidents usually run in a two-round majority system. The new democracies both borrow from Western Europe and tinker with their own innovations. Table 3 presents a comprehensive summary of the electoral structures of most of the post-communist states through 1996.

The election laws for the initial anti-communist referenda in 1989–90 were necessarily written in haste. The expedient in each country was to use the election system of their past: Central European states reverted to the proportional representation systems of the inter-war period, while the still-Soviet Republics relied mainly upon the Soviet-era single member majoritarian system. Poland, holding the first such election, and Hungary in delaying its election, each innovated with different combinations of electoral rules.[70]

Each set of participants, roughly defined as the surviving Communist parties and the opposition, sought election rules in their own favour. Communists, still believing themselves to have the advantage, wanted single member majority systems, while reformers wanted the more 'democratic' proportional representation. In subsequent elections, most parties and groups have opted for either a proportional or a mixed system; while each expects some gains, none is willing to risk the debilitating loss which would accompany another party's massive win in a single member plurality system. In the Ukraine, however, the 'party of power' continues its preferences for single member majority system,[71] while Russia now uses a mixed system.[72]

While a majority single member system is thought to incline toward a stable two party system over time,[73] one of the short-range effects of this system in the new democracies has been to encourage direct electoral competition among parties that are currently in the government coalition. In the 1996 Czech Senate election, for example, the two minor government parties ran directly against candidates of the major government party in runoff elections, the bulk of which

---

[69] J. McGregor, 'How Electoral Laws Shape Eastern Europe's Parliaments', RFE/RL Research Report, 2,4 (22 January 1993), 11–18. C. Flores Juberias, 'Electoral Systems in Eastern Europe', Paper read at International Political Science Association, Berlin, 1994). M. S. Shugart, 'Building the Institutional Framework: Electoral Systems, Party Systems, and Presidents', (Manuscript, University of California at San Diego, September 1995).

[70] J. Syllova, 'The Transition to Democracy in Czechoslovakia in the Field of Electoral Law', in Ziemowit J. Pietras and Marek Pietras (eds), *The Transnational Future of Europe* (Lublin, Maria Curie-Sklodowska University Press, 1992). D. M. Olson, 'Compartmentalized competition: the managed transitional election system of Poland', *Journal of Politics*, 55 (1993), 415–41. J. Hibbing and S. Patterson, 'A democratic legislature in the making: the historic Hungarian elections of 1990', *Comparative Political Studies*, 24 (1991), 430–54. S. Bach, 'From Soviet to Parliament in Ukraine: The Verkhovna Rada during 1992–1994', in David M. Olson and Philip Norton (eds), *The New Parliaments of Central and Eastern Europe* (London, Cass, 1996). Remington, 'Introduction: Parliamentary Elections and the Transition from Communism'. Jasiewicz, 'The Enfranchised, the Re-enfranchised and the Self-disenfranchised: The Politics of Electoral Reforms in Post-communist Poland'.

[71] Bach, 'From Soviet to Parliament in Ukraine: The Verkhovna Rada During 1992–1994'.

[72] Remington, 'Introduction: Parliamentary Elections and the Transition from Communism'.

[73] M. Duverger, Maurice, Political Parties, (New York, Wiley, 1954). V. Bogdanor, Introduction', in Vernon Bodganor and David Butler, eds., *Democracy and Elections: Electoral Systems and their Political Consequences*, (Cambridge, Cambridge University Press, 1983).

were won by the minor partners.[74] It was immediately noticeable that the partners were less comfortable with one another in government after the election than together in opposition before.

The election results tend to be very different in each country from one election to another. Whether or not the election law is changed, previous winners and incumbent government parties tend to be defeated in a subsequent election. But on the whole, new parties do not enter parliament; the alternating results tend to occur among the parties already in, or recently formed within, parliament.

The party system consequences of electoral law provisions have not been unidirectional in the early years of diverse experiments in the new democracies. Two separate sets of statistical simulations on the Polish Sejm elections (of 1991 and 1993) both suggest, however, that the sheer number of electoral groups has had a greater impact on the resulting party system in parliament than have other features of the electoral law, including district magnitude and the vote counting rules.[75]

It is striking that in the two countries which use very different election systems for their two parliamentary chambers, the party results are similar in each election.[76] Both Poland and the Czech Republic employ proportional representation and multi-member districts for the more powerful chamber, but a single member system (whether plurality or majority) for the second chamber.

Electoral Filter

Election systems provide a series of steps to reduce the number of parties to those that are genuine contenders for political power. While in each country, a hundred or more 'parties' are officially registered, anywhere from 10 to 40 offer candidates in parliamentary elections. The highest number of reported electoral lists offered in any one election was 112 in Poland, in the 1991 election.[77] The number of parties and other electoral groupings is successively limited at each stage of the electoral process. In Lithuania, for example, 33 parties were registered in 1996, while 27 offered candidates, and 14 parties won at least one office.[78]

The use of these numbers for comparative analysis is bedeviled, however, by two considerations: they are not collected or reported uniformly by any one source, and, more important, they reflect the diversity of practices of each country. The diversity of electoral group formation is itself a barrier to accurate numbers within any one country and to consistent numbers across countries.

The 1994 Hungarian election illustrates the varieties of practice and the resulting ambiguities of numbers: 35 parties offered candidates. There were, in

[74] Czech Press Agency (CTK), 'Volby 1996' (email transmission, 1996).

[75] S. Gebethner, 'System Wyborczy: Deformacja czy reprezentacja?', in Stanislaw Gebethner (ed.), *Wybory Parlamentarne 1991 i 1993* (Warsaw, Wydawnictwo Sejmowe, 1995), 9–48. Bach, 'From Soviet to Parliament in Ukraine: The Verkhovna Rada During 1992–1994'. J. Gibson, and A. Cielecka, 'The Polish Electoral System: An Unrepresentative Outlier?', Paper read at Annual Meeting of American Political Science Association, San Francisco, 29 August–1 September 1996).

[76] Gebethner, 'System Wyborczy: Deformacja czy reprezentacja?'. J. Wiatr, 'Fragmented Parties in a New Democracy: Poland', Paper presented to conference, Political Parties in the New Democracies, Vienna, 24–26 April 1992. Olson, 'Democratization and Political Participation: the Experience of the Czech Republic'.

[77] Lewis, 'Political Institutionalisation and Party Development in Post-Communist Poland'.

[78] Open Media Research Institute (OMRI), *Daily Digest* (17 September 1996).

TABLE 3. Electoral Systems of Post-Communist States, 1989–1996

A. Central European States

Country	Election year	Chamber structure	Chamber names	Districts				Vote method	Electoral threshold (%)
				Number	Type	Size	Total seats		
Poland	1989	Bicameral	Sejm	108	MM	2 to 5	425	Maj	N/A
				1	NL	35	35	Maj	N/A
					Total Seats		460		
			Senate	49	MM	2 to 3	100	Maj	N/A
	1991		Sejm	37	MM	7 to 17	391	PR	N/A
				1	NL	69	69	PR	5
					Total Seats		460		
			Senate	49	MM	2 to 3	100	Plur	N/A
	1993		Sejm	37	MM	3 to 17	391	PR	5
				1	NL	69	69	PR	7
					Total Seats		460		
			Senate	49	MM	2 to 3	100	Plur	N/A
Czech Republic	1990 & 1992	Unicameral	Chamber of Deputies	8	MM	8 to 32	200	PR	5
	1996	Bicameral	Chamber of Deputies	8	MM	8 to 32	200	PR	5
			Senate	81	SM	1	81	Maj	N/A

Slovak Republic	1990	Unicameral	National Council	4	MM	12 to 50	150	PR	3
	1992 & 1994		National Council	4	MM	12 to 50	150	PR	5
Hungary	1990	Unicameral	National Assembly	176	SM	1	176	Maj	N/A
				20	MM	4 to 28	152	PR	4
				1	NL	58	58	PR	4
				Total Seats			386		
	1994		National Assembly	176	SM	1	176	Maj	N/A
				20	MM	4 to 28	152	PR	5
				1	NL	58	58	PR	5
				Total Seats			386		

Legend: Districts: MM = Multi-Member, SM = Single Member, NL = National List, Vote Method: PR = Proportional Representation, Maj = Majority, Plur = Plurality.

Sources: Inter-Parliamentary Union, 'PARLINE Database', at http://www.ipu.org; K. Jasiewicz, 'Elections and Political Change', in White, Batt and Lewis (eds), *Developments in East European Politics* (1993); D. Olson, 'Compartmentalized competition', *Journal of Politics*, 155,2 (1993); Parliament of the Czech Republic, at http://www.psp.cz; Parliament of Hungary, at http://www.mkogy.hu; Parliament of the Republic of Poland, at http://www.sejm.gov.pl and at http://www.senat.gov.pl.

TABLE 3. Continued

B. Balkan and South-Eastern European States

Country	Election year	Chamber structure	Chamber names	Districts Number	Type	Size	Total seats	Vote method	Electoral threshold (%)
Albania	1991	Unicameral	People's Assembly	250	SM	1	250	Maj	N/A
	1992		People's Assembly	100	SM	1	100	Maj	N/A
				1	NL	40	40	PR	4
					Total Seats		140		
	1996		People's Assembly	115	SM	1	115	Maj	N/A
				1	NL	25	25	PR	4
					Total Seats		140		
Croatia	1992	Bicameral							
	1993		House of Counties	21	MM	3	66*	PR	5
	1995		House of Representatives	28	SM	1	28	Maj	N/A
				1	NL	80	80	PR	5
					Total Seats		108*		

	Year		Chamber	Districts			Total Seats	Maj	N/A
Bulgaria	1990	Unicameral	Grand National Assembly	200	SM	1	200	Maj	N/A
				28	MM	4 to 12	200	PR	4
	1991 & 1994						400		
			National Assembly	31	MM		240	PR	4
Romania	1990	Bicameral	Chamber of Deputies	42	MM	4 to 39	396	PR	N/A
			Senate	42	MM	2 to 14	119	PR	N/A
	1992		Chamber of Deputies	42	MM	4 to 29	341*	PR	3
			Senate	42	MM	2 to 13	143	PR	3
	1996		Chamber of Deputies	42	MM	4 to 29	341*	PR	3
			Senate	42	MM	2 to 13	143	PR	3
Slovenia	1996	Unicameral	National Assembly	8	MM	11	88	PR	N/A

Legend: Districts: MM = Multi-Member, SM = Single Member, NL = National List Vote Method: PR = Proportional Representation, Maj = Majority.

Sources: Inter-Parliamentary Union, 'PARLINE Database' at http:/www.ipu.org; K. Jasiewicz, 'Elections and Political Change', in White, Batt and Lewis (eds), *Developments in East European Politics* (1993); J. McGregor, 'The Presidency in East Central Europe', RFE/RL Research Report, 3, 2 (January, 1994); Parliament of the Republic of Croatia, at http://www.sabor.hr; Parliament of the Republic of Romania, at http://dias.vsat.ro; Parliament of the Republic of Slovenija, at http://www.sigov.si.

*Additional reserved seats.

TABLE 3. Continued

C. Baltic States

Country	Election year	Chamber structure	Chamber names	Districts Number	Districts Type	Districts Size	Total seats	Vote method	Electoral threshold (%)
Estonia	1990	Unicameral	Supreme Council	11	MM	8 to 11	105	STV	N/A
	1992 & 1995		State Assembly	11	MM	8 to 11	101	PR	5
Latvia	1990	Unicameral	Supreme Council	201	SM	1	201	Maj	N/A
	1993		Saeima	5	MM	14 to 27	100	PR	4
	1995		Saeima	5	MM	14 to 27	100	PR	5
Lithuania	1990	Unicameral	Supreme Council	141	SM	1	141	Maj	N/A
	1992 & 1996		Seimas	71	SM	1	71	Maj	N/A
				1	NL	70	70	PR	4
				Total Seats			141		

Legend: Districts: MM = Multi-Member, SM = Single Member, NL = National List, Vote Method: PR = Proportional Representation, Maj = Majority, STV = Single Transferable Vote.
Sources: Estonian Ministry for Foreign Affairs, at http://www.vm.ee; Inter-Parliamentary Union, 'PARLINE Database', at http://www.ipu.org; K. Jasiewicz, 'Elections and Political Change', in White, Batt and Lewis (eds), *Developments in East European Politics* (1993); Latvian Saeima, at http://www.saeima.lanet.lv.

TABLE 3. Continued

D. Other Former Soviet Union States

Country	Election year	Chamber structure	Chamber names	Districts			Total seats	Vote method	Electoral threshold (%)
				Number	Type	Size			
The Russian Federation	1995	Bicameral*	State Duma	225	SM	1	225	Maj	N/A
				1	NL	225	225	PR	5%
				Total Seats			450		
Ukraine	1994 & 1995	Unicameral	Verkhovna Rada	450	SM	1	450	Maj	N/A
Moldova	1993 & 1994	Unicameral	Parlamentul	1	MM	104	104	PR	4%

Legend: Districts: MM = Multi-Member, SM = Single Member, NL = National List; Vote Method: PR = Proportional Representation, Maj = Majority.

Sources: Inter-Parliamentary Union, 'PARLINE Database', at http://www.ipu.org; K. Jasiewicz, 'Elections and Political Change', in White, Batt and Lewis, (eds), Developments in East European Politics (1993).

*Although the Russian Parliament is bicameral, only the Duma is popularly elected.

addition, 103 independent candidates, while six candidates appeared on more than one party list, making a total of 1877 candidates.[79] On the other hand, of the 35 candidate lists in the 1993 Polish election, only 15 offered candidates in most of the 52 electoral districts.[80]

The Vote Threshold

The size of the vote cast for below-threshold parties and the degree of proportionality of the parliamentary distribution of party seats are inversely related. It is only with the large voter exclusion rates of the new democracies that this effect has been noticeable. The electoral threshold varies between 3 and 5% for single parties. The threshold increases, however, for electoral coalitions. This provision is legal recognition of the different organizational forms through which candidates may combine to run for office.

The voter exclusion rates by country and year, in Table 4, were at their highest in the 1991–93 period. The exclusion rate has varied from a low in Albania in 1992 of 1.79% to a high in Poland in 1993 of 34.6%. They were lower in the initial elections because of the prominence of the single anti-communist reform movement, such as Civic Forum and Solidarity. As those umbrella conglomerates split into successor groups and parties, the apparent confusion among both putative candidates and questioning voters increased. An indicator of the possibility of less confusion is that the mean exclusion rate declined in the 1994–96 period.

The high exclusion rates of the new democracies contrasted sharply especially in contrast with Western European experience.[81] There seems, however, to have been no discernable consequences in either public attitudes or elite behaviour. It may be that a 5% barrier is overly high in new democracies with many parties. One consequence has been to exclude moderate and centrist parties, though the intention in Western Europe has been to exclude the extremist parties. Perhaps a threshold slowly increasing over time, starting for example at 3%, would have had a somewhat different effect on the party system.

It should be noted, however, that state finance of parties has a lower threshold. In states with a 5% electoral threshold, the financial subsidy threshold is at 3%. In several instances, the vote threshold has been increased, usually up to 5% for single parties and higher for coalitions; in no case has the vote threshold been lowered.

Proportionality Index

The degree of proportionality of parliamentary seat distribution to party shares of the vote was lowest in the 1991–93 period, reflecting the intersection of the emergence of many small parties with the 3–5% threshold requirement (Table 5). The lowest proportionality index has been found in Poland 1993,

---

[79] A. Agh and S. Kurtan, 'The 1990 and 1994 Parliamentary Elections in Hungary: Continuity and Change in the Political System', in Attila Agh and Sandor Kurtan (eds), *Democratization and Europeanization in Hungary: The First Parliament, 1990–1994* (Budapest, Hungarian Centre for Democracy Studies, 1995), 15.

[80] Millard, 'The Polish Parliamentary Election of September 1993', 320–23.

[81] A. Lijphart, *Electoral Systems and Party Systems* (Oxford, Oxford University Press, 1994). Shugart, 'Building the Institutional Framework: Electoral Systems, Party Systems, and Presidents'.

TABLE 4. Elections in Central European States: Elections in Central European States: Exclusion Index, 1990–1996

Region	Country	Year of Election							Mean
		1990	1991	1992	1993	1994	1995	1996	
Central Europe	Poland		7.08		34.6				20.84
	Czech Republic	18.90		19.1				11.20	16.40
	Hungary	15.85				12.66			14.26
	Slovak Republic	7.70		23.8		13.06			14.85
Balkans	Albania			1.79				9.35	5.57
	Bulgaria		24.95			7.59			16.27
	Croatia						6.30		6.30
	Romania	4.59		16.21				19.90	13.57
	Slovenia			17.50				11.30	14.40
Baltic States	Estonia			8.00			12.80		10.40
	Latvia				10.75		12.48		11.62
	Lithuania			10.03				13.00	11.52
	Mean	11.76	16.02	13.78	22.68	11.10	10.53	12.95	

Notes: Exclusion index is calculated by summing the total vote not represented in parliament.

TABLE 5. Elections in Central European States: Proportionality Index, 1990–1996

Region	Country	Year of Election							
		1990	1991	1992	1993	1994	1995	1996	Mean
Central Europe	Poland		87.0		62.5				74.7
	Czech Republic	81.1		80.9				94.4	85.5
	Hungary	78.0				78.9			78.4
	Slovak Republic	92.3		76.2		87.0			85.2
Balkans	Albania			94.2				73.1	83.6
	Bulgaria	9.50	75.1			88.0			86.0
	Croatia						87.1		87.1
	Romania	96.0		83.8				89.9	89.9
	Slovenia			95.4				94.3	94.9
Baltic States	Estonia			82.4			87.2		84.8
	Latvia				89.2		86.6		87.9
	Lithuania			89.7				79.8	84.8
	Mean	88.5	81.1	86.1	75.9	84.6	87.0	86.3	

Notes: Proportionality index is calculated by dividing the proportionality difference by 2 and then subtracting from 100.
Source for Proportionality Index: R. Rose, 'Elections and Electoral Systems: Choices and Alternatives', in V. Bogdanor and D. Butler (eds), *Democracy and Elections* (Cambridge, Cambridge University Press, 1983).

Bulgaria 1991 and Slovakia 1992. While there have been some dramatic declines (Hungary), both the Czech Republic and Slovakia have increased the proportionality of their parliaments in the most recent elections. It is only in 1996 that some of the new parliaments have become as proportional as are the western European parliaments. The 1996 Czech rate of 90.84, for example, resembles the western European average of 94.[82]

Effective Number of Parties

The relative sizes of the parties can be reduced, by means of the Taagepera and Shugart method, to a single index of the number of *effective parties* both in the electorate and in parliament (Table 6). The trend over the several elections, similar to the other indicators, is for the effective number of parties to increase in the second election over the initial post-communist referendum, and to decrease in the third set of elections. With the exception of Slovakia, countries have a lower number of effective parties in the third election than in the second, while in all, with the exception of Hungary, all countries had a higher effective number of parties in the second than in the initial elections.

In each instance, the number is smaller in parliament than in the electorate. The largest differences between electorate and parliament are found in Hungary's first, in Poland's third, and in Romania's second election, reflecting the disproportionality of seat distribution within parliament.

TABLE 6. Party System Change by Electoral Sequence: Effective Number of Parties

Country	Election 1		Election 2		Election 3	
	Votes	Seats	Votes	Seats	Votes	Seats
Bulgaria	2.75	2.14	4.19	2.41	3.87	2.73
Czech Republic	3.18	1.89	7.69	4.80	4.89	4.15
Hungary	6.76	3.74	5.54	2.89		
Poland			14.69	10.93	9.81	3.87
Romania	2.25	2.19	7.04	4.80		
Slovakia	5.76	4.98	4.22	3.24	5.37	4.41
Mean value	4.14	2.99	7.23	4.85	5.99	3.79

Sources: 'Effective Party' formula: Taagapera and Shugart, 1989, pp. 78–79; Country Indices: Mansfeldova and Kitschelt, 1995; McGregor (1993); Bielasiak, 1995, p. 31; Original calculations: Slovakia & Czech Republic, Election 3.
Notes:
1. In countries with bicameral parliaments, only data from the lower chamber are shown.
2. Reported number sometimes vary by source.

[82] Rose, *What is Europe?*, 163. The proportionality index is half of the sum of percentage points difference between the party share of votes and seats, subtracted from a perfect score of 100%. Though we find the same trends, our calculations lead to somewhat different numbers for Central European parliaments than reported by Rose.

Party Volatility

Over time, do the parties and the party systems of the new democracies show evidence of stability? Stability in parties across elections and parliamentary terms as well as consolidation at any one time is a key trait of party systems. The party volatility rate could be expected to be high between the initial and second elections, reflecting the fragmentation of the anti-communist reform movement from the initial election (Table 7). In that first pair of elections, the party volatility rate (with a maximum of 200 percentage points) has been as high as 178 and 160, in the Czech and Slovakian Republics. That rate, however, has dramatically declined in the second pair of elections (inclusive of the second and third elections). While the volatility index has been much higher both in Central Europe and in Western Europe in the beginning democratic elections, in both regions the index has declined over time.[83]

TABLE 7. Electoral Volatility Index by Region, Country, and Electoral Sequence

Region	Election sequence		Longer span
Country	1 to 2	2 to 3	
Central Europe			
Bulgaria	44		
Czech Republic	178	58	
Hungary	52		
Poland		53	
Romania	126		
Slovakia	160	57	
Western Europe			
Germany	52		16
Italy	46		
Spain	25		10

Note: Maximum variation = 200.
Source: Rose, 1996b, p. 153 Table 7.2; and author calculations.

A high volatility index could stem from several different circumstances. In Slovakia, the volatility in the second pair of elections occurred because of the formation of new political parties, while in the Czech Republic, the approximately same volatility rate occurred because of major changes in vote shares among continuing parties. The latter circumstance was also associated with the approximately same volatility rates in Hungary (first election pair) and in Poland. As the voter exclusion rate changes, that factor, too, could result in changes in vote shares among existing parties.[84]

---

[83] Rose, *What is Europe?*, 152–53.
[84] The party volatility index is the sum of the vote percentage difference between parties in pairs of successive elections. The Rose index is calculated for all parties obtaining over 1% of the vote. We, by contrast, sum the percentage for all parties below the vote threshold into a single figure. Thus our numbers will differ slightly, while retaining comparability among countries and across years.

Vote Structure and Issue Dimensions

All post-communist elections have shown a patterning in the vote. Both by geography[85] and through exit polls and public opinion data,[86] voting for parties is differentiated by age, gender, place of residence, region, education and occupation. Income differences, given their ambiguous status in current post-communist society, have less relationship to the vote than do other characteristics.

In addition, the demography-vote relationship has some stability over the several democratic elections. Furthermore, the geography of the vote is often related to pre-Communist and inter-War vote patterns, even though there has been a wholesale turnover of population.[87] Nevertheless, neither demographic categories nor putative 'interests' lead directly to political party formation. While all countries in this region have rural electorates, for example, few have rural parties.

Issue dimensions and cleavages, both by number and content, in public opinion and in parliament vary by country. In one four-country study, the Czech Republic provided the clearest example of economic issues dominating party definitions, and thus most amenable to a left-right dimension similar to western democracies. Hungary also showed the dominance of a single issue dimension, but not on economic questions. Poland and Bulgaria showed far more complex circumstances of several different issue dimensions. Economic reform was one of several major issues in Poland, but not in Bulgaria.[88] One characteristic of Bulgarian parties is that they are deeply divided in their issue attitudes.[89]

[85] T. Kostelecky, 'Changing Party Allegiances in a Changing Party System: the 1990 and 1992 Parliamentary Elections in the Czech Republic', in Gordon Wightman (ed.), *Party Formation in East-Central Europe* (Hants, UK, Edward Elgar, 1995). P. Jehlicka, T. Kostelecky and L. Sykora, 'Czechoslovak Parliamentary Elections 1990: Old Patterns, New Trends and Lots of Surprises', in John O'Loughlin and Herman van der Wusten (eds), *The New Political Geography of Eastern Europe* (London, Belhaven, 1993). V. Krivy, 'The Parliamentary Elections 1994: the Profile of Supporters of the Political Parties, the Profile of Regions', in Sona Szomolanyi and Grigorij Meseznikov (eds), *Slovakia Parliamentary Elections 1994* (Bratislava, Slovak Political Science Association, 1995), 114–35. J. Ragulska, 'Democratic Elections and Political Restructuring in Poland, 1989–91', in John O'Loughlin and Herman van der Wusten (eds), *The New Political Geography of Eastern Europe* (London, Belhaven, 1993). M. Gregor and L. Cama, 'Volby a okresy', *Sociologicky casopis*, 29,4 (1993), 493–515.

[86] J. Bielasiak, 'Institution Building in a Transformative System: Party Fragmentation in Poland's Parliament', in Lawrence Longely (ed.), Working Papers on Comparative Legislative Studies, (Appleton WI, Research Committee of Legislative Specialists, International Political Science Association, 1994). Z. Buterova, 'The Citizen as a Respondent and a Voter: Reflection on Election Polling', in Sona Szomolanyi and Grigorij Meseznikov (eds), *Slovakia Parliamentary Elections 1994* (Bratislava, Slovak Political Science Association, 1995).

[87] Kostelecky, 'Changing Party Allegiances in a Changing Party System: the 1990 and 1992 Parliamentary Elections in the Czech Republic'. A. Korosenyi, 'Revival of the Past or New Beginning? The Nature of Post-Communist Politics', in Gyorgy Szoboszlai (ed.), *Democracy and Political Transformation* (Budapest, Hungarian Political Science Association, 1991). Z. Kovacs, 'The Political Geography of Hungarian Parliamentary Elections, 1989', in John O'Loughlin and Herman van der Wusten (eds), *The New Political Geography of Eastern Europe* (London, Belhaven, 1993).

[88] Toka, 'The Programmatic Structuring of Party Competition: Bulgaria, the Czech Republic, Hungary, and Poland in Spring 1994'. Markowski, 'Ideological Dimensions in Eastern European Context'.

[89] Kitschelt, 'Patterns of Competition in East Central European Party Systems'.

Three sets of issue dimensions were identified in a multi-country study, including several post-Soviet Republics: ethnicity, social liberalism, and political liberalism. These issues did not combine into a single dimension in any country, and varied in their configuration among the several countries.[90] A review of Polish parties, elites, and public opinions suggested six major dimensions,[91] while region-wide typologies suggest a pattern of nine or ten main parties.[92] In parliamentary roll call votes, party alignments are fluid. The parties often are not uniform in voting, and apparently opposite parties actually vote together, depending upon specific issues.[93] Interviews with party leaders in Poland, found both that each party was internally divided on economic issues and that economic views were shared across parties.[94] This varied pattern of issue alignments, as measured both by public opinion and parliamentary roll calls, is consistent with our earlier observations about the flux and variability in organizational types and electoral strategies among parties and countries in the initial democratic decade.

Emergent Trends

Several trends in party organization and the party system appeared during the first-half decade of democracy in central Europe after communism. The first generation of parties reflect the institutional innovation made possible, if not also necessary, by the context of unprecedented social conditions. The trends include: (1) types of party electorates, (2) the parliamentary-centered character of party dynamics, (3) consolidation of the party system, (4) differentiation among the countries, and (5) emergence of the *cadre-catchall* party.

First, the broad distinction between the historical parties and the new parties symbolizes a more fundamental distinction than the mere passage of time; the parties with older roots have a more clearly identified and stable electorate than do the more recently created parties. The newly created parties in Central Europe tend to be the post-transitional parties, the survivors of Solidarity in Poland and of the Civic Forum in the Czech Republic, to refer to two of the more prominent conglomerate reform movements. Their leaders tend to be based in parliament, and are often in direct conflict with one another to identify and claim the electorates that support a combination of democratic and

[90] S. Whitefield and G. Evans, 'Mass Ideology and Political Competition in Post-Communist Societies', Paper read at conference on Party Formation and Public Opinion in Eastern Europe, Duke University, 1995.

[91] Wesolowski, 'Formation of Political Parties in Post-communist Poland'.

[92] Rose, *What is Europe?*, 138–46. Kitschelt, 'Patterns of Competition in East Central European Party Systems'.

[93] Wiatr, 'Fragmented Parties in a New Democracy: Poland'. J. Wiatr, 'The dilemmas of reorganizing the bureaucracy in Poland during the democratic transformation', *Communist and Post-Communist Studies*, 28,1 (March 1995). S. Gebethner, 'Political Parties in Poland (1989–1993)', in Gerd Meyer (ed.), *Die politischen Kulturen Ostmitteleuropas im Umbruch* (Tuebingen, Francke Verlag, 1993), 311–38. D. M. Olson, 'The Sundered State: Federalism and Parliament in Czechoslovakia', in Thomas F. Remington (ed.), *Parliaments in Transition* (Boulder CO, Westview, 1994), 97–124. P. Kopecky and L. Nijzink, 'Party Discipline and the Relations between Ministers and MPs: A Comparison between The Netherlands and the Czech Republic', Paper read at ECPR Workshop, Bordeaux, 1995. A. Agh and S. Kurtan (eds), *Democratization and Europeanization in Hungary: The First Parliament, 1990–1994* (Budapest, Hungarian Centre for Democracy Studies, Tables', 1995).

[94] E. Nalewajko, 'Partie polityczne w Polsci – geneza i instytucjonalizacja'.

DAVID M. OLSON 41

economic reform. The older parties, by contrast, can rely upon known and relatively stable electorates. The connections between voters and leaders may be more symbolic than organizational, but their shared party names and traditions survive as viable political symbols in post-communism. The historical parties include a diversity of electorates and issue positions, including the religious and the economic. Among the latter are post-communist parties in all countries, and distinctively in Poland, the Peasants' Party.

Second, the major party leaders are assembled in parliament, and the main dynamics in the formation of coalitions and of party splits occur either in parliament or are directed toward parliamentary elections. Contending organizations in the direct presidential elections both reflect and become components of the parliamentary party. Parliament contains most of the offices they seek, and party leadership both gravitates to, and emerges from, that institution.

A third trend has been party system fragmentation followed by beginning signs of consolidation of the party system, for which the aggregate measures serve as indicators. The effective number of parties in particular, accompanied by a declining exclusion rate, has begun to moderate since the 1991–93 period.

A fourth trend in the party system is that a taxonomy of countries is emerging within the wider region. One set, including Poland, the Czech Republic and Hungary, appear to have developed a more stable party system than the others, especially in that parties and coalitions of parties are the main actors in electoral and parliamentary politics. Many of the ex-Soviet Republics are at the opposite end of a developmental continuum, in that political parties as an organizational form are in competition with other electoral groupings, and there is a high degree of party volatility from one election to the next. Virtually all political activity in the former Soviet Republics is based upon the former Communist Party, while in central Europe and also in the Baltic States, parties are based upon a wider range of experiences. A middle set of countries include most of central Europe outside the USSR, along with the Baltic states.

Fifth, party organizations and other electoral groupings are mainly cadre in structure and catch-all in appeal. Their activity and leadership tend to centre in parliament.

It is by no means clear whether, over a decade or longer, these incipient trends will continue. The party system interacts with other components of the wider political system, and all are conditioned by unpredictable economic and ethnic stress.

Next Step Questions

Just as political parties themselves are at their beginnings in the new post-communist democracies, so *research* on party developments is also at its beginnings.[95] Certainly no comparable set of political changes in history has been so well-chronicled by the scholarly community as has been the process of transition from communism. The range of inquiry is so wide, that I am emboldened to suggest an inventory of relatively specific research targets, at least within the realm of political parties. This concluding section will suggest

[95] A. Pacek, 'New political parties in Eastern Europe: building a research agenda', *VOX POP Newsletter*, 10,3 (1992), 1, 8ff.

some of the next questions to be examined in advancing the understanding of political parties and party systems at their beginnings.

Candidate nominations. Party lists can be formed by regional or central party leaders, while single member candidacies can be decided at either constituency or higher levels of the party. While there has been some discussion of 'primaries' in the Czech parties, little is known in any country of how party decisions are made, and who makes them, about candidacies. Candidate selection, one of the elemental functions of political parties, is an unknown process from municipal councils up to national parliaments and presidents.

Party finance. As is the nomination process, the flow of funds is a tracer element in party organization. While there are occasional reports and constant rumours of scandals, little press reporting and even fewer official records are available. While this essay has made reference to the importance of state finance to political parties, there is also a flow of funds from foreign sources and an admixture of funds from business enterprises, many of which still have state funding.

Party participants and organizational form. Who are the activists in electoral groupings, from parties to more loosely structured associations? The elemental questions are of numbers and location: how many participants are there, and where are they? Perhaps our estimate of the prevalence of the cadre type party structure is based on evidence about few public participants, while there could be many more activists than are visible at first glance. What are the organizational varieties of 'electoral groupings' and 'proto-parties'?

Parliamentary and external party units. To what extent is there a personal union between parliamentary and external units of the same party? How often do disagreements arise, over what matters, and how are they resolved?

Coalitions. What are the strategic calculations of party leaders that lead them to enter, reject, or withdraw from coalitions, in both elections and in parliaments? What do they learn from their experience?

Patterns of system and country. What types of parties emerge; in what patterns do whole party systems develop? Not all parties are alike, and increasingly we can observe that not all countries in this regional set are alike either.

Developmental paths. How do parties and party systems form initially, and how do they change over time? The electoral sequence perspective leads us to closely monitor each election and ensuing parliamentary term as they occur. While in established democracies, the question of origins is an exercise in history, we have an opportunity in new democracies to observe parties at their early stages. We have the rare opportunity to observe at first hand those events and dynamics which, at some future time, will retrospectively be designated as the 'freezing moment'.

The Post-communist Transition and Institutionalization of Lithuania's Parties

Introduction

Lithuania's transition from a one-party communist state to a multi-party system is a good example of a *negotiated revolution*. That transition, however, was not linear, but rather phased, with each phase having a different impact on party organization and politics. Three facets of the transition will be examined here:

- the impact of the general logic of post-communist transition on emerging multi-partyism and on particular parties
- the legal and institutional bases of Lithuania's parties and
- the relation of organizational patterns and party government in the institutionalization of the parties.

Lithuania's experience with competetive parties did not begin in 1990. Historic experience, dating back to the late 19th century, has been relevant to recent developments. That history is the starting point for my discussion here.

Historic Roots of Parties and Multipartyism in Lithuania

Multi-party competition is not a historical novelty in Lithuania. The first political parties emerged in the late 19th and early 20th centuries, generally in the same historical period as in most other countries of East Central Europe. The Lithuanian Social Democratic Party (LSDP) was founded in 1896, the Democratic Party (LDP) in 1902, and the Christian Democrats (LChDP) in 1905. (See Appendix for a full list of relevant parties and their abbreviations.) Most of these and other parties emerged from various ideological streams within the national liberation movement started at the end of the 1880s.

The Lithuanian Council, the political institution that declared independence in 1918, was dominated by party politicians from the moment of its establishment in September of 1917. The LSDP, LChDP, National Progress, Democratic and Socialist People's parties were represented in the Council from the outset.

The early development of multi-party competition, however, did not offer much promise of political stability. The two-year period of 1918–1920 saw five cabinet crises, brought on by partisan disagreement. It was only after the election of the Constituent Seimas in 1920 that a fully functioning parliamentary democracy came into being, with parties granted legal and practical means to implement their representative function in Lithuanian society.

The 1922 Constitution made the parliament responsible for the election of the President and for the appointment of the Cabinet. As a consequence of these legal provisions, parliamentary parties moved to the centre of power in the

TABLE 1. Parliamentary Democracy and Lithuania's Parties, 1919–1926

	Membership	Constituent Seimas, 1920		1st Seimas, 1922		2nd Seimas, 1923		3rd Seimas, 1926	
		Votes (%)	Seats N	Votes (%)	Seats N	Votes (%)	Seats N	Votes (%)	Seats N
Christian Democratic Bloc:									
LChDP	28.000 (1931)	35	24	17	15	14	14	13	14
Labour Federation	15.000 (1920)	10	15	12	11	15	12	8	5
Farmers' Union	4000	1	20	12	12	14	14	11	11
Peasants Peoples Alliance:									
LSPDP*	33.000 (1926)	6	9	1	5	18	16	22	22
LPU*		17	20	17	14	–	–	–	–
LSDP	3.000 (1926)	13	13	10	11	11	8	17	15
LNPP**	13.000 (1928)	1.7	–	2.9	–	2	–	4	3
LFP	?	0.4	–	–	–	–	–	1.8	2
Others***		15.9	11	28.1	5	26	14	23.2	13
Total:			112		78		78		85

*LSPDP and LPU founded Lithuanian Peasants Peoples Party in 1922.
**After 1924 Lithuanian Nationalists Union.
***Ethnic parties and pro-communist groups.

Lithuanian state. The 1919–1926 period was one of relatively stable competition between two party blocs. The right wing was dominated by the Christian Democratic coalition; the left wing was led by the Peasant People's and Social Democratic parties. The major parties, such as the Christian Democrats, Social Democrats, and Peasant Peoples' parties, developed broad rank and file memberships that exceeded the numbers found in contemporary Lithuania's leading parties (see Table 1).

In the 1919–1926 period, the strongest political force was clearly the Lithuanian Christian Democratic Party, together with its satellite organizations, the Labour Federation and the Farmers Union. This combination held a majority of seats in all parliaments in the period, with the exception of the 3rd Seimas, elected in 1926 (see Table 1). The major competitor to the LChDP was the so-called Peoples coalition. Initially, it included the Lithuanian Socialist Peoples and Lithuanian Peasants parties. A third major political group was represented, of course, by the Lithuanian Social Democratic Party, which overcame the virus of communism in 1918 and 1919. Later the LSDP joined the Left wing coalition led by the social-liberal Peasants Peoples Party.

The results of elections to the Constituent Seimas, in 1920, was 'a bolt from the blue' to the National Progress Party (NPP), which had been in a leading position, along with LChDP, in the Lithuanian Council and several Cabinets in 1918 and 1919. During the elections of 1920 the NPP was unable even to get into the Constituent parliament. Moreover, the NPP (in 1924 it was renamed the *Lithuanian Nationalists Union – LNU*) played only a role of minor party during the remaining years of the inter-war parliamentary democracy.

The growth and stabilization of the parties and the multi-party system was dramatically reversed after the 1926 *coup d'etat*, led by the Nationalist Union. The causes of the *coup* can be traced to both external and internal conditions. Lithuania's next-door neighbour, Poland, suffered the Pilsudski-led *coup* in May, 1926. The LNU learned the Polish lesson, despite the hostile relations between the two countries in the 1920s. Democracy in the other neighbouring countries was either weak – Estonia, Latvia, Weimar Germany – or did not exist at all – Russia. Yet one cannot attribute the Lithuanian democratic collapse primarily to mere diffusion. Its principal causes were domestic.

All conditions that might have been supportive of democracy in Lithuania were clearly underdeveloped in the inter-war period. Democratic culture was a weak and short-lived phenomenon, the level of literacy was low, socio-economic development was based predominantly on agriculture. Society in itself was highly conservative and religious (dominated by Roman Catholics).

The constitutional design of democratic institutions also had its imperfections. The proportional electoral system produced a high level of party fragmentation, leading to unstable majorities in the Seimas. Lithuanian politics was extremely personalized, in addition to 'hypertrophied partisanship', as in the case of Czechoslovakia between the two world wars.[1] The parliament's use of its power over cabinet decision making proved meddlesome. The President was appointed by, accountable to, and controlled by the Seimas. A clear functional separation of powers between legislature and executive was never implemented or even properly designed in Lithuanian laws in the 1920s.

The political behaviour of parties, especially of the Christian Democrats, was in many ways completely irresponsible. The LChDP was inclined towards a policy of hardly manageable broad coalitions. Until 1924 it refused to form a single-party government and to take full responsibility for the Cabinets' performance, even though it had a parliamentary majority. Imbalances between centres of power, permanent clashes among political parties, along with the society's inexperience with democracy, guided Lithuania's political ship into waters of authoritarian rule.

The 'overheating' of the young democracy was finally reached in 1926. The collapse of the competitive multi-party system after the *coup d'etat* was not sudden but rather a gradual process. The only party that was banned outright after the Lithuanian Nationalist Union came to power was the Communist Party. All others survived for shorter or longer period after the coup. The LNU, led by Antanas Smetona, sought initially to preserve a parliamentary form of government. Moreover, the coup leaders needed the tacit support of the Christian Democrats in order to create an impression that the LNU had taken power in a more or less constitutional manner and with a formal approval of the Seimas. This political diplomacy was fruitful for the LNU, and it was able to

[1] See: E. Broklova, 'Historical Roots for the Restoration of Democracy in Czechoslovakia,' in I. Gabal (ed.), *The 1990 Election to the Czechoslovakian Federal Assembly. Analyses, Documents and Data* (Berlin, Sigma, 1996), p. 33.

concentrate power in its hands without major resistance. The only attempt to organize a *contra-coup*, by a group of LSDP members, failed in September 1927. Nevertheless, activities of the LSDP were not prohibited until 1933. All other parties, except the LNU, were banned *de facto* in November 1935.

In 1938 the 'soft' authoritarian rule by the Nationalists came back to policy of 'tolerance' towards a 'loyal opposition', due to increasing international tensions in the Baltics and Europe. One-party dictatorship was finally introduced only after Lithuania's occupation by the Soviets in 1940. However, after World War II some Lithuanian parties were re-established in exile. In 1948 the Lithuanian Christian Democratic Party in exile joined the Christian Democratic International. Two years later, it joined the Union of Christian Democrats of Central Europe. The LSDP in exile took part in activities of the Socialist International.

The point I am making is that the traditions of Lithuanian party politics were never wholly stopped or forgotten between 1940 and 1988. Without a doubt, Lithuania's political stage was dominated by the Communist Party for almost fifty years in the 20th century. But former political affiliations and preferences were alive in cultural and social consciousness, at least in some parts of society. A definite sign of this influence was the rapid re-establishment of all major historical parties after 1988.

In the 20th century Lithuanian political parties developed through, at least, six different phases:

- the emergence of traditional right- and left-wing parties from the end of the 19th century until the declaration of Lithuania's independence in 1918, when parties were able to enter the stage of nation-state politics as principal actors
- the period of parliamentary multipartyism between 1918 and 1926
- restricted multi-party system under the supremacy of the Lithuanian Nationalists Union, 1926–1935
- the one-party system of the LNU in the period 1935–1940
- totalitarian and authoritarian rule by the Communist Party and final collapse of the competitive multi-party system in 1940–1941 and from 1944 to 1988
- the establishment of Sajudis[2] and the gradual revival a of competitive party system after 1988.

The rebirth of multi-party system is a different story. It might be divided in various phases too. But before examining that process it will be helpful to look on the general logic of the democratization process, as well as the roles of parties in this process both in Lithuania and in comparative perspective, since 1988.

Institutional Democracy and Political Parties

In 1988 Lithuania, along with Estonia and Latvia, was forced by many objective and subjective circumstances to lead a historical mission to destroy the former Soviet Union, the authoritarian and imperial monster. The signal of freedom and democracy sent from the Baltics was heard in East Central Europe, which

---

[2] The Lithuanian Reform Movement – a secessionist group that cut across partisan lines. After 1993, it was re-organized as the *Homeland Union* (Lithuanian Conservatives).

produced the anti-Communist, national, and democratic transformations of 1989.

The post-communist metamorphoses can be and are described by different concepts and terms in various countries. It took a form of *devolution of autarchy* in Romania, but it is usually characterized as a *self-limiting revolution*[3] in the case of Hungary. However, the post-communist democratization is a highly dynamic phenomenon always and everywhere. Claus Offe has reflected upon this feature of the post-communist changes in the following way:

> There is no time for slow maturation, experience, and learning along the evolutionary scale of nation building, constitution making, and the politics of allocation and redistribution. And neither are there model cases which might be imitated nor for that matter, a victorious power that would impose its will from the outside.[4]

A paradox of the post-communist transition is not that it was caused mainly by internal processes. Here, in contrast to the preceding experiences of democratization in the 20th century, political reform was not only a precondition of economic changes, but 'at the same time [economic and social] stability is needed to ensure a peaceful political transition'[5]. According to Samuel Huntington's logic, a market economy prepared the soil for democratic order and the liberal state from the beginning of the 19th century until the post-communist transitions in the late 1980s and early 1990s. Moreover, if all previous transitions to democracy included only political reconstruction of one or another country, the post-communist democratization covers all spheres of the internal and external environment of the transforming country. Briefly speaking, a scenario of transition in Eastern Europe was based on a motto: 'mass democracy first, capitalism later'.[6]

Lithuania's model of transition to democracy is similar to the other East Central European and Baltic countries. There are several commonalities in that pattern. It means that democratic traditions are based, at least to some extent, on the inter-war experience. Institutional democracy was introduced through a 'negotiated revolution' or political dialogue between an emerging alternative political elite and reform communists. The new political order is a product of relatively gradual changes and failed attempts to reconstruct the *ancien regime* into 'socialism with a human face'. And the changes are implemented mainly by legal and political means as well as in a non-violent way.

Without a doubt, a major element of the post-communist democratization is a revival of parties and multi-party systems. This element is important not only as a structural part of political or institutional democracy, but also as a basic component of the polity through which citizens can express their alternative demands and preferences, that is, a role of the parties as intermediate structures

---

[3] A. Arato, 'Revolution or Restoration?', in *The New Great Transformation?* (New York, Routledge, 1994), p. 67.

[4] Quoted from J. Musil, 'Czechoslovakia in the Middle of Transition,' in S. T. Graubard (ed.), *Exit from Communism* (London, Transaction, 1993), p. 181.

[5] M. Glenny, '*The Rebirth of History: Eastern Europe in the Age of Democracy,*' London, Penguin Books, 1990), p. 15.

[6] L. Balcerowicz, 'Eastern Europe: Economic, Social and Political Dynamics', in: B. Goralczyk et al. (eds), In *Pursuit of Europe. Transformations of Post-Communist States, 1989–1994* (Warsaw, PAN ISP, 1995), p. 110.

in a democratic political system. The parties serve as the channels through which societal interests are articulated and aggregated. They serve also as the procedural and institutional instruments for creating a competitive political environment. Finally, from examples of transitions to democracy in Southern Europe, it is clear that consolidation of democracy takes the form of more or less stable party government.[7]

There are things that can be changed virtually overnight. Unfortunately or, maybe, fortunately, it is not a case of the post-communist transition. In 1990 Ralf Dahrendorf admitted that the transforming countries need only a period of about six months to introduce democratic institutions, and to meet minimalist requirements of political democracy. Indeed, the speed with which communist autocrats were replaced by colourful reformers in Eastern Europe is amazing. But the changes were not so fast as it seemed to be in 1989 or 1990. Moreover, as time passes, from the departure point in 1989, more and more analysts are recognizing that the liberalization and democratization in many countries (as Poland, Hungary, even the former Soviet Union) was much more gradual and started long before the famous 1989 – 1991 revolutionary period. Unfortunately, in all countries where liberalization started earlier, the way to go, in sense of time, was longer. The turning point in the chain of liberalization, especially for the Baltics and for the external Soviet satellite countries in Eastern Europe, was the policy of *perestroika* and *glasnost* launched by Mikhail Gorbachev in 1985.

Because the new democratic order has started to shape the polities of Eastern Europe, not from the ashes of the communism but rather through attempts to reconstruct the old regime, a perception that the collapse of communism left a political vacuum is highly misleading. On the contrary, the Communist Party was in power and tried to preserve its positions as long as possible and by every possible means until the founding elections. Following the first competitive elections the communists were exchanged for broad coalitions of opposition reformers, ranging from radical nationalists to westernized liberals. From the very beginning, the political stage of the transforming countries was overcrowded by diverse sets of political actors. Their seemingly unstructured interactions confound the effort to understand the complexity of the transitional political scene. Moreover, the essential feature is that 'the transformation process itself is not a continuum but a sequence of distinct phases'.[8] It means that each phase of transition has very specific and distinctive goals. It has leading political players in every sphere – institutional, legal, social, and economic – affected by the ongoing changes.

Institutional democracy is not introduced so easily as it was thought by Dahrendorf in 1990. Furthermore, political democracy cannot be created by a single act or a decision of a single institution, even if it would be a Constituent Assembly. The development of a democratic institutional order could be measured by two theoretical conditions: structural stability and functional autonomy of political players in the transition. This focus allows us to see the most influential political actors during each phase of the transformation.

[7] See: L. Morlino, 'Consolidation of party government in southern Europe', *International Political Science Review*, 16 (1995), p. 145.

[8] Z. Brzezinski, 'The great transformation', *The National Interest*, 3 (1993), p. 5.

TABLE 2. Political Actors in the Transition: Stability and Autonomy

Phase of transition	Stable and autonomous political actors
Pre-transitional crisis	Embryonic interests groups, **Communist party***
Confrontation	Interests groups, **political parties** (megapolitical conglomerates-LCP and Sajudis)
Reform of system	Interests groups, political parties, **Constituent parliament**
Consolidation of democracy	Interests groups, political parties, parliament, **executive and state's bureaucracy**
Stable democracy (polyarchy)	Interests groups, political parties, parliament, executive and state's bureaucracy, courts**

*Dominant political actor is in bold.
**All political actors are stable and autonomous.

Looking from this angle, the transition has had five different phases in Lithuania (Table 2).

During the transition process, not only can different political actors be characterized by different influence on the process of changes in certain phases, and by speedy correction of their positions, but also *the whole logic of transformation is based on asynchronous development of basic structures of democratic polity.* It is not enough to legalize political opposition or to pass a law on independent courts, on the assumption that all these political structures will from that moment automatically turn into stable and autonomous institutions. A 'corridor' of political pluralism is widened gradually, and during every new phase of the transition new political structures gain independence and acquire relative stability.

Political parties are not exempt from this rule. The general logic of the transition was not avoided by political parties. The rebirth of multipartyism was not a linear process but rather developed through certain phases, as illustrated in Table 3.

The pre-transitional crisis or liberalization within the old regime revived hopes of would-be reformers that the *ancien regime* might be changed. These hopes united the reformers' efforts in broad political movements. But in the case of the former Soviet Union the major political issue was establishment of the boundaries of partial liberalization and a guarantee for the Communist party to control activities of semi-independent interests groups and new citizens' associations. Clearly, during the pre-transitional crisis the LCP was able to preserve its monopoly of power.

But in a further development of democracy, a crucial role was played by two sets of factors: (a) creation of conditions for party competition and electoral choice; and (b) establishment 'of consultative and decisional mechanisms, more or less explicitly designed to circumvent accountability to popularly elected representatives'.[9]

A main precondition of real institutional reforms was a birth of megapolitical forces in every transforming country, such as *Sajudis* in Lithuania or

[9] G. O'Donnell and P. C. Schmitter, *Transitions from Authoritarian Rule: Tentative Conclusions about Uncertain Democracies* (Baltimore, Johns Hopkins University Press, 1991), p. 9.

TABLE 3. Phases of Transition for Parties

Phase	Type of party system	Dominant political actor	Dominant function of parties	Type of inter-party relations
Pre-transitional crisis (1985–1988)	hegemonic party system	LCP	mobilization	domination
Confrontation (1988–1989)	political plurality within one-party system	LCP and Sajudis	mobilization	confrontation
Reform of system (1990–1992)	megapolitical plurality and megapolitical fragmentation	Independent LCP and Sajudis, new parties	articulation of macro-interests, mobilization	limited competition, politics of non-cooperation
Consolidation of democracy (1992–1996)	confrontational multi party system	right-left wing parties	embryonic articulation and aggregation of interests	limited cooperation, non-adversary competition
Stability	consensual multi-party system	stable right-left wing parties	articulation and aggregation of interests	cooperation and competition

Solidarnozc in Poland, as instruments of collective political opposition. Their emergence was a sign that the pre-transitional crisis was over and the confrontational phase had begun.

The first real achievement on the institutional level was a democratization of electoral procedures, allowing non-radical oppositional forces to take part in the elections. Moreover, the elections became a mechanism of electoral choice and a vehicle of democratic changes, in contrast to their former function as a voting-machine to increase the legitimacy of the *ancien regime*. In Lithuania the bulk of the effort of two dominant political players, the Lithuanian Communist Party and Sajudis, was concentrated on establishing rules and procedures for democratic elections in the phase of confrontation. In spite of the LCP's efforts to preserve its political positions and role, crucial changes occurred within this party.

From the Baltics perspective, the Lithuanian Communist Party was substantially different from its counterparts in Estonia and Latvia. As a consequence of these distinctions, the role and evolution of the LCP during the transition is only partially comparable to that in neighbouring countries.

A crucial distinguishing feature of the LCP role was its ethnic composition. The LCP was a 'lithuanized' party *vis-a-vis* the 'russified' communist parties in

TABLE 4. Ethnic Composition of the Baltic Communist Parties: 1989

	Estonia	Latvia	Lithuania
Members of the CP per 1000 adult population	98	92	78
Representatives of titular nations in the CP (%)	50	40	71
Russians (%)	39	43	17
Others (%)	11	17	12

Estonia and Latvia (see Table 4). The LCP was not only dominated by the native population, but the rate of membership to population was lower than in either Estonia or Latvia. Ethnicization of the LCP has led to a relatively high degree of legitimacy for the party on the domestic political stage compared to the other Baltic countries, where the communist parties were perceived mostly as external and alien institutions. Lithuanian reform communists were supported by the opposition forces from the very beginning, and they came to the top of the LCP easily in 1988. Furthermore, in 1989–1990 the LCP was able to transform itself into a representative parliamentary party, while all attempts to form more or less lasting ex-communist parties had failed in Estonia and Latvia.

Shortly after the founding of Sajudis in June of 1988, the LCP nomenklatura was divided into three political factions: hard-liners, moderates, and reformers. Moreover, many non-nomenklatura communists joined and even took part in the creation of Sajudis.

The leading political actors of the second phase of party transition, that of confrontational politics (Table 3), were Sajudis and the divided CP. Both political groups could hardly be described as political parties, in a traditional sense, due to their ideological heterogeneity, their macro-political appeals for 'democracy', 'independence', and 'preservation of reformed socialism', on the one hand, and their attempts to mobilize anyone and everyone behind macro-political slogans, on the other. But during the phase of confrontation the hegemonic one-party system was changed by proto-multipartyism, where the dominant political forces were the LCP and Sajudis. A final point of the confrontational period was the 'founding' election in February of 1990.

A victory of Sajudis in the founding election initiated the phase of system reforms. During this phase of transition the most important political player was the constituent parliament, the only institution which was able to institution-alize and legitimize political democracy on the basis of law. Indeed, political parties played a marginal role in these developments (somewhat in contrast to the historic example of the Constituent Seimas in 1920). But changes during the recent systems reforming period within political parties have had long-lasting effects for the parties themselves. First, hard-liners of the former LCP became more and more isolated. Their organization disintegrated finally in 1991. Second, the political distance between moderate ex-communists and radical opposition was increasing and broadening as such fundamental macro-political goals as institutional democracy and major economic reforms were imple-mented. From this moment, different ideological preferences began playing an increasing role in political discourse. Ideological differences reach a point of division among the new political parties and the former partners of the reform coalition. Both leading actors of reforms – Sajudis and the independent LCP –

adopted different strategies of development. The independent LCP was transformed into a moderate social democratic organization, the Lithuanian Democratic Labour Party. The story of Sajudis was much more complicated.

The major trend within Sajudis was gradual fragmentation 'from above', that is factionalization of Sajudis within the constituent parliament. At the same time, new parliamentary factions of Sajudis started to search for extra-parliamentary bases of support. It was a two-way traffic. On the one hand, parliamentary factions from Sajudis initiated development of some extra-parliamentary parties (such as the Lithuanian Centre Union in 1992, whose roots are in the Centre faction of Sajudis). But it was more common for new extra-parliamentary parties to merge their efforts with certain parliamentary factions (such as the Liberal Union and the Liberal faction of the Constituent parliament). The fragmentation of megapolitical conglomerates produced the so-called one hundred party system. In 1992 more than 30 political associations and parties were registered in the Ministry of Justice. This may be compared to 177 in Poland, and 79 in the Czech and Slovak Republic in 1991.

All in all, the fragmentation of Sajudis was a very positive process for the institutionalization of Lithuania's multi-party system. At the end of the system reform phase (see Table 3), the parties had become the principal players shaping electoral choice in Lithuania. The parliamentary elections of 1992 might be called the first multi-party elections in the country since 1926.

The adoption of a new constitution in 1992 is a formal point of departure in the consolidation of democracy phase. The traditional branches of institutional power – legislature, executive and courts – acquired structural stability as a direct effect of the introduction of a new constitution. Political parties were transformed into autonomous structures within a democratic policy, and their initial institutionalization phase was over.

On the other hand, democratic stability is not only a matter of a multi-party system. Even after their initial institutionalization, parties are still involved in confrontation and struggle to preserve their newly developed ideological niches. Connections between parties and the social groups whose interests they claim to represent are relatively weak. The best illustration of these facts is electoral volatility and the *frozen* electorates of the major Lithuanian parties in the elections of 1995 and 1996 (see Tables 9, 10 and 11). But stabilization of democracy is not only a problem of parties, as such. It is also, and probably more fundamentally, a problem of emerging social strata and new social values. The latter aspect has crucial significance, because continuing structural social instability leaves the parties as nearly the sole efficient instruments to aggregate interests and to mobilize voters, that is, to set up new ideas, values and beliefs *from above* that are at least partially conducive to the socio-economic positions of the parties' electorates.

During the fourth phase, consolidation of democracy (see Table 3), major innovations took place in the area of inter-party relations. The adversarial model of parties' interactions was changed by some limited cooperation and non-adversarial competition. These tamed relationships come about as a consequence of both institutionalization of parties as well as stabilization of party elites. Only marginal parties continued to follow a non-cooperative path, because they each still had to solve their individual dilemma of survival.

Where is a final point at which one can declare a new democracy consolid-ated? The question has no definite answer. Theoretically speaking on the level of political parties, it is quite clear that a consensual party system would be a sign of stable democracy. When losers accept the right of winners to rule and where winners accept the right of losers to engage in opposition a significant level of maturity has been reached. But even in some recognized stable democracies (for example, in Italy), the party system may still be very unstable and highly fluid. Nevertheless, if we will follow the previous hypothesis, that the stability of a party system is an indicator of polyarchic democracy, we could expect that a stable party system might be constituted after the second or third multi-party parliamentary elections (excluding the 'founding' elections as mostly non-party, but plural elections), if they will meet some structural requirements such as stable number of relevant parties, relatively stable level of electoral participation, continuous ideological identity of major political parties, and so on. At this moment only one thing is definite: consensual party politics come about gradually. In some transforming countries it will take a longer period of time than in others.

Looking back on the revival of party competition in Lithuania in recent years, it is obvious that this process was consistent with the general logic of democratic transition. Nevertheless, political parties acquired their traditional political roles very quickly, such that a more detailed examination of the process party institutionalization in Lithuania is in order.

Institutionalization of Lithuania's Parties

In the transforming societies, the processes of party institutionalization might be described on the basis of two parameters:

- formal or legal and institutional regulations of party development, including the legal basis of party formation, the electoral system as it conditions parties' electoral performance, and parliamentary rules of party activities
- organizational structuring of political parties through development of specialized bodies suitable for representative politics, mobilization of electoral support, and political efficiency of party activities.

Legal Bases of Lithuania's Parties

The legal regulations of parties'activities is an essential point in the analysis of party structure and performance. Moreover, laws are initiated and formulated by political groups and organizations. It means that all the laws necessarily reflect the interests of certain groups. The question is only to what degree these interests are put forward?

Political parties are mentioned only twice in Lithuania's 1992 Constitution. Article 35 states that 'citizens have a right freely to unite themselves into communities, political parties and associations, if their goals are not contradicting the Constitution and [Lithuania's] laws'.[10] The same article remarks that the formation and activities of political parties are regulated by other laws. Article 83 of the Constitution refers to political parties rather negatively: 'person, who is elected President of Republic, must cancel his activities in

---

[10] *Lietuvos Respublikos Konstitucija* (Vilnius, LR Seimo leidykla, 1993), p. 22.

political parties and political organizations until a new electoral campaign for President of the Republic'.[11]

Despite the brevity of these direct references to political parties, the Constitution established very definite guarantees for collective and individual political self-expression. It included the freedom of thought, right to privacy, the principle of equal treatment before the law, the rights to vote and to representation, the right to criticize the government and governmental officials etc. in other words those guarantees that constitute the basis of group and individual autonomy *from* and influence *on* political institutions.

The Constitution is the only general legal document that allows and regulates party activities. But nonetheless the road travelled on the way to this document was long and rough. Sajudis, founded in June 1988, as the first mass opposition movement was an illegal organization according to the Soviet legal code. Furthermore, the only way to legalize Sajudis was for it to be registered as a social movement. Articles 6 and 7 of the Constitution of Soviet Lithuania stated that the LCP was 'an integral part' of the CPSU and that the latter was the only legal political party, playing 'the leading and directing role' in the society. These articles of the Constitution were removed entirely in December 1989.

However, reconstruction of multi-partyism *de facto* was started not only by and through Sajudis. In late 1988 and early 1989 such historical organizations as the Democratic, the Christian Democratic, the Social Democratic parties, as well as the Nationalists Union and 'Young Lithuania' formed the initial groups and announced that they were the continuation of their inter-war predecessors. At the same time a few new parties, such as the Humanists and the Greens, were established. In April 1989 Sajudis passed a motion that the LCP must be transformed into an autonomous political party, and that all other parties should be legalized and receive equal treatment under the law.[12]

The actual rebirth and formation of political parties was more speedy than were changes in the legal regulations. The 1989 legal changes served to codify changes that had already taken place and practices that had become more or less customary.

Major efforts to introduce formal legal regulations for the political parties were made by the Constituent parliament in September 1990 with adoption of a *Law on political parties and political organizations*. The law described rules and procedures of party formation and activity. The so-called *parties law* granted the right to all citizens of Lithuania to form and participate in activities of political parties. The law suspended the right of party membership only for military and police servicemen, staff of national security agencies, and judicial officials during the period of their service or employment. Requirements and procedures of party formation and registration included five basic components:

- to have, at least, 400 founding-members
- to pass a party statute and basic programme
- to elect leadership
- to form party institutions at a conference or congress of the founding members or their delegates;
- to register the political party with the Ministry of Justice.

[11] *Lietuvos Respublikos Konstitucija*, p. 51.
[12] See *Lietuvos Kelias* (Vilnius, Viltis, 1990), p. 31.

Lithuania's rules of party registration might be characterized as strict, because each new party was required to present a list of founders with names and signatures, data about their citizenship, addresses, personal codes, professions, confirmation that she/he is not a member of another party, a protocol of the founding conference, party statute, and even designs of party symbols. Another important regulation, established by the parties law, was a detailed definition and description of party financial sources. Legal sources of party incomes include membership fees, profit from publishing, and private donations. Support of parties from public funds was prohibited, except the right of parliamentary parties to receive some governmental funding. The parties law completely ignored the allocation of material and financial resources for electoral campaigns. Campaign finance was regulated by separate laws on parliamentary and local elections. These laws require political parties to open special accounts for electoral campaigns. They also set a maximum level of electoral expenses for every party in order to preserve equal opportunities in competition for votes. Because of difficulties controlling actual election expenses, this regulation of parties has not been implemented accurately and properly.[13]

Since 1990 a very sensitive issue for Lithuania's parties was the problem of governmental support. Actually, only parties represented in the parliament are able to get indirect public funding through an institution of secretary-assistants to MPs. Every member of the Seimas was entitled 'to have a personal secretary-assistant or joint secretary-assistants with other members of parliamentary groups [factions], whose salaries shall be paid from the State Budget'.[14] Moreover, every MP had a right to additional funds for the reimbursement of office, postal, transportation and other expenses incurred from parliamentary activities. The latter provisions, in a broad sense, can quite easily be used to provide public funds to cover some party activities of MPs.

All these laws favour and increase competitiveness of the parliamentary parties, and it is a common trend in Lithuanian legislation on parties, regardless of what party is in power. Preferential treating of existing parliamentary parties, especially the largest parties, is even more explicit in the election laws.

The first post-communist election law was passed by the Constituent Parliament in July 1992. Previously the founding election was based on a majoritarian system of representation. The debate over a profile of an electoral system was extremely sharp and controversial in 1992. The right-wing of Sajudis argued for a majority formula, while the moderates of Sajudis and the left-wing parties expected to get dividends from a proportional system of elections. Both opposing groups believed that the different electoral systems promoted by them would allow them at least to secure their parliamentary seats and would restrict political fragmentation in the parliament through cutting off entry into the Seimas of small extra-parliamentary parties.

After a prolonged political crisis from April to July of 1992, a mixed majoritarian-proportional electoral system was introduced in Lithuania. This

---

[13] In 1992 a maximum level of electoral expenses for a single candidate was fixed at the level of 20 statistical monthly salaries (SMS), and 200 SMS for a party list. This level of expenses was increased in 1996 respectively to 50 and 1000 SMS, but still little more than 500,000 Litas (4 Litas = 1 US$) was not enough to organize electoral campaigns of major political parties. Every party taking part in the elections was allowed to use national TV and radio for one and half hours on a free of charge basis to present its views and programme to voters.

[14] *Lietuvos Respublikos Seimo Statutas* (Vilnius, 1994), p. 7.

decision was an outcome of political compromise. Nevertheless, the mixed representation system was one of the best options available to provide balance between representativiness and fragmentation in the parliament after the first multi-party elections of 1992.

The law on the Seimas elections fixed that 71 member would be elected in single-mandate constituencies, and 70 seats of the parliament would be filled on a proportional basis. All parties needed 4% of total votes to enter the Seimas, except political organizations representing ethnic minorities. After the amendments to the law in June of 1996, the threshold for a single party was increased to 5% and for an inter-party coalition to 7%. The special threshold of 2% for minority ethnic parties was abolished. These changes were made by efforts of the strongest parties – the LDLP, HU(LC), LChDP – and reflected their desire to tighten the circle of electoral competition around a small set of competitors. Moreover, the higher threshold for party coalitions compared to single parties could be cited as violating a principle of equal opportunity in representative democracy. By increasing the price of pre-election inter-party coalitions, the law has almost eliminated opportunities of smaller parties to compete against their bigger competitors.

The outcomes of the 1992 and 1996 parliamentary elections disappointed the expectations of the larger competing groups regarding the effects of proportional and majoritarian electoral systems. The expectations of the right-wing Sajudis failed because the majoritarian representation yielded seats in the the Seimas for 13 parties in 1992 and 14 in 1996 – hardly the expected reduction of small parties' influence. With the exception of the LSDP, the moderates failed to get into the parliament in 1992. And in both elections only 5 political organizations were able to enter the Seimas through the proportional formula. It means, paradoxically according to theory, that the majority system produced party fragmentation and the proportional representation decreased it in the Lithuania's parliament.

The law on local elections, passed by the Seimas in 1994, adopted proportional representation, with parties as the only entities able to nominate candidates. A 4% threshold was set for entry into local self-government bodies. During the local elections of 1995, 16 parties were able to get seats in the local governments.

The differing electoral systems on the national and local level allow for a majority of parties to be represented either on one or another level of government as well as to reach a *modus vivendi* between multiple parties, as well as to secure representation of various political identities of voters. On the other hand, the large number of competing parties in the elections indicates that all of them are playing consequential roles for interest articulation, and even major parties still are in trouble with respect to their capacity to aggregate interests. For instance, two leading parties in the national election of 1996 – the HU (Homeland Union, formerly Sajudis, and also currently known as the Lithuanian Conservatives, or LC) and LChDP – received only 15.76 and 5.24%[15] votes from the eligible electorate.

If the mixed electoral system is maintained in the future, it is quite easy to predict that, with on-going stabilization of the party system, voters' behaviour may change considerably. We may expect an electoral learning process to yield

[15] A. Lukosaitis, *Parlamentarizmo raidos etapai Lietuvoje 1990–1997m.* (Vilnius, LR Seimas, 1997), pp. 19–20.

such change. The proportional formula, with the 5% threshold presumably favouring major parties, ignored the desires of 36% of voters in 1996. That was the proportion of votes going to parties failing to pass the threshold. The present electoral rules will eventually lead a significant portion of voters to change their behaviour and turn to a split-ticket voting, that is, to vote for different parties along the proportional and majoritarian formulas.

The picture of parties' legal bases would be incomplete without mentioning their status and influence in the Seimas. Especially since all new parliaments carry a double burden of responsibility. They act as agents of political socialization for the parliamentary elite while simultaneously performing standard legislative functions.[16] Nevertheless, the essential structure of parties' representation in the parliament are parliamentary factions.

The first parliamentary factions were established in the Supreme Council in the early 1990s. On the eve of the elections of 1992 there were nine parliamentary factions (see Table 5). Among them seven were founded on the basis of Sajudis, and the other two represented the Polish Union and the LDLP. The majority of these factions could be hardly characterized as parliamentary parties because of the lack of connections to the extra-parliamentary organizations, low internal discipline, and ideological differences among members of same faction.

TABLE 5. Political Composition and Factions of the Supreme Council: 1990–1992[17]

Party	MPs (N) March, 1990	Faction	MPs (N) November, 1992
Sajudis*:	96	Centre	20
Green Party	4	LDLP	9
LSDP	9	Polish Union	8
LDP	3	United faction of Sajudis	14
LChDP	2	Nationalists	9
Independent LCP*	46	Moderate	18
CPSU	6	Liberal	9
		National Progress	9
		Sajudis Unity	11
		[Independents]	31
Total:	140		138

*Part of the ILCP members were supported by the Sajudis, and it is why the total number of MPs from these organizations is higher than the overall number of seats in the Constituent Parliament.

The standing orders of the Supreme Council took little notice of the parliamentary factions in the legislative process. Despite the fact that during the 'founding' elections some candidates mentioned their party affiliations on the Sajudis list, it was overshadowed by the Sajudis label. The fragmentation of Sajudis and partially of the ILCP in 1990–1992 confirms the megapolitical character of these organizations at the moment of the 1990 elections.

[16] M. D. Simon and D. M. Olson, 'Parliamentary Committees and Parliamentary Development in Poland's Democratic Transition', Paper delivered at the annual MidWest Political Science Association Meeting, Chicago, 18–22 April 1996, p. 1.
[17] Figures from Lukosaitis, *Parlamentarizmo radios etapai Lietuvoje 1990–1997*, pp. 9–10.

The situation of parliamentary factions changed fundamentally after the first multi-party elections in 1992. From that moment the Seimas was organized along party lines. The most obvious indicator of increasing strength of parliamentary parties was a sudden decrease of the number of non-affiliated MPs from 22.1% in 1990 to 4.9 in 1992, and to nil in 1996. Even independent MPs joined parliamentary factions in 1996 because they, along with the Seimas committees, became into the most influential centres in the legislative process. A relatively low requirement for parliamentary faction membership – at least, three members of Seimas can register a faction – facilitated the uniting of all MPs into the factions in 1996.

According to the Statute of Lithuania's Seimas, parliamentary factions perform the following formal functions:

- prepare the agenda for the Seimas plenary sittings and Seimas sessions
- propose candidates for membership on parliamentary committees, commissions and the Board of Seimas
- submit drafts of decisions
- may declare themselves parliamentary opposition and announce an alternative to the government's programme.[18]

Two institutions of the Seimas are crucial for the influence of parliamentary factions. The committee system and the assembly of spokespersons of factions. The permanent standing committees of the Seimas are formed along party lines from top to down. Article 46 of the Seimas' Statute recommends that the chairperson and deputy chair of committees shall represent different parliamentary factions. Even more, a certain number of chairs and deputy chairs of the committees accorded to the parliamentary majority and minority must be in a proportion to the number of MPs belonging to them.[19] All other members of the committees are delegated by the individual parties on the basis of their professional experience and the political importance of a particular committee (except small factions, which may be formed as inter-party clubs or by non-party members).

The assembly of factions' speakers is a very influential decision-making institution of the Seimas, because it is entitled to set up a preliminary agenda of plenaries and to present proposals on organization of the Seimas works in general. The representational quota in the assembly is one MP from each 10 members of a parliamentary faction. This rule, of course, strengthens the positions of the parliamentary majority.

The essential internal instrument of factions are their formal meetings, where policy positions are decided and where internal unity is preserved. The democratic consolidation and election of a multi-party parliament with a stable majority reinforced the voting discipline of factions in the Seimas after 1992.

Two questions remain regarding the role of the parliamentary factions. One regards the opportunities for organization of separate groups of MPs based on ideological differences within the parliamentary factions. In the period from 1993 to 1996 the ruling LDLP successfully blocked out all attempts to establish formal factions within its parliamentary ranks. After the elections of 1996 the situation changed because the previous single-party majority was replaced by

[18] *Lietuvos Respublikos Seimo Statutas*, pp. 18–19.
[19] *Lietuvos Respublikos Seimo Statutas*, pp. 21–22.

two parties, the HU(LC) and the LChDP. There are circumstances working against possible splits in the parliamentary factions of the ruling coalition: (1) partnership in the coalition encourages both leading factions to be more concerned with their internal cohesion; (2) the more centralized and hierarchical type of leadership of the HU(LC) and LChDP, compared to the LDLP, discourages fragmentation; and (3) increasing political competitiveness along party lines in the parliament enhances the relative unity of the governing coalition. Of course, there are conditions which could provoke developments on the opposite direction, and the broad area for potential internal disagreements and tensions within the ruling coalition could be opened by poor performance in implementation of economic and social policy objectives. Certain program-matic differences are already accepted within the coalition, given that the HU(LC) has accepted a policy of economic efficiency, based on expansion of support for the private sector, while the LChDP stresses its commitment to social welfare.

A second question regarding parliamentary factions concerns views toward institutionalization of opposition. One view is that of the Homeland Union (the descendent of Sajudis), as the former leader of the right wing opposition potentially capable of providing a pole around which smaller factions can coalesce, argues for a united opposition. Such a united opposition would enjoy broad rights and privileges in a model of the Conservatives. The LDLP and LSDP, due to their internal competition for the leadership on the left wing of the political spectrum, are for a split opposition. In this case the same rights in parliamentary decision making might be enjoyed by all factions declaring them-selves in opposition. The first model favours larger parties, while the second gives an advantage to medium and smaller parliamentary factions. Because the present rules of the parliamentary game do not restrict freedom of opposition, it is very likely that no changes at all will occur.

A shift towards the committee system and parliamentary factions as the main vehicles of decision making has changed the overall organization and style of Lithuania's Seimas. These changes might be summed up in the following way:

- representation in all institutions of the Seimas is based on party lines
- the role of plenary sessions decreased, with the main political discussions redirected to the party factions, committees and commissions
- the influence of individual MPs was specified, but the role of collective entities, first of all, parliamentary factions, has substantially increased in parliamentary decision-making.

The form of legal regulations is an extremely important variable in deter-mining the efficiency of parties in new democracies. However, the internal party organization is no less an important element in this process.

Organization of Parties: Structure and Efficiency.

A basic condition affecting the political efficiency of parties is their organ-izational capacities to articulate and aggregate societal interests, or to be responsive to citizens' demands. From this angle, three structural segments of party organization have crucial importance:

- whether the party is in power
- the party's bureaucracy, and
- the nature of the party *rank-and-file* members or/and the party of electorate.

Because many of the post-communist parties, from genetic point of view, are products of a *territorial penetration*, that is, they were developed and structured from the top down by a party elite, the most appropriate way to begin analysis of parties' structure is from the top by an examination of the party leadership.

Three of the five major Lithuanian parties – the HU(LC), LCU and LDLP (till 1992) – could be characterized as having personalized leadership and an influential party elite. The leading elites of HU(LC) and the LDLP, as successors of the former megapolitical conglomerates (respectively Sajudis and the LCP), was very interested in preserving the former organizational networks. An important basis for the institutionalization of those parties was the socialization of their elites during the Constituent parliament.

The LChDP and LSDP developed in a slightly different way. The restoration of both parties was based on a reconstruction of historical political traditions. Furthermore, a strong component of their legitimacy was the organizational units in exile, which became members of respective international party organizations in the 1950s.

In the course of consolidation of democracy, the roles of party elites are tending to change in two different directions. In the right and centre parties the original elite continues to be very influential, with highly personalized leadership (except the LChDP). In contrast, the leadership of the left wing parties is becoming more and more collectivist as in cases of the LDLP and LSDP (Table 6).

Extremely important as an organizational element of all influential parties is their representation in various governmental and parliamentary structures. Seen from an internal organizational perspective, parliamentary factions lack clear integration into the overall structure of parties and their decision making,

TABLE 6. Organizational Pattern of Lithuania's Parties

	Style of leadership	Influence of party's leader	Regulation of membership*	Relations between party and its faction
HU(LC)	personalistic	strong	restrictive	dominance
LChDP	mixed	medium	restrictive	integration
LCU	personalistic	strong	mixed	dominance
LSDP	collectivist	medium	open	integration
LDLP	collectivist	medium	mixed	autonomy

*Scale of evaluation from: H. Smith-Sivertsen, 'Towards Parties of Elites – or Populism?', Paper delivered at the International Conference 'The Challenges of Regime Transformation: New Politics in Central and Eastern Europe', Vilnius, December 10–15, 1996, p. 6.

except within the Christian Democrats. The latter formally integrated its parliamentary faction into the party's governing council. The parliamentary factions of all other major parties are rather autonomous and linked to a particular party only through direct leadership-faction connections. Such pattern of relations is leading to a situation whereby recruitment of future MPs will be a highly centralized and hierarchical process, despite the fact that, after 1992, the major Lithuanian parties succeeded in developing relatively broad networks of local organizations. The voice of local branches in the nomination of parliamentary candidates is still low. Of course, the parties having a collectivist pattern of leadership are more open in this procedure compared to the parties with strong personalized leadership.

Over the few years following the breakup of the USSR, there has been a clear tendency in Lithuania toward strengthening the roles of executive structures of all leading parties, with the only exception being the LDLP. Being the ruling party, the LDLP lacked the will (and scarce human and financial resources) to be other than cavalier about the influence and efficiency of its bureaucracy. I should note again that parties with charismatic leadership have more centralized organization and a greater role for the national bureaucracy as well as a more significant role for executive institutions in formulation of the policy agenda, development of organizational initiatives and overall decision making inside the party. However, local party bureaucracy is underdeveloped, and, more important, it has a low profile in the socialization of the future party elite.

The central bureaucracies of even the leading parties are still small and concentrated in national headquarters of each party (Table 7). Because it is organized around the institution of secretaries/assistants to MPs, a primary task of party bureaucracy is to satisfy the needs of the parliamentary faction rather than to organize extra-parliamentary activities. Nevertheless, a gradual expansion of local party networks and the necessity to improve the efficiency of extra-parliamentary campaigns are forcing parties to give more autonomy and responsibility to the de-centralized elements of their bureaucracies.

The rank-and-file and, in a broader sense the *party in the electorate*, are fundamental elements of party organization. Moreover, these are the first indicators of organizational stabilization of parties in new democracies. The experience of democratic transitions in Southern Europe illustrates that party membership rates increased gradually only in Spain. In all other cases, including post-war Italy, the beginning of democratic consolidation produced relatively

TABLE 7. Party Staff Size: National Headquarters and Local Branches

	Staff (N)	Local Branches (N)		
	1997	1995*	1997	Change
HU(LC)	7	69	76	+7
LChDP	4	55	55	0
LCU	2	35	45	+10
LSDP	3	48	52	+4
LDLP	7	51	52	+1

*Data from H. Smith-Sivertsen, 'Towards Parties of Elites- or Populism?', p. 8.

sudden growth of party membership.[20] As Lithuania entered the phase of democratic consolidation, there was substantial growth of parties. In 1993 only 1.3% of all eligible voters were members of political parties. By the end of 1996 overall party membership had more than doubled, increasing to 2.8%.[21]

Viewed from a Baltic perspective, Lithuania's parties are well-structured and developed. Median party membership in Estonia and Latvia is below 1000, whereas it is over 3000 in Lithuania. In 1995, membership in the Estonian Centre party was only 1407, 1200 in the National Independence party, and 452 in the Coalition party. This is in spite of the fact that all these parties were strongly represented in the parliament. The largest Latvian party, the Farmers' Union, was able to mobilize 4225 members, but all other parties were far behind the LFU.[22]

On the other hand, whereas the major Lithuania's parties – the HU(LC), LChDP, LDLP, LSDP and LDLP – accounted 90% of total party membership in 1993, their proportion decreased to 56% in 1996. The lack of capacity of major Lithuanian parties to attract new supporters was strikingly manifested through the dynamics of their electoral support. The LDLP (successor to the Lithuanian Communists) suffered by far the greatest losses of electoral support, losing over 650,000 between the national elections of 1992 and 1996 (Table 8). The only party that was able to increase support was the Lithuanian Centre Union. Even in this case, however, the electoral basis of the LCU is not sufficient to pave a way to the position of a governing party. The Homeland Union (HU/LC) has a *frozen* electorate, that is, the level of its support has been stable since 1992, with no sign of ability to attract undecided voters. In 1992 it led to the defeat of the former Sajudis in the parliamentary elections. Again the Conservatives were unable to mobilize new supporters, except those few who defected from the Christian Democrats in 1996.

TABLE 8. Electorates of Lithuanian Parties: 1992–1996 ('000)

	Seimas elections '92	Seimas elections '96	Change
Lithuanian Conservatives	393	409	+16
Christian Democratic Party	234	136	−98
Labour Democratic Party	817	130	−687
Social Democratic Party	112	90	−22
Centre Union	47	113	+66

Furthermore, a poor electoral mobilization by Lithuanian parties was associated with a sharp decrease of voter turnout in national and local elections after 1992 (Table 9). Looking at voter turnout from the Baltic perspective, the Lithuanian phenomena, when in between two consequent parliamentary elections in 1992 and 1996 as much as 23% of eligible voters became politically inactive, cannot be explained by the peculiarity of such institutional factors as electoral competitiveness and proportionality, unicameralism vs bicameralism,

[20] Morlino, 'Consolidation and party government in southern Europe', pp. 150–152.
[21] Excluding membership the Union of ex-Political Prisoners and Deportees, which was rather interests' group than party.
[22] See H. Smith-Sivertsen, *Towards Parties of Elites – or Populism?*, p. 7.

TABLE 9. Voter Turnout in the Parliamentary Elections: 1990–1996 (%)

	The 'founding' elections	1st multi-party elections	2nd multi-party elections	Average
Estonia	78	67	70	71.6
Latvia	80	89	72	80.6
Lithuania	72	75	52	66.3
Total:	76.6	77.0	64.6	

multipartyism, or electoral laws.[23] The only substantial institutional difference between the Baltic countries is that Lithuania has adopted the mixed electoral system, and other two – Estonia and Latvia – have a proportional one.

There are two scenarios that may explain the current Lithuanian situation. On the one hand, it might be seen as a consequence of such short-term factors as continuing economic troubles, inefficiency of the LDLP governments in the social policy area in 1995 and 1996, or corruption scandals. These Lithuanian experiences may have combined to enhance voters' disillusion with politics. An alternative explanation is more clearly cultural. During the transition Lithuanian political culture moved far away from the so-called *subject* political culture, but still a *participatory* one is only developing and has not yet stabilized. Furthermore, since 1988 political discourse has been based very much on protest mobilization and has been very expressive in terms of political means and forms, especially, in the context of Lithuanian's Catholic culture. As consolidation of democratic political life acquired more routine forms and ways of decision making. Electoral participation lost its former glamour. A combination of the above described scenarios would offer a quite realistic explanation of Lithuania's exceptionalism in terms of voter turnout in recent years.

Of course, frozen or decreasing electorates of major parties reflect potential instability for the party system and suggest that the institutionalization of Lithuania's parties is as yet unfinished. Volatility scores, calculated by a method initially developed by Przeworski,[24] shows that a score of electoral volatility of 25.5 for the leading Lithuanian parties was slightly higher than in Poland and Slovakia (respectively in 1991–1993: 22.78, and 1992–1994: 24.68), but less than in Hungary (in 1990–1994: 28.02).[25] But these scores are far higher than Western European countries' volatility scores,[26] even taking account of the fact that the methodology of volatility evaluation itself is imperfect (Table 10).[27]

[23] Institutional attributes of voter turnout are analysed in detail in: R. W. Jackman and R. A. Miller, 'Voter turnout in the industrial democracies during the 1980s', *Comparative Political Studies*, 28 (1995), 468–477.

[24] See: A. Przeworski, 'Institutionalization of Voting Patterns, or is Mobilization the Source of Decay?', in *American Political Science Review*, 69 (1975), pp. 47–67.

[25] K. Janda, 'Restructuring the Party Systems in Central Europe', Paper prepared for the International Symposium, Democratization and Political Reform in Korea, Seoul, 19 November 1994, pp. 13–16.

[26] See data in S. Bartolini and P. Mair, *Identity Competition, and Electoral Availability: The Stabilisation of European Electorates, 1885–1985* (Cambridge, Cambridge University Press, 1990), p. 69.

[27] For instance, a volatility score of the HU(LC) is +4.6, but actual increase electorate was only 3.9% in elections of 1996.

TABLE 10. Electoral Volatility in Lithuania: 1992–1996

	Votes (%) 1992	Votes (%) 1996	1992–1996 difference	Volatility
LDLP	42.5	9.5	−33.0	16.5
HU(LC)	20.5	29.7	9.2	4.6
LChDP	12.2	9.9	−2.3	1.15
LSDP	5.8	6.6	0.8	0.4
LCU	2.4	8.1	5.7	2.85
Total:	83.4	63.8	51.0	25.5

Obviously, efficient political mobilization of voters is a major challenge for Lithuanian parties over the next few years.

Yet, in spite of considerable instability in support bases, the question 'Who are the supporters of particular parties?' is still relevant. Ongoing social transformations restrict development of stable party preferences and identities, but some general features of leading party electorates might be noted. Standard variables such as sex, age, education, living place, income, and ethnicity reveal interesting patterns. Preliminary evaluations of social profiles of party electorates reflect the following tendencies: (a) the majority of leading political parties are heavily dependent on middle aged and older supporters; (b) non-Lithuanian ethnics (mainly Russian) favour the left-wing parties; (c) electoral groups with low and medium incomes tend to support the left-wing parties and the Christian Democrats; (d) females tend to support the right-wing parties rather than the left-wing.

The structural organization of Lithuanian parties clearly westernized in the first 5–6 years after independence. Since 1990 all parties based their organization on a territorial principle[28] instead of the *territorial-occupational* principle of the Soviet era. Nevertheless, the mixed electoral system does not allow local branches of parties to be matched strictly to single-mandate electoral districts. Only the Conservatives made a serious effort to connect their local branches with the boundaries of electoral constituencies. Other parties organized their local groups along the lines of the administrative territorial division of the country. Since 1993 the major parties have founded specialized and autonomous youth and women sections. Nevertheless, women are still underrepresented in the elite of almost all parties, except the Women Party (Table 11).

The overall organization of Lithuania's parties is neither strictly hierarchical nor pyramidal, but rather all the basic segments of party structure – parliamentary faction, party bureaucracy, and the rank-and-file members – are interdependent. Structural organization is not the only indicator reflecting political efficiency of parties in new democracies. Their effectiveness cannot be analysed without also looking at the parties' performance in government.

Government and Political Efficiency

The common theory of representative democracy defines political parties as the main political actors responsible for government policy. Jean Blondel points out

[28] It was required by Law on Political Parties and Political Organizations from 25 September 1990.

TABLE 11. Representation of Women in Lithuania's Parliament

	1992–1996	1996–2000
HU(LC)	4 (17.39)	15 (21.42)
LChDP	0	1 (6.25)
LCU	0	2 (15.3)
LSDP	0	2 (16.66)
LDLP	3 (4.28)	2 (16.66)
Total:	10 (7.09)	24 (17.52)

that 'the articulation between governments and the parties that support them is one of the key mechanisms, if not the key mechanism, enabling democratic politics to operate, and it is therefore essential that this articulation function efficiently'.[29] There is little doubt that, after the 1992 election, Lithuania's government can be characterized as a *party government*, according to Katz's well-known formula (despite the fact that it was not until 1994 that a single party government could be formed – by the LDLP).

Parties' efficiency in government cannot be evaluated without investigation of their influence in the parliament. The simplest indicator of a party's parliamentary influence is number of seats in the Seimas. The total number of parties holding seats in the Seimas, at thirteen to fourteen, is relatively high and stable after 1992. The same tendency towards stabilization of numbers of parliamentary parties is evident in the other Baltic countries as well. Nevertheless, an assumption that all parties holding seats might called as 'efficient' or 'relevant' would be misleading, because some of them were unable even to form single-party factions in the parliament. The alternative and more precise way to define efficient parties is to take into account only parties that were able to create their own factions in the Seimas.[30] After the elections of 1996 only 5 parties that had entered the parliament through the proportional electoral formula founded single-party factions. In this case only the HU(LC), LChDP, LCU, LSDP, LDLP could be named as relevant parties.

However, it is still a challenge to choose indicators useful in the evaluation of the relevant parties. Obviously, size of parliamentary faction is an appropriate indicator of party influence in legislature. But fractional strength of party may be used in different ways or even stay unused in some cases. Parliamentary parties are collective political actors and they are acting in the Seimas as collective decision-making entities. Looking at the question from this perspective, it would be appropriate to measure the influence of relevant parties by their presence in the main institutes of the Seimas: the Board, committees and commissions. According to this methodology, after the Seimas elections of 1996 the most influential party was the HU(LC) (Table 12).

The institutional influence of the Conservatives was higher than their fractional potency. However, the actual fractional strength of their parliamentary majority increased because of the formal coalition with the Christian

[29] J. Blondel, 'Toward a Systematic Analysis of Government–Party Relationship', *International Political Science Review*, 2 (1995), p. 127.
[30] A formal minimal requirement is a membership of, at least, 3 MPs on a single-party or cross-party basis.

TABLE 12. Scores of Parliamentary Influence of Lithuania's Parties

	Seimas of 1992–1996: Institutional influence*	Fractional influence*	Medium	Seimas of 1996–2000: Institutional influence	Fractional influence	Medium	Average scores
HU(LC)	8.6	16.3	12.4	52.7	50.7	51.7	32.1
LChDP	nil	7.1	3.5	18.0	11.6	14.8	9.2
LCU	6.6	1.4	4.0	11.1	9.4	10.2	7.1
LSDP	6.6	4.9	5.7	11.1	8.7	9.9	7.8
LDLP	66.2	51.7	58.9	2.7	8.7	5.7	32.3
Others	12.0	18.6	15.3	4.4	10.5	7.6	11.3

*Institutional influence measured through a position analysis of number of members of the Seimas Board, chairs and deputy chairs' positions of parliamentary committees and commissions hold by each party.
Institutional influence (I) is calculated along the formula: $I = (a/x + b/x + c/x)/3 \times 100$ (a = representation in the Seimas Board; b = in the Seimas committees; c = in the Seimas commissions, x = number of posts actually taken by parties in each institution). Fractional influence (F) equals a percentage of total party seats in the parliament.

Democrats. The LChDP and LCU extended their overall power on parliamentary decision making through entering into the alliance with the HU(LC) too. In 1992–1996 the LDLP and in 1996–1997 the HU(LC) used the same strategy to minimize each other's institutional influence. But both parties practiced different tactics to achieve it. The LDLP did it through giving positions to the 'third' or small parties; the HU(LC) preferred the closest allies – the Christian Democrats and Centre Union (Table 12).

Theoretically patterns of party-government relationships might be placed on a continuum from *dependence* to *independence*. Blondel suggested an additional dimension of *autonomy* vs *interdependence* to measure party-government relationships.[31] There are three distinct types of party-government relationship in this triangle: (a) autonomous government, with party playing a minimal role in a formation and performance of government (the USA); (b) government dependent on party (coalitional cabinets in Belgium, Netherlands) and (c) party dependent on government (France, the UK).[32]

What model is the closest to Lithuania's experience? A few variables are crucial for defining the party-government relationships in Lithuania. The constitutionally mixed presidential-parliamentary system leads towards autonomy of the cabinet from party. In some cases (for instance, implementing foreign and security objectives) the cabinet can rely on interactions with the President rather than with the parliamentary majority. Nevertheless, appointment of ministers is controlled by the ruling party in the Seimas.

Two other factors affecting party-government relationships might be characterized as political ones: the continuous single-party majority in the parliament after 1992 and the degree of cohesion of the ruling party. After 1992 we could mention a few different directions along which actual party-government relations developed. In a period from 1993 to the middle of 1994,

[31] Blondel, 'Toward a Systemic Analysis of Government–Party Relationship', p. 131.
[32] Blondel, 'Toward a Systemic Analysis of Government–Party Relationship', p. 132.

the LDLP government was supported and controlled by the parliamentary faction. Later on, things changed and the Cabinet of Slezevicius became more autonomous and began to influence party decisions more than the party influenced the government. After a banking crisis at the end 1995 to early 1996 the LDLP regained power on the government to some extent.

The 1996 elections changed again the pattern of party-government relations. The formal coalition agreement between the HU(LC) and the Christian Democrats put the Vagnorius cabinet under the control of coalition parties. Moreover, the previous experience in power of the Landsbergis-Vagnorius (former leaders of the right-wing Sajudis and present leaders of the HU(LC)) team in 1991–1992 supports an assumption that the post-96 cabinet will be more strictly subordinated to the will of the parliamentary majority than was the case with the LDLP. Additionally, such short-term political circumstances as the presidential elections at the end of 1997 or early 1998, as well as a higher level of organizational and ideological cohesion within the Conservative Party, compared to the LDLP, will probably reinforce the dependence of the government on the party.

Over the long-term, the *surplus winning coalition*, with dominance of the HU(LC), may serve to increase independence of the government from the Conservative Party as well as to open additional space for the autonomous pursuit of policy objectives by the government. The influence of the LChDP and LCU (as an informal member of the governing coalition) on elaboration of governmental policies will be as weak as it was from the very beginning.

Clearly, the common policy objectives of the Vagnorius' cabinet are constrained by the electoral programme of the HU(LC). The other two parties – the LChDP and LCU – can affect the performance of government through control of particular ministries. Looking statistically, the HU(LC) power in the cabinet is only slightly disproportional to its share of seats in the surplus winning coalition in the parliament (Table 13). The actual political weight of the Conservatives is even higher in the government because the party selected the Prime Minister and appointed its own representatives to most important ministerial positions (Finance, Economy, Internal Affairs, excepting only the post of minister of Foreign Affairs, which went to the leader of LChDP.

Obviously, the right-wing coalition is based on *primus inter pares* relationships, with the HU(LC) enjoying greater influence on the government. However, the power of the Conservatives' elite is not a translation of the influence of the rank-and-file party on the cabinet. The lower levels of the

TABLE 13. The Influence of Coalition Parties on the Cabinet, 1996–97

	HU(LC)	LChDP	LCU	Total number of seats
Number of seats in the Cabinet	13	3	2	18*
Share of seats in the Cabinet (%)	72.2	16.7	11.1	–
Share of seats in the parliamentary coalition (%)	70.8	16.1	13.1	99

*Prime Minister plus 17 ministers.

Conservatives' organization do have some very limited opportunities and channels to affect the governmental policy through:

- the party's electoral programme
- channeling of communication between party electorate and the government and
- monitoring the policy and performance of party in the office.

Significant sources for political efficiency of the ruling parties are their connections with interests groups from both the office-seeking and the policy pursuit perspectives. Party-interest group interactions are not only a factor necessary for adequate aggregation of societal demands but also they work for consolidation of power in the hands of new political elites and parties in the transforming countries.

In the Lithuanian case, the party-interest groups relationships are still quite ambivalent. First of all, the interests groups lack both legal status and traditional channels of communication with parties and party governments. The LDLP government made efforts to institutionalize a tripartite linkage between the cabinet, the employers' associations, and the trade unions. Unfortunately, these relationships suffered from the lack of clear rules and no history of standing, direct influence on governmental decision making. Only a few major interest groups, such as the Confederation of Industrialists and some trade unions, established direct links with the Seimas and the Cabinet. On the level of individual parties, in recent years a few of them have developed links with interest groups. Examples include the LSDP and the trade unions or the LChDP and the Catholic Church. The HU(LC) even signed formal agreements of cooperation with some entrepreneurial organizations on the eve of the 1996 national elections. Moreover, after the victory in the elections V. Babilius of the Lithuanian Confederation of Industrialists (LCI) was appointed to the Minister of Economy in accord with the pre-election agreement between HU(LC) and the LCI.

The alliance of the HU(LC) and the LCI may well be a sign that party-interest group relationships are entering an era of cooperation and that the previous period of mutual neutrality, at best, as well as distrust is over. Meanwhile, among the more positive developments on the horizon is further institutionalization and legal regulation of party-interest groups relations.

The HU(LC) and the LCI interactions are based on a corporatist pattern. Smaller interest organizations are acting on a pluralist basis, but due to lack of legally defined channels of lobbying, underdevelopment of associational networks and culture among interest groups, they are highly inefficient in satisfying their interests through negotiations with parties. On the other hand, the major parties are themselves recognizing that the linkage with interest groups would increase their political efficiency.

Conclusions

The competitive party system is a political reality in Lithuania. And stable party government is a factor of successful ongoing consolidation of democracy. Some problematic aspects of party performance include voter volatility and political mobilization and a certain ambivalence of party-interest group linkages.

Further, emphasis on *vertical* vs *horizontal* relationships inside of parties present obstacles on the way of party institutionalization. However, in general Lithuania's parties are well advanced on the way to institutionalization and successfully performing the functions of the intermediary structures in consolidating democracy.

Appendix: Lithuanian Parties and Abbreviations

CPSU – Communist Party of the Soviet Union
HU(LC) – Homeland Union (Lithuanian Conservatives)
LChDP – Lithuanian Christian Democratic Party
LCP– Lithuanian Communist Party
LCU – Lithuanian Centre Union
LDLP – Lithuanian Democratic Labour Party
LDP – Lithuanian Democratic Party
LFP – Lithuanian Farmers' Party
LLU – Lithuanian Liberal Union
LNPP – Lithuanian National Progress Party
LNPU – Lithuanian National Progress Union
LPU – Lithuanian Peasants Party
LSDP – Lithuanian Social Democratic Party
LSPDP – Lithuanian Socialist People Democratic Party
NP 'Y. L' – National Party 'Young Lithuania'
U ex-P&D – Union of ex-Political Prisoners and Deportees

Consolidation and Stabilization of the Party System in the Czech Republic*

MICHAL KLÍMA

Introduction

The current Czech party system is the result of a process of gradual transformation which has been taking place since the breakdown of the communist regime, or, in the case of the Czech Republic as such, since the split of Czechoslovakia at the end of 1992.

The Constitution of the Czech Republic, as adopted in December 1992, established a parliamentary form of government. In other words, political parties became the major instruments of government. This means that the Czech parliamentary system of government is also one of party government. Parliament is now conceived of as a moderate arena in which political parties compete. Parties have the responsibility to stand for particular policy programmes and to attempt to implement those programmes if elected.

The transformation of the political and economic systems was not a straightforward and simple process. The aim of this paper is to give a definition and brief description of the main periods of development of the party system: from a one-party state system to a more mature and stabilized party pluralism. The latter stages of this development have seen a considerably fragmented party system transformed via a process of concentration into a system of moderate pluralism.

The level of the individual political parties will be examined from an evolutionary viewpoint. Parties will also be scaled along a left-right axis. The internal organizational structure of the parties is analysed as well as the role of the parliamentary party (officially referred to as the *deputy club*) in the organization and functioning of the Czech Parliament. Other important factors to be analysed in this paper are the influence of parliamentary electoral systems on the formation of the party system, and, last but not least, the phenomenon of cartelization which is currently manifesting itself in the Czech party system.

Development of the Party System

The post-1989 transition to a pluralistic democracy, and thus to a pluralistic party system, took place against a backdrop of simultaneous processes of continuity and discontinuity with the past. The establishment and formation of the party system in Czechoslovakia exercised a decisive influence on its own specific pattern of sharp cleavages within a brief span of history.[1] Differences

---

* This article refects the political situation in the Czech Republic until January 1997.
[1] For more detailed discussion of these cleavages, see: S. W. Rivera, 'Historical cleavages of transition mode? Influences on the emerging party systems in Poland, Hungary and Czechoslovakia', *Party Politics*, 2,2 (1996), 177–208.

previously held in check – old conflicts from the pre-Socialist period, to some extent modified and muted during the period of Socialist development – were suddenly let out of the bag in the turmoil of states undergoing democratization and general transformation. These conflicts escalated and then acted as time bombs in the social organism. Newly revived nationalistic, class, and to some extent religious cleavages surfaced in full force in an atmosphere where swelling social energy did not encounter the inhibitory barriers of the long-standing written or unwritten rules that are customary in standard democracies. In nationally heterogeneous countries, this unique post-socialist development created a hierarchical pattern of mutually aggravating cleavages, dominated at the top by national conflict. This scenario eventually led to the trauma of the break-up of Czechoslovakia (as well as of the Soviet Union and of Yugoslavia).

The emergent system consisted of separate Czech and Slovak parties. This pattern was established in the early days of the Velvet Revolution of November 1989, when the Czechs and Slovaks set up their own citizens' movements, Civic Forum (OF) and Public Against Violence (VPN), respectively. The division of the party system was endorsed in the first free elections, held in June 1990 when the country was still a Federal Republic, in which only one of the parties standing in both republics – the Communist Party of Czechoslovakia – obtained seats in both national legislatures.[2] The separate party system generated a series of problems when the citizens' movement split early in 1991. The issue of Czechoslovakia will not concern this discussion any further, but attention will be focused primarily on the establishment, formation and development of the party system in the Czech environment.

The transition from a single-party state system to a pluralistic party system has its own dynamics. In the context of political development it is possible to identify four periods:

1. *Anti-party sentiment and proliferation of parties*
   (November 1989 to February 1991)
2. *Emergence and crystallization of the party system*
   (February 1991 to June 1992)
3. *Formation and consolidation of the party system*
   (June 1992 to May/June 1996)
4. *Stabilization of the party system*
   (after May/June 1996)

The first short period is defined by its salient features: November 1989, the first parliamentary elections in June 1990, and the split of the citizens' movement. This phase is characterized primarily by the dominant position of the newly founded OF (Civic Forum), which enjoyed mass support and was widely perceived as a substitute for the monolithic power of the Communist Party. The anti-party sentiment was connected with the historical experience of the First Republic (1918–1938), with the party state of the communist regime and the dissident movement, and with the attitudes of newly elected President Havel. Nevertheless, after January 1990, when the resolution was passed on the adoption of an electoral system based on proportional representation, there was a proliferation of parties and political movements. In the wake of the June 1990

---

[2] The Czech and Slovak National Councils came into existence as a result of federalization at the beginning of 1969.

elections, 66 political entities were registered on the basis of the Act on Association in Political Parties and Political Movements. The overwhelming majority of political parties and movements were created without mass membership or any organizational structure.

It would be misleading, however, to say that the establishment of the party system *per se* created the core of the political system. Rather, it was a transitional period, during which a variegated cluster of power centres operated: the Co-ordinating Centre of Civic Forum, the President, the Ministry of the Interior, and the Ministry of Defence (according to the round-table decisions) and to a certain extent Parliament itself.[3]

The second period is marked by the consequences of the disintegration of the electoral victors. Both of the broad political movements, OF (Civic Forum) with 49.5% of the votes in the Czech part and VPN (Public Against Violence) with 29.3% in Slovakia, split into a number of successor parties.[4] An unconsolidated party system, in which party identities and organizational structures were weak, led to a number of party splits and mergers. A regrouping of political forces took place, both within and between parties. To give an example, the original four deputy clubs which formed the Czech legislature in early 1990 had proliferated into 11 party factions by the time of the 1992 parliamentary elections.[5] At the same time, the parties became the real key centres of decision making as the parliamentary form of government began to function. The regime/anti-regime cleavage ceased to be central to political life. The spectrum of Czech parties began to be distributed largely along a left-right axis, with the addition of the KDU-CSL, a party which is more or less defined by its Christian stance, a stance dominated by Catholicism (Table 1).

During the third phase, which saw the break-up of Czechoslovakia,[6] there is a clear consolidation and concentration of the party system in the Czech Republic. *A multi-party system with the dominant party* on the right was estab-

TABLE 1. Parties in the First Chamber and Left-Right Self-Placement of their Supporters (%)

Parties*	1	2	3	4	5
SPR-RSC	5	12	40	21	22
ODS	–	2	21	54	23
ODA	–	1	46	47	6
KDU-CSL	1	8	61	26	4
CSSD	4	32	60	4	–
KSCM	40	46	12	1	1

*See Appendix for full English-language names of parties
Source: STEM/Stedisko empirických výzkumù – Centre for Empirical Research, Trends 1–97, 1 – clear left; 2 – somewhat left; 3 – centre; 4 – somewhat right; 5 – clear right.

[3] For further discussion on this matter, see: V. Dvoráková and J. Kunc, 'The Czech Party System and its Dynamic', in E. Matynia (ed.), *Grappling with Democracy, Deliberations on Post-Communist Societies (1990–1995)* (Prague, Sociologické nakladatelství, 1996), pp. 159–66.
[4] The split-up of OF was formally approved in February 1991, that of VPN in March 1991.
[5] See: J. Reschová and J. Syllová, 'The Legislature of the Czech Republic', *Journal of Legislative Studies*, 2,1 (1996), p. 100.
[6] The Czech Republic came into being as an independent state on 1 January 1993.

Table 2. Results of 1992 and 1996 Parliamentary Elections (over 5% of votes)

Parties Movements coalitions	1992 (%)	1996 (%)
ODS-KDS	29,73	29,62
LB[a]	14,05	(1,40)
CSSD	6,53	26,44
LSU[b]	6,52	–
KDU-CSL	6,28	8,08
SPR-RSC	5,98	8,01
ODA	5,93	6,36
HSD-SMS[b]	5,87	–
KSCM[a]	–	10,33

[a]The Communists left the club of the Left Block in January 1994.
[b]LSU a HSD-SMS split and merged with other parties and deputy clubs.
More detail in Table 5.

lished for four years (1992–1996), with almost one third of the votes going to ODS (Civic Democratic Party), as seen in Table 2. The majority principle was used on a governmental level. Within the coalition government ODS possessed ten members whilst ODA (Civic Democratic Alliance) and KDU-CSL (Christian and Democratic Union/Czech People's Party) had only nine.

The marked regrouping of political forces lasted right up to the time of the parliamentary elections held in May/June 1996. As a result of the concentration of political forces into a small number of political entities, the established parties entered a phase of gradual internal consolidation, during which they strengthened their bonds with society and thereby 'dug themselves in' on the political scene.

The fourth period began with the 1996 parliamentary elections to the Chamber of Deputies and to the newly established Senate. The spring 1996 elections to the First Chamber served as confirmation of the further concentration of the party system. Only six parties were able to overcome the 5% electoral threshold. These elections, however, gave birth to a new political situation. The significant gain in votes by CSSD (Social Democrats), an increase of 20% on the 1992 elections (see Table 2) resulted in the creation of a *multi-party system with two dominant parties*. A classic party system thus sprung into being, with one strong party on the left and another on the right. At the same time, the more or less extreme parties of the KSCM (Communists) and SPR-RSC (Association for the Republic/Republican Party), with approximately 20% of the votes between them, can be seen operating at opposite ends of the political spectrum. The three partners, ODS, KDU-CSL and ODA managed to form a right-centrist coalition, but this time as a minority government.[7] From a party point of view, this government is more balanced: ODS no longer occupies such a dominant position, and although it is still the party with the largest number of ministers (8), KDU-CSL and ODA between them also share 8 portfolios between them.

[7] The Chamber of Deputies is composed of 200 members, elected for a four-year period by the proportional representation method. The coalition government, made up of ODS, KDU-CSL and ODA has the support of a minority of 99 parliamentarians.

The Senate elections held in November 1996 reinforced the hitherto somewhat rickety balance of forces on the political scene (see below). Nonetheless,
the establishment of the Senate entailed the creation of a new centre of political
power and the rise of a new power group in the framework of the political
parties.[8] In this sense, the formation of senatorial deputy clubs may represent a
much-needed stimulus to the development of intra-party democracy and
decentralization.

Parties – Individual Level

The Constitution of the Czech Republic mentions political parties only in the
broadest of terms: Article 5 of the Constitution states that the party system is
founded on the basis of 'free competition between political parties' which
respect fundamental democratic principles. In addition, the Charter of Basic
Human Rights and Freedoms, which is an integral part of the constitutional
order of the Czech Republic, makes direct or indirect reference to political
parties in the section on political rights – Articles 20 and 22.[9]

From an evolutionary viewpoint, it is possible to divide the political parties of
the Czech party system into three categories:[10]

1. *traditional parties – permitted* during socialism (the Communist Party
   and its satellites)
2. *traditional parties – prohibited* during socialism
3. *new parties*

The first category, that of traditional parties which enjoyed a continuous
development, includes of course the *Communist Party of Bohemia and Moravia
(KSCM)*, which, as a result of its specific form of development (during the First
Republic of 1918–1938 and after November 1989), still retains a strong social
base on the left – despite the fact that it is the least reformed Communist Party
in Central Europe. This category of traditional parties also includes the current
Christian Democratic Union/Czech People's Party (KDU-CSL). This predominantly Catholic party transferred its base in exile to London during the Fascist
occupation, and its natural development was also considerably disturbed during
the socialist period, when its leadership collaborated to a greater or lesser extent
with the state Communist party. Nevertheless, its existence, primarily from a
regional level downwards, helped at least to maintain minimum standards of an
alternative civic life. If we compare over the century the concentration of voters
for this Christian party, it is noticeable that it has maintained a remarkably
stable geographic constituency – in the regions of southern Moravia and
eastern and southern Bohemia.

In this first category it is also possible to include the ever-weakening *National
Socialist Party*, renamed during Socialism as the Socialist Party, and after 1989
adopting the name Liberal Socialist National Party (LSNS). In December 1995,

---

[8] According to the Constitution, the Czech Parliament is constructed as an asymmetrical
bicameral body. This means that a negative vote on the part of the Senate may be overturned by a
simple majority of all deputies. The government is not responsible to the Senate, but exclusively to
the First Chamber.

[9] *Ústava Ceské republiky a Listina základních práv a svobod* (Aries, Ostrava).

[10] For further details, see: M. Klíma, 'The Emergence of the Czech Party System', in B. Ríchová
(ed.), *Anthology of Political Science Studies* (Prague, University of Economics, 1995), pp. 23–36.

this centre party merged with the Free Democrats, but is still in danger of disappearing.

The most significant member of the second category of traditional parties, those which were prohibited during the socialist era, is the newly established *Czech Social Democratic Party (CSSD)*.[11] This party entered the 1992 Czech parliament with 6.5% of the votes, making it the second largest opposition party on the left. Four years later, the CSSD achieved a remarkable success by gaining 26.4% of the votes (Table 2).

The third category, that of newly established parties without historical roots, developed mostly from the mass democratic movement (Civic Forum – OF), which succumbed to internal differences after winning the elections in 1990, and thus split into three successor parties: the *Civic Democratic Party (ODS)*, *Civic Democratic Alliance (ODA)*, *and Civic Movement (OH)*.[12] Since 1992, the first two of these parties, together with KDU-CSL, have comprised the ruling coalition. Both are oriented to the right or centre-right.

The new extreme right-wing opposition party, the *Association for the Republic/Republican Party of Czechoslovakia (SPR-RSC)* arose outside Parliament. It aims to attract protest voters by means of its strongly anti-establishment slant. In the 1996 elections it gained even more votes than four years previously (an increase from 6% to 8%). The remainder of the new parties, including the Green Party and several Moravian parties, are very weak. A similarly negligible influence may be felt on the part of the right-wing *Democratic Union (DEU)*, founded in 1994, although this party has become a parliamentary party by virtue of its victory in one single-member constituency in the framework of the majoritarian electoral system applied to the Senate (see below).

The prevailing discontinuity of the existing array of political parties is evident not merely from the dominant role of entirely new political entities. It is also manifested in the ill-defined boundaries of their constituencies, in the confusion and variability of their election manifestos, and in the stunted development of their internal structures. This applies to newly established parties which emerged at an elite level, usually within Parliament (frequently successor parties of the disintegrating OF). Such internally created parties built their organization top down. On the whole, the newly established political parties, including the strongest ones, have not gained more than some tens of thousands of members (ODS, 23,400; ODA, 2,800; CSSD, 13,700). These parties still do not possess a sufficiently developed organizational structure. This became particularly evident in the November 1994 municipal elections when ODS, ODA and even CSSD registered a very small percentage of votes in smaller towns and in countryside areas in general. In 1997, the two strongest parties tried their utmost to recruit as many members as possible, so as to have something to choose from when it came to compiling lists of candidates for the 1998 municipal and Senate elections.[13] The weak membership base of the new

---

[11] Until spring 1993 the party leader was Jirí Horák, formerly a member of the Social Democrats until 1948, subsequently an émigré.

[12] OH, later renamed as the Free Democrats (SD), merged with LSNS in December 1995 to form the SD-LSNS. After the most recent parliamentary elections this centrist party (2.05% of votes) is in danger of extinction.

[13] Municipal candidate lists may require up to 56,000 party members. See: *MF Dnes*, 20 January 1997.

political parties can also in part be attributed to the deep-rooted tradition of anti-party sentiment in Czech political culture (see above).

On the other hand, basically denominational parties like KSCM and KDU-CSL are based on a traditionally well-developed organizational structure that has a solid grass-roots foundation at the municipal level. These classic denominational parties are more or less dependent on a stable, relatively disciplined and geographically identifiable constituency. Both parties may also be regarded as the only mass parties (KSCM, 200,000 members; KDU-CSL, 80,000 members). These parties not only benefit from a relatively large and stable membership and a highly developed nationwide organization, but they have also inherited considerable material assets from the past.

The total membership of the Czech parties is between 420,000 and 430,000. This amounts to about 6% of the electorate.[14] As is happening in Western Europe, the Czech political parties are loosening their bonds with specific groups of voters, and beginning to appeal to the electorate at large. The evidence suggests a consistent trend toward a much less structured electorate and toward the fragmentation and individualization of political preferences. Between the years 1990 and 1995 a clear decline may be detected in the extent to which voters identify very strongly with parties. Very strong party identification fell from 40 % in 1990 to 27% in 1992, and again to 18% in 1995. The highest sense of identification may be seen with voters for KSCM (44%) and KDU-CSL (30%). On the other hand, the lowest number of voters strongly attached to their party is found in the case of CSSD (8%) and ODA (7%).[15]

As has already been mentioned, the Czech party system was formed predominantly along a left-right axis (Table 1). This reflects the broader factor of citizens' own self-placement on the left-right scale in the period 1990–1996. From the data given (Table 3), it is clear that a centrist orientation dominated during the early phase of the democratization of society, when the broad-based Civic Forum was in power. A move away from this centrist orientation in favour of a markedly right focus was associated with the period of the second parliamentary elections (June 1992), i.e. with the disintegration of OF and the instigation of economic reforms. The left-right dichotomy typical of other Western European democracies was manifested in the Czech Republic as a dichotomy in attitudes for and against the radical transformation of society – transformation first and foremost in the economic sense.

TABLE 3. Left-Right Self-placement Distribution: 1990, 1992, and 1994

	May 1990	July 1992	June 1994
Left	19.2	16.4	20.2
Centre	50.9	33.1	39.2
Right	29.9	50.5	40.4

Source: STEM/Stedisko empirických výzkumù – Centre for Empirical Research, 1994.

[14] According to estimates, SPR-RSC has 40,000 members. The *Pensioners for Life Security (DZJ)*, which was the only non-parliamentary party to exceed the 3% threshold (3.09) as the condition for receiving state subvention, boasts a surprising 53,000 members. But its nature is more that of an interest organization, politically inactive between elections. The other non-parliamentary party, SD-LSNS has 8000 members (2.05% of votes).
[15] *MF Dnes*, 22 September 1995.

TABLE 4. Citizens' Self-Placement Across the Left/Right Spectrum (November 1996 – in percentage[a])

1	2	3	4	5	6	7
2	5	14	32	17	17	3

Source: IVVM/Institut pro výzkum verejného mínení – Institute for Public Opinion Research, November 1996.
1 – extreme left; 2 – left; 3 – centre-left; 4 – centre; 5 – centre-right; 6 – right; 7 – extreme right.
[a]10% do not know.

During the implementation of economic reform, when the essential foundations of the market economy were laid down, centrist tendencies again came to the forefront, despite the fact that public opinion in favour of the right remains a constant phenomenon for the time being. This is confirmed by the public opinion poll of November 1996, in which citizens were asked to place themselves on a seven-degree scale of left to right (Table 4).The tendency to a more right-wing orientation is evident from the table, even though citizens most often place themselves in the centre category. The extremes (both left and right) are rather rare.

Party Organizational Structure

As far as internal party activity is concerned, the law states that parties may not come into existence or develop their activity if they lack democratic statutes or democratically established bodies, or if their policy programme or activity poses a threat to morality, to public order or to the rights and freedom of citizens. These general principles are further specified only in the case of party statutes (*by-laws*). The Act on Association in Political Parties and Political Movements defines the formal requirements for the statutes: name and abbreviation of party, official party headquarters, policy objectives, rights and obligations of members, provisions concerning organizational units and party bodies (statutory bodies, organs of arbitration and auditing committees), the principles governing its financial management and the manner of disposal of the balance of assets in case of the party's liquidation.[16] The legal regulations establishing the general and formal requirements of the statutes leave a considerable amount of leeway for the discretion of the political parties themselves.

The *division of power* in political parties operates in both a vertical and horizontal direction. The *vertical organizational structure* is to a large extent defined by the law, under which parties may be 'organized in principle on a territorial basis'.[17] The system usually applied in the Czech Republic is that of a three- or four-tier hierarchy of party bodies: local, district, (regional) and national. The vertical structure of the parties is not only based on the territorial division of the state as contained in the law, but is also closely tied to the electoral system (division into electoral districts) and to the size of the individual parties.

[16] Act no. 118/1994 Sb. on Association in Political Parties and Political Movements, Article 4 and Article 6, paragraph 2.
[17] Act no. 118/1994 Sb., Article 5, paragraph 3.

The intra-party division of power on a *horizontal level* is founded on the basis of *representative, executive, judicial* and *controlling bodies*. The representative bodies comprise the assembly of members (delegates) on all levels of the vertical organizational structure. The executive element of party power consists of the elected bodies (party leader, Executive Committee) and appointed bodies (party apparatus). Any judicial power the party may have is represented by its internal organs of arbitration. Control functions are exercised by the auditing committees. Here we shall be dealing mainly with the representative and executive bodies on the national level.

The supreme body of a political party is the party convention. This, according to the statutes of most parties, takes place once every two years. The relative infrequency of conventions means that they are often overburdened with work, and that the ceremonial aspect of them is emphasized to the detriment of their working function. The extraordinary nature of party conventions is sometimes intensified by the fact they are held prior to parliamentary or municipal elections. The actual discussion and criticism of particular matters at conventions are also limited, owing to the fact that the executive bodies responsible for the preparations frequently present the convention documents just before the meeting, or even during the course of it.[18]

The decisive criterion for delegating members at the convention is the size of the membership base. Delegates at the convention are thus elected by the appropriate district organizations, with the exception of the *ex officio* membership of certain top state offices (minister, deputy) and party posts (party leader and deputy leader, other high-ranking party officials). The provision on *ex officio* membership also relates to the special position of certain party organizations. According to the CSSD statues, the Young Social Democrats and the Social Democratic Women have the right to send their delegates to the party convention.

Elected central executive party bodies responsible to the convention include the party leader, the Executive Committee, and the conference. Party leaders usually have a special position based more on their informal standing than on a formally regulated position (e.g. by the statutes). In the case of an electoral victory, they aim to occupy the highest state office, and have considerable influence on the personnel and programme policy of the party. All of the major parties elect their leaders at the convention, for terms of office of 2–4 years.

The Executive Committee plays the role predominantly of initiator and coordinator. In cases where there is no such body as the conference, the Executive Committee has a greater degree of authority. An example of this might be the ODS executive council, which possesses the right to decide on the final composition of candidate lists or on the establishment and dissolution of local organizations. In general, the Executive Committee is made up of both elected and non-elected members. The *ex officio* members include the leader and deputy leader of the party, the chairperson of the deputy club, ministers etc. Whilst the ODS executive council is almost one third composed of members elected by the convention (8), ODA's executive council consists exclusively of non-elected members.

---

[18] For more detail, see V. Simícek, 'Vnitrní zivot politických stran', *Politologický casopis*, No. 2 (1996), 105–121.

The conference serves as the supreme party body between conventions, and is a connecting link between the executive elected bodies (deputy leader, Executive Committee) and the supreme representative body (the convention). In practically all the parties it mostly consists of elected members. The majority of parties practise the proportional principle of regional representation in this body.

To round up this study of the division of power in the organizational structure of a party, it only remains to mention the organs of 'judicial' power. The purpose of the arbitrating bodies within a party is to settle intra-party conflicts. Some parties (ODS, KSCM) have a two-tier system operating at national and district level, whereas others (ODA, KDU-CSL) use a single-tier system. Most parties apply the principle of permanent organs of arbitration (ODS, KSCM, ODA, KDU-CSL). CSSD is an exception, in that it sets up *ad hoc* arbitrating bodies for settling particular disputes. In general it is safe to say that the role of the organs of arbitration is not sufficiently specified in the statutes, and that its role is often perfunctory.

Amongst the conditions for the formation and consolidation of the party system in the Czech Republic, the elements of direct democracy are undervalued. Intra-party referenda are used neither for the election of the party leader nor for the nomination of party candidates for parliamentary elections or for resolutions on party mergers. The only exception to this is the intra-party referendum in KSCM on changing the name of the party.

Overall, it may be argued that the organizational structure of parties in the Czech Republic is not directly determined by the orientation of their policy programmes. The exception here would be the protest/extreme party SPR-RSC. This is the only party to possess a two-tier system as far as its vertical organizational structure is concerned – at local and national level. This party holds its convention only once every four years. The leader of SPR-RSC is elected for a 4-year period, and a privileged position is accorded to him by the party statutes.[19] The Executive Committee has only five members, and enjoys extensive authority, closely tied to the party apparatus and the dominant influence of the party leader.

The Parliamentary Party

One important unit of the overall party organization also operates in Parliament. There exist party groups by means of which political parties play a central role in the organization and functioning of the Czech Parliament. Although there is a significant overlap of personnel at the top of party organizations, *the parliamentary party*, officially designated as the *deputy club*, plays a relatively independent role.

In theory, deputies may remain without membership in any deputy club, or an independent deputy club can be established. In practise, this tends to happen only rarely, since according to the electoral system the incoming representatives can enter the Chamber only on a party list of candidates. According to the new Standing Orders, passed in April 1995, the formation of a deputy club in the

---

[19] According to SPR-RSC statutes, the party leader appoints and recalls the treasurer, and appoints two deputy leaders in an advisory capacity.

newly elected Chamber of Deputies requires a minimum of 10 deputies, as opposed to the former 5.

The raising of the threshold for establishing a deputy club, in addition to other measures (see below) in the new Standing Orders are designed to prevent the phenomenon known as 'political tourism'. In the 1992–1996 deputies' term of office, more than 70 deputies out of 200 went over to a different party from the one on whose behalf they were elected.

Massive fluctuation among the deputy clubs was accompanied by the frequent extinction and formation of new clubs. This process is shown in Table 5. Nine deputy clubs were established after the June 1992 parliamentary elections, but by June 1994 their number had risen to 12, plus several independent deputy clubs. At the end of the term, in May 1996, the number of clubs decreased back to 9, but the personnel composition of all of them was changed and 3 of them were newly established.

In this context, it must be emphasized that the governmental coalition was stable during the years 1992–1996. The phenomenon of party factionalism and party splits was confined largely to the opposition parties.[20] The high level of instability within parliamentary parties, however, can be ascribed to weak party identity, organizational instability and insufficient personal experience.

Deputy clubs receive subventions according to the number of deputies who are members of individual clubs, and are also provided with rooms and with the technical equipment necessary for their activity. They are entitled to proportional representation[21] in the bodies of the Chamber of Deputies: Standing Committees, Commissions and Investigative Commissions. During the course of an electoral term, new deputy clubs may be established, but they are not entitled to proportional representation in the above-mentioned bodies of the Chamber.

The most important arena for deputy work is not the Standing Committee, but the deputy club. This is also clearly visible in the context of the legislative process. The legislative procedure of three readings determines that a draft should be available to committees only after the first reading, i.e. after a vote based on party grounds at a plenary meeting. As deputy clubs, as a rule, tend to submit to party discipline, the draft has a strong political bias even before being discussed in the committees.[22] In general the deputy clubs show a high level of voting cohesion. In the years 1992–1996 this applied mainly to the coalition deputy clubs as well as to LB/KSCM, but in the post-1996 Chamber the voting cohesion of all deputy clubs rose to 90–95%.

---

[20] While only one deputy defected from coalition deputy clubs to the opposition side, nine opposition deputies joined the government coalition. For details see: Z. Mansfeldová, 'The First Czech Parliament in the View of the Members of Parliament', in L. D. Longley and D. Zaljc (ed.), *Working Papers on Comparative Legislative Studies III*: The New Democratic Parliaments – The First Years (Appleton WJ: Research Committee of Legislative Specialists, forthcoming).

[21] The proportional representation system is not applied to the election of officials. Between 1992 and 1996, coalition clubs held the chairing positions in the Chamber itself and the individual Standing Committees. This situation changed after the spring 1996 elections, when a minority government was formed, but notwithstanding the more or less anti-system parties KSCM and SPR-RSC are still excluded from these leading parliamentary posts.

[22] For further details, see M. Klíma, 'The New Standing Orders in the Light of the Relationship of the Legislative and Executive Power', in *Budapest Papers on Democratic Transition* (Budapest, Hungarian Centre for Democracy Studies Foundation, 1996), no. 168.

TABLE 5. Deputy Club Membership in the First Chamber

Deputy club	post-1992 elections	pre-1996 elections	post-1996 elections
ODS	66	72	68
KDS	10[a]	–	–
KDU-CSL	15	24	18
ODA	14	16	13
CSSD	16	22	61 (58)[e]
SPR-RSC	14	5	18
LB	35	23	–
KSCM[b]	–	10	22
LSU	16	–	–
HSD-SMS[c]	14	–	–
CMUS[c]	–	15	–
ONAH[d]	–	6	–
Independent	–	7	(3)[e]

[a]After KDS merged with ODS in March 1996, several deputies left for KDU-CSL.
[b]The Communists left the club of the Left Block (LB) in January 1994.
[c]In January 1993 HSD-SMS changed its name to HSDMS and again in 1994 to CMSS – Czech Moravian Party of the Centre. In December 1994 the deputy clubs LSU and CMSS merged and the deputy club CMUS – Czech Moravian Union of the Centre came into existence.
[d]In November 1994 the deputy club ONAH – Civic National Movement – was founded by three deputies from SPR-RSC and two deputies from LSU.
[e]In December 1996 two CSSD deputies were excluded from the party itself because of voting in favour of the governmental budget proposal during the first reading. In January 1997 another member was excluded, this time for unwarranted use of an academic title. As a result, its deputy club numbers 58 members at present; the three deputies mentioned have become independent.

The governmental parties make use of an institution known as the Coalition Ten. This body is composed of the Chairperson and the Deputy Chairpersons of the Chamber, the three leaders of the coalition deputy clubs and the three leaders of these parties. The Coalition Ten meets prior to the plenary sessions and prepares recommendations for their deputy clubs. This has the effect of increasing Parliament's dependence on party bargaining.

The growing power of the deputy clubs in the functioning of the Chamber is determined by the process of consolidation taking place within the political parties themselves. By 1996 parties had succeeded in gradually forming a more developed party organizational structure. Not only did the management of the deputy clubs became more centralized, but also the influence from extra-party organizations, from the party national executive, and from the party in government (in the case of the government coalition), became more tangible.[23] This progressive party evolution in the context of the parliamentary form of

[23] As many as 74% of deputies in the Chamber said that the party national executive sometimes or often tried to give instructions to their parliamentary party. For further discussion, see P. Kopecký, 'The Organization and Behaviour of Political Parties in the Czech Parliament: From Transformative Towards Arena Type of Legislature', in P. G. Lewis, (ed.), *Party Structure and Organization in East-Central Europe* (Aldershot, Edward Elgar, 1996).

government increased the influence of the political parties in the Chamber. In this sense, the Chamber functions more or less as a kind of arena where the differing views and political opinions of the governmental and opposition deputy clubs confront one another.

The Influence of the Electoral System

The particular nature of the electoral system always has a palpable influence on the creation and formation of a party system. It is not by chance that there was heated discussion about whether it was appropriate for a democratizing and transforming Czechoslovakia to use a majoritarian system or proportional representation. It has become clear that the selection of a system of proportional representation for the Chamber, a system as yet employed in only the three parliamentary elections held from 1990 to 1996, has not led to the over-atomization of the party system or to regime instability, as some had warned. In addition, the proportional representation method neither eliminated minority interests nor basically distorted the representation of political interests in Parliament. Thus it did not create fertile ground for political radicalism and the potential formation of an extra-parliamentary opposition. On the contrary, the proportional system of representation integrated embryonic political interests into a united pluralistic framework for a party system. In this way, a much-needed legislative space was created for expressing and applying the broadest political interests in the conditions of the emerging democracy. The party system could thus develop and grow naturally. A broad spectrum of political parties formed. Although at first it seemed that the political scene was too fragmented, this factor indicated a fullness and depth in a variety of political directions and eventually exercised a positive influence on the crystallization of the party system in the development of a mature political culture.

However, the system of proportional representation is applied in a somewhat moderated version, incorporating a number of built-in mechanisms designed to curtail excess political fragmentation. The greater influence of the stronger at the expense of the weaker parties is in particular reinforced by two measures: the quorum for entry into Parliament and the payment of fees upon registration of a candidate for elections. The years 1992 and 1996 saw an increase on 1990 in the threshold for the entry of political parties or party coalitions into Parliament. In 1990, the threshold for individual political parties was set at 5% of the votes. In the 1992 elections, this basic threshold remained, but new quora were intro-duced at a higher level for party coalitions: for two- and three-party coalitions, 7%; for coalitions of four or more parties, 10%. The new electoral law passed in September 1995 raised the barrier even further for multi-party coalitions: three-party coalitions, 9%; coalitions of four or more parties, 11%.

As for the establishment of fees for registering party lists of candidates, even this mechanism improves the prospects of the larger and wealthier parties. For parliamentary elections in the Czech Republic, it is obligatory to deposit 200,000 CZK for each party list per electoral region. As the Republic is divided into eight electoral regions, the total sum for parties that want all regions covered by their candidates is 1.6 million CZK. This deposit is returnable only in the case that the given quorum for entry into Parliament is met. This can lead to considerable financial difficulties, particularly for smaller parties. Moreover, only parties and coalitions with at least 3% of the votes (until 1995, 2%) are entitled to receive the state subsidy of 90 CZK (previously 15 CZK) per vote obtained.

In general it can be said that the electoral system is one of the factors which contribute to the tendency for small parties to lose votes. It is not by chance that the number of parliamentary parties was reduced from 9 (in 1992) to 6 (in 1996). The vote share of non-parliamentary parties (below 5%) have also fallen: whilst in the 1992 elections they won 19% of the vote, in 1996 this figure fell to only 11%.

Notwithstanding, the system of proportional representation not only helps to achieve a greater concentration of political forces, but it also strengthens the standing of the political parties themselves in the political system of the Czech Republic. The law on elections to the Chamber allows lists of candidates to be submitted only through political parties and party coalitions. Neither individuals nor groups can act as independent candidates or associations (in contrast to municipal elections).

The second factor reinforcing the position of parties and their apparatus is the manner in which the second count is carried out: on the basis of a Republic electoral number (Hegenbach–Bischoff method), all remaining seats from the first count in the regional voting districts are re-distributed. The order of candidates not elected from the regional districts is determined by the party leadership.

Even the fact that the electoral law allows limited preferential voting does not effectively alter the dominant standing of parties on the political scene. On one party ballot paper, voters have the right to mark only four candidates for whom they wish to express their preference. Preferential voting is only valid if at least 10% of voters for the given party use this option. In this case, the seat belonging to the given party goes first to the candidate who receives, in the form of preferential votes, at least 10% of the total number of votes cast for the party in the relevant regional district (the average district magnitude is 25 mandates). In practice, the impact of preferential voting is negligible. In the 1996 elections no candidate was elected in this way.

Another factor which may contribute to the concentration of the party system is the functioning of the Upper House of Parliament. At the end of September 1995, after almost 3 years of provisional constitutional arrangements, the Chamber passed a law specifying the electoral rules for the establishment of the Senate. The 'Act on Elections to the Chamber of Deputies and to the Senate of Parliament' enabled elections to the Senate to be held in 1996. Thus the letter of the new Constitution, approved at the end of 1992 in connection with the split of Czechoslovakia, was finally fulfilled. The alternative principle of electoral system applied to the Senate corresponds to the asymmetrical nature of the bicameral Parliament. For the Senate, a two-ballot system in single-member districts was approved.

The new electoral law established 81 constituencies. In November 1996, full elections to the Senate were held for the first and also for the last time. The reason for this is that a system was used in which senators in one third of the electoral districts were elected for a period of only 2 years, in the second third for 4 years and in the rest of the country for 6 years. Thus the Senate will be replenished, not all at once in all districts, but by one third every 2 years on a 'mosaic' principle. Candidates are elected by absolute majority. Should no candidate receive an absolute majority of votes in the first ballot, a second run-off ballot is held between the two best placed candidates.

On the basis of such limited experience, it would be premature to evaluate the impact of the first Senate elections on the existing pattern of the Czech party system. The fact remains that SPR-RSC refused to participate in the elections. The biggest surprise was the success of the Democratic Union in fighting its way through to join the other parliamentary parties, albeit with a gain of only one seat. From the point of view of the balance of forces on the political scene, the Senate elections had a somewhat stabilizing effect, as the minority coalition government gained a majority of seats in these elections. In the long-term perspective, however, the situation is not so clear-cut, as CSSD was the most successful party in the six-year constituencies (Table 6).

TABLE 6. Number of Senators – According to Length of Term of Office

Parties	2 years	4 years	6 years	Total
ODS	13	13	6	32
CSSD	5	9	11	25
KDU-CSL	4	3	6	13
ODA	4	0	3	7
KSCM	0	1	1	2
DEU	0	1	0	1
Independent[a]	1	0	0	1

[a]The only independent senator is R. Falbr – President of the Czech Trade Unions. Nevertheless even he is indirectly supported by CSSD.

Cartelization of the Party System

A new party model has entered the political debate in the form of the cartel party, a model which is characterized by the interpenetration of party and state and by a pattern of collusion between parties. Parties become agents of the state and employ the resources of the state to ensure their own collective survival against the challenge of new parties. In the case of cartel parties, traditional hierarchical party organization and sheer size and commitment of party membership are not such important factors in the organization of an effective electoral strategy. The introduction of public subsidies for parties and privileged access to state-regulated channels of communications is a major help to the established parties in maintaining their position.[24]

Of what relevance to the Czech party system is the discussion on the new type of political party? Is there a 'cartel party' in the Czech Republic, on an individual level and/or on the level of the party system? Is there a real danger that party competition will be stifled and that we will witness the subsequent rise of protest parties?[25]

First and foremost, it must be stated that Mair and Katz define their *cartel party* as a purely theoretical model. Actual parties in a given country tend to appear on the borderline between particular types of party, and are more or less

---

[24] For a more detailed discussion of this issue, see P. Mair and P. Katz, 'Changing models of party organization and party democracy: the emergence of the Cartel Party', *Party Politics*, 1,1 (1995), 5–28.

[25] See: M. Klíma, 'Strana kartelového typu', *Politologický časopis*, no. 1, (1996), 4–11.

similar to one type or other. In the conditions prevailing in the Czech Republic, KSCM and KDU-CSL may in general be classified as mass parties; they are distinguished from the other parties by their relatively extensive membership base, complex organizational structure, strong party identification (stable voting preference) and clear denominational orientation. CSSD and ODS, on the other hand, may be ranked among the so-called 'catch-all' parties. These parties are oriented less towards narrow interest groups, and have a much wider field of activity. Nevertheless, their links to civic society are of fundamental importance. In this respect, one still cannot overlook the influence of the membership base, even though this may operate on a lesser scale, or the importance of the organizational structure and a certain degree of voter identification with the party. ODA comes closest to the cartel style of party. This is a party with a tenuous membership base, a weak organizational structure and an almost negligible degree of direct liaison with the voters (and not only at grass-roots level). Decisions on tactics and strategy in ODA are made almost exclusively within the central party bodies. SPR-RSC, on the other hand, is a type of party to be characterized rather by its reaction against official policy. In its own way, it portrays itself as a protest party, adopting an oppositional stance towards the established parties.

This division of the Czech parties is to be taken only as a rough guide, and it must be remembered that many of these parties are still fledglings, and in this respect the categorization sketched above may prove to be somewhat premature. At the same time it is worth noting that both KSCM and KDU-CSL are attempting to expand their voting clientele, and their election campaigns exhibit marked symptoms of a management style of leadership.

In any case it has to be admitted that, even in the Czech environment, a party system is developing which corresponds more or less to the characteristics of the cartel style of party. Parties are receiving quite considerable state subventions, as well as access to the electronic media, which is subject to substantial state control.

Concerning state grants to political parties, the biggest recipients are, needless to say, those parties with the largest number of votes in elections. The current system of state contributions calculates the amount of money to be assigned according to the results of elections (see above). In addition, exceeding the 5% margin brings with it both entry into Parliament and the so-called mandate grant.[26] State grants to parties make up a substantial portion of a party's budget; in the case of ODS and ODA the state contribution is the highest item of party revenue.[27]

The following considerations serve to illustrate the fact that the financing of parties is to a large extent being shifted onto the state:

- the political parties do not in general have a mass membership base
- party business activity is limited by the law

---

[26] Parties which gain representation in the Chamber are entitled to a yearly grant of 0.5 million Czech crowns per deputy mandate, and to an additional 5 million crowns a year. The state also allocates money for the activity of deputy clubs.

[27] In 1995 ODS received a state contribution of nearly 37 million crowns, ODA 12.5 million (of the others, LB received nearly 15 million, CSSD 14 million, KDU-CSL 12.5 million etc.). See *Lidové noviny*, 11 April 1996.

- donations from sponsors do not amount to large sums in the case of most parties
- the concentration of the party system means that the parliamentary parties enjoy ever higher financial gain in proportion to their election results
- there is also a gradual process of increases in state grants to political parties in connection to the first elections to the Senate.

A tendency to discriminate against small parties in favour of large parties has been gradually emerging in the context of the electoral regulations (see above). This is reflected in the increase in the electoral threshold and in the increase in the limit for the distribution of grants per vote received, in the establishment of the condition of obtaining 3% of votes (in the case of the Chamber) for the return of deposits, in the absence of restrictions on electoral campaign expenses and in the acceptance of the single-member constituency option for elections to the Senate.[28]

The application of the benefits of state grants and of access to the state media as well as the electoral barriers imposed on small parties could in the near future lead to the formation of a cartel of parties here which is capable of blocking the way for political alternatives (smaller parties).

Conclusion

The end of communist totalitarianism, coupled with the need to instigate and carry through a radical economic transformation, swung the pendulum of political sympathy in favour of the right. This right-wing tendency appeared constantly during the period from 1990 to 1996, and is likely to become a long-term factor on the Czech political scene. It is connected primarily to the relative success of economic reform. To a certain extent we can expect a repetition of the so-called German syndrome, when a significant left party entered the government only later on in the proceedings. In this context, it may also be expected that as the most crucial economic and political transformation processes draw to a close, public opinion will not only stop moving in favour of the right, but will start to move gradually in the opposite direction, towards a strengthened centrist or even left position.

On an individual level, the political parties were divided into three categories. The traditional parties (KSCM, KDU-CSL, and to some extent LSNS) take advantage of their highly developed organizational structure and strong party identity. The new parties on the other hand, whether they grew out of parliamentary soil (ODS, ODA, OH) or arose outside Parliament (CSSD, SPR-RSC) have had to form their own party base, internal organizational structure and party affiliation from scratch.

The initial fragmentation of the party system manifested itself on the level of the parliamentary parties – the so-called *deputy clubs*. Massive fluctuation among deputies was accompanied by the frequent extinction and formation of new clubs. The crystallization of the party system, the more centralized

---

[28] It was KDU-CSL and ODA who in the coalition negotiations with ODS advocated the option of 27 three-member constituencies.

management of deputy clubs as well as the toughening of party discipline increased the influence of political parties in the Parliament. The result was the formation of a moderate arena type of parliament (the Chamber).

The formation of the party system in the Czech Republic has entered a phase of stabilization, in which a broad spectrum of political parties with limited fragmentation has been established on a parliamentary level. A party system has emerged in the form of a moderate pluralism where only six parties play a central role on the Czech political scene.

Most recently, since the two parliamentary elections in 1996, a pattern of multi-party system with two dominant parties has been established. Thus the Czech party system is now based on the balancing out of the power ratio between right and left, a scenario which leaves open the possibility of a gradual transition to the originally German version of the 'two-and-half' party system. The precipitation of parties on the right, left, and centre would lead to the entrenchment of the two strongest parties in their dominant position, one on the right and one on the left (ODS and CSSD), with a greater or lesser degree of participation on the part of the smaller centrist parties. As for the extreme parties on both left and right, it is unlikely that they will constitute a significant political power in the future. It may be expected that, in time, KSCM will lose power in consequence of the loss of its older electorate. The nationalist or regional parties (after the break-up of Czechoslovakia and municipal elections in November 1994) currently represent a dwindling number of supporters. The Moravian parties, for instance, have effectively disappeared.

The established parliamentary parties are taking advantage of their privileged access to state subventions and to the media. They are also in the process of creating electoral regulations which effectively limit the entry of new parties into the party system. Thus the near future could see the formation of a cartel of parties in the Czech Republic. In this case, the irresponsibility of the established parties might create room for heightened activity on the part of extreme protest parties.

It is clear that the tendency to accelerate the concentration of the party system is strongly supported by the main political parties on the grounds that the less parties there are, to a degree, the simpler and clearer everything is, and the better for democracy. The opposite of this may be the case, especially in an environment of 'unsettled' transformation and an as yet immature political culture. In places where a natural renewal of the face of government by means of elections has not yet taken place, there is a danger of heightening political arrogance on the part of those who have been in power for a long time.

Appendix: Full Names of Parties[29]

OF – Civic Forum
VPN – Public Against Violence
ODS – Civic Democratic Party
CSSD – Czech Social Democratic Party
KSCM – Communist Party of Bohemia and Moravia

---

[29] For a summary description of all the parties and party-like organizations since the 1989 revolution, see Arthur S. Banks, Alan J. Day and Thomas C. Muller, *The Political Handbook of the World: 1997* (Binghamton NY, SA Publications, 1997), pp. 218–220.

KDU-CSL – Christian Democratic Union/Czech People's Party
SPR-RSC – Association for the Republic/Republican Party of Czechoslovakia
ODA – Civic Democratic Alliance
DZJ – Pensioners for Life Security
DEU – Democratic Union
SD-LSNS – Free Democrats/Liberal Social National Party
LB – Left Block
KDS – Christian Democratic Party
LSU – Liberal Social Union, a political movement which in 1992 consisted of three parties: the Czechoslovak Socialist Party (later LSNS), the Agrarian Party, and the Green Party
HSD-SMS – Movement for Self-Governing Democracy/Association for Moravia and Silesia

Who Survives? Party Origins, Organizational Development, and Electoral Performance in Post-communist Russia

GRIGORII V. GOLOSOV*

Introduction

Initial proliferation of parties is one of the characteristic features of post-authoritarian politics. Arguably, the intrinsic uncertainty of the process of regime change creates environments that encourage political actors to try their luck in exploring new issue dimensions and addressing their appeal to previously non-mobilized sectors of the electorates.[1] Those parties which fail to attract voters in the founding elections subsequently disappear, while the vote for the surviving parties tends to gradually stabilize.[2] Such trends are observable in the post-communist countries of Eastern Europe. While the emerging party systems of these countries are often viewed as especially unstable and fragmented,[3] attrition takes place primarily among those parties that lose the founding elections. This may be illustrated with an *ad hoc* invented quantitative index, the *party survival rate*, defined as a proportion of the vote jointly received in the second elections by those parties each of whom gained no less than 3% of the vote in the founding elections. In Hungary, the party survival rate is as high as 90%; in Poland, where the process of party system formation has been often viewed as damaged by an especially unfavourable combination of country-specific factors,[4] the party survival rate nevertheless approaches 72%.[5] In this

---

* Research for this article was supported by a grant from the Central European University Research Support Scheme. I would also like to thank Vladimir Gel'man whose generous help and advise contributed a lot to my work. All errors are entirely mine.

[1] See Guillermo O'Donnell and Philippe Schmitter, 'Tentative Conclusions about Uncertain Democracies' in Guillermo O'Donnell *et al.* (eds), *Transitions from Authoritarian Rule: Prospects for Democracy* (Baltimore, Johns Hopkins University Press, 1986), p. 58; Rein Taagepera and Matthew Soberg Shugart, Seats and Votes: *The Effects and Determinants of Electoral Systems* (New Haven, Yale University Press, 1989), p. 88.

[2] Arthur W. Turner, 'Post-authoritarian elections: testing expectations about "first" elections', *Comparative Political Studies*, 26 (1993), 341–3.

[3] See, for instance, Frances Millard, 'The Polish parliamentary elections of October 1991', *Soviet Studies*, 44 (1992), 837–56.

[4] See Grzegorz Ekiert, 'Peculiarities of post-communist politics: the case of Poland', *Studies in Comparative Communism*, 25 (1992), 341–6.

[5] Calculations based on the data provided in AndrAs KÖrÖsÉnyi, 'The Hungarian parliamentary elections, 1990', *Electoral Studies*, 9 (1990), 337–45; Barnabas Racz and Istv(n Kukorelli, 'The "second-generation" post-communist elections in Hungary in 1994', *Europe-Asia Studies*, 47 (1995), 251–79; and Paul G. Lewis, 'Political institutionalisation and party development in post-communist Poland', *Europe-Asia Studies*, 46 (1994), 779–99.

respect, Russia, with its party survival rate of only about 53%,[6] displays a distinctive pattern.

To explain the observed peculiarity of party system formation in Russia, a variety of theoretical perspectives can be productively employed. Two such perspectives have featured most prominently in the on-going debate on post-communist politics. One of them bases explanatory models primarily on *system level* variables. For instance, it is not unusual to explain the under-development of the emerging party systems with reference to such systemic factors as the lack of recognizable social bases to new political parties, the absence of mezzo-structures, or the lack of civic orientations among the population.[7] While many of such explanations apply equally to the whole universe of post-communist democracies, the system-level perspective also allows for identifying country-specific factors, such as the emergence of a strong presidency in Russia.[8] This theoretical perspective tends to produce valid but often too general explanations. In particular, the question of why some parties do survive despite all system-level constraints, while others do not, remains unsolved.

After the 1993 parliamentary elections in Russia, a different perspective became increasingly popular among political scientists and analysts. This perspective uses primarily *individual party level* variables, explaining party electoral performance with reference to more or less successful competitive strategies and tactics employed in the course of the pre-electoral campaign. For instance, many analysts viewed the structure of the vote in the 1993 elections as being defined by tactical advantages gained by the winning party as a result of its skilful use of the electronic media.[9] Strategic ideological choices made by party leaderships in post-communist countries, including Russia, also bear heavily on party electoral performance.[10] The validity of this theoretical perspective cannot be denied, as it does allow for attaining a better understanding of those factors that facilitate party survival. The major problem here is that by concentrating attention on the environments within which parties operate, this perspective tends to underestimate the importance of intra-party developments. More or less explicitly, parties are considered as something nearly equivalent to their leaders who make right or wrong tactical and strategic choices. But, as Przeworski and Sprague remind us, 'to assume that party leaders can pick any strategy, address themselves to any group with any programme, reduces the study of parties and elections to empty formalisms'.[11]

[6] See Robert W. Orttung, 'Duma elections bolster leftist opposition', *Transition: Events and Issues in the Former Soviet Union and East-Central and Southeastern Europe*, 2, No. 4 (1996), p. 7. For reasons which will be clarified in the course of this analysis, I consider the 1993 parliamentary elections as the 'founding' elections in Russia.

[7] For an overview, see Geoffrey Evans and Stephen Whitefield, 'Identifying the bases of party competition in eastern Europe', *British Journal of Political Science*, 23 (1993), 521–48.

[8] Richard Sakwa, 'Parties and the multiparty system in Russia', *RFE/RL Research Report*, 2, No. 31 (1993), 7–15.

[9] For a critical exposition of this 'media theory', see Vladimir Shlapentokh, 'The 1993 Russian Election Polls', *Public Opinion Quarterly*, 58 (1994), 597–602.

[10] See Herbert Kitschelt, 'The formation of party systems in east central Europe', *Politics and Society*, 20 (1992), 7–50; Grigorii V. Golosov, 'Modes of communist rule, democratic transition, and party system formation in four east European countries', *Donald W. Treadgold Paper in Russian, East European and Central Asian Studies*, No. 9 (Seattle, Henry M. Jackson School of International Studies, University of Washington, 1996).

[11] Adam Przeworski and John Sprague, *Paper Stones: A History of Electoral Socialism* (Chicago, University of Chicago Press, 1986), p. 120.

While the systems-level and party-level approaches are in many respects different, they share an important methodological property. Both are focused on the processes occurring on the level of party systems. Paradoxically enough, such a vision is most widely applied to the Russian polity, where, as many scholars argue, there is no party *system* but only individual parties.[12] The truth of such claims may be denied on theoretical grounds, yet in principle, such a methodological bias in favour of the party-system level of analysis is scarcely justifiable. True, the majority of Russia's political parties are still in the state of flux, with myriads of formations constantly emerging, holding congresses, changing their names, proposing programmes and bylaws, forming coalitions, splitting, reuniting, and disappearing, often without a trace. Observing, not to say explaining, these developments is a bewildering and not very rewarding business. In this analysis, I will attempt to examine mainly those developments that occur on the level of individual party organizations. This is not to say that the systems-level theoretical perspectives briefly outlined above should be – or will be – totally abandoned. Within their own heuristic domains, they are indispensable. What is needed is to complement them with an approach that allows for giving consideration to intra-party developments as well.

The major goal of this analysis is thus to examine *how party organizational development influenced party performance in the 1993 and 1995 national parliamentary elections in Russia*. In the field of comparative research on political parties, there is a thoroughly theoretically elaborated assumption that 'the characteristics of a party's origins are in fact capable of exerting a weight on its organizational development even decades later'.[13] In fact, none of Russia's major political parties, including even the Communist party, which reconstituted itself only in 1993, measures its age in decades. Organizational structures almost immediately coincide with origins and cannot be understood without reference to them – hence a retrospective character of a part of this essay. Three of the following sections examine the origins of those parties that contested the 1993 and 1995 elections. Indeed, the process was so peculiar that without such an examination the electoral outcomes would be hardly explainable, at least as far as the effects of party organization are concerned. The presidential election of 1996, however important it may have been for the development of Russia, will not be examined. In fact, the impact of existing party organizations on the structure of choices confronted by the electorate in that election was negligible, with only three of ten competitors representing recognizable political parties. The reasons for such an unusual situation will be clarified in the course of the analysis, although I do not address the question directly. In my conclusion, the prospects for party system institutionalization in Russia will be briefly discussed.

Collective and Selective Motives for Party Activity

The formative phase of any party system is a period when, for a variety of reasons, people join previously non-existing political parties. Analytically, these

---

[12] See Ronald J. Hill, 'Parties and the Party System', in Stephen White *et al.* (eds), *Developments in Russian and Post-Soviet Politics*, 3rd ed. (Durham, Duke University Press, 1994), p. 107.

[13] Angelo Panebianco, *Political Parties: Organisation and Power* (Cambridge, Cambridge University Press, 1988), p. 50.

reasons – or incentives – may be divided into two major categories, *collective* and *selective*.[14] The former are primarily the incentives of identity and solidarity. Joining a political party provides an individual with psychological advantages obtained from belonging to a team. Those groups offering collective incentives may be labeled *communities of fate*. Those entities in which the incentive for individual engagement is more material than psychological, that is, selectively rewarded, may be called *communities of fortune*.

Communities of Fate

Because it is normally through the ideological code of communication that political identities are expressed, collective incentives are strongly related to the ideology presented by the party. The more the party is a *community of fate*, defined primarily by a specific identity that has no equivalent in the external market, the stronger are the psychological advantages of belonging to it. Thus, in communities of fate, collective incentives prevail in the sense that their members consider their commitment to certain common goals to be the most important rationale for getting together.

Of course, political organizations are not the only context in which identities can be formed. One is tempted to ask what makes people identify themselves with parties rather than, say, basketball teams or churches. The simple answer is that, when faced with a plethora of such options, people choose those organizations that are defined in ways corresponding to the dominant agenda of the given society. In a society dominated by religious concerns, joining a church might be a better option. Party-based identities attract people only when and where politics are perceived to be important, that is, when and where mass publics become politically mobilized. Transitions to democracy in the former communist countries differ from other democratizations across the world exactly in that they involve mass political mobilizations rather than elite pacts.

Selective incentives are the incentives of status and material benefits associated with party membership. Status comes first. This means that membership is often seen as an honour, a symbol to be flaunted with friends. Beyond a certain threshold, party activism becomes a professional or semi-professional activity, and begins to be rewarded in more material ways, either directly (as in the case of the party bureaucracy) or indirectly, in forms of salaries tied to elective offices or other remunerations.

A distinction between party members whose participation depends upon collective incentives and those whose participation depends upon selective incentives can be drawn only for analytical purposes. However, there are real-world parties that are not *communities of fate*, in the sense that for their activists selective incentives are quite viable and important. Such organizations can be dubbed *communities of fortune* (to be discussed in more detail later). In fact, the vast majority of western political parties belong to this category, while communities of fate are rare and unusual in well-established democracies. But for the reason that selective incentives for joining political parties are important elements of the decision making process, which is not the case in transformative

---

[14] Panebianco, *Political Parties: Organisation and Power*, p. 24. See also Peter B. Clark and James Q. Wilson, 'Incentive systems: a theory of organisations', *Administrative Science Quarterly*, 6 (1961), 129–66.

societies with their lack of electoral competition for offices, communities of fate proliferate during the early phase of democratization.

Up to 1990, fully independent political associations could not exist in the Soviet Union. Article 6 of the 1977 Constitution identified the Communist Party of the Soviet Union (CPSU) as 'the leading and guiding force of Soviet society, of all state organs and public organizations'. In the second half of the 1980s, however, the political reality of the country became more complex than had been expected by the drafters of the Constitution. During the summer and fall of 1986, Mikhail Gorbachev broke sharply with the policies pursued earlier and initiated his new strategy, *perestroika*.[15] One of the important steps in implementing this strategy was to support the growth and spread of informal groups. By this, Gorbachev apparently sought to create a non-party support base for his reformist agenda, which would enhance his positions *vis-a-vis* powerful competitors in the Communist party leadership.[16] Some of the informal groups became politically active as early as 1987.[17]

Gorbachev's agenda aspired to create neither a liberal democratic polity nor a capitalist economy. In his public rhetoric, the Soviet leader presented himself as a neo-Leninist who wanted to update and modernize the system but, at the same time, to keep it indisputably socialist, in vigorous competition with the West.[18] The same orientation had been evident among some of the early informal groups.[19] By the end of 1988, however, neo-Leninism as the ideological basis of the informal movement had been almost totally replaced with a different variety of political discourse, sometimes dubbed the *mainstream democratic* ideology.[20] Narrative expositions of this ideology may be found in the programmes of several parties that emerged from the informal movement.[21] For the sake of brevity, it might be quite illuminating to cite a Moscow journalist who, when asked about his political goals, referred to the necessity of building a normal society, 'one founded on human rights, civil liberties and granting to people of economic freedom'.[22] This formulation revealed the core element of the mainstream democratic ideology: it was imbued with references to the central tenets of western liberal philosophy, such as the universality of fundamental human rights, with the West itself representing the way in which these rights had

---

[15] For an analysis of Gorbachev's political agenda, see John Miller, *Mikhail Gorbachev and the End of Soviet Power* (London, Macmillan, 1993).

[16] See Victoria Bonnell, 'Voluntary Associations in Gorbachev's Reform Program', in Alexander Dallin and Gail Lapidus (eds), *The Soviet System in Crisis: A Reader of Western and Soviet Views* (Boulder CO, Westview, 1991).

[17] For useful overviews of the 'informal movement', see Judith B. Sedaitis and Jim Butterfield (eds), *Perestroika from Below: Social Movements in the Soviet Union* (Boulder CO, Westview, 1991); *Neformal naia Rossiia* (Moscow, Molodaia Gvardiia, 1990); *Neformaly: Kto Oni? Kuda Zovut?* (Moscow, Politicheskaia Literatura, 1990); Vera Tolz, *The USSR's Emerging Multiparty System* (New York, Praeger, 1990).

[18] See John B. Dunlop, *The Rise of Russia and the Fall of the Soviet Empire* (Princeton, Princeton University Press, 1993).

[19] See Vladimir Brovkin, 'Revolution from below: informal political associations in Russia, 1988–89', *Soviet Studies*, 42 (1990), p. 239.

[20] The term suggested in Richard Franklin, 'The emerging democratic parties in the Russian Federation', *VOX POP: Newsletter of Political Organizations and Parties*, 12, No. 1 (1993), p. 8.

[21] See, for instance, *Sotsial-Demokratiia: Informatsionnyi Byulleten*, 1990 G., pp. 1–4.

[22] Judith S. Kullberg, 'The ideological roots of elite political conflict in post-Soviet Russia', *Europe-Asia Studies*, 46 (1994), p. 941.

to be protected. By implication, the Soviet Union had been viewed as an abnormal, totalitarian system.

Many causal factors jointly facilitated the rise of the mainstream democratic ideology to political prominence.[23] Any explanation, however, should take into account that Gorbachev did not launch his political mobilization in institution-free environments. Quite the reverse, the system already embraced a huge variety of institutions intended to provide the population with channels of political participation, from the Communist party itself to trade-unions, youth organizations, and elected state bodies.[24] Moreover, one of the official goals of *perestroika* was to revitalize these institutions. There were thus a lot of options available to those who wanted to participate in politics, the informal groups being only one possibility. Under these conditions, it was essential to shape the *identity set* of the informal movement in a way that would define its actual – and, more importantly, potential – participants more precisely than the officially formulated goals of the movement allowed.[25] Here again, the existence of the Soviet-type participatory institutions provided the informal movement with a pivotal reference point. The rationale for becoming an informal could be explicated with reference to the fact that other institutions were insufficient or, as it soon became widely accepted among the informals, insufficiently democratic, abnormal. The mainstream democratic ideology provided the movement with an adequate identity set. Hence the movement's gradual radicalization in the course of 1987–88.[26]

The acceptance of the mainstream democratic ideology had several important consequences for the organizational structure of the informal movement. Since the major goal of the movement had been defined as promoting western-style democracy, internal democracy was highly valued, while hierarchical structures had been viewed as associated with the Stalinist past and thus thoroughly rejected by virtually all informals. Some of the groups lacked any leadership structures, self-consciously operating as gatherings of equals. In others, governing organs took the form of broad, nonhierarchical multimember bodies.[27] As Fish has put it, 'the organizational forms found in Russia's democratic movement indeed represented symbolic challenges to traditional Soviet forms of organization, with their subordination and sham participation'.[28] One might argue that for such groups, creating nationwide coalitions would have been a tremendously difficult task. So it was. Many groups preferred to operate on their own. Later, they became what was commonly referred to as *sofa*

[23] See Judith Devlin, *The Rise of the Russian Democrats: The Causes and Consequences of Elite Revolution* (London, Edward Elgar, 1995).

[24] For contrasting views on functions of Soviet political participation, see Philip G. Roeder, 'Modernization and participation in the Leninist developmental strategy', *American Political Science Review*, 83 (1989), 859–84; and Donna Bahry and Brian D. Silver, 'Soviet citizen participation on the eve of democratization', *American Political Science Review*, 84 (1990), 821–47.

[25] On the concept of 'identity set', see Patrick Dunleavy, *Democracy, Bureaucracy and Public Choice* (New York, Harvester Wheatsheaf, 1991), pp. 54–5.

[26] For a factually rich description of gradual 'radicalization' of the 'informals' in Moscow, see Vyacheslav Igrunov, 'Public Movements: From Protest to Political Self-Consciousness', in Brad Roberts and Nina Belyaeva (eds), *After Perestroika: Democracy in the Soviet Union* (Washington DC, Center for Strategic and International Studies, 1991).

[27] See M. Steven Fish, *Democracy from Scratch: Opposition and Regime in the New Russian Revolution* (Princeton, Princeton University Press, 1995), pp. 113–8.

[28] Fish, *Democracy from Scratch*, p. 117.

parties – those whose whole membership could comfortably sit on a single sofa. There was, however, a strong incentive to unite, stemming from one of the basic elements of the mainstream democratic ideology, its commitment to a multi-party democracy.[29] When, in March 1990, Article 6 of the Soviet Constitution had been abolished, this commitment could finally find its realization. Some of the informal groups engaged themselves even earlier in what they viewed as the process of party formation.

Many students of this process notice that ideologically, the emerging proto-parties were practically indistinguishable from one another.[30] This is quite understandable, taking into account that the mainstream democratic ideology defined their identity sets in a basically uniform way. Why, then, did several – not just one – democratic parties emerge? Unfortunately, the amount of survey data and other firm evidence that could clarify this problem are scarce. The available data, however, unambiguously point at the fact that, being defined by their rejection of the Soviet order, the informal groups viewed the intensity of this rejection as a major basis for party building.[31] For this end, it apparently did not matter to what extent potential political partners distanced themselves from the regime in their public rhetoric. Commitment to the mainstream democratic ideology could be safely taken for granted. What really mattered was the intensity of anti-regime attitudes as expressed in the life trajectories of the members of the groups.

From this perspective, the informal movement fell into two distinctive categories. On the one hand, there were those who during the informal phase of their political careers retained Communist party membership, thus not breaking completely with the past. This group of the informals formed a network of party discussion clubs, which transformed itself into the Democratic Platform within the CPSU and eventually, into the Republican Party of the Russian Federation (RPRF).[32] On the other hand, many informals never joined the CPSU, or left it long before it was safe to do so, thus displaying a perceivably stronger commitment to the cause of democracy. These people formed the basis of the Social Democratic Party of the Russian Federation (SDPRF).[33] The union between the RPRF and the SDPRF, widely advocated by some of the leaders of both parties, never materialized.[34]

This brief discussion of the *communities of fate* would be incomplete without mentioning that, while the mainstream democratic ideology did play the central role in shaping the informal movement, two other ideological trends were also evident. Neither of them attracted a particularly large following in 1987-91, but

[29] For a variety of expositions of this commitment, see M. A. Babkina (ed.), *New Political Parties and Movements in the Soviet Union* (New York, Nova Science, 1991).

[30] See Michael Urban, 'Party Formation and Deformation on Russia's Democratic Left', in Robert T. Huber and Donald R. Kelley (eds), *Perestroika-Era Politics: The New Soviet Legislature and Gorbachev's Political Reforms* (Armonk, M. E. Sharpe, 1992).

[31] See Sergei Mitrokhin and Michael Urban, 'Social Groups, Party Elites and Russia's New Democrats', in David Lane (ed.), *Russia in Flux: The Political and Social Consequences of Reform* (London, Edward Elgar, 1992); Fish, *Democracy from Scratch*, pp. 88–93.

[32] See Vladimir Pribylovskii, *Dictionary of Political Parties and Organizations in Russia* (Washington DC, Center for Strategic and International Studies, 1992), pp. 72–5.

[33] Pribylovskii, *Dictionary of Political Parties and Organizations in Russia*, pp. 91–4; Aleksandr Sungurov, *Stanovlenie Politicheskikh Partii i Organov Gosudarstvennoi Vlasti v Rossiiskoi Federatsii* (St Petersburg, Strategiia, 1994), pp. 13–4.

[34] Fish, *Democracy from Scratch*, p. 91.

their organizational residua did survive into the next phase of the country's political development. One of these trends may be called *nationalist*, although its representatives more often defined themselves as *patriots*. The origins of the contemporary Russian nationalism can be traced to the late 1950s, and this movement – or, rather, a state of mind, occasionally supported by the authorities, survived through the whole period of communist rule in the country.[35] In 1983, the nationalists obtained a kind of legal status in Moscow under the *Pamyat'* (Memory) Society of History and Literature Amateurs. With the emergence of the informal movement, groups of nationalists started to make their appearance in major Russian cities, often adopting the name of *Pamyat'*. For example, the Pamyat' Historical and Patriotic Association of Novosibirsk, founded in February 1986, started to advocate a distinctively political agenda well before any other informal group became politicized.[36]

Some of these groups were as moderate as many of the early pro-reform informals, while others displayed a xenophobic and, occasionally, anti-communist attitude, viewing the regime as a marionette of a worldwide Judeo-Masonic conspiracy.[37] One might argue that for such groups, the logic of gradual radicalization of the informal movement created quite a favourable opportunity structure. At some moment in 1988, it did seem that the nationalists emerged as an important centre of attraction for all who were dissatisfied with the regime.[38] To become such a centre, however, the nationalists had to forge an identity set more credibly non-communist than that of the rising mainstream democrats. This proved to be a difficult task. While some of the Pamyat' activists held a negative view of the Bolshevik revolution, their hostility towards the contemporary West – both towards its perceived geo-political ambitions and towards its execrated *mass culture*, as well as towards the idea of a market economy – served as a bond conjoining them with the old regime. For the nationalists, therefore, radicalization often meant rapprochement with the authorities, which severely damaged their capacity to expand their membership base. None of the numerous nationalist groups active in Russia in 1991 exceeded 600 members.[39]

At the same time, the nationalist groups turned out to be no more capable of creating an effective nationwide organization than did their mainstream democratic rivals. In fact, Pamyat' never constituted a unified organizational entity. Rather, it was a collection of groups using the same label.[40] The nationalists were definitely not inclined towards internal democracy, and

[35] See Stephen R. Carter, *Russian Nationalism: Yesterday, Today, Tomorrow* (London, Pinter, 1990); John B. Dunlop, *The Faces of Contemporary Russian Nationalism* (Princeton, Princeton University Press, 1983); Alexander Yanov, *The Russian Challenge and the Year 2000* (Oxford, Basil Blackwell, 1987).

[36] See Grigorii V. Golosov, 'Political Parties in Western Siberia, August 1991–October 1993', Kennan Institute for Advanced Russian Studies Occasional Paper, No. 257 (Washington DC, Woodrow Wilson International Center for Scholars, 1994), p. 12. Similar groups had been created in about 30 cities, see *Spravochnik po Neformal'nym Obshchestvennym Organizatsiiam i Presse* (Moscow, SMOT Informatsionnoe Agentstvo, 1989), p. 61.

[37] See Francis Fukuyama, 'Varieties of Russian Nationalism', in John H. Moore (ed.), *Legacies of the Collapse of Marxism* (Fairfax, George Mason University Press, 1994).

[38] See Julia Wishnevsky, "The origins of Pamyat'", Survey 30, No. 3 (1988), 82–3.

[39] See Pribylovskii, *Dictionary of Political Parties*, passim.

[40] See Michael Hughes, "The Rise and Fall of Pamya'", *Religion, State and Society*, 20 (1992), 213–29.

however small, their groups were hierarchically organized and directed by single leaders. This organizational form, associated with the principle of strong leadership highly valued among the nationalists, turned out to be inappropriate for communities of fate, as it led to numerous splits resulting from leadership struggles. In contrast to the democrats, the nationalists viewed the very idea of a multiparty system with suspicion.[41] In combination, these factors determined the extremely fragmented character of the nationalist segment of Russia's political spectrum.

Both the democrats and the nationalists, although not with equal success, based their identity sets on their rejection of the official channels of political participation. This was not exactly the case with the third ideological trend evident in the years of perestroika, the neo-communists. For them, the Soviet system was not intrinsically bad. Rather, it deteriorated as a result of incorrect policies pursued by Gorbachev, with concessions allegedly made to black marketeers, petty bourgeois, and so on at the expense of the labourers.[42] Consequently, the major goal, as viewed by the neo-communists, was not to replace the Communist Party of the Soviet Union (CPSU) but to improve it. Lacking its *vanguard* role, and the advantage that conferred, this goal had to be achieved by means of independent political action. Two closely interconnected organizations emerged: first the United Workers' Front and later the Communist Initiative Movement.[43] In 1989–91, none of them achieved a mass membership.[44] It must be mentioned, however, that the neo-communist informals did not share the principled loathing for strong organization typical of the democrats; nor did they tend to split to the same extent as the nationalists. In fact, the idea of the unity of the working class constituted an important part of their identity set. As a result, their nationwide structures, even though fairly small in membership, were relatively well-organized along the familiar lines of democratic centralism.

Communities of Fortune

The March 1989 elections to the Congress of People's Deputies of the Soviet Union were held in the country where only one political party, the CPSU, was officially recognized, and under a system which allowed the non-competitive allocation of a significant share of seats.[45] (See the Appendix for a list and brief description of the consequential parties in Russia.) By holding these elections, Gorbachev further strengthened his positions *vis-à-vis* the party apparatus.[46] At the same time, the 1989 elections dramatically increased the scope of opportunities available to independent political actors. Henceforth, communities of fate

---

[41] See Robert W. Orttung, 'The Russian right and the dilemmas of party organisation', *Soviet Studies*, 44 (1992), 445–78.

[42] *Sovetskaia Rossiia*, 13 September 1989, p. 2.

[43] For a detailed description, see Orttung, 'The Russian right'.

[44] For a rough estimate of the United Workers' Front membership, see Pribylovskii, *Dictionary of Political Parties*, p. 109.

[45] See Stephen White, 'From acclamation to limited choice: the Soviet elections of 1989', *Coexistence*, 28 (1991), 77–103.

[46] See Richard Sakwa, *Gorbachev and His Reforms 1985–1990* (Englewood Cliffs, Prentice Hall, 1990), pp. 18–19.

as the dominant form of proto-party organizations in Russia became supplemented with groups seeking elected offices.

To be sure, in 1989 the new structure of opportunities was in its very initial phase. Independent associations did not even have the right to nominate candidates for office.[47] The vast majority of the candidates, including the democratic ones, ran under the CPSU label. Some of them, however, were actively supported by the informals. All over the country, a plenitude of *voters' clubs* and *citizens' committees* were organized to promote the democrats striving for the Congress mandates. In Moscow and Leningrad, these efforts resulted in a number of impressive victories of the democrats.[48] This led to two important organizational developments. Within the newly-elected body, the democrats created their own faction, the Interregional Group.[49] On the grassroots level, voters' clubs and electoral support teams united to form the Moscow Association of Voters, which began planning strategy for the forthcoming electoral campaign to the Congress of People's Deputies of the Russian Federation. In January 1990, the pre-electoral programme developed by the Association was accepted by the meeting of democratic candidates from a wide range of Russia's regions. They agreed to form a nationwide electoral alliance, Democratic Russia, directly connected with the Interregional Group.[50]

The March 1990 elections were generally successful for the democrats, especially in large cities.[51] As a result, the representative of the democrats, Boris Yeltsin, was elected as the Chairman of the Congress.[52] This, however, did not lead Democratic Russia to organizational consolidation. In fact, the alliance effectively ceased to exist after the elections. Voters' clubs and citizens' committees, as well as the informal movement as a whole, did help a number of candidates to win elections. Many of the elected deputies, however, had little reason to view the support of such groups as a crucial factor of their success. Individual efforts, popularity, and media exposure were generally more important. The very fact of electoral success further increased the winners' independence from their support teams. Even the leaders of informal groups who gained election to legislative bodies acted without responsibility toward their organizations, and contributed little if any effort to sustain these groups.[53] Instead, they preferred to accommodate to their new institutional environments.

The real meaning of the 1989–90 campaigns for the development of party entrepreneurship in Russia was that this experience had made a lot of individuals who contemplated launching political careers aware of the new structure of opportunities. Lacking either personal popularity or access to the media, these people sought alternative vehicles of promotion. At the same time, some of the members of the new political class that emerged within the new

---

[47] For a detailed analysis, see Michael Urban, *More Power to the Soviets: The Democratic Revolution in the USSR* (Aldershot, Edward Elgar, 1990), pp. 37–43.

[48] Brendan Kiernan and Joseph Aistrup, 'The 1989 elections to the Congress of People's Deputies in Moscow', *Soviet Studies*, 43 (1991), 1049–64.

[49] See *Sovetskaia Molodëzh'*, 26 January 1990, p. 2.

[50] Arkadii Murashev, 'Mezhregional'naia Gruppa', *Ogonëk*, No. 32 (July 1990), p. 8.

[51] See Thomas Remington, 'The March 1990 RSFSR Elections', in Darrell Slider (ed.), *Elections and Political Change in the Soviet Republics* (Durham, Duke University Press, 1991).

[52] For an insightful analysis of Yeltsin's political career, see Timothy J. Colton, 'Boris Yeltsin, Russia's All-Thumbs Democrat', in Timothy J. Colton and Robert C. Tucker (eds), *Patterns in Post-Soviet Leadership* (Boulder CO, Westview, 1995).

[53] Fish, *Democracy from Scratch*, p. 134.

legislatures sought to strengthen their power bases by means of party building. As a result, the idea of creating a mass democratic party, capable of removing the CPSU from power, soon gained popularity. An ardent proponent of this idea, Nikolai Travkin, launched his Democratic Party of Russia (DPR) in May 1990. Travkin held that to fight an effective trench war against the CPSU his party had to be organized along similar lines, with a single leader and strict discipline exercised over the activities of its members.[54] While the former idea materialized, with Travkin himself being elected as the Chair of the DPR, implementing the latter proved to be problematic. On the one hand, Travkin did invest tremendous organizational efforts into creating a network of new party organizations all over the country. As a survey of the participants in the DPR Congress in April 1991 demonstrated, 44% of them had joined the party in May–December of 1990 (compared to 11% in the SDPRF).[55] But on the other hand, creating mass membership could not be achieved without recruiting the informal organizations, and in several regions, they formed the local branches of the DPR.[56] This brought the organizational ethos of the informal movement into the DPR.

After a brief period of associating itself with the independent workers' movement, the DPR accepted the mainstream democratic ideology.[57] Two other proto-parties tried to enhance their opportunities in competition for potential members by defining their ideological stances in more specific ways. Both of them, the Russian Christian Democratic Movement (RCDM)[58] and the Constitutional Democratic Party (CDP),[59] emerged from the informal movement. Both, however, aspired to become real parties basing their electoral appeal either on recognizable social constituencies or, in the latter case, on historical legacies. They assumed leadership styles quite reminiscent of that of the DPR. This strategy proved to be not so successful as that of the DPR. The regional networks created by the RCDM and the CDP were not very large, and they consisted mostly of the informals. This resulted in the same kind of problems that ruined the nationalist groups – leadership struggle, splits, and factionalism. It would seem that the RCDM and the CDP stood in the midway between the categories of communities of fortune and communities of fate: their leaders and activists were apparently inclined towards political entrepreneurship, but the informal bases of these parties' membership were scarcely adequate to this purpose.

A different strategy was employed by those groups that tried to utilize the tremendous resources of the declining regime for their own benefit. One such group was the Liberal Democratic Party of the Soviet Union. At first glance, the party did not differ much from other mainstream democratic groups. Its leader, Vladimir Zhirinovsky, when asked to sum up his political credo, exclaimed: 'My programme? It is like everybody else's: perestroika, free market, and

[54] On the formative phase of the Democratic Party of Russia, see K. Zavoiskii and V. Krylovskii, *S Chego Nachinaetsya Partiia* (Moscow, Ekspress-Khronika, 1990).

[55] Mitrokhin and Urban, 'Social Groups', p. 75.

[56] Pribylovskii, *Dictionary of Political Parties*, p. 20.

[57] See *Demokraticheskaia Rossiia*, No. 1 (July 1990), pp. 2–6.

[58] See Richard Sakwa, 'Christian Democracy in Russia', *Religion, State and Society*, 20 (1992), 135–200.

[59] See V. F. Levicheva and A. A. Nelyubin, 'Novye Obshchestvenno-Politicheskie Organizatsii, Partii i Dvizheniia', *Izvestiia TsK KPSS*, No. 8 (1990), pp. 149–50.

democracy!'[60] Soon it became clear that the new party, as well as a number of other previously unknown groups, enjoyed a quite extraordinary degree of attention at the top of the Soviet hierarchy. These groups' representatives were granted audiences by the state leaders, and received an extensive coverage in the Communist party-controlled media.[61] For the Communists, Zhirinovsky's party could be viewed as a safe coalition partner under the conditions of the emerging multiparty system.[62] For Zhirinovsky himself, the support of the authorities was essential for maximizing his political gains in these strongly competitive environments.

The party-building efforts of Travkin and others were viewed not entirely favourably by those democratic leaders, especially among the elected people's deputies, who started to feel themselves unexpectedly deprived of any access to the channels of political mobilization. Lacking organizational bases of their own but enjoying instead enormous personal popularity, they sincerely feared the emergence of what had been referred to as a *populist dictatorship* within the democratic movement.[63] In order to counterbalance this perceived danger, the Moscow and Leningrad democrats initiated the formation of a new political movement, once again labelled *Democratic Russia*. In contrast to the Democratic Party of Russia (DPR), the organizational structure of Democratic Russia was designed as a loose coalition of democratic parties, groups, and individuals, directed by several co-chairs and not imposing any kind of discipline over its participants.[64] Obviously, such an organizational basis was quite acceptable for the *communities of fate*, and indeed, the SDPRF and the RPRF provided Democratic Russia with many local branches. For small *communities of fortune* and numerous *sofa parties*, the rationale for joining was also clear: without losing their organizational autonomy, they could benefit from belonging to a large coalition. For the DPR, however, the emergence of Democratic Russia posed a formidable challenge. The major target of the founders of Democratic Russia were the members of Travkin's party and, even more importantly, its potential members. For those striving to launch a political career within the democratic movement, there was now quite a visible alternative to the DPR.

Not surprisingly the debate between Travkin and his opponents in the organizing committee of Democratic Russia resulted in his withdrawal from the movement.[65] Travkin's position, however, was strongly resisted by the largest local branches of the DPR – that is, primarily by those which emerged from the informal movement. Some of these branches simply ignored Travkin's rejectivism and formed the core of Democratic Russia's local chapters.[66] Under these conditions, Travkin apparently realized that not to join Democratic Russia meant to threaten the very existence of the DPR, and he reluctantly reversed his initial stance. Thus Democratic Russia emerged as the largest organization of

[60] Cited in Pribylovskii, *Dictionary of Political Parties*, p. ix.

[61] See, for instance, *Pravda*, 1 April 1990, p. 1.

[62] See *Demokraticheskaia Rossiia*, No. 3 (September 1990), p. 4.

[63] See Yitzhak M. Brudny, 'The dynamics of "Democratic Russia", 1990–1993', *Post-Soviet Affairs*, 9 (1993), 141–70.

[64] *Partiinaia Zhizn'*, No. 2 (January 1991), pp. 44–7.

[65] See Vladimir Glotov, 'Oktyabr' Demokraticheskoi Rossii', *Ogonëk*, No. 45 (November 1990), p. 6.

[66] Pribylovskii, *Dictionary of Political Parties*, p. 21.

the democrats, with membership estimates varying from 300,000[67] to 1,300,000.[68] In January 1991, the movement openly declared its opposition to Gorbachev; later it backed Yeltsin in his fight for the Russian presidency.[69] At that time, the major form of the movement's activities was staging demonstrations in support for Yeltsin.[70] From the organizational point of view, demonstrations were important for several reasons. First, they provided the movement with a perfect setting for consolidating its membership and recruiting new members. Second, they provided the movement with media exposure. Third, collections taken up at demonstrations proved to be the major source of funds available to Democratic Russia.[71]

More than the 1990 republican elections, the June 1991 presidential election in Russia was conducted along partisan lines. However, competing parties as such were largely absent. The candidacy of Yeltsin was endorsed by several parties, including Democratic Russia, the Democratic Party of Russia, the Social Democrats, the Republican Party of the Russian Federation, the Christian Democrats, and the Constitutional Democrats.[72] Hence Yeltsin emerged as the joint candidate of the democratic opposition. The Communists (CPSU) produced as many as four candidates, representing different trends within the disintegrating party. The only explicit party candidate was Zhirinovsky, whose party did not have any significant membership at that time. Of course, the mercurial political entrepreneur could not challenge Yeltsin on the grounds of the mainstream democratic ideology originally accepted by his party. There was, however, a segment of the political spectrum virtually unexplored by the communities of fortune: nationalism. During the campaign, Zhirinovsky based his rhetoric on promising to defend Russians and the Russian-speaking population over the whole territory of the USSR. It was, in fact, in his bid to become Russian president that Zhirinovsky attracted widespread public attention and succeeded in establishing regional branches of his party.[73]

Yeltsin won the 1991 election with 57.3% of the vote. Pro-communist candidates fared poorly: the best of their results was a low 16.9%. Surprisingly for many observers, Zhirinovsky with 7.8% managed to capture third place in the election.[74] As a result of the election, Russia apparently entered into a new phase of political development. With the largest of the former republics of the USSR controlled by the pro-reform president, the credibility of the Communists as a potential ruling party sharply declined. This brought about two potentially important, but inconclusive, consequences. On the one hand, Travkin resumed his attempts to create a well-organized mass democratic party, this time by merging his DPR with smaller democratic parties.[75] On the other hand, Yeltsin's victory helped him to garner loyal support of the old political, managerial and administrative elites in the periphery of the country. Strongly

[67] Pribylovskii, *Dictionary of Political Parties*, p. 24.

[68] *Nezavisimaia Gazeta*, 25 April 1991, p. 1.

[69] See Michael Urban, 'Boris Yeltsin, Democratic Russia and the campaign for the Russian presidency', *Soviet Studies* 44 (1992), 187–207.

[70] *Kuranty*, 12 March 1991, p. 1

[71] Fish, *Democracy from Scratch*, p. 179.

[72] *Vybory-95*, Issue 2 (Moscow, Informatsionno-Ekspertnaia Gruppa 'Panorama', 1995), p. 21.

[73] Vera Tolz *et al.*, 'Profiles of the main political blocs', *RFE/RL Research Report*, 2, No. 20 (1993), p. 24.

[74] *Rossiiskaia Gazeta*, 20 June 1991, p. 1.

[75] See *Nezavisimaia Gazeta*, 11 July 1991, p. 2.

reluctant to join the democratic movement, which appeared to be too radical and thus hostile to their own interests, they sought alternative political organizations.[76] One such option was the pro-reform wing of the CPSU, which in 1991 started to break off as the Democratic Party of Russian Communists led by Vice President Aleksandr Rutskoi.[77] The summer of 1991 was the golden age of party political entrepreneurship among the democrats. There was a widespread expectation that a coalition of democratic forces would challenge the CPSU during the next parliamentary elections and would probably win. Remarkably few attempts to create a competitive party can be registered among the nationalists and neo-communists. A dubious exception was Zhironovsky who, after all, originated from the democratic camp. As the democratic movement grew in strength, both opposing tendencies increasingly connected themselves with the old regime. They therefore remained *frozen* in the informal phase of their political development.

The Interlude from August 1991 to December 1993

The attempted coup of August 1991 changed the whole structure of opportunities available to Russia's major political actors.[78] The leaders of the democratic movement were among the first to come out in support of Yeltsin's decree banning the CPSU; yet the collapse of that ageing organization meant that the task of the democratic parties had been largely accomplished.[79] Upon the receipt of extraordinary powers from the Congress of People's Deputies, Yeltsin invited none of the leading democrats to participate in drafting and implementing the programme of economic reform. Instead this task had to be accomplished by a team of individuals who owed their promotions exclusively to their connections and personal loyalties to Yeltsin.[80] The SDPRF claimed that one of the members of the *government of reforms* was its nominee, but in fact, the man was not even a member of the party.[81] Within the Russian legislature elected in March 1990, the role of parties was also modest. Parliamentary fractions grew in importance, but only one of them claimed to be party-based (the united fraction of RPRF-SDPRF, in April 1992 comprising 67 members of the 1086-member legislature).[82]

---

[76] See *Nezavisimaia Gazeta*, 2 July 1991, p. 1.77. *Rossiskaia Gazeta*, 3 August 1991, p. 1. On the process of gradual ideological diversification within the CPSU, see Mark R. Beissinger, 'Transformation and Degeneration: the CPSU under Reform', in James R. Millar (ed.), *Cracks in the Monolith: Party Power in the Brezhnev Era* (Armonk, M. E. Sharpe, 1992).

[77] Later to be known as the People's Party Free Russia.

[78] For an analysis of the August coup, see Richard Sakwa, 'The revolution of 1991 in Russia: interpretations of the Moscow coup', *Coexistence*, 29 (1992), 27–67. A useful overview of party politics in Russia in 1991–93 can be found in A. Salmin *et al.*, *Partiinaia Sistema v Rossii v 1989–1993 Godakh: Opyt Stanovleniia* (Moscow, Nachala-Press, 1994).

[79] Marcia A. Weigle, 'Political participation and party formation in Russia, 1985–1992: institutionalizing democracy', *Russian Review*, 53 (1994), p. 206.

[80] On the composition of the 'government of reforms', see Richard Sakwa, *Russian Politics and Society* (London, Routledge, 1993), p. 74.

[81] Michael McFaul, 'Party Formation after Revolutionary Transitions: the Russian Case', in Alexander Dallin (ed.), *Political Parties in Russia* (Berkeley, Center for International and Area Studies, University of California, 1993), p. 21.

[82] A. A. Sobyanin (ed.), *VI S"ezd Narodnykh Deputatov Rossii: Politicheskie Itogi i Perspektivy* (Moscow, Organizatsionnyi Otdel Prezidiuma Verkhovnogo Soveta Rossiiskoi Federatsii, 1992), p. 11.

In the periphery of Russia, the regime change did not result in any significant elite change.[83] In 1990–91, the institutional shift of power from the Communist party to the state was accompanied by a corresponding move of personnel, so that during the period of Gorbachev's reforms, the old peripheral elites lost few power positions.[84] In the aftermath of the August 1991 events, Yeltsin undertook a massive effort to ensure the loyalty of the local elites by means of appointing Heads of Administrations in the provinces and territories of Russia. A significant number of provincial leaders either supported Yeltsin or remained neutral during the coup attempt.[85] For them, this proved to be an effective strategy for securing their power positions, even though the local democrats vigorously condemned such a practice.[86] Where necessary, new provincial heads had been appointed. Few of them, however, could be considered as democrats.[87] One of the reasons was that in his bargaining with the Congress of People's Deputies, Yeltsin conceded that the new local heads would have to be approved by the corresponding soviet deputies from that territory.[88] Given the conservative composition of provincial representative bodies, the chances for the democrats to gain such approval were negligible. Even where this was possible, the lack of administrative competence and experience on the part of the democrats practically prevented them from obtaining significant positions. There were cases when the democratic parties and activists themselves actually requested that Yeltsin appoint experienced administrators as provincial heads.[89] On the lower levels of provincial administrations, there was some influx of democratic activists into the structures of power. But this infusion was clearly insufficient to alter the course of the decision-making process. As a result, the democrats either came to terms with the old establishment, thus effectively ceasing to belong to the democratic movement, or eventually found themselves defeated by their more experienced competitors in the field of bureaucratic power games.[90]

As a result of these developments, both the national leaders and the local activists of the political parties found themselves in a rather ambiguous situation. On the one hand, the cause they were fighting for had apparently been won. On the other hand, their own political gains were, as a rule, miserable. For those parties whose membership recruitment strategies were based primarily on

---

[83] On the lack of elite change in Russia, see Eric Hanley et al., 'Russia – old wine in a new bottle? The circulation and reproduction of Russian elites, 1983–1993', Theory and Society, 24 (1995), 639–68; Ol'ga Kryshtanovskaia, 'Transformatsiia Staroi Nomenklatury v Novuiu Rossiiskuiu Elitu', Obshchestvennye Nauki i Sovremennost', No. 1 (1995), 51–65.

[84] See Gavin Helf and Jeffrey W. Hahn, 'Old dogs and new tricks: party elites in the Russian regional elections of 1990', Slavic Review, 51 (1992), 511–30; Mary McAuley, 'Politics, economics and elite realignment in Russia: a regional perspective', Soviet Economy, 8 (1992), 46–88; Joel Moses, 'Soviet provincial politics in the era of transition and revolution', Soviet Studies, 44 (1992), 479–509.

[85] See Vera Tolz and Melanie Newton (eds), The USSR in 1991: a Record of Events (Boulder CO, Westview, 1993), passim.

[86] Zerkalo: Vestnik Obshchestvennykh Komitetov Rossiiskikh Reform, No. 2 (February 1992), p. 6.

[87] This was the case in the Krasnodar territory, for instance. See Rossiiskii Sbornik (Moscow, Informatsionno-Ekspertnaia Gruppa 'Panorama', 1995), p. 177.

[88] Rossiiskaia Gazeta, 5 November 1991, p. 1.

[89] Rossiiskii Sbornik, p. 273.

[90] See Vladimir Gel'man and Ol'ga Senatova, 'Politicheskie Partii v Regionakh Rossii: Dinamika i Tendentsii', Vlast', No. 5 (1995), p. 41.

selective incentives, this created an especially severe problem. For party leaders, a possible outcome was to change their ideological positions in a way that would provide them with the role of the official opposition. This, indeed, was what the leaders of all three major communities of fortune – the Russian Christian Democratic Movement, the Democratic Party of Russia, and the Constitutional Democratic Party – attempted to do as early as late 1991. All three parties sharply opposed the dissolution of the Soviet Union and started to advocate its maintenance as a federation, and an indivisible Russia.[91] After the beginning of radical economic reform, they rejected the concept of price liberalization and sharply criticized the government's strategy as 'ruinous for Russia'. Moreover, in early 1992, all three parties began openly seeking an alliance with the nationalists.[92]

The effects of this ideological leapfrogging on the organizational structures of the parties under consideration were not very favourable. The membership of the DPR had fallen from an estimated 50,000 in early 1992 to barely 15,000 by the end of that year.[93] Moreover, the initially centralized structure of the DPR had largely disintegrated. With Travkin's efforts concentrated primarily on coalition building on the elite level, local party organizations became increasingly independent from Moscow and often preferred to act on their own. The Civic Union, a centrist coalition of pressure groups and opposition parties, including the DPR, had not been joined by several local branches of the party.[94] This resulted in what was sometimes referred to as the 'two-storey' structure of the DPR, with local organizations being neither effectively connected to the Moscow leadership nor represented in that leadership.[95] A possible explanation for this fractious situation would be that there was a tacit agreement between Travkin and local activists: each of the parties to that agreement enjoyed maximum latitude while benefiting from belonging to (and, in the case of Travkin, leading) one of a few nationwide organizations. The local organizations of the RCDM and CDP also experienced sharp membership declines and increasing alienation from the national leaders.[96]

The Republicans (RPRF) and Social Democrats (SDPRF) confronted a different kind of problems. For these parties, their democratic identity was something that could not be sacrificed at any circumstances. But to be sustainable, ideology must be translated into a credible political strategy, and if this does not happen, the party's identity suffers.[97] Before the coup attempt, both the RPRF and the SDPRF pursued a rather well-defined strategy of defeating the Communists. Under the new conditions, however, this strategy became utterly irrelevant. One possible option was to support Yeltsin unconditionally, and another was to keep distance from the government and criticize it for being 'insufficiently democratic'. The SDPRF effectively split over which of

[91] *Nezavisimaia Gazeta*, 12 December 1991, p. 2.

[92] Sungurov, *Stanovlenie Politicheskikh Partii*, p. 24.

[93] Sakwa, *Russian Politics and Society*, p. 148.

[94] *Rossiiskii Sbornik*, p. 138. On the origins of the Civic Union, see Eric Lohr, 'Arkadii Volsky's political base', *Europe-Asia Studies*, 45 (1993), 811–29.

[95] Vladimir Gel'man and Ol'ga Senatova, 'Politicheskie Partii v Regionakh Rossii', in Vladimir Gel'man (ed.), *Ocherki Rossiiskoi Politiki: Issledovaniia i Nablyudeniia 1993–1994 Gg.* (Moscow, Institut Gumanitarno-Politicheskikh Issledovanii, 1994), pp. 17–18.

[96] See *Rossiia: Partii, Assotsiatsii, Soiuzy, Kluby: Dokumenty i Materialy v 10 Knigakh*, Book 1, Part 2 (Moscow, RAU-Press, 1992), pp. 299–300, 330–31.

[97] Panebianco, *Political Parties*, pp. 41–2.

the options was more consistent with its ideological foundations. The RPRF, even though it displayed a higher degree of organizational stability, also witnessed the emergence of deep internal divisions. This undermined the already loose organizational structures of the democratic parties.[98] In many regions, the democratic movement effectively reverted to the state of affairs typical of 1987–88.[99]

The organizational degradation of the remnants of the democratic movement had been accompanied by the gradual activation of two rival ideological tendencies, the nationalists and the neo-communists. One of the early attempts to create a mass nationalist organization was the Russian Popular Union (RPU) led by Sergei Baburin.[100] Baburin was elected to the Congress of People's Deputies of Russia as a representative of the democratic forces, but later he started to advocate views emphasizing Russian nationalism and chauvinism.[101] From the very beginning, however, the RPU included not only noted nationalists originating from the informal movement and democrats-turned-nationalists like Baburin himself, but also a number of politicians previously associated with the Communist party. One of them was Gennadii Zyuganov, the future leader of the Russian Communists.[102] Yet another nationalist coalition, the Russian National Assembly, also had prominent ex-Communists in its leadership.[103]

This signalled the emergence of a new type of party entrepreneurship in Russia – the political involvement of those former CPSU members and functionaries who did not ally themselves with the new political order. One of the options available to these increasingly active politicians was to join the major organization which evolved from the informal neo-communist movement, the Russian Communist Workers' Party (RCWP). Founded in November 1991, the party advocated establishing a dictatorship of the proletariat based on workers' self-management, Marxist-Leninist ideology, and a planned economy.[104] Organizationally, the RCWP claimed to have essentially the same structure as the disbanded CPSU. In particular, the statute of the party emphasized that party cells must be at the workplace, not residential.[105] In fact, the activities of the RCWP and its close affiliate, the Working Russia movement, more closely resembled Democratic Russia of the previous phase of the country's political development than they did the CPSU. The major form of the RCWP's activities were demonstrations, in 1992 occasionally attended by large numbers of protesters, and other forms of unconventional political participation.[106] Little is

[98] See V. Ia. Gel'man, "Iabloko': Opyt Politicheskoi Al'ternativy", *Kentavr*, No. 6 (1995), pp. 44–5.

[99] Sungurov, *Stanovlenie Politicheskikh Partii*, p. 41.

[100] On the founding of the RPU, see *Glasnost'*, 30 October–6 November 1991, p. 2.

[101] Pribylovskii, *Dictionary of Political Parties*, p. 85.

[102] Sven G. Simonsen, 'Leading the communists through the '90s', *Transition: Events and Issues in the Former Soviet Union and East-Central and Southeastern Europe* 1, No. 12 (1995), p. 60.

[103] *Izvestiia*, 3 December 1992, p. 3.

[104] See *Political Parties and Movements*: A Quarterly of the INTERLEGAL Center for Political and Legal Studies, No. 1 (1992), p. 13.

[105] *Glasnost'*, 28 November–5 December 1991, p. 2.

[106] See Ia. Yermakov *et al.*, 'Kommunisticheskoe Dvizhenie v Rossii v Period Zapreta', *Kentavr*, No. 3 (1993), 65–80. For general overviews of early communist successor parties in Russia, see Peter Lentini, 'Post-CPSU communist political formations', *Journal of Communist Studies*, 8 (1992), 280–92; Jeremy Lester, *Modern Tsars and Princes: The Struggle for Hegemony in Russia* (London, Verso, 1995), pp. 213–23; Stephen White and Ian McAllister, *Communists after Communism* (Glasgow, University of Strathclyde Center for the Study of Public Policy, 1994).

known of the internal structure and social composition of the RCWP in 1992. One observer of activities in Novosibirsk, saw the RCWP members as divisible into two categories: the middle-aged activists, often with their backgrounds in the informal pro-communist organizations of 1990–91, and elderly pensioners longing for the ideological scenery of their youth. While no claim is made that these observations are representative of other Russian regions, they do provide some basis for explaining the further development of the neo-communist movement in Russia. It must be noted that by mid-1992, the RCWP claimed to have 150,000 members, which if true would have made it the largest party in Russia.[107]

In late 1992, the Constitutional Court of Russia upheld Yeltsin's action banning the CPSU with regard to the central organs of the party but not to those at the local level. This decision ignited a comprehensive campaign to revive the Communist party, and beginning in January 1993, local party conferences were conducted in nearly every region of Russia.[108] This process culminated in the *revival-unification* Congress of Communists in February 1993. The representatives of more than 500,000 newly registered party members attended.[109] The organizational basis for the Communist Party of the Russian Federation (CPRF) was provided not by the RCWP or any other previously established group but rather by independent party organizations.[110] When invited to join the new formation, the leaders of the RCWP not only refused but also sharply criticized the CPRF leadership for, in particular, 'deviations from the class position'.[111] Such an accusation was not entirely unrealistic, given that the new party's elected leader, Zyuganov, had a long history of flirtation with noted nationalists. The appeals of the RCWP leaders to class consciousness, however, did not help save their organization. Local branches of the RCWP started to disintegrate, with sometimes large groups of their members joining the CPRF.[112]

To explain these developments, it is important to take into account that, according to many estimates, the CPRF was overwhelmingly dominated by pensioners.[113] One might safely assume that for these people selective incentives did not matter much. For them, the Communist party membership was, on the one hand, an important part of their identities; on the other hand, it was something that shaped their everyday activities in the course of their lifetime. By joining the Communist party again, they sought to create environments maximally reminiscent of the society they were accustomed to. From this perspective, the militant activities of the RCWP were irrelevant. Hence the success of the CPRF in attracting some of the former RCWP members. At the same time, the informal or, rather, non-system[114] character of the RCWP did not correspond to the selective incentives of a fairly large group of the former CPSU functionaries. An overview of the personal composition of the CPRF

[107] Sakwa, *Russian Politics and Society*, p. 141.
[108] *Glasnost'*, 9–15 February 1993, p. 5.
[109] For a description of the Congress, see *Nezavisimaia Gazeta*, 16 February 1993, p. 1.
[110] See, for instance, *Rossiiskii Sbornik*, pp. 159–60.
[111] *Molniia*, No. 52 (February 1993), p. 1.
[112] See *Rossiiskii Sbornik*, p. 459.
[113] See D. V. Badovskii and A. Iu. Shutov, 'Regional'nye Elity v Postsovetskoi Rossii: Osobennosti Politicheskogo Uchastiia', *Kentavr*, No. 6 (1995), p. 12.
[114] For a more detailed analysis, see Golosov, 'Political Parties in Western Siberia', pp. 34–40.

regional leadership in some twenty provinces of Russia demonstrates that these people have come from the middle levels of the CPSU hierarchy and, in sharp contrast to the activists of the RCWP, they often retained managerial positions after regime change.[115] The ideological rigidity of the RCWP leadership and its unwillingness to accept new political realities posed a major problem for such people. This was clearly indicated by the fact that the revival-unification Congress, with its participants coming largely from this stratum, elected the 'flexible' Zyuganov as the CPRF leader.[116]

In the fall of 1992, the nationalists of different origins launched a broad coalition, the National Salvation Front. The new entity brought together the remnants of the nationalist informals, the leaders of the RCDM and CDP, the Baburin's RPU and the like, and some of the Communists, including Zyuganov.[117] In the course of 1993, the Front became increasingly involved in the acute conflict between Yeltsin and the Congress of People's Deputies of Russia sided by Yeltsin's Vice President, Rutskoi. This conflict resulted in the September–October 1993 events in Moscow, leading to the dissolution of the Congress and scheduling fresh parliamentary elections for December 1993.[118]

Party Organization and Party Performance in the 1993 Parliamentary Elections

The 1993 elections were unusual in several important respects.[119] In contrast to many other post-authoritarian elections, the electoral rules emerged not as a result of compromise between competing political forces but were imposed by one political actor, the presidential administration, upon all other actors.[120] One of the goals pursued by the drafters of the law was to avoid extreme atomization characteristic of the Congress of People's Deputies, for such atomization had been viewed as a property conducive to conflicts between the executive authorities and the legislature. From this perspective, it was essential to encourage the development of a multiparty system.[121] The law provided for a mixed system, with half the deputies of the lower chamber, the State Duma, elected by a proportional formula in a national district and the other half by a

---

[115] See *Rossiiskii Sbornik*, passim.

[116] For an exposition of Zyuganov's ideological discourse in 1992, see *Molodaia Gvardiia*, No. 9 (September 1992), pp. 50–52.

[117] See Gordon M. Hahn, 'Opposition politics in Russia', *Europe-Asia Studies*, 46 (1994), 306–14.

[118] See Thomas F. Remington, 'Representative Power and the Russian State', in Stephen White *et al.* (eds), *Developments in Russian and Post-Soviet Politics*, 3rd ed. (Durham, Duke University Press, 1994), pp. 77–80.

[119] For general descriptions of the 1993 elections, see Jerry F. Hough, 'The Russian election of 1993: public attitudes towards economic reform and democratization', *Post-Soviet Affairs*, 10 (1994), 1–37; Peter Lentini, 'Elections and national order in Russia: the 1993 elections to the Russian State Duma', *Journal of Communist Studies and Transition Politics*, 10 (1994), 151–92; Yuri V. Medvedkov *et al.*, 'The December 1993 Russian elections: geographical patterns and contextual factors', *Russian Review*, 55 (1996), 80–98; Richard Sakwa, 'The Russian elections of December 1993', *Europe-Asia Studies*, 47 (1995), 195–227; Matthew Wyman *et al.*, 'Public opinion, parties and voters in the December 1993 Russian elections', *Europe-Asia Studies*, 47 (1995), 591–614; Stephen Whitefield and Geoffrey Evans, 'The Russian elections of 1993: public opinion and the transition experience', *Post-Soviet Affairs*, 10 (1994), 38–60.

[120] See Michael Urban, 'December 1993 as a Replication of late-Soviet electoral practices', *Post-Soviet Affairs*, 10 (1994), 127–58.

[121] *Moskovskie Novosti*, 20 June 1993, p. A9.

plurality system in single-member districts. In order to be eligible to run, a party or bloc required at least 100,000 nominations with no more than 15,000 signatures drawn from any one of Russia's 89 territorial units. A 5% barrier was used to prevent the proliferation of small parties.[122]

Many analysts have emphasized the impact of the extensive use of the electronic media on the 1993 election results.[123] Theoretically, however, the electoral law provided ample opportunities to utilize party organization for maximizing electoral gains. First, for the purpose of nomination, having a regional network was an important asset. Second, one might reasonably assume that those parties that managed to fill their lists with locally prominent politicians could increase their vote shares in respective localities. Third, local party organizations could heavily supplement the media campaign with grassroots activities. Fourth, parties capable of winning elections both by the list system and in single-member districts were obviously in a more advantageous position than others. All these considerations, however, had to be weighed against the background of the lack of party structures characteristic of virtually all participants in the 1993 elections.

In 1992–93, Russia witnessed several attempts to create a governing democratic party.[124] One of these attempts had been undertaken in July 1992 at a meeting called the Forum of Democratic Forces. The Forum brought together two kinds of participants. On the one hand, the Forum included some of the national leaders of Democratic Russia, so called *pragmatists* who tended to unconditionally support the government. On the other hand, the government itself had been represented by a number of senior officials, such as the principal drafter of the reform programme Yegor Gaidar and Anatolii Chubais, the head of the State Committee on Property, the entity responsible for privatization.[125] The Committee effectively ran a coalition of state-related interest groups, the Association of Privatized and Privatizing Enterprises.[126] The process of the formation of the governing party continued through 1992 and 1993, and in October 1993 culminated at the Founding Congress of *Russia's Choice*.

In addition to democratic activists and government leaders, the new coalition included local Heads of Administrations and other officials.[127] Thus what had been commonly referred to as the *party of power* finally took its shape. Integrating the democrats into the new entity, however, caused three important problems. First, some of the officials sought to turn Russia's Choice into a fully professional and well organized political party. Although supportive of the government, the leaders of Democratic Russia thoroughly rejected the idea. Instead, they favoured preserving a loose organizational framework, and this position prevailed. Second, the excessive number of prominent personalities in

[122] For a detailed analysis of the law and its political consequences, see V. I. Vasil'ev and A. E. Postnikov, *Vybory v Gosudarstvennuiu Dumu: Pravovye Problemy* (Moscow: BEK, 1995).

[123] See James Hughes, 'The "Americanisation" of Russian politics: Russia's first television election, December 1993', *Journal of Communist Studies and Transition Politics*, 10 (1994), 125–50.

[124] For an overview, see Gel'man and Senatova, 'Politicheskie Partii v Regionakh Rossii', pp. 21–23.

[125] Michael McFaul, *Post-Communist Politics: Democratic Prospects in Russia and Eastern Europe* (Washington, DC: Center for Strategic and International Studies, 1993), pp. 66-72.

[126] See Ye. Krasnikov, 'Politicheskoe Predstavitel'stvo Biznesa', *Predely Vlasti*, No. 4 (1994), pp. 138–9.

[127] See *Spravochno-Informatsionnye Materialy*: Uchreditel'nyi S"ezd Obshchestvenno-Politicheskogo Bloka *Vybor Rossii*. Moscow, 1995.

the leadership of Russia's Choice was naturally disadvantageous for the activists of Democratic Russia, with their chances to be placed high on the party list being reduced at this juncture. In fact, only 7% of the names on the list of Russia's choice were those of professional party activists.[128] Third, and arguably related to the previous problems, the national leaderships of two major constituent parts of Democratic Russia, the RPRF and the SDPRF, refused to join the new entity.

On the grassroots level, however, an even more complicated situation emerged. For many local organizations of Democratic Russia and other democratic parties, joining Russia's Choice was a possible way out of the political ghetto where they found themselves during the 1991–93 interlude. In the Novosibirsk province, for instance, the regional branch of the RPRF not only joined Russia's Choice but effectively formed its local chapter.[129] At the same time, many chapters of Democratic Russia, led by not-so-pragmatic activists, refused to join irrespective of the position of the leaders of the movement.[130] Finally, there were regions in which all three entities – Democratic Russia, the RPRF, and the SDPRF – split on the issue.[131] The non-pragmatic participants of the democratic movement founded the regional organizations of the Yavlinsky–Boldyrev–Lukin Bloc (*Yabloko*).

Officially, Yabloko had been established by the RPRF, the SDPRF, and a small democratic break-off group of the RCDM. Practically, as reflected in its label, the coalition was dominated by a number of prominent personalities including Grigorii Yavlinsky, an economist who owed his popularity to the *500-day* programme of market reforms published in 1990. In October 1993, Yavlinsky and a number of other high profile individuals formed their own list and then invited the democratic parties to join.[132] After some hesitation, especially evident in the case of the RPRF,[133] the founders accepted the invitation. What was the rationale for joining? First, none of the parties proved to be capable of collecting the required number of signatures on its own. The RPRF, for example, collected only 70,000 signatures.[134] The second reason was that in the RPRF and SDPRF many local organizations accepted the line of democratic alternative to Yeltsin, now explicitly advocated by Yavlinsky, as early as in 1992. Not to join meant to lose a chance of pursuing a credible political strategy, something that the members of both parties desperately lacked. Like Russia's Choice, Yabloko thereby managed to utilize the organizational resources of the remnants of the democratic movement. In both cases, these scarce resources were heavily supplemented with non-party assets: close ties with the state apparatus and state-related interest groups (Russia's Choice), and Yavlinsky's situational charisma combined with an attractive ideological stance (Yabloko).

[128] V. A. Kolosov, 'Sdvigi v Politicheskikh Orientatsiiakh Izbiratelei i Geografiia Golosovaniia za Partiinye Spiski', in V. A. Kolosov (ed.), *Rossiia na Vyborakh: Uroki i Perspektivy* (Moscow: Tsentr Politicheskikh Tekhnologii, 1995), p. 18. The party lists for all parties appeared in *Rossiiskaia Gazeta*, 12 November 1993.

[129] See Nadezhda Borodulina, 'Novosibirskaia Oblast': Ekonomika, Partii, Lidery', *Vlast'*, No. 9 (1995), 34–9.

[130] See *Rossiiskii Sbornik*, pp. 302–3.

[131] *Rossiiskii Sbornik*, p. 357.

[132] See *Federal'noe Sobranie: Spravochnik* (Moscow: Informatsionno-Ekspertnaia Gruppa 'Panorama', 1996), p. 174.

[133] See *Moscow News*, 22 October 1993, p. 2.

[134] Sakwa, *The Russian Elections*, p. 201.

In contrast to the Republicans and the Social Democrats, the Democratic Party of Russia (DPR) contested the elections on its own, and filled its party list primarily with names of its leaders and activists.[135] This clearly indicated that in contrast to other democratic parties, the DPR to an extent succeeded in preserving the very existence, if not the integrity, of its regional network. Other resources available to the DPR were scarce.

The Party of Russian Unity and Concord (PRUC) entirely lacked any roots in the democratic movement, thus representing another extreme. Created by Sergei Shakhrai, Head of the State Committee for Nationalities, on the eve of the campaign, PRUC based its organizational structure almost exclusively on the regional centres of that rather powerful committee, joined by several sympathetic provincial administrations and interest groups like the Union of Small Cities.[136] Probably the most important asset of the PRUC, however, was the role played by Shakhrai in distributing state subsidies among the ethno-based federal units (republics) of Russia. As a result, the *minister of nationalities* enjoyed fairly cosy relations with many leaders of the republics.[137]

Many other participants in the 1993 elections, irrespective of their ideological orientations, closely followed the pattern of the PRUC. They included the Civic Union for Stability, Justice and Progress, based on the most important interest group of the military-industrial complex; the Women of Russia movement, based on the remnants of the vast network of *zhensovety* (women's councils) that emerged in 1988 as a part of Gorbachev's social mobilization effort;[138] and the Agrarian Party of Russia (APR). The latter group so closely allied itself with the Communists that it was often characterized as a rural subdivision of the Russian Communists (CPRF).[139] In fact, the APR was based not on the rural cells of the former CPSU, but rather on the organizational infrastructure of the old system of collective and state farms, largely unchanged in 1991–93. The elements of this infrastructure included the aggressive lobby of collective farm managers called the Agrarian Union, the official trade unions of the agro-industrial complex, and agricultural departments of provincial administrations.[140] The elections were contested by a number of other corporatist and interest groups organized along similar lines.[141]

Overall, as many as 35 electoral associations collected signatures required for official registration, but only 13 succeeded. Those which failed were mostly small interest groups and remnants of the informal movement, including the largest of the groups originating from Pamyat'.[142] It must be mentioned that parties identified with the opposition confronted many difficulties in collecting signatures against the backgrounds of widespread fear engendered by the

[135] Kolosov, 'Sdvigi v Politicheskikh Orientatsiiakh', p. 16.
[136] Gel'man and Senatova, 'Politicheskie Partii v Regionakh Rossii', p. 23.
[137] For example, see *Rossiiskii Sbornik*, pp. 49–54.
[138] See *Rabotnitsa*, No. 6 (1988), p. 5.
[139] See Eberhard Schneider, *The Nationalist and Communist Parliamentary Groups in the Russian State Duma* (Cologne: Bundesinstitut für Ostwissenschaftliche und Internationale Studien, 1995), p. 31.
[140] V. A. Kolosov and R. F. Turovskii, 'Partii v Regionakh Rossii: Geografiia Golosovanii, Rezul'taty i Vozmozhnosti', *Sapere Aude: Selected Works of the Moscow School of Political Studies*, No. 2 (1995), p. 128.
[141] See Peter Lentini, 'Electoral associations in the 1993 elections to the Russian state Duma', *Journal of Communist Studies and Transitional Politics* 10 (1994), 1-36.
[142] For a complete list, see *Vybory-95*, p. 137.

violent dissolution of the previous parliament.[143] The Popular Union (RPU) claimed that the police had raided its offices and stolen 20,000 signatures, and the Christian Democratic Movement (RCDM) had been disqualified by the Central Electoral Commission, for not entirely clear reasons.[144] One of the consequences was that among the nationalists only Zhirinovsky's Liberal Democratic Party of Russia (LDPR) gained registration.

It is not certain how much of a party the LDPR was in late 1993. While some of the analysts held that Zhirinovsky had preserved a network in the provinces,[145] and it might be fair to assume that at least some of the LDPR local branches established in 1991 were still active in 1993, few such instances can be viewed as sufficiently documented.[146] The lack of organizational structures was clearly reflected in its list, which included – in addition to Zhirinovsky's comrades in arms such as his relatives – many people previously unnoticed in any connections with the LDPR, even occasional Communist party members.[147] Much of the electoral success of the Liberal Democrats had to be attributed to Zhirinovsky's excellent media campaign, as well as to the fact that the LDPR most successfully combined an unmistakably nationalist ideological stance with a well-articulated anti-government position,[148] and to the lack of ideologically similar competitors. It is important to mention that during the campaign, Zhirinovsky undertook massive efforts to create a regional network for his party. In contrast to virtually all other party politicians in Russia, he travelled to many regions of the country in a zealous attempt to recruit party members and to create local branches of the LDPR.[149]

Both the Russian Communist Workers (RCWP) and the Communist Party of the Russian Federation (CPRF) were initially banned after the October 1993 events in Moscow. But if the former boycotted the December elections, calling for a campaign of civic disobedience, the latter easily collected the required number of signatures and was added to the list of registered parties. Still, running an effective vote-maximizing campaign in the aftermath of the October events was a difficult task for the Communists who were widely portrayed in the media as the 'party of civil war'. Rather, the CPRF had to gain recognition as a legitimate political actor.[150] As a result, the party's pre-election rhetoric, as expressed in Zyuganov's speeches, was overcautious, obscured with quasi-academic terminology, and generally vague. Consciously avoiding sharp issues, Zyuganov emphasized his nationalism, and stressed such values as labour, justice, and 'civil peace'.[151] In sharp contrast to the LDPR, the CPRF did not run any significant media campaign, relying instead on its regional network.

---

[143] See Urban, 'December 1993', p. 137.

[144] *Vybory-95*, pp. 179, 184.

[145] Alexander Rahr, 'Preparations for the parliamentary elections in Russia', *RFE/RL Research Report* 2, No. 47 (1993), p. 6.

[146] *Rossiiskii Sbornik*, pp. 211, 281.

[147] For the list of deputies elected on the LDPR ticket, with 42 per cent of them not even party members, see *Byulleten' Tsentral'noi Izbiratel'noi Komissii Rossiiskoi Federatsii*, No. 12 (1994).

[148] See Golosov, 'Modes of Communist Rule', pp. 65–7.

[149] See *Izvestiia*, 27 November 1993, p. 2.

[150] Vladimir Gel'man, 'Kommunisty v Strukturakh Vlasti: Analiz Deiatel'nosti', *Vlast'*, No. 6 (1996), pp. 20-21.

[151] See V. G. Gel'bras *et al.*, *Kto Yest' Chto? Politicheskie Partii i Bloki, Obshchestvennye Organizatsii* (Moscow: Ministerstvo Ekonomiki Rossiiskoi Federatsii, 1994).

In single-member districts, electoral associations pursued a variety of strategies reflecting their differential opportunities.[152] Corporatist and interest groups tried to reach their specific constituencies by recruiting their candidates from the respective strata. Two associations, the Democratic (DPR) and the Communist (CPRF) parties, tended to nominate their members. Among the candidates supported by Yabloko, many belonged to the founding parties, but there was also a significant number of nationally and locally known personalities of democratic alternative stances. Candidates advanced by the parties of power, Russia's Choice and the PRUC, often belonged to the administrative apparatus, although in the former case, democratic activists also ran. The most characteristic feature of the single-member races, however, was that they were dominated by the independent candidates, not affiliated with any of the electoral associations. On the one hand, this resulted from the use of non-partisan ballot in this section of the elections.[153] On the other hand, the weakness of regional networks obviously contributed to the unwillingness of locally prominent personalities to associate themselves with any of the parties.

The results of the 1993 elections scarcely demonstrated any positive effects of organization on party electoral performance.[154] The poorly organized LDPR, with its 22.9% of the vote fared better than the well-organized CPRF (12.4%), while corporatist and interest groups like Women of Russia and the Agrarians (8.1 and 8.0%, respectively) gained better results than the DPR (5.5%). Of two parties of power, Russia's Choice (15.5%) fared better than the PRUC (6.8%), but this could be attributed to the former's stronger base in the state apparatus rather than to its democratic component. Yabloko, with its 7.9%, emerged as the major party of democratic alternative. Again, it was unclear what part of this fairly limited success could be attributed to the movement's formal founders. One could plausibly argue that the voters were attracted by the personality of Yavlinsky and/or the monopolistic position of Yabloko in an important segment of Russia's political spectrum. In single-member districts, only three parties won significant amounts of seats – Russia's Choice (30), the Communists (16), and the Agrarians (12). Here, the effects of party organization were more evident, but these results faded in comparison to 141 seats gained by independents.

It may be concluded that, instead or revitalizing party building efforts in Russia, the 1993 elections logically concluded the previous phase of party system formation (or rather deformation) in the country. The role of party organization proved to be at best unclear, while strong personalities, attractive ideologies, the use of the media, and power bases in the state apparatus and specific constituencies did matter. This, however, could be interpreted in two different ways. On the one hand, given the lack of party organization among nearly all participants, with the exception of the CPRF, in the 1993 elections, one could argue that by building a strong party, an important asset for winning the following elections could be secured. On the other hand, it was possible to

[152] For a comprehensive overview, see R. F. Turovskii, 'Gde i Kakie v Rossii Partii? ("Partiinye" protiv "Nezavisimykh" v Odnomandatnykh Okrugakh)', in V. A. Kolosov (ed.), *Rossiia na Vyborakh: Uroki i Perspektivy* (Moscow: Tsentr Politicheskikh Tekhnologii, 1995).
[153] Robert G. Moser, 'The impact of the electoral system on post-communist party development: the case of the 1993 Russian parliamentary elections', *Electoral Studies*, 14 (1995), p. 392.
[154] For election results, see *Rossiiskaia Gazeta*, 28 December 1993, p. 1; *Byulleten' Tsentral'noi Izbiratel'noi Komissii Rossiiskoi Federatsii*, No. 12 (1994), p. 67.

concentrate on maximizing different resources without paying much attention to party organization. Both strategies were evident on the political arena of Russia in 1994–95, with the crucial test provided by the 1995 parliamentary elections.

Party Organization and Party Performance in the 1995 Parliamentary Elections

The 1993 elections were ruinous for the parties of power. Both Gaidar and Shakhrai resigned from the government. After that, the PRUC continued to exist only as a minor parliamentary fraction, while Russia's Choice proceeded to transform itself into a full-fledged political party, Russia's Democratic Choice.[155] This move alienated the leaders of Democratic Russia, resulting in their withdrawal from Russia's Choice even before the step was officially announced. The transformation left outside of the new grouping those democratic celebrities and state officials who did not want to subject themselves to any party discipline, especially with Gaidar lacking governmental status. Many of them started to form their own parties and movements. This led to the extreme fragmentation of the democratic part of Russia's political spectrum.[156] Some of the entities, including Russia's Democratic Choice and the newly-formed movement *Forward, Russia*, sincerely attempted to create party organizations. These attempts, however, met little understanding among the politically inactive mass publics, particularly in the periphery of Russia. Scores of other democratic parties did not even try to establish themselves organizationally. Instead, they tried to provide maximum publicity to their leaders, and to articulate their programmatic differences from the government and other democrats.[157]

As a result, a huge variety of democratic alternatives emerged. Even Russia's Democratic Choice, which continued to support the economic policy of the government, sharply split with it over its policy in the North Caucasian republic of Chechnya and over a number of other issues.[158] The proliferation of democratic alternatives created a formidable challenge to Yabloko. In January 1995, the coalition reaffirmed its loose structure by declaring itself an 'all-Russian public association', with provision for membership extended to individuals, national parties, and regional parties.[159] This made Yabloko fairly reminiscent of the early democratic movement, but with a crucial contextual difference: in contrast to 1991, in 1994–95 Russia lacked any conditions for mass pro-democratic political mobilization. Only in few localities, such as St. Petersburg, did fairly large and stable organizations affiliated with Yabloko emerge.[160]

[155] See Vera Tolz, 'Significance of the new party Russia's Democratic Choice', *RFE/RL Research Report* 3, No. 26 (1994), 25–30.

[156] See A. Iu. Zudin, 'Politicheskii Spektr Kampanii 1995 G.', *Sapere Aude: Selected Works of the Moscow School of Political Studies*, No. 2 (1995), pp. 81–3.

[157] See Michael McFaul and Nikolai Petrov (eds), *Previewing Russia's 1995 Parliamentary Elections* (Washington, DC: Carnegie Endowment for International Peace, October 1995).

[158] *Kommersant-Daily*, 20 June 1995, p. 3.

[159] *Segodnya*, 12 January 1995, p. 2.

[160] On the origins of St Petersburg's Regional Party of Centre, see M. B. Gornyi *et al.*, *Gorodskoi Sovet Leningrada – Sankt-Peterburga v 1990–1993 Godakh* (St. Petersburg: Strategiia, 1996).

According to one estimate, in early 1995 the number of such regions did not exceed 10–12.[161]

Despite the ideological diversity and organizational disarray of the democratic camp, none of the democrats supported the government fully and unconditionally. In April 1995, Prime Minister Viktor Chernomyrdin announced that he would lead a new centre-right electoral bloc, pretentiously labelled *Our Home is Russia*. The bloc, joined by several cabinet members and other key figures in the government apparatus, as well as by high-ranking officials in most provinces of the country,[162] had been unanimously identified as a reincarnation of the party of power by Russian political observers.[163] Indeed, much like Russia's Choice of 1993, Our Home is Russia effectively combined state administration with private capital. But in contrast to its predecessor, Our Home is Russia did not define itself in the democratic idiom. In fact, it lacked any coherent ideology, substituting for it with vague calls for 'stability' and a government of 'professionals' who would lead without 'shocks' and 'experimentation'.[164] In many regions, the organizations of Our Home is Russia practically coincided with state administrative offices. But there was also some influx of the break-off groups of Russia's Choice into the new movement.[165] Originally, Our Home is Russia was a part of a larger project conceived in Yeltsin's administration. Another part of that project was the centre-left variety of the party of power led by the Chairman of the Duma, Communist-turned-Agrarian-turned-Yeltsinist Ivan Rybkin.[166] The Bloc of Rybkin, however, failed to secure participation of the Agrarians (APR) and the official trade-unions which were to form the bloc's basis.[167] In addition to these centrist parties, dozens of other self-declared centrists emerged, many of them representing interest groups and personal political vehicles.

The nationalist Duma opposition was represented primarily by Zhironovsky's Liberal Democrats. In contrast to Yavlinsky, Zhirinovsky took the problem of party building seriously. On the one hand, he reaffirmed his monopolistic control over the LDPR in April 1994, when he was elected as the sole leader of the LDPR for a term of 10 years.[168] On the other hand, he continued his vigorous efforts aimed at establishing party branches in virtually all regions of Russia. Given the rarity of potential party activists in the provinces, this was a difficult task. In part, it was solved by recruiting the former activists of democratic parties.[169] In other instances, regional branches of the LDPR were led or sponsored by local businessmen.[170] One of the most efficient organizations of Zhirinovsky's party emerged in the Krasnodar territory, where it managed to receive 10 of 49 seats in the regional legislature. More often,

[161] Gel'man, 'Iabloko', p. 57.
[162] *Segodnya*, 26 April 1995, p. 1.
[163] *Novaia Sibir'*, 7 August 1995, p. 3.
[164] *Rossiiskaia Gazeta*, 13 May 1995, pp. 1–2.
[165] Zudin, 'Politicheskii Spektr', p. 87.
[166] See *Segodnya*, 31 May 1995, p. 3.
[167] See Robert W. Orttung, 'Rybkin fails to form a viable left-center bloc', *Transition: Events and Issues in the Former Soviet Union and East-Central and Southeastern Europe* 1, No. 15 (1995), 27–31.
[168] *Federal'noe Sobranie*, p. 169.
[169] For examples, see *Rossiiskii Sbornik*, pp. 194, 265.
[170] *Rossiiskii Sbornik*, pp. 93, 257.

however, the LDPR lost local elections.[171] The imposition of the *Führerprinzip* on the local branches of the LDPR often caused acute struggles among individuals striving for leadership. In the Sverdlovsk province, for example, at one moment four people claimed to be local LDPR leaders.[172] Nevertheless, Zhirinovsky generally succeeded in creating the regional network of his party. In 1995, the LDPR proved to be the only electoral association capable of nominating its candidates in all single-member districts. Many of these candidates obviously had little chance to win.[173] The goal pursued by these nominations was most probably providing additional publicity to the LDPR as a whole.

The organisational efforts of Zhirinovsky found an imitator in the same segment of Russia's political spectrum, in the person of former Vice President Rutskoi. He claimed that Zhirinovsky had been able to steal his support in the previous elections only because he (Rutskoi) had been stuck in prison after the October 1993 events.[174] To correct this mistake, the *Derzhava* (Great Power) social-patriotic movement had been launched. But, in contrast to the Liberal Democrats, the new movement lacked any serious organizational basis. The remnants of Rutskoi's personal political vehicle, once called the *Democratic Party of Russian Communists* and then twice renamed, were not only insufficient but also unreliable. For this party's members, the post-1993 Rutskoi was too radical. This forced Rutskoi, who permanently travelled Russia in much the same way as Zhirinovsky,[175] to rely upon a variety of pre-existing nationalist groups, including the offsprings of Pamyat', the Constitutional Democrats (CDP), and the Christian Democrats (RCDM). Several defectors from the LDPR, including its major campaign organizer, also joined the movement. In the fall of 1995, a number of prominent figures, dissatisfied with their placement on the party list, not only left Derzhava but also accused Rutskoi of filling the list with the names of criminals.[176] For a party which based its public rhetoric on 'Christian morality' and promised to fight crime, these accusations, widely disseminated by the media, resulted in its complete disarray. This was the price paid by Rutskoi for his ill-conceived attempt to build a centralized party structure on the basis of the remnants of the informal movement.

Yet another attempt to invade into the ideological space of the LDPR had been undertaken by a coalition which imitated the organizational model of Yabloko, the Congress of Russian Communities (CRC). The leadership of the coalition included three high-profile personalities at once – a noted representative of the military-industrial complex, Yurii Skokov, Lieutenant General (retired) Aleksandr Lebed, who had received immense publicity for his defence of the Russian-speaking minority in Moldova, and the leader of the Duma fraction of the Democratic Party (DPR), Sergei Glaz'ev (the DPR itself

---

[171] See O. Grigor'ev and M. Malyutin, *Regional'naia Situatsiia v Rossii Posle Dekabr'skikh Vyborov: Analiz Novykh Tendentsii i Politicheskikh Itogov Mestnykh Vyborov Vesnoi 1994 G* (Moscow: Fond 'Diskussionnoe Prostranstvo', 1995).

[172] *Rossiiskii Sbornik*, p. 472.

[173] Nikolai Petrov, 'Analiz Rezul'tatov Vyborov 1995 G. v Gosudarstvennuiu Dumu po Okrugam i Regionam', in *Parlamentskie Vybory 1995 Goda v Rossii* (Moscow: Carnegie Endowment for International Peace, 1996), pp. 12–13.

[174] *Segodnya*, 4 April 1995, p. 2.

[175] *Izvestiia*, 9 August 1995, p. 1.

[176] *Russkii Vostok*, 18 September 1995, pp. 1–2.

effectively disintegrated soon after the 1993 elections, in large part no doubt
due to its disappointing performance).[177] A charismatic leader with dynamic
oratorical skills, Lebed was expected to complement Skokov's political
experience and financial resources, while the presence of Glaz'ev had to
symbolize the coalition's commitment of the strategy of gradual economic
reforms.[178] In contrast to Rutskoi, the leaders of the Congress of Russian
Communities (CRC) did not even try to build a strong regional network.
Instead, they chose to rely upon a huge variety of structures already available in
the periphery, including some of the local branches of the DPR, local clientelist
networks like that of the former head of the Chelyabinsk provincial legislature,[179] and the remnants of Pamyat' like the ultra-nationalist *Fatherland*
movement in Novosibirsk.[180] Local branches of a small and inactive communist
successor group, the Socialist Working People's Party, also participated.[181]
Such a miscellany of groups was scarcely equivalent to a political party. During
the campaign the leaders of the CRC apparently placed its organizational
consolidation low on the priority. Instead, they concentrated on providing
extensive electronic media exposure to themselves.

The leaders of the Communists (CPRF), with an already existing regional
network, faced a different kind of problem. In general, the ideological evolution
of the party's leadership in 1994–95 was characterized by its gradual rejection of
Marxist orthodoxy, accompanied by the shift towards a more nationalist
stance.[182] Hence, the intention to invade the ideological niche occupied in 1993
by Zhirinovsky's Liberals was also evident. This trend, however, was constrained
by the unwillingness of some of the regional branches (including the strongest
ones, such as in Volgograd province)[183] to follow this line. While such tacit
disagreements did not lead to any significant splits, the danger always remained,
because the majority of the CPRF members and activists based their notion of
the Communist party on its explicit commitment to Marxism-Leninism.

The continuing presence of the Workers Party (RCWP) was an important
contextual factor. After uneasy negotiations, the RCWP refused to enter
coalition with the CPRF, accusing the latter of unwillingness to provide proper
representation to the workers.[184] Instead, the informal communists formed their
own bloc under a lengthy label, *Communists – Workers' Russia – For the Soviet
Union*. Yet another challenge to the CPRF came from *Power to the People*, a
coalition that adopted basically the same organizational strategy as Yabloko
and the Congress of Russian Communities (CRC). The leaders of Power to the
People were Baburin of the Russian Popular Union (RPU) and the former
Soviet Prime Minister Nikolai Ryzhkov.[185] This alliance of convenience,

[177] *Segodnya*, 8 August 1995, p. 2.
[178] See interview with Glaz'ev in *Zavtra*, No. 40 (October 1995), pp. 1, 3.
[179] V. A. Kolosov, R. F. Turovskii, 'Kampaniia 1995 Goda: Regional'nye Strategii Predvy-
bornykh Blokov', in V. A. Kolosov (ed.), *Rossiia na Vyborakh: Uroki i Perspektivy* (Moscow:
Tsentr Politicheskikh Tekhnologii, 1995), p. 154.
[180] *Vechernii Novosibirsk*, 22 March 1996, p. 5.
[181] On that 'party', see Yermakov *et al.*, 'Kommunisticheskoe Dvizhenie'; and Boris Kagarlitskii,
'Levye v Rossii: Nadezhdy, Neudachi, Bor'ba', *Svobodnaia Mysl'*, No. 11 (1994), pp. 35–6.
[182] For an exposition of Zyuganov's ideological discourse during the 1995 campaign, see
Sovetskaia Rossiia, 24 October 1995, pp. 1–2.
[183] *Rossiiskii Sbornik*, p. 87.
[184] *Segodnya*, 17 August 1995, p. 1.
[185] *Pravda*, 27 October–2 November 1995, p. 2.

apparently based on its participants' hopes to capitalize on combining the modest organizational resources of the RPU with the perceived (or mis-perceived) personal popularity of Ryzhkov, had been supplemented with a large number of locally prominent personalities in the periphery of Russia. Typically, these people had their backgrounds in communist opposition to Yeltsin but did not join the CPRF because their high profiles allowed them to play on their own.[186]

The 1995 Duma elections, therefore, were characterized by the proliferation of mini-parties, stemming both from the peculiarities of the political context and from fairly loose party registration rules.[187] Forty-three electoral blocs registered to party-list ballots, up from 13 in 1993. The major corporatist and interest groups contesting the elections included Women of Russia, the APR, and a coalition based on the official trade unions, the Union of Labour. Only four of the competing parties – the CPRF (22.3% of the vote), the LDPR (11.2%), Our Home is Russia (10.1%), and Yabloko (6.9%) – managed to cross the 5%. The results of other parties were disappointing: Women of Russia received 4.6% of the vote; the Communists – Workers' Russia – For the Soviet Union, 4.5%; the CRC, 4.3 per cent; the Workers Self-Government Party, a pro-reform group virtually synonymous with its leader, 4.0%; Russia's Democratic Choice, 3.9%; the APR, 3.8%; Derzhava, 2.6%; Forward, Russia!, 1.9%; and the Union of Labour and Power to the People, 1.6% each. Other electoral associations fared even worse, with the Bloc of Ivan Rybkin receiving slightly more than 1% of the vote. In single-member districts, most successful results were obtained by the CPRF (58 seats), the APR (20), Yabloko (14), and Our Home is Russia (10); Power to the People and Democratic Russia's Choice received nine mandates each. Many leaders of the mini-parties also won district races. This reduced the number of independents or unaffiliated members in the Duma to 77.[188]

Conclusion

Who survives? Or, perhaps more importantly, who does not? The message of the 1995 elections implies answers that are in many respects different from the common expectations engendered by the experience of 1993. It turned out to be that none of the anticipated substitutes for party organization worked particularly well. The failures of the Congress of Russian Communities, Power to the People, Derzhava and various pro-democratic mini-parties indicates that placing high-profile personalities on party lists does not win a significant number of votes. The extensive media coverage secured, for instance, by the Bloc of Ivan Rybkin, also proved to be insufficient, given that the Communists hardly used television commercials.[189] In contrast to 1993, corporatist and interest groups failed. The list of survivors included both relatively well-organized parties, the Communists and the Liberal Democrats, and even ranked them according to the

---

[186] Kolosov and Turovskii, 'Kampaniia 1995 Goda', pp. 151–3.

[187] See Vladimir Gel'man, 'Vybory Deputatov Gosudarstvennoi Dumy: Pravila Igry, Zakono-datel'naia Politika i Pravoprimenitel'naia Praktika', *Konstitutsionnoe Pravo: Vostochnoevropeiskoe Obozrenie*, No. 4 (13), 1995–1 (14), 1996, pp. 25–6.

[188] For election results, see *Rossiiskaia Gazeta*, 6 January 1996, pp. 4–7.

[189] See Laura Belin, 'Television plays a limited role in Duma elections', *Transition: Events and Issues in the Former Soviet Union and East-Central and Southeastern Europe*, 2 No. 4 (1996), 20–23.

levels of their organizational stability. Given that, despite general programmatic differences, both parties belonged to the anti-Yeltsinist opposition, this ranking appears to be suggestive in two respects. On the one hand, the better 1995 organizational resources of the CPRF allowed it to attract a large part of the 1993 LDPR electorate.[190] On the other hand, ideological constraints imposed upon the CPRF by its mass membership did not allow it to squeeze the LDPR completely out of its nationalist niche. At the same time, the superiority of the LDPR's organizational resources *vis-à-vis* its nationalist rivals had been clearly reflected by the fact that it managed to defeat both other parties that claimed for themselves the role of non-communist nationalist opposition to the government, the CRC and Rutskoi's Derzhava.

The extreme fragmentation of the pro-reform vote suggests that within this part of the ideological spectrum none of the parties managed to establish a firm leading role. The 1995 performance of Our Home is Russia was even poorer that that of Russia's Choice in 1993, clearly indicating that its reliance on the state apparatus was not a safe electoral strategy. Although Yabloko replicated its modest success of 1993, it failed to occupy the ideological space of democratic alternative to the same extent as the CPRF and the LDPR did in their respective ideological niches. A simple calculation shows that while the CPRF received 69.2% of the vote jointly cast for the leftist parties (including the APR), and the LDPR – 56.1% of the vote cast for the nationalist parties, Yabloko had been supported by only 35.1% of the pro-reform voters. Given that some of the latter voted for Our Home is Russia, the figure might be even lower.[191] While it is impossible to judge with precision what part of this variation can be explained with reference to the lack of organizational resources on the part of Yabloko, one might speculate that the presence of a stronger democratic alternative party would have forced some of the mini-parties to wither away, and prevent pro-reform voters in many regions of Russia where Yabloko failed to establish itself organizationally from voting for other electoral associations.

In contrast to some observers who assert that Russia might have lost its chance to develop viable political parties simply because all over the world, 'the time of mass parties has passed',[192] this analysis suggests that party organization does matter in Russia. What had been lost was the chance to develop it in proper time. It appears that to create viable well-organized parties in a democracy from scratch, two conditions are needed:

- mass political mobilization that mobilizes *communities of fate* by means of collective incentives for the prospective party members, and
- institutional environments favourable for the gradual enhancement of *communities of fortune* by means of selective incentives.

These conditions, unfortunately, cannot coincide temporally, and indeed, their incongruence damaged the development of party politics in other post-communist countries. For instance, the anti-party legacies of Solidarity in

[190] Petrov, 'Analiz Rezul'tatov Vyborov', p. 29.

[191] For a taxonomy of ideological trends used in this calculation, see Robert W. Orttung, 'Duma elections bolster leftist opposition', *Transition: Events and Issues in the Former Soviet Union and East-Central and Southeastern Europe*, 2, No. 4 (1996), p. 7.

[192] See discussion between Denis Dragunskii and Martin Malia, 'The Sorcerer's Apprentice', *Twentieth Century and Peace*, No. 9 (1990), p. 20.

Poland[193] can be interpreted in basically the same way as the legacies of the informal movement in Russia. In none of the countries of East/Central Europe, however, has the lack of selective incentives been so evident as in Russia (and some other former Soviet republics). Moreover, the 1996 presidential election further complicated the picture for the emerging political parties. The winner, Yeltsin, consistently dissociated himself from any political party in the course of his campaign, while the presidential aspirations of three major party politicians, Zyuganov, Yavlinsky, and Zhirinovsky, were ruined. For all three parties, even though in different ways, this may have disastrous consequences. Many analysts note that in presidential systems, parties tend to be more ideologically and organizationally flexible than in parliamentary systems.[194] In Russia, flexibility is definitely not what most parties lack. Some of them are already too flexible in all possible respects (if, of course, we view the total lack of rigidity as equivalent to *flexibility* rather than *fragility*). Others, like the CPRF, cannot maximize their ideological flexibility without minimizing organizational stability.

In the on-going debate on party institutionalization, three factors impeding this process have been identified:

- the rise of parties from local organizations that congeal into a national organization (territorial diffusion)
- the sponsorship of existing institutions (external legitimation), and
- the presence of charismatic founders.[195] As we have seen, all these factors are very salient in Russia.

Of all the surveyed electoral associations, only one – the nationalist LDPR – did not develop through diffusion; even the CPRF emerged as a coalition of already existing independent committees. The role of external sponsors was all too evident in the development of such important parties as Russia's Choice, Our Home is Russia, and the APR. Zhirinovsky of the LDPR, Yavlinsky in Yabloko and many others illustrate the role of the charismatic leader, the third negative factor, quite convincingly. The prospects for party institutionalization in Russia are therefore vague. One might safely predict that in future parliamentary elections, whenever they happen, the party survival rate will be not much higher than in 1995. Whether the emerging party system will start to freeze after that, depends on many contextual factors. But to a significant extent, it depends on the willingness of Russian politicians, especially those who confess their commitment to democracy, to invest their efforts into democratic institution building by taking party organization seriously.

Appendix: Major Parties in Russia
Pre-1990

Communist Party of the Soviet Union (CPSU, *Kommunisticheskaia Partiia Sovetskogo Soiuza*): Sole legal party from 1921 to March 1990, suspended in August 1991, banned in November 1991.

---

[193] See Lewis, 'Political Institutionalisation', pp. 785–90.
[194] See, for instance, Matthew S. Shugart and John M. Carey, *Presidents and Assemblies: Constitutional Design and Electoral Dynamics* (New York: Cambridge University Press, 1992), p. 223.
[195] See Panebianco, *Political Parties*, pp. 49–68.

1990 – August 1991

Liberal Democratic Party of Russia (LPDR, *Liberal'no-Demokraticheskaia Partiia Rossii*): Founded in March 1990 as the Liberal Democratic Party of the Soviet Union, assumed current name in 1992, the most important nationalist party in the 1993 elections and afterwards.

Russian Christian Democratic Movement (RCDM, *Rossiiskoe Khristiansko-Demokraticheskoe Dvizhenie*): Founded in April 1990, participated in Democratic Russia, shifted to 'nationalism' in late 1991, helped launch Derzhava in 1995.

Social Democratic Party of the Russian Federation (SDPRF, *Sotsial-DemokraticheskaiaPartiia Rossiiskoi Federatsii*): Founded in May 1990 out of the 'informal movement', participated in Democratic Russia, effectively disintegrated in 1992–93, formally co-founded Yabloko in 1993.

Democratic Party of Russia (DPR, *Demokraticheskaia Partiia Rossii*): Founded in May 1990, participated in Democratic Russia, disintegrated in 1994–95, one of its factions joined the Congress of Russian Communities in 1995.

Constitutional Democratic Party (CDP, *Konstitutsionno-Demokraticheskaia Partiia*): Founded in May 1990, participated in Democratic Russia, shifted to 'nationalism' in late 1991, changed its name to 'All-Russian National Right Centre', helped launch Derzhava in 1995.

Republican Party of the Russian Federation (RPFR, *Respublikanskaia Partiia Rossiiskoi Federatsii*): Founded in November 1990 out of the Democratic Platform of CPSU, participated in Democratic Russia, helped launch Russia's Choice, formally co-founded Yabloko.

August 1991 – December 1993

Russian Communist Workers Party (RCWP, *Rossiiskaia Kommunisticheskaia Rabochaia Partiia*): Founded in November 1991 out of the Communist Initiative Movement and other 'informal communist' groups, briefly banned in October 1993, launched the 'Communists–Workers' Russia–For the Soviet Union' bloc in 1995.

Russian Popular Union (RPU, *Rossiiskii Obshchenarodnyi Soiuz*): Founded in December 1991, 'nationalist', a member of the 'Power to the People' bloc in 1995.

Agrarian Party of Russia (APR, *Agrarnaia Partiia Rossii*): Founded in February 1993, closely allied with the Communists (CPRF).

Communist Party of the Russian Federation (CPRF, *Kommunisticheskaia Partiia Rossiiskoi Federatsii*): Founded in February 1993 as a successor to the CPSU, briefly banned in October 1993, eventually emerged as the largest party in Russia.

Russia's Choice (*Vybor Rossii*): Founded in October 1993 as a 'governing democratic movement', lost this status and split in 1994, many of its former leaders helped launch Our Home is Russia and Forward, Russia! in 1995, unsuccessfully contested the 1995 elections as Democratic Russia's Choice – United Democrats.

Yabloko: Founded in October 1993 as a coalition of parties and individuals presenting a 'democratic alternative to the government', transformed itself into an 'all-Russian public association' in January 1995.

Party of Russian Unity and Concord (PRUC, *Partiia Rossiiskogo Edinstva i Soglasiia*): Founded in October 1993, helped launch Our Home is Russia in 1995, effectively ceased to exist as a separate party after the 1995 elections.

January 1994–1995

Congress of Russian Communities (*Kongress Russkikh Obshchin*): Founded in January 1995 on the basis of a small break-off group of the CDP, emerged as a major 'moderate nationalist' party after being joined by a number of prominent personalities in April 1995, effectively ceased to exist after the 1995 elections.

Forward, Russia! (*Vpered, Rossiia!*): Founded in February 1995 out of Russia's Choice and other 'democratic' groups, became inactive after the 1995 elections.

Great Power (*Derzhava*): Founded in April 1995 by amalgamating several 'nationalist' groups, split in August 1995, effectively ceased to exist after the 1995 elections.

Our Home is Russia (*Nash Dom – Rossiia*): Founded in May 1995 as a reincarnation of the 'governing democratic party'.

The Turkish Party System in Transition: Party Performance and Agenda Change

ALİ ÇARKOĞLU*

Introduction

The general election of 24 December 1995 marked a turning point in Turkish politics. For the first time in Turkish electoral history, with 21.4% of the vote, the pro-Islamist party obtained the highest electoral support. The Welfare Party has its roots in the pre-1980 National Salvation Party, which followed the National Order Party founded in 1970. For most of the post-1960 period electoral support for pro-Islamist parties remained on the fringes of the system. These parties often openly challenged the secular basis of the Republic, interjecting a cause for political polarization in the country. Consequently, for being against the secular regime, both the National Order Party and the National Salvation Party had been banned by the military regimes of 1971 and 1980 respectively. The recent electoral successes of the Welfare Party are intrinsically related to the bottlenecks of the party system in responding to the needs and expectations of large segments of Turkish society. The decline of the centre left and right parties signals a high level of alienation from the political system in general, in all likelihood stemming from a serious degree of dissatisfaction with government policies. Many have claimed that it is precisely this irresponsiveness of mainstream politics to the aspirations of the masses that gave rise to the recent electoral surge of pro-Islamist parties.[1] Accordingly, the victory of the Welfare Party in the 1995 general elections, following the one in 1994 local elections, potentially marks the end of traditional centre-right politics in Turkey. It also poses a series of questions about the popular appeal of Islam and of the ideological shifts among the elites and masses that give support to pro-Islamist parties. Below I will focus on two central questions: Has the Turkish party system moved toward more or toward less stability, in terms of volatility, fractionalization, or the content of party agendas? What are the underlying characteristics of public ideological change in Turkey and how are those changes reflected in the party system?

I shall evaluate changes in the Turkish party system by means of macro-level measures based on election results as well as through an examination of changes in ideological perspective as reflected in party manifestos. I first present a brief discussion of the historical development of the Turkish party system,

* I would like to thank Fikret Adaman and Richard I. Hofferbert for their insightful and helpful comments on an earlier version of this article as well as İlkay Sunar for discussion of developments in Turkish parties' ideological rhetoric. The usual caveat applies.
[1] See B. Toprak, 'Islam and the Secular State in Turkey', in Ç. Balım, E. Kalaycıoğlu, C. Karataş, G. Winrow and F. Yasamee (eds), *Turkey: Political, Social and Economic Challenges in the 1990s* (Brill, 1995), pp. 90–96 and I. Sunar and B. Toprak, 'Islam in politics: the case of Turkey', *Government and Opposition*, Autumn (1993), 421–441 for similar assertions.

underlining its theoretically salient features to be discussed at greater length in the ensuing sections. This section ends with a diagnosis of dominant centrist positions among the Turkish electorate that is in stark contrast with rising electoral support for the right-of-centre parties, especially of pro-Islamist tendencies such as the Welfare Party. Following a short evaluation of agenda transformation in the Turkish party system within a single dimensional left-right ideological context, I develop an alternative two-dimensional framework that captures some of the salient features of Turkish politics. I conclude with emphasizing the rising instability in ideological emphases, as reflected in party manifestos and discuss the peculiar stands of different parties' strategies in response to rising electoral support for the Welfare Party.

Volatility and Fragmentation of the Party System

Several developments in world politics, with important theoretical and practical policy significance, remarkably overlap with the character of the Turkish political system. Turkey represents a test case for not only the difficulties faced in consolidation of democratic rule in a politically unstable part of the world. It also offers potentially valuable insights for the process of democratization under a continuing radical economic transformation with rising religious and ethnic tensions. The Turkish experience can provide a valuable perspective for the analysis of newly democratized countries in the destabilizing international as well as domestic political contexts. Accordingly, the study of the Turkish party system should be of interest to students of comparative politics.

Before examining the emerging trends in ideological orientation of the Turkish party system, it is important to note some of its salient features during the multi-party democracy period of 1950–1996.[2] The elitist tradition of politics

[2] For a lengthy discussion of the basic tenets of Turkish politics and party system see A. Çarkoğlu, 'The Turkish general election of 24 December 1995', *Electoral Studies*, 16 (1997), 86–95, A. Eralp, M. Tunay and B. Yeşilada (eds), *The Political and Socioeconomic Transformation of Turkey* (Praeger, 1993), E. Kalaycıoğlu, 'Multi-party politics in the 1980s', *Current Turkish Thought*, 56 (1985), 2–30, E. Kalaycıoğlu, 'The by-election of 1986: a scrutiny of the Turkish electoral politics', *Current Turkish Thought*, 60 (1986) 2–23; E. Kalaycıoğlu, 'Elections and party preferences in Turkey, changes and continuities in the 1990s', *Comparative Political Studies*, 27 (1994), 402–424, E. Kalaycıoğlu, 'Decentralisation of government' in M. Heper and A. Evin (eds), *Politics in the Third Turkish Republic* (Westview, 1994) pp. 87–102, K. H. Karpat, *Turkey's Politics: the Transition to a Multi-Party System* (Princeton, Princeton University Press, 1959); K. H. Karpat, 'The Turkish elections of 1957', *Western Political Science Quarterly*, 14 (1961), 439–459; E. Özbudun, 'Turkey', in M. Weiner and E. Özbudun (eds), *Competitive Elections in Developing Countries* (Duke University Press, 1987), pp. 107–143; E. Özbudun, 'The Turkish party system: institutionalisation, polarisation and fragmentation', *Middle Eastern Studies*, 17 (1981), 228–240; E. Özbudun, 'Voting behaviour: Turkey', in J. Landau, E. Özbudun and F. Tachau (eds), *Electoral Politics in the Middle East: Issues, Voters and Elites* (Stanford, Hoover Institute Press, 1980), pp. 129–35, E. Özbudun, *Social Change and Political Participation in Turkey* (Princeton, Princeton University Press, 1976) E. Özbudun and F. Tachau, 'Social change and electoral behaviour in Turkey: toward a critical realignment?', *International Journal of Middle East Studies*, 6 (1975), 460–480; S. Sayarı, 'The Turkish party system in transition', *Government and Opposition*, 13 (1978), 39–57, J. S. Szyliowicz, 'The political dynamics of rural Turkey', *Middle East Journal*, 16 (1962), 430–442; J. S. Szyliowicz, 'The Turkish Elections: 1965', *Middle East Journal*, 20 (1966), 473–494; F. Tachau, *Turkey: The Politics of Authority, Democracy and Development* (New York, Praeger, 1984); B. Toprak, *Islam and Political Development in Turkey* (Leiden, Brill, 1981); B. Toprak, 'The state, politics and religion in Turkey', in M. Heper and A. Evin (eds), *State, Democracy and the Military: Turkey in the 1980s* (Berlin, Walter de Gruyter, 1988), pp. 119–136; A. H. Ulman and F. Tachau, 'Turkish politics: the attempt to reconcile rapid modernisation with democracy', *Middle*

in Turkey has dominated party politics, and contributed to its intense and non-consensual nature effectively impeding its institutionalization.[3] In especially its initial stages, the Turkish party system was shaped by 'intra-elite conflicts rather than through the materialization of the cleavages of society in the national political life'.[4] Domination by elite politics with weak social foundations was effectively coupled with patronage relationships.[5] Due primarily to rapid modernization, social cleavages started to play a significant role only in the 1970s.[6]

Frequent military interventions, which dissolved some of the political parties and prosecuted their leadership, resulted in serious disruption of the party system's developmental dynamics.[7] Disruption of political socialization of the masses and the resulting weakening of party identification among the electorate led to an opportunist attitude among the voters. Voters frequently switched their votes, especially but not exclusively, to ideologically adjacent parties with little regard to partisan preferences.[8] This prepared a floating partisan base for especially the right wing parties. Instead of party identification, simple short-term party preferences came to dominate electoral choice.[9]

East Journal, 19 (1965), 153–169; B. Yeşilada, 'New political parties and the problems of development in Turkey', *New Perspectives on Turkey*, 1 (1987), 35–62; W. F. Weiker, *The Modernisation of Turkey, from Atatürk to the Present Day* (Holmes & Meier, 1981).

[3] See Sayarı, 'The Turkish party system in transition', p. 40; U. Ergüder and R. I. Hofferbert, 'The 1983 elections in Turkey: continuity or change in voting patterns', in M. Heper and A. Evin (eds), *State, Democracy and the Military, Turkey in the 1980s* (Berlin, Walter de Gruyter, 1988), p. 82; F. W. Frey, 'Patterns of elite politics in Turkey', in G. Lenczowski, (ed.), *Political Elites in the Middle East* (Washington DC, 1975), pp. 41–82; F. W. Frey, *The Turkish Political Elite* (Cambridge MA, MIT Press, 1965).

[4] Sayarı, 'The Turkish party system in transition', p. 40.

[5] See A. Kudat, 'Patron-client relations: the state of the art and research in eastern Turkey', in E. D. Akarlı and G. Ben-Dor (eds), *Political Participation in Turkey, Historical Background and Present Problems* (Boğaziçi University Publications, 1975), pp. 61–88; S. Sayarı, 'Some notes on the beginnings of mass political participation', in E. D. Akarlı and G. Ben-Dor (eds), *Political Participation in Turkey, Historical Background and Present Problems* (Boğaziçi University Publications, 1975), pp. 121–134, İ. Sunar, 'The politics of state interventionism in "populist" Egypt and Turkey', in A. Öncü, Ç. Keyder and S. E. Ibrahim (eds), *Developmentalism and Beyond* (The American University in Cairo Press, 1995), pp. 94–111; İ. Sunar, 'Populism and patronage: The Demokrat Party and its legacy in Turkey', *Il Politico*, 4 (1990), 745–757 on patronage relations in Turkey.

[6] See Özbudun, *Social Change and Political Participation in Turkey*; Özbudun, 'Voting behavior: Turkey'; Özbudun and F. Tachau, 'Social change and electoral behaviour in Turkey'; F. Tachau and M. D. Good, 'The anatomy of political and social change, Turkish parties, parliaments and elections', *Comparative Politics* (1973), 551–73.

[7] With the exception of the first 1960 military regime that prosecuted 3 members of the ruling Democrat Party in no instance was the military successful in effectively eliminating the leadership of political parties for long. Even in the case of the 1960 coup the parties that played to the political inheritance of the Democrat Party did receive the majority of the votes in the first post-coup elections of 1961. The most successful of these inheritors the Justice Party single-handedly obtained the majority of votes in 1965.

[8] See E. Kalaycıoğlu and A. Y. Sarıbay, 'Çocukların parti tutmasını belirleyen etkiler' (On factors affecting party identification of children), in Turkish, *Toplum ve Ekonomi*, 1 (1991), 137–150 for an analysis of the breakdown of party identification in early childhood political socialization in the aftermath of 1980 military coup.

[9] See U. Ergüder, 'Changing patterns of electoral behavior in Turkey', *Boğaziçi Üniversitesi Dergisi (Social Sciences)*, 8–9 (1980–1), 45–81; U. Ergüder, 'The Turkish party system and the future of Turkish democracy' in Ç. Balım, E. Kalaycıoğlu, C. Karataş, G. Winrow and F. Yasamee (eds), *Turkey: Political, Social and Economic Challenges in the 1990s* (Leiden, Brill, 1995),

A reflection of weak partisan attachments among the electorate has been increasing electoral volatility.[10] Figure 1 shows the historical development of volatility, as measured by Pedersen's index.[11] Volatility of election results has an upward trend with significant fluctuations, due primarily to newly founded parties.[12] The level of instability in the system reaches its maximum in 1987 when the leadership of the pre-1980 parties were allowed, after a referendum, to return to active politics, each with their own party. Although the 1991 and 1995 elections' volatility scores were lower than that of the 1987, the average volatility over the entire 1954–1995 period is 21.2%. This means that on average about 20 per cent of the electorate shifted their votes from one party to another in consecutive elections. Considering that in no election was this vote shift lower than 10% of the vote, we see that the Turkish electorate has had a very fluid aggregate-voting pattern.

From a comparative perspective, we again observe that Turkish electoral volatility is among the highest. Shamir presents the volatility scores of 530 elections in 19 developed democracies covering all available elections from 1840 to 1977.[13] Shamir's sample has a mean score of 11. The Turkish mean volatility score is second only to Iceland's score of 23. Considering that Iceland's staggering volatility in the pre-1930 period is the reason why it has such a high mean level of electoral instability, we observe that average Turkish volatility is higher than all developed countries' in Shamir's sample.[14]

Is Turkey's electoral volatility a national phenomenon, or is it concentrated in particular regions? Table 1 presents the geographical distribution of volatility in Turkey. Electoral volatility is calculated on a provincial basis for three election pairs (1991, 1995 general and 1994 local elections). There is a clear increase in the volatility indexes across provinces. When we test for differences across seven geographical regions, we observe that the Eastern and Southeastern regions

pp. 61–73, Kalaycıoğlu, 'Elections and party preferences in Turkey, changes and continuities in the 1990s', 402–24.

[10] See Özbudun, 'The Turkish Party System'; Erguder and Hofferbert, 'The 1983 Elections in Turkey' and A. Çarkoğlu, '24 Aralık 1995 seçimlerinde bölgeselleşme, oynaklık, parçalanma ve temsil adaleti' (Regionalisation, volatility, fractionalisation and representational justice in Turkey's December 24, 1995 elections) in Turkish, *Görüş* TUSIAD (1996), 50–54.

[11] M. N. Pedersen, 'The dynamics of European party systems: changing patterns of electoral volatility', *European Journal of Political Research*, 7 (1979), 1–26; M. N. Pedersen, 'On measuring party system change: a methodological critique and a suggestion', *Comparative Political Studies*, 12 (1979), 387–403.

[12] Since the volatility index uses one period lagged value of parties' vote shares two observations are lost; one for the first multi-party election of 1950 and the other for the first post coup election of 1983 when all pre-1980 parties were abolished by the military regime. Similarly, the military regime of 1960 abolished the Democrat Party and executed its leadership. However, three parties emerged as successors to the Democrat Party political heritage. I used the sum of these three parties' vote shares as the continuation of the Democrat Party in 1961 to calculate the volatility index.

[13] M. Shamir, 'Are Western party systems "Frozen"?', *Comparative Political Studies*, 17 (1984), 35–79.

[14] As Ergüder and Hofferbert, 'The 1983 elections in Turkey', p. 85 argue one reason for Turkey's high electoral volatility might be its relatively low socio-economic development compared to developed democracies. Since we are not in a position to test for this assertion with additional data on developing democracies we have to rely on two alternative assertions mentioned above. First, is that volatility increases after the disruptions imposed on the party system due to closed parties and prosecuted leaders. Second, is low party identification among the electorate. This however, is primarily an assertion at the individual level about which we again do not have enough empirical evidence.

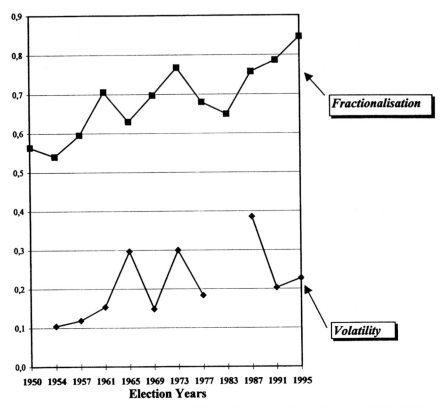

Figure 1. Fractionalization and Volatility in Turkish Elections 1950–1995

have significantly higher mean volatility. The remaining five regions do not exhibit significant differences in their mean volatility among themselves. Also significant in this juncture is that variation in provincial volatility is explained by regional differences in increasing percentages as we move from 1991 to 1995. In other words, there seem to be greater instability differences in parties' electoral support from one region to another. It should also be noted here that the People's Democracy Party of ethnic Kurdish origin successfully obtained considerable electoral support in the Eastern and Southeastern regions. However, it gained no parliamentary seats, due to its failure to pass the 10% nationwide threshold. The failure also of the Nationalist Action Party to get representation for the same reason created a situation where the two extremist parties, one ultra-Turkish nationalist and the other ethnic secessionist fringe party, are pushed outside of the parliament. This creates a potential for further polarization in the system.

As a result of surfacing socio-political cleavages in the society, two decades of centre-right domination in the Turkish party system came to an end with the 1973 general election.[15] New parties took hold among the electorate, which also contributed to the weakening of party identification.

---

[15] See Ergüder, 'Changing patterns', pp. 50–61; Sayarı, 'The Turkish party system in transition' and Özbudun, 'The Turkish party system'.

Table 1. Regional Electoral Volatility and Fractionalization in Turkey 1991-1995

Volatility index	Central Anatolia	Marmara	Eastern Anatolia	Southeastern Anatolia	Black Sea	Aegean	Mediterranean	Mean for Turkey	Explained (%) variation across regions
1991–1995	21.7	18.7	37.0	46.8	19.1	21.5	25.1	26.1	66.4
1994–1995	15.0	16.3	28.2	33.4	17.2	15.0	20.8	20.2	39.5
1991–1994	14.8	12.5	23.9	34.1	15.5	1.7	17.5	17.8	51.9

Fractionalization index	Central Anatolia	Marmara	Eastern Anatolia	Southeastern Anatolia	Black Sea	Aegean	Mediterranean	Mean for Turkey	Explained (%) variation across regions
1995	80	79	79	79	79	81	81	79	5.9
1994	82	80	79	79	81	81	81	80	14.8
1991	76	77	73	68	75	75	73	74	31.8

*Since the mean for Turkey is calculated as unweighted average across provinces they deviate from index values calculated from aggregate country values for parties.

The Volatility index (V) is calculated by using $i = 1, \ldots N$ parties in the following formula: $V = \{(1/2)\Sigma_N(|\text{Vote}\%_{i,t} = \text{Vote}\%_{i,t-1}|)\}$. The index lies between 0 and 1. $V = 1$ represents a completely unstable system whereas $V = 0$ represents one where all parties obtained the same vote shares as they did in the previous election (see Pedersen, 1979).

The fractionalization index F is calculated by using election outcomes for $i = 1, \ldots N$ parties in the following formula: $F = \{1 - \Sigma_N(\text{Vote}\%)^2\}$. F also varies between 0 and 1. The fractionalization index reaches a minimum of zero when one party receives all of the popular vote. When too many parties receive relatively small electoral support the index will approach to zero; i.e. extreme vote concentration corresponds to zero fractionalization. and when one party receives all of the votes it will give a value of 1 (see Rae, 1967).

Explained (%) variation across regions refers to the R-squared in the equation where provincial volatility and fractionalization indexes are explained by regional dummy variables. Accordingly, it refers to the amount of variation accounted for by regional dummy variables alone.

Fractionalization is the extent of electoral support's spread across multiple parties.[16] Figure 1 shows the historical development of fractionalization, as measured by Rae's index.[17] Over the 1969 and 1973 elections an increase in dispersion within the party system is observed. However, in the last pre-1980 coup election of 1977 we observe a drop in the extent of the spread of electoral support across parties. The military regime's restrictions on the 1983 elections kept the fragmentation of the party system at an artificially low level. Ever since the 1987 election fractionalization continually increased, reaching an all time high in the 1995 election. Fractionalization of election results has a somewhat more stable upward trend than does the volatility index. Ever since the first general election of the post-1980 military regime, in 1983, fractionalization has been increasing. The 'effective-number-of-parties' index, after Taagepera and Shuggart, also shows that, due to rising fractionalization in the system, by 1995 there are 6 approximately equal size parties and a marginal party.[18] Contrary to the previously illustrated regional differences in volatility, we see that fractionalization becomes more and more homogenous all across the country (see the lower portion of Table 1). The variation explained by regional differences declines between 1991 (31.8 percent) and 1995 (5.9 percent).[19] As the whole system becomes more and more fractionalized, regional differences in provincial fractionalization indexes disappear. Accordingly, the system came to accommodate more and more parties, despite legal arrangements (most notably, the 10% hurdle) imposing representational quotas to discourage smaller parties.

With increased electoral success of fringe parties, single party government became impossible. The lack of parliamentarian majorities led to frequent changes of coalition governments that typically were unable to deliver policies to resolve mounting social and economic problems. Dependence on patronage distribution and dominant party leadership in all relevant parties made it virtually impossible to run stable coalitions.[20]

Military interventions resulted in virtually new constitutions during the regimes of 1960 and 1980. These were followed by smaller constitutional adjustments after only long and heated debates. There still does not seem to be a consensus around the fundamental rules of the game. All major parties at one point in their existence had been against all or parts of the

[16] See Sayarı, 'The Turkish party system in transition'; Özbudun, 'The Turkish party System' and Çarkoğlu, '24 Aralık 1995 seçimlerinde bölgeselleşme'.

[17] D. Rae, *The Political Consequences of Electoral Laws* (New Haven and London, Yale University Press, 1967).

[18] See R. Taagepera and M. S. Shugart. *Seats and Votes: the Effects and Determinants of Electoral Systems* (Yale University Press, 1989), p. 79. Effective number of parties $N = 1/(1 - \text{Fractionalization Index})$. $N = 6.49$ in 1995 whereas 2.85 in 1983. In pre-1980 period the highest it ever got was 4.3 in 1973 elections.

[19] D. A. Gross, 'Units of analysis and Rae's fractionalisation index', *Comparative Political Studies*, 15 (1982), 85–98 notes that calculation of Rae's fractionalisation index at a lower level of aggregation; i.e. at provincial level rather than regional or country level, will increase the value of the index and overestimate the level of interparty competition in a system as measured by the mean level of fractionalisation. With limited regional data on the last 3 elections between 1991 and 1995 we also observe here the same tendency of an overestimate in fractionalisation. However, even after correcting for this overestimation we still observe a considerable level of fractionalisation in the Turkish system.

[20] See Ergüder, 'The Turkish party system'; Ergüder and Hofferbert, 'The 1983 elections in Turkey', p. 82; and Özbudun, 'The Turkish Party System'.

constitution.[21] This alone constitutes a major source of the mass alienation from mainstream politics, and it creates a serious legitimacy problem.

The military leadership often targeted the party system in its diagnosis of the country's problems, citing party fragmentation as the major reason for intervention. However, simple observation of Figure 1 shows that each military intervention actually resulted in a subsequently higher level of electoral fragmentation. Disruption of political socialization and artificial legal arrangements imposed by the military regimes also significantly contributed to increases in electoral volatility. As a result of increasing voter volatility and fragmentation, the party system has reached a stage in its development where coalition governments are unavoidable. However, the historical tradition of elite domination and weak mass membership stands in front of cooperation among the parties. In recent years for example, aside from some relatively minor political reasons, such as competition for the same electoral constituency, the main obstacle to coalition partnership between the Motherland and the True Path parties, the two centre-right competitors, is their respective bottlenecks in party leadership. The same explanation can also be given for the centre-left wing parties; the Republican People's Party and the Democratic Left Party.[22]

Interpersonal animosities at the very top of the party leadership fall very much in line with Turkish historical experience. What is relatively hard to explain is the reason for the impotence of party constituencies in taking over these seemingly superficial, uncooperative attitudes in party leadership that exasperate the fragmentation and polarization in the system. The animosities among the two centre-left and the two centre-right parties stand in contrast to ideological similarities in their constituencies. Esmer notes that there are significant differences between the left and right end of the spectrum's mean self-placement scores along the left-right ideology scale. In other words, the self-placement scores of the Social Democrat Populist Party supporters and those of the Welfare Party are significantly different. However not much of a difference is observed between the mean self-placement scores of Democratic Left and Republican People's Party as well as Motherland and True Path Party supporters. The ideological differences among the centre-left and centre-right parties seem negligible at least from the perspective of their supporters.[23]

Figure 2 shows the results of three surveys conducted in 1977, 1990 and 1995. The first of these surveys was conducted just prior to 1977 general election.[24] The respondents were asked to place themselves on the centre-left, centre or centre-right of the political spectrum. Besides the 20.9% who claimed to have no opinion on this question, the rest were distributed almost equally across the

[21] E. Kalaycıoğlu, 'Cyclical breakdown, redesign and nascent institutionalisation: the Turkish Grand National Assembly' in U. Liebert and M. Cotta (eds), *Parliament and Democratic Consolidation in Southern Europe: Greece, Italy, Portugal, Spain and Turkey* (London, Pinter, 1990), pp. 184–222.

[22] During the electoral campaign for the 1995 election, the animosities between the centre-right party leaders have occupied the centre stage especially during the televised debates where open dislike between the Motherland Party leader Mesut Yılmaz and the True Path Party leader Tansu Çiller reached a climax. See Çarkoğlu, 'The Turkish general election' for a longer discussion of the campaign of 1995).

[23] Y. Esmer, 'Parties and the electorate: a comparative analysis of voter profiles of Turkish political parties', in Ç. Balım, E. Kalaycıoğlu, C. Karataş, G. Winrow and F. Yasamee (eds), *Turkey: Political, Social and Economic Challenges in the 1990s* (Leiden, Brill, 1995), pp. 83–84.

[24] See Ergüder, 'Changing patterns'.

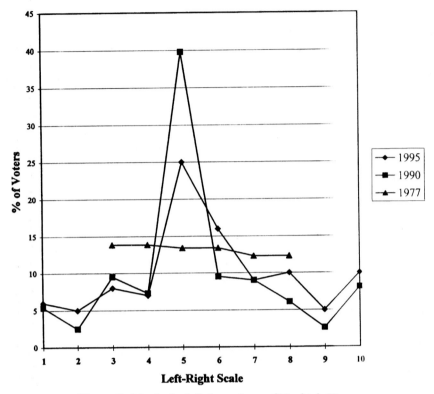

Figure 2. Ideological Orientations of Turkish Voters

three options given; 24.6% were at the centre-right, 26.8 at the centre and 27.7 at the centre-left.[25] Since respondents were not given the extreme-left or extreme-right positions as options we are limited in our ability to compare these results with those taken in 1990 and 1995. Nevertheless the fact that relative strengths of these three centrist positions being of roughly equal size is an important observation to note.

[25] When distributing the voters on a 10 point scale I created groups of 2 scale points to represent 5 groups running from the extreme-left to centre-left, centre, centre-right and lastly the extreme-right. The distribution of the electorate along the left-right continuum for 1977 is obtained by assuming that within the centre-left, centre and centre-right, voters are uniformly distributed. Since extreme right and extreme-left positions were not offered for 1977 these categories are left empty. To clarify my terminology the terms used in describing positions along the 10 point left-right scale is summarised below:

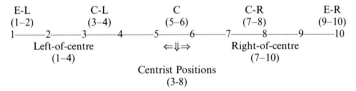

where E-L: Extreme Left, C-L: Centre Left, C: Centre, C-R: Centre Right, E-R: Extreme Right.

Nationwide representative samples taken in 1990 and 1995 both use a 10 point left-right scale instead of the one composed of centre-left, centre and centre-right in 1977. The recent surveys indicate that a shift towards the right-of-centre is taking place. The 1990 sample shows that 81.2% of the respondents place themselves at centrist positions, whereas only 7.9% were on the extreme-left and 10.7% were on the extreme-right positions.[26] The sample taken in 1995 shows that 75% of the electorate place themselves on centrist positions along the left-right scale.[27] While the distribution of the electorate across left-of-centre positions (positions 1 through 4 on the left-right scale) remains approximately the same in both 1990 and 1995 samples, those of the right-of-centre positions (positions 7 through 10 on the left-right scale) are persistently higher in 1995. From 1990 to 1995 the very centre of the left-right scale drops from 49.3% to 41%. It seems that the centre has lost its appeal for 8.3% of the electorate who shifted predominantly towards the right-of-centre positions. However, despite significant gains for the right-of-centre, an overwhelming majority of the Turkish electorate still identifies with a centrist positions.

At this juncture we are faced with a problematic phenomena in need of an explanation. How is it possible to have extreme-right parties such as the Welfare Party as well as the National Action Party playing the role of key parties in the Turkish party system, if not simply dominating the electoral scene, while the centrist tendencies among the electorate continue? Ergüder provides two possible explanations that help clarify these circumstances.[28] First, is the frequent manipulation of the election system by the incumbents to obtain electoral gains. However, if this were to be an important factor, the rise of the extremist parties could have been halted by the incumbents.[29] Second, Ergüder also seem to assert that the party system is simply having difficulties in responding to the demands of the rapidly growing and fast changing Turkish society: 'The party system is bursting at the seams because of rapid mobilization, and population growth'.[30] Surveys by the International Republican Institute about attitudes in urban settlements provide strong evidence that supports this claim.[31] As the system fails to respond to the electorate's needs and expectations, untried parties, old leaders operating under non-democratic inner party machines, as well as new parties with ethnic appeal, seem to attract and mobilize electoral support that further contributes to the fragmentation of the system. The Welfare Party successfully used the fact that it has never been in power as the dominant party to put into effect its programme. Successful municipal administrations by

[26] See U. Ergüder, Y. Esmer and E. Kalaycıoğlu, *Türk Toplumunun Değerleri* (Turkish Values) (İstanbul, TUSIAD, 1991); and Kalaycıoğlu, 'Elections and party preferences in Turkey'.

[27] See Strateji/MORI, *Aylık Siyasi ve Ekonomik Endikatörler Araştırması, Temmuz 1995* (Monthly Political and Economic Indicators, July 1995) in Turkish (Istanbul, Strateji/MORI Monthly Reports, 1996).

[28] Ergüder, 'The Turkish party system', p. 71.

[29] Ergüder's second explanation asserts the disturbing impact of military interventions on the political system and voter behaviour that is touched upon above.

[30] Ergüder, 'The Turkish party system', p. 71.

[31] International Republican Institute, *Turkey, Survey Results: Attitudes and Priorities of City Dwellers, April 22–30, 1995* (Washington D.C., 1995), International Republican Institute, *Turkey, Survey Results: Attitudes and Priorities of Citizens of Urban Areas, November 9–23, 1995,* (Washington D.C., 1995) see also Çarkoğlu, 'The Turkish general election' for a lengthy discussion of the results in the above International Republican Institute studies.

the Welfare Party after their electoral victory in 1994 local elections also helped to attract voter support.

However, the question still remains: some of the centrist voters might provide a portion of the support base for the Welfare Party but have the Welfare Party stands that positioned it on the fringes of the Turkish ideological spectrum changed? Can we still call the Welfare Party an extreme right-wing party or did the Welfare Party fill the vacuum in the Turkish centre?

Party Agendas in Transition

The volatility and fragmentation of the Turkish party system no doubt has many roots, not the least of which have been the interruptions imposed by military governments. However, there may also be an even more fundamental structural source of instability, namely the transitional status of the public and party agendas as reflections of Turkey's socioeconomic transformation. Turkey may be passing through what could be considered, in statistical parlance, a rotation of cleavages. That is, the major dimensions of political alignment are only recently moving from a more traditional to the left-right dimension so central to industrialized democracies.

Recent research on party election manifestos offers a new vantage from which to view such a possibility. The research programme of the Manifesto Research Group of the European Consortium for Political Research has adopted a common coding scheme for the analysis of post-World War II party election manifestos for content analysis of issue dimensions in modern party systems in a score of countries.[32] The coding procedure consists of assigning each sentence in party manifestos into a unique category. A total of fifty-four categories are designed to measure change in issue content over time, across parties and nations. The percentage of sentences a party devotes to each category in its manifesto provides a measure of party emphasis on the issue domain represented by that category.[33]

Pioneering works of the Manifesto Research Group have shown that a 'left-right' dimension unambiguously emerges as the dominant element summarizing the general tendency of party programmes in most countries.[34] Issues grouped under 'left' and 'right' dimensions represent polarization around issues of redistribution, reliance on market or planning in economic policy, traditional morality and national defence. The dominant position of this dimension led to the left-right party programme scale developed by Laver and Budge.[35] This

[32] See I. Budge, D. Robertson, and D. Hearl (eds), *Ideology, Strategy, and Party Change: Spatial Analyses of Post-War Election Programs in Nineteen Democracies* (London, Cambridge University Press, 1987); M. Laver and I. Budge (eds), *Party Policy and Coalition Government in Western Europe* (London, MacMillan, 1993); H-D. Klingemann, R. I. Hofferbert and I. Budge, *Parties, Policies and Democracy* (Westview, 1994).

[33] For details of the coding procedures and descriptions of the coding categories refer to Budge *et al.*, *Ideology, Strategy, and Party Change: Spatial Analyses of Post-War Election Programs in Nineteen Democracies* and Klingemann *et al.*, *Parties, Policies and Democracy*.

[34] See Budge *et al.*, *Ideology, Strategy, and Party Change: Spatial Analyses of Post-War Election Programs in Nineteen Democracies*.

[35] See Laver and Budge, *Party Policy and Coalition Government in Western Europe*. See also R. I. Hofferbert and S. Blinn, 'Left-right orientations of party election programs in modern democracies: some unanticipated findings', paper presented at the Midwest Political Association Meetings in Chicago (1992); Klingemann *et al.*, *Parties, Policies and Democracy*; and A. Çarkoğlu,

scale is the sum of all party emphasis categories under pre-determined left and right dimensions. The difference between the left and right scores gives a net left tendency for a given manifesto. A positive left-right score indicates that more left emphases were made in the manifesto, thus indicating a left tendency.[36]

The left-right conceptualization of the Turkish electorate has long been seen as secondary to the *centre-periphery* cleavage, Mardin's analysis being the most often cited.[37] Following Mardin's lead others have also argued that Turkish politics is built around a strong and coherent state apparatus run by a distinct group of elites. The *centre* is confronted by a heterogenous, sometimes hostile periphery, composed mainly by peasantry, small farmers and artisans. For all practical purposes the periphery was seen as the complement of the centre.[38] The 'centre' is organized around Kemalist secular principles and represents a centralist, nationalist and state protectionist attitude. The *periphery*, on the other hand, reflects all the salient features of subject and parochial orientations depicted a generation ago by Almond and Verba.[39] It includes conflicting and openly hostile regional, religious and ethnic groups whose most binding common tenet is their hostility towards the 'centre'. The Republican People's Party, a typical centre party, transformed itself into a modern left-wing party during the 1960s. The right-wing Democrat Party of the 1950s, the Justice Party of the 1960s and 70s, and the contemporary Welfare Party and all other centre-right as well as extreme-right wing parties also shared elements from the periphery *a la* Mardin.[40] However, we still cannot claim a one to one correspondence between the left-right and the centre-periphery dichotomy.

Figure 3 shows the positions of the leading Turkish parties' programme emphases on the left-right dimension for the 1950–1995 period. The more right wing the emphases are in a manifesto, the more the party falls to the bottom of the graph; the more left-wing the emphases are, the higher up it will rise on the graph.

We see that for all elections of the period, except the first post-coup election in 1961 and the last election in 1995, the traditionally left and right parties are clearly separated. The Democrats of 1950, who held a clear majority in that decade, are clearly to the right of the Republican People's Party (RPP), the spiritual and organizational descendent of Atatürk's original creation. (We do

---

'Election manifestos and policy-oriented economic voting: a pooled cross-national analysis', *European Journal of Political Research*, 27 (1995), 293–317 for different applications of the left-right scale.

[36] Left issue emphases are the sum of percentages for the following categories: Decolonization, Military negative, Peace, Internationalism, Democracy, Regulation of Capitalism, Economic Planning, Pro-Protectionism, Controlled Economy, Nationalization, Pro-Social Services, Pro-Education, Pro-Labour. Right issue emphases are the sum of percentages for the following categories: Military positive, Freedom and Human Rights, Constitutionalism, Effective Authority, Free Enterprise, Economic Incentives, Anti-Protectionism, Economic Orthodoxy, Anti-Social Services, National Way of Life, Traditional Morality, Law and Order, Social Harmony.

[37] Ş. Mardin, 'Center-Periphery Relations: A Key to Turkish Politics?', *Daedalus*, 102 (1973), 169–190.

[38] See Frey, 'Patterns of elite politics in Turkey', M. Heper, *The State Tradition in Turkey* (Walkington, Eothen, 1985), İ. Sunar, *State and Society in the Politics of Turkey's Development* (Ankara, AÜSBF, Yayınları, 1975); and F. Tachau, *Turkey: The Politics of Authority, Democracy and Development* (New York, Praeger, 1984).

[39] G. Almond and S. Verba, *The Civic Culture* (New Jersey, Princeton University Press, 1963).

[40] Mardin, 'Center-periphery relations'.

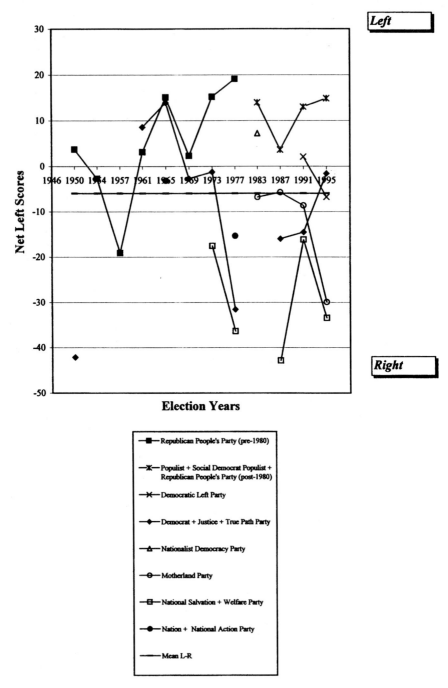

Figure 3. Left-Right Ideological Positions of Parties in Turkey, 1950–1995

not have any useable documents for the Democrat Party's 1954 and 1957 elections). We also see that the Republican People's Party first moves towards the centre in 1954 and eventually shifts down the graph by 1957. This indicates an ideological move about 20 points to the right of the spectrum by the RPP. Such a strategy by the RPP signals an effort to chip away the electoral advantage of the Democrats during the 1950s by staying clearly on the right side of the ideological spectrum. By 1961 the RPP moves back up to the left of the spectrum, following a period of military rule, during which the Democrat Party was outlawed. The successor of the Democrats, the Justice Party, should be expected to take over the rightward position. However, it emphasizes left issues more than the Republican People's Party, thus exhibiting the first one of the two 'leap-frogging' incidents between a right and a left wing party. However, the very fact that this election took place following extraordinary circumstances of a military regime that executed leading figures of the Democrat Party is probably the main reason for an artificial ideological leap-frog of the representatives of the Democrat heritage.

Elections in the 1970s show increasing ideological polarization in the system.[41] The ideological distance tends to increase especially between the centre-left Republican People's Party, and the centre-right Justice Party, prior to the 1980 coup. Sayarı observes that 'during the four years following the 1973 election the *Justice Party's* ideological stand was discernibly closer to the extreme-right than to the centre'.[42] We observe a similar tendency in the move of the Justice Party programmes towards the right end of the spectrum. The Justice Party actually passes the ultra-nationalist Nationalist Action Party, in 1977, and gets close to the right-most National Salvation Party in emphasizing right-wing issues. The moderate position of the Nationalist Action Party is due to several emphasis areas. Practically feeling unchallenged about its credibility in nationalistic stands by the move of the Justice Party towards the extreme-right, the Nationalist Action Party seems to stress the moderate right, as well as some traditionally left arguments such as the dominant role of government in the economy. This effort to moderate itself ideologically is aimed to attract electoral support from the centre-right constituencies of especially the Justice Party. For the case of the National Salvation Party, however, a similar type of moderation is not observed.

Until 1995, the post-1980 elections reflect a clearly differentiated party system along the left-right spectrum. In the 1983 post-coup election both the Populist Party and the Nationalist Democracy Party were reflecting clear left tendencies in their programs. Only the winner of the election, the Motherland Party, has a moderate right-wing stand. The pattern that emerges after three military inter-ventions (1961, 1972, and 1980) is a tendency to move to the left of the spectrum by emphasizing more government role in the economy, which seems like a safe argument in a sensitive period of transition. Given the overall similarity between the Populist Party and the Nationalist Democracy Party in 1983, the Mother-land Party easily differentiated itself from the rest of the group in the first post-coup elections by occupying the empty centre-right position (under restrictive regulations imposed by the military). However, we should also recognize the fact that Motherland Party of 1983 was the most centrist party of all Turkish

---

[41] See Sayarı, 'The Turkish party system in transition'; Özbudun, 'The Turkish party system'.
[42] Sayarı, 'The Turkish party system in transition', p. 50.

electoral history up to that time, conveniently riding the 1980s centrist tendencies among the electorate.

Clear inter-party differentiation continues through the 1991 election where there seems to be some ideological convergence to the centre-right positions by the Motherland, Welfare and the True Path parties. A somewhat moderated Welfare Party still remained as the right-most party of the system. The Social Democrat Populist Party differentiates itself by turning back to the left end of the spectrum. The Democratic Left Party remains moderately to the left-of-centre.

The possible stability of the relative positions comes to an end in the 1995 elections, where several parties leap-frog each other's positions. The Democratic Left Party shifts to the right by emphasizing particularly freedom and human rights, economic orthodoxy through savings and thrift, and smaller and more efficient government. The True Path Party's move to the left is characterized by emphasis on internationalist, pro-European Community, democracy, pro-social services, and pro-education arguments. On the other hand, the Motherland Party moved further down to the right end of the spectrum by emphasizing freedom and human rights, economic orthodoxy through smaller and more efficient government, traditional morality, and national way of life. The Welfare Party moves back down and maintains the leadership of the right end of the spectrum.

The Welfare Party emphasis in the 1995 election manifesto is concentrated on freedom and human rights, especially emphasizing religious liberties (17.87% of the manifesto). Arguments in favour of democracy (6.81%), decentralization (2.55%), administrative efficiency (3.4%), strong government, self-declaration of competence in government (12.77%) and other parties' lack of such competence (8.51%), general economic goals (17.02%) and general appeal for the paradigm of growth (9.36%). Similar to the position of the Nationalist Action Party in 1977, the Welfare Party of 1995 does not allocate much space to arguments in favour of national way of life or traditional morality; only 1.71% of the manifesto is dedicated to these two categories.

Two points deserve to be underlined here about the moves of the Welfare Party during the post-1980 period. The first observation is that, throughout the period, the Welfare Party always remained the right-most party in the system. Second, in 1995, the Welfare Party turned back from its apparent leftward tilt in 1991 and again headed rightward. This move however, should be evaluated within the context of a similar move by the Motherland Party down the right-end of the spectrum. Before the elections, the Motherland Party was engaged in an election coalition with the Grand Union Party, a more religiously oriented splinter from the ultra-nationalist Nationalist Action Party. Such a move, coupled with our findings from the content analysis of the Motherland Party manifesto, was clearly targeted to appeal to the Welfare Party constituencies. The Welfare Party then correctly diagnosed this objective and moved further right in order to differentiate itself as the only credible owner of the right-end of the spectrum.[43]

---

[43] Although the answer to the question will remain inherently speculative, one is led to question of whether it would be more probable that the centralizing tendencies in the Welfare Party manifestos would continue had the Motherland Party not moved to the right targeting the constituencies of the Welfare Party. There is evidence from the geographical distribution of electoral

The above discussion of competition in the party system clearly provides some hints of destabilizing changes in Turkish politics. We can see reflections of these changes not only in election outcomes, in the form of increasing fractionalization and electoral volatility, but also in the shifting agendas of the parties. Furthermore, the uni-dimensional left-right conception of ideology reflected in election manifestos also shows some unprecedented changes, especially in the 1995 general election. The uni-dimensional left-right scale plotted above (Figure 3) relies on a specific selection of party emphases used by other scholars in cross-national research.

In order to obtain a more general picture, consistency in election manifesto emphases taken as a whole is presented below. Following Janda *et al.*, I present correlations between subsequent elections across the 1950–1995 period.[44] Figure 4 plots the correlations of each party's programme in an election with its prior programme. If the issue profile in one election (or simply the percentage of space allocated to different issue categories in one election) is highly correlated with the issue profile in the subsequent election we infer that the party in question did not change the structure of its issue profile much. The higher the correlation, the more stable the patterns of programmatic thematic emphases from election to election for each party in the system.[45]

In Figure 4 we see first of all that pre-1980 stability in issue emphasis profiles in the system as a whole was higher than in the post-1980 period. In other words, parties tend to change their issue profiles to a larger extent in the most recent elections. The highest issue profile consistency is obtained by the pre-1980 Justice Party and post-1980 Motherland Party with each getting an average of 0.79 correlation. Interestingly, for a party identified with traditional Islamist causes, the Welfare Party obtains the lowest average correlation between programmes in adjacent elections. The issue profile of the Welfare Party has been changing rapidly especially in the last two elections. In the 1995 election, the True Path Party also reduced its consistency considerably compared to 1991. Given that all its competitors have been rapidly changing their issue profiles, and also that the Motherland Party has been losing electoral support almost continuously for the last three elections, one is led to the conclusion that sticking to its issue profile really does not help the Motherland Party. A similar observation can also be made about the only party which had generally increased its election to election consistency in the issue profiles emphasized – the Republican People's Party. It, too, saw serious erosion of its base. All other

support across Turkish provinces that indicate similarity of support bases between the Motherland Party and the Welfare Party. Çarkoğlu, '24 Aralık 1995 seçimlerinde bölgeselleşme' show that electoral support of both Welfare Party and Motherland Party is concentrated on the same cluster of provinces composed of eastern and central Anatolia. Both parties' support decline considerably in the western regions.

[44] K. Janda, R. Harmel, C. Edens and P. Goff, 'Changes in party identity, evidence from party manifestos', *Party Politics*, 1(1995), 171–96.

[45] I start from 1954 election to trace the consistency in Republican People's Party manifesto profiles. In 1983 I took Republican People's Party as the precursor of the Populist Party; the only left-wing party of the post-coup election. The first correlation of the True Path Party in 1987 is calculated using 1977 issue profile of the Justice Party. The same convention is applied to the Welfare Party and its correlation for 1987 is calculated using the National Salvation Party issue profile in 1977.

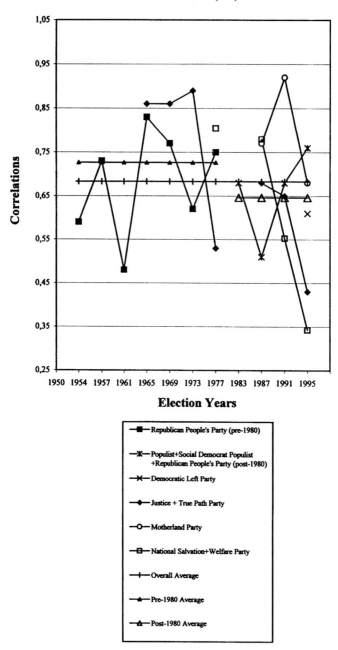

Figure 4. Consistency of Election Across Elections

parties in the system were rapidly changing the structure of their issue emphases.[46]

---

[46] For a more rigorous analysis of the relationship between election outcomes and manifesto change see Janda *et al.*, 'Changes in party identity'.

The essential message of Figure 4 is that, not only do we observe electoral fluidity reflected in the increased fractionalization and electoral volatility, but we also see that parties' consistency in the composition of their programmatic emphases is declining. This result gives yet another empirical support to the claim that Turkish politics has been undergoing a fundamental change, especially over the past few elections.

Towards a New Conceptualization: a Two-Dimensional Analysis

As the above evaluation of the Turkish electoral history from a uni-dimensional left-right ideological perspective shows, the use of party manifesto data is very helpful in illustrating the central divide in the party system and the resulting strategic moves by the parties. A focus on left-right, however, assumes that the centre-periphery cleavage also does not seem any longer to offer a strong explanatory framework for the Turkish experience. As Toprak underlines, 'social and geographical mobility, coupled with development of modern communication networks, to a large extent have integrated the periphery with the centre. The typical villagers of earlier decades, who lived in closed communities and had little contact with outsiders, are fast disappearing. Rather the typical villager today is likely to have relatives or former neighbours in the big cities of Turkey or Europe.'[47]

Although Turkish society is unequivocally more open and has access to a much wider set of communication channels, the extent to which expansion of access to modern tools of communication has transformed the society is not so clear.[48] Thus, although very important, the left-right axis may not yet be the central dimension in Turkish politics. My objective here is not to resolve complicated questions about social change in Turkish society. Instead, I want to concentrate on the reflections of political issues in election manifestos. I ask whether an alternative conceptualization of salient cleavages in Turkish society can be seen in the Turkish election manifestos – a conceptualization that will improve our understanding of Turkish politics along a centre-periphery as well as the left-right cleavage paradigms.

In order to provide a summary of the general structure of issues raised in elections and to diagnose trends in this structure across time and parties, I use factor analysis to derive salient dimensions in party manifestos. For this purpose 35 election manifestos over the 1950–1995 were pooled together. Table 2 below shows the results of a two-factor pooled analysis. The first dimension underlines support for the middle class and labour groups. It stresses

---

[47] Toprak, 'Islam and the secular state in Turkey', p. 94.

[48] The difference between the value systems of the elites and the masses seem to be narrower than expectations on many issues such as attitudes towards development and technological advances (See Ergüder *et al.*, *Türk Toplumunun Değerleri*, p. 36). Equally surprising finding of the survey conducted in Turkey as part of the World Values Survey is the support for the so-called post-materialist values reflected in support for environmental protection (See Ergüder *et al.*, *Turkish Values*, pp. 49–50). However, the same survey also show that a significant portion of Turkish society believe in destiny, distrustful of most people outside of their immediate family surroundings, do not take part in voluntary or civic organizations of any kind. The characteristics of those who have conservative and progressive attitudes show no discernible pattern across different demographic or economic variables except age, education and religiosity. Especially the political attitudes and voting tendencies are closely related to religiosity, age and education (See Ergüder *et al.*, *Türk Toplumunun Değerleri*, pp. 40–45 and Esmer, 'Parties and the electorate').

TABLE 2. Factor Analysis Results: New Cleavages in Turkish Politics (Varimax Rotation)

Factor 1: Local/Traditional vs. Universalist Cleavage.
Factor 2: Government Controlled Economy vs. Market System/Civil Society Cleavage

	Factor 1	Factor 2
Internationalism (−)	0.72	0.12
Traditional Morality (+)	0.68	0.03
European Community (−)	0.64	−0.07
Special International Relations (−)	0.58	−0.10
Anti-Imperialism	0.57	−0.17
National Way of Life (+)	0.54	0.10
Political Corruption	0.49	−0.30
Middle Class. Small Merchants (+)	0.48	0.19
Military (+)	0.32	0.57
Labor Groups (+)	0.31	0.13
Social Justice	0.24	0.42
Nationalization	0.21	0.43
Freedom and Human Rights	0.01	−0.62
Productivity	0.00	−0.31
Democracy	−0.04	−0.48
Controlled Economy	−0.05	0.66
Economic Planning	−0.05	0.52

	Factor 1	Factor 2
Controlled Economy	−0.05	0.66
Education Expansion	−0.43	0.63
Military (+)	0.32	0.57
Protectionism (+)	−0.06	0.56
Economic Planning	−0.05	0.52
Econ. Incentives	−0.21	0.51
Nationalisation	0.21	0.43
Social Justice	0.24	0.42
Welfare State Expansion	−0.64	0.24
Middle Class. Small Merchants (+)	0.48	0.19
Internationalism (+)	−0.44	0.16
Labour Groups (+)	0.31	0.13
Internationalism (−)	0.72	0.12
National Way of Life (+)	0.54	0.10
Economic Goals	−0.44	0.07
Traditional Morality (+)	0.68	0.03
Technology and Infrastructure	−0.64	−0.04

	Factor 1	Factor 2
Economic Orthodoxy	-0.06	-0.45
Protectionism (+)	-0.06	0.56
Multiculturalism (+)	-0.19	-0.14
Economic Incentives	-0.21	0.51
Non-Economic Demographic Groups (+)	-0.28	-0.34
Free Enterprise	-0.35	-0.19
Environmental Protection	-0.42	-0.09
Education Expansion	-0.43	0.63
Economic Goals	-0.44	0.07
Internationalism (+)	-0.44	0.16
Decentralization (+)	-0.46	-0.25
European Comm. (+)	-0.49	-0.32
Welfare State Expansion	-0.64	0.24
Technology and Infrastructure	-0.64	-0.04

	Factor 1	Factor 2
European Community (−)	0.64	-0.07
Environmental Protection	-0.42	-0.09
Special International Relations (−)	0.58	-0.10
Multiculturalism (+)	-0.19	-0.14
Anti-Imperialism	0.57	-0.17
Free Enterprise	-0.35	-0.19
Decentralization (+)	-0.46	-0.25
Political Corruption	0.49	-0.30
Productivity	0.00	-0.31
European Community (+)	-0.49	-0.32
Non-Economic Demographic Groups (+)	-0.28	-0.34
Economic Orthodoxy	-0.06	-0.45
Democracy	-0.04	-0.48
Freedom and Human Rights	0.01	-0.62

Factor	Eigenvalue	% of Variation explained	Cumulative % of variation explained
1	5.4	17.5	17.5
2	3.9	12.6	30.1

demands for social justice as well as favourable mentions of national independence and sovereignty, as opposed to internationalism. Still on the same side of the dimension, favourable mentions of traditional moral values, opposition to the European Community and negative mentions of particular countries blended with anti-imperialistic jargon surface. Appeals to patriotism and nationalism, need to eliminate corruption, support for middle class and small merchants, support for the military and labour groups, arguments in favour of equality and social justice, nationalization and government ownership in general also appear on this side of the dimension.

This factor has negative loadings that define the other end of the spectrum. Arguments in favour of multiculturalism, use of economic incentives, favourable mentions of women, youth and linguistic groups, support for free enterprise and environmental protection, expansion of education, general economic goals, need for international cooperation, support for decentralization, support for the European Community, arguments in favour of welfare programmes' expansion and importance of modernization of industry, methods of transport and communication take place on this side of the first factor. As such, this dimension contrasts arguments in support of local, traditional constituencies to arguments for more universalistic values supporting an open market economy in good working relations with the rest of the world. I call this factor *local/ traditional vs. universalist cleavage*, which could be viewed as a reasonable working operationalization of the periphery vs. centre concept.

The second dimension reflects a cleavage I call *government controlled economy vs. market system/civil society*, which might be considered a broad cognate of left vs. right. This dimension is dominated by economic issues that clearly reflect a market vs. government sector debate. Added to this well-known dimension are political principles regarding democracy, freedom and human rights and support for non-economic demographic groups such as youth and women.[49]

It should be noted here that the two factors reflect issue emphases that differ somewhat from the expected centre vs. periphery and left vs. right cleavage. Positive loadings of the first dimension, on the one hand, reflect closed traditional social values that are combined with isolationist anti-imperialist, anti-internationalist jargon stressing patriotism and nationalism. However, support for labour groups and the military as well as appeals for social justice are not the typical issues of the periphery. The negative loadings on the other hand run much more strongly against the expectations of a centrist issue emphasis.[50] Support for multiculturalism, women, youth, linguistic and other specialized interest groups as well as support for decentralization are all issues that run against the traditional Turkish centre positions. Similarly, only in recent years, support for free enterprise, economic incentives, as an effective policy tool as well as policy support for the environment became part of the governments'

---

[49] See Budge *et al.*, *Ideology, Strategy, and Party Change: Spatial Analyses of Post-War Election Programs in Nineteen Democracies*; S. Bartolini and P. Mair, *Identity, Competition and Electoral Availability, the Stabilisation of European Electorates, 1885–1985* (Cambridge, Cambridge University Press, 1990); Laver and I. Budge, *Party Policy and Coalition Government in Western Europe*; P. Mair, 'Locating Irish political parties on a left-right scale', *Political Studies*, 34 (1986), 456–465 and Çarkoğlu, 'Election manifestos' for similar factor analysis results showing the relevance of government vs. markets cleavage in economic issues.

[50] Mardin, 'Center-periphery relations'.

policy positions. Nevertheless it is yet too early to claim that elites close to the state did integrate these issues into their political agenda in full.

Loadings of the second dimension seem at first sight to reflect a left-right cleavage. However, in several important aspects it represents drastic deviations from it. It should be admitted that positively loaded economic issues, except the support for governmental economic incentives, are all typical left issue stands. However, support for the military has not been the position of the Turkish left for at least the post-1970 period. Similarly, besides the economic positions of the left, not much of traditional left policies such as peace, internationalism, democracy and support for labour groups appear to be important in this dimension. Instead of labour groups, support for small merchants and the middle class have a relatively more important position. On the negative loading side, economic policy positions are dominated by traditionally left positions of support for democracy and freedom and human rights. Although traditional right issue stands such as support for free enterprise and policies to create small and efficient government structure and similar orthodox economic policies appear on the negative side of this dimension, issues such as support for decentralization, and non-economic demographic groups also appear to be important aspects of this dimension. Demands for restructuring of government into not only an economically more efficient, small and incorrupt entity, but also one which respects human rights of its citizens, abiding the rules of democracy, and necessarily decentralizing its powers in the process, are clearly represented in this second dimension. Such demands find reflections on both sides of the traditional left-right ideological divide in the post-1980 Turkish party system. The underlying idea behind these demands for a new form of Turkish state is simply a gradual dissolution of state powers.[51]

The content analysis of Turkish election manifestos of the last forty-five years provides valuable information on the ideological rhetoric of political competition among political parties. First of all, the dominant factor that arises out of election manifesto emphases is one that resembles the centre-periphery framework. However, there exists a significant deviation from the conventional version of Mardin's framework in the combination of issue emphases included in the first dimension that argues against straightforwardly call it a *centre-periphery* cleavage. Secondly, the other issue dimension that arises from my analysis reflects some modernizing forces in Turkish society that mirror an issue combination with traits of a Western type left-right divide. However, as with the first dimension, one observes peculiarities in the Turkish issue combinations dominating the second dimension that deviate from the conventional left-right divide, as seen from a comparative perspective.

The above analysis shows that together with a modernizing set of issues in the *government controlled economy vs. market system/civil society* cleavage, that act as a Turkish approximation of the conventional left-right divide, the *local/traditional vs. universalist cleavage*, with similarities to the conventional

[51] See N. Göle, 'Toward an autonomisation of politics and civil society in Turkey', in M. Heper and A. Evin (eds), *Politics in the Third Turkish Republic* (Westview, 1994), pp. 213–222 and F. Birtek, 'Prospects for a new centre or the temporary rise of the peripheral asabiyah?' in M. Heper and A. Evin (eds), *Politics in the Third Turkish Republic* (Westview, 1994), pp. 223–230 for two insightful interpretations and speculations of the post 1980 experience in Turkey. See also E. Kalaycıoğlu, 'Decentralisation of government' in M. Heper and A. Evin (eds) *Politics in the Third Turkish Republic* (Westview, 1994), pp. 87–102 on recent decentralization debates in Turkey.

centre-periphery framework, surface as the two dominant dimensions of the Turkish ideological rhetoric. The deviations in these two dimensions from their counterparts in other democracies is due, in all likelihood, to the fact these issue emphases are reflections of primarily a party elite undertaking the preparation of an attractive issue package for the potential constituencies. Within an impurely democratic institutional framework of the Turkish party system and the pressures of a strong network of patron-client relationships these reflections could well be deceptive. However, the linkage between mass ideological orientations and their reflections in the political elites' rhetoric and actions is a distinct area of study beyond the scope of the present analysis. Nevertheless, the findings above raise questions about the structure of issue dimensions in Turkish politics underlining future research needs.

The question of whether popular demands have been raised that are in line with the above outlined transformation scenario is also beyond the focus of the present analysis. One should admit that there seem only hints of politically potent demands for the transformation of the centralized powers of the Turkish State. As a result mainly of strict control over protest behaviour, mass demands have not been raised through any popular demonstration or organized movement. Nevertheless, political parties' issue emphases do reflect a tendency to incorporate this cleavage into their issue mix.

Figures 5 and 6 show the development of party stands on the two dimensions. Respectively, they show a broad trend from localism to universalism (Figure 5) and from governmental control to market economy (Figure 6). But there is variation in the extent to which particular parties share these trends. On both dimensions the Welfare Party is placed on the extremist positions. We observe that the Welfare Party and its predecessor the National Salvation Party have always been on the local/traditional side of the first dimension. Its emphasis on local/traditionalist arguments steadily increased from the early 1970s National Salvation Party period up until the 1991 election. After a poor showing in the 1987 election with the lowest ever, since the early 1970s, 7.2% vote share, the Welfare Party moved to the centre by emphasizing some 'universalist' arguments. As a result Welfare in 1995 almost equally emphasized both sides of the local/traditionalist vs. universalist cleavage, coming very close to the centre. However, despite this apparent centrist move Welfare still remains the only party with a net local/traditionalist emphasis in the system. The Republican People's Party of the pre-1980 period has been mostly on the 'universalist' side of the cleavage. Only during the 1950s did it move to the local/traditionalist side as a result of competition with the Democrat Party. Again for the critical election of 1973 we find the RPP on the local/traditionalist side. The electoral losses in the 1973 election seem to have drastically pushed the Justice Party to the local/traditionalist side. For both the 1973 and 1977 elections the National Salvation Party and the Nationalist Action Party remain clearly separated from the other parties.

During the post-1980 coup period the general trend in the system has been one of shifting towards more emphasis on the 'universalist' arguments. While the Motherland Party remains consistently around a moderate universalist net emphasis throughout the period, the True Path Party and the inheritors of the RPP tradition, except the Democratic Left Party, have drastically changed their positions, especially in the last two elections, in favour of the universalist emphases. All in all, over the last three elections the Turkish party system has

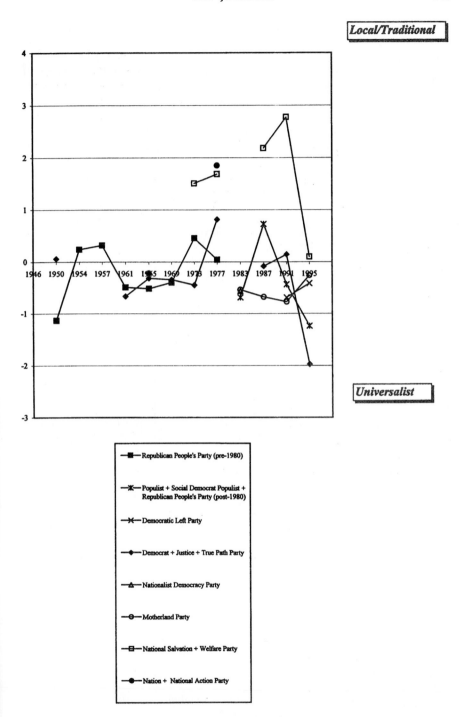

Figure 5. Factor 1: Local/Traditional vs. Universalist Cleavage

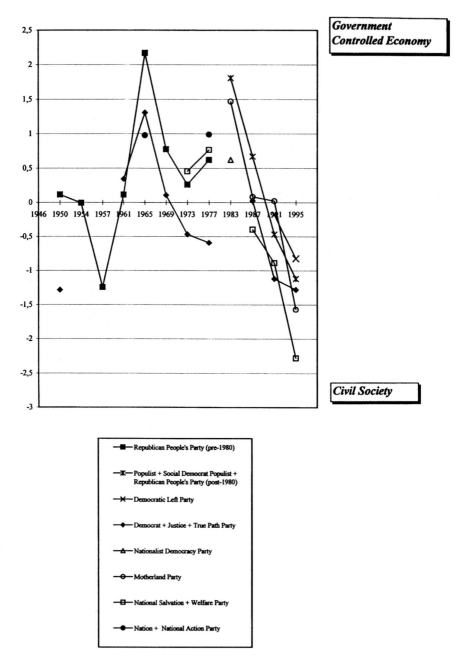

Figure 6. Factor 2: Government Controlled Economy vs. Market System/Civil Society Cleavage

shifted its emphases in favour of the 'universalist' arguments. The discrepancy between the Welfare Party and the rest of the parties have sharply declined as a result of the Welfare Party's moderation along this dimension.

The general trend in the government control vs. market/civil society dimension has been one of a clear shift away from state involvement in the economy and polity. Or the move has been from the *left*, to the *right*, if one wishes to make that jump in measurement interpretation. During the pre-1980 period, the Republican People's Party and the National Salvation Party have been in favour of state involvement in different aspects of economic life. The Justice Party steadily shifted towards more emphasis of 'market/civil society' issues and the last election of this period in 1977 resulted in the largest divide between the Justice Party and the other parties in the system. In contrast, the post-1980 period witnessed a continuous shift by all parties in the system towards more emphasis of the 'market/civil society' issues. This drastic shift of emphasis from state controlled economic policy-making to one of emphasis on decentralized free enterprise system, which underlines also the political components as democracy and human rights, is shared by all parties.

The relative positions of the parties along the salient two dimensions are outcomes of two composite indexes. Accordingly, it should be stressed here that not all parties equally emphasize the diverse group of issues embedded in our two dimensions. For example, the Welfare Party seems to have emphasized 'civil society' issues more than anybody else in the 1995 election. This is due to the huge portion of the Welfare Party manifesto (approximately 26.6%) that is devoted to favourable arguments for democracy and human rights. Moreover, the Welfare Party does not use these issues to make an argument similar to others. Welfare's emphasis on freedom and human rights is concerned more with religious freedoms than anything else, with overtones of oppressive attitudes for other belief systems and minority groups. The Motherland Party on the other hand emphasizes shrinking the government sector, the need to eliminate political corruption, decentralization, and the need to boost economic growth and productivity.

The evidence from the election programmes also shows that there has been a clear shift of issue priorities in the Turkish party system away from a local/ traditionalist and from state-centred, government controlled economy to one that emphasizes universal values and civil society concerns in general. Surprisingly, the rise of the Welfare Party coincides with these fundamental changes in Turkish political rhetoric. The Welfare Party has successfully adapted to shifting issue emphases in the system. It has adapted its party manifesto especially in the 1995 election to moderate its emphases on the local/ traditionalist vs. universalist cleavage by moving down towards the centre position. Nevertheless, despite its moderation moves the Welfare Party still remained as the party that has the highest local/traditionalist views in the system. It remains the most extreme party on that dimension. Similarly, Welfare has adapted to shifting emphases in favour of issues I call the 'civil society' issues. On this second dimension it has again successfully adjusted its position maintaining its distinct extremist position in the system relative to the other parties. In short, one should recognize that the rise of the Welfare Party does not correspond to a rise of electoral support for a right-of-centre pro-Islamist party sticking to its extremist positions in a static way. Just to the contrary, the Welfare Party modified its relative emphases on issues skilfully so that it can project a dynamic capacity to adjust to new contexts. At the same time it was successful in distinguishing itself from the rest of the system parties by remaining clearly on the fringes of the newly developed ideology ranking in the system.

Conclusions

The Turkish party system has been undergoing a fundamental change. The political system cyclically creates its own bottlenecks, which seem to remain largely unresolved. On the electoral scene instability and fragmentation has been constantly increasing. Various reflections of these changes can be seen in the parties' election manifestos. The manifesto data also reveal a deeply rooted shift in the parties' structure of argumentation corresponding to electoral shifts. The available data simply do not give an opportunity to test whether these shifts in electoral preferences have been the underlying cause of the changes in party issue emphases or whether the causation runs from the party elites' formulations to public opinion shifts. On the basis of preliminary analyses by Janda *et al.* there are indications that electoral performance is closely linked to manifesto change.[52] The above analysis also suggests that parties have changed their strategy to appeal to the masses in Turkey. Some issue categories closely associated with what I call the 'universalist' dimension as opposed to 'local/ traditional' have been emphasized to a growing extent. Similarly, all significant parties in the system have been stressing the 'market/civil society' themes more and more intensely. Moreover, those parties who seem to share, if not to lead, larger portion of these system trends also surface to be the more successful ones. Democratic logic necessitates that there should be an electoral basis for changing party issue emphases. If there were no real electoral gain in these changing party strategies the parties simply would not retain them for long. The foundations of these changes lie in political behaviour of the Turkish electorate. The above findings should be tested by survey data to determine the underlying issue bases of the Turkish electorate. Only then can the picture be made to offer a more accurate rendition of reality.

On the basis of my analysis, one must conclude that the Turkish party system, near the end of the century, does not seem to have fulfilled the purposes expected of its counterparts in more fully modernized democracies. Peculiar historical factors, most notably the anti-party policies of the intermittent military governments, have clearly destabilized the party system. As of this writing the coalition government of the pro-Islamist Welfare Party and the True Path Party have resigned and were replaced by a minority coalition of secularist parties. Claims of behind the scenes backing of the Military to the new government have been voiced and numerous scandalous dealings involving some parties' leadership have been exposed to the public. There are two major developments that slowly seem to surface in the public agenda with potential capacity to totally reshape the Turkish party system. One is the resurfacing demand by some circles of a new presidential system. The other involves legal initiatives apparently supported by the new coalition government to prosecute the leadership of the True Path Party due to charges of corruption and even to close down the Welfare Party for being unconstitutionally anti-secular. Despite

[52] Janda *et al.* 'Changes in party identity'.

these ongoing investigations and scandals of corruption that continually alienate masses from the system, Turkey still experiences its longest period of elective governance. However, it remains to be seen whether these steps taken to reshape the party system will result, as they did in previous attempts of 1960 and 1980 military regime periods, in eventual rejection of the precautions taken in the name of injecting more stability into the party system.

Underlying all these developments is a socioeconomic transformation that has created a confusing overlay of value cleavages, which significantly complicates party strategy. The evidence hints strongly that there is a movement toward a more stable left-right dimension of competition, and a commensurate lessening of centre-periphery relevance. If, indeed, that process proceeds to a reasonable equilibrium, the Turkish party system may have the opportunity to do its democratic job. The apparent chaotic political situation certainly has its roots in the fluid transitional character of socio-economic structure in Turkey. The reflection of such an uncertain context in ideological rhetoric of parties and their constituencies unquestionably contributes to persisting political flux in the country.

Parties, Party Systems, and Satisfaction with Democratic Performance in The New Europe

CHRISTOPHER J. ANDERSON[1]

Introduction

Political parties and the party systems they form constitute the major channels of interest aggregation and citizen input in contemporary democracies. They are the vehicles through which political elites supply policy alternatives, and they constitute the major route for citizens to organize the demand for such alternatives.[2] Parties also play a crucial role in the nature of democratic governance because they help legitimize the state. After all, free and fair elections in which parties compete for office are a prime criterion for whether a system should be considered a democracy in the first place. Outside of elections, political parties also have long been the most important mediating institutions between citizens and the state, in particular as parties have taken on the roles as simultaneous agents both of the state and its citizens.[3]

While virtually all democracies have political parties that compete for office, political systems differ in a number of important ways with regard to how they go about channeling inputs or providing policy alternatives, and with regard to the roles they assign parties in this process. Moreover, and perhaps most importantly, the ways in which political institutions condition the formation, functioning, and development of political parties and party systems varies as well. While there is an extensive literature linking electoral systems and the development of party systems, few researchers have investigated their link with how citizens – the ultimate arbiters of democratic governance – feel about the way the political process performs.

This essay focuses on two types of political performance that are expected to affect citizen attitudes about the political system: *party* and *party system* performance. While *party* performance focuses on how individual political parties perform their roles as mobilizing and organizing agents in elections, *party system* performance involves the aggregate constellation of parties in a political system and its electoral consequences in the form of party system fragmentation and volatility. This essay investigates whether, and how, cross-national differences in both party and party system performance affect citizens' evaluations of their country's political system.

[1] Many thanks to Richard I. Hofferbert, participants at the SUNY-Binghamton political science graduate colloquium, and the political science department at Washington University in St. Louis for thoughtful comments on earlier ideas and drafts.
[2] H. D. Klingemann, R. Hofferbert, and I. Budge, *Parties, Policies, and Democracy* (Boulder, CO, Westview, 1994).
[3] R. Katz, and P. Mair, 'Changing models of party organization: The emergence of the cartel party', *Party Politics* 1,1 (1995), 5–28.

On the basis of directly comparable survey evidence from about 20 democracies collected between 1993 and 1995, this article examines the determinants of cross-national differences in democratic support in both old and new democracies. Specifically, I focus on satisfaction with democracy in the 15 member states of the European Union as well as in several of the emerging democracies of east central Europe. I investigate whether and to what extent electoral rules and party system performance help us understand differences in levels of satisfaction with the political system in both old and new democracies.

The next section reviews the literature on electoral systems and party performance; subsequently, I develop a model of how these may be related to levels of democracy satisfaction in contemporary democracies. The empirical analysis then tests these relationships systematically, and a concluding section discusses the results and spells out implications for further research.

Electoral Systems, Party Systems, and Performance

What are the relationships between a country's electoral institutions and the outcomes they produce? For one, it is well known that electoral systems are the primary institutional factor that constrains the development and nature of a country's party system. Moreover, it is widely assumed that the laws governing electoral systems have politically non-neutral consequences.[4] Simply put, it is believed that the nature of the electoral system in place in a country affects the type of party system that develops (two-party versus multi-party) by influencing the strategic considerations of voters and political elites. The more proportional the electoral system, the more likely it is that the party system is fragmented.[5] Consequently, much of comparative political science has sought to extend the notion that political institutions affect parties and party systems in democracies.[6]

Electoral rules, however, do not simply impose such non-neutral consequences on the participants in the governing process; they also provide them with strategic opportunities. Moreover, electoral rules are not dictated by some magic force, but structured and used by citizens and elites alike. Electoral rules can be said to have two kinds of consequences: first, they delineate the probabilities that particular political parties will gain representation in parliament. Second, they influence the electoral strategies of both voters and political parties. Hence, they also constrain both the representative and policy making processes in a country and affect how citizens evaluate the performance of the democracy they live in.

Aside from institutional determinants of party and party system development and performance, a number of scholars have pointed to factors rooted in the socio-structural environment as important determinants of party and party

[4] M. Duverger, *Political Parties* (New York, Wiley and Sons, 1954). D. W. Rae, *The Political Consequences of Electoral Laws* (New Haven, Yale University Press, 1967). W. H. Riker, 'The number of political parties: A re-examination of Duverger's law', *Comparative Politics* 9 (1976): 93–106. A. Lijphart, 'The political consequences of electoral laws, 1945–85', *The American Political Science Review* 84,9 (1990): 481–496.
[5] A. Lijphart, *Electoral Systems and Party Systems: A Study of Twenty-Seven Democracies, 1945–1990* (New York, Oxford University Press, 1994).
[6] A. Lijphart, 'Constitutional choices for new democracies', *Journal of Democracy* 2,1 (1991), 72–84. D. W. Rae, *Political Consequences of Electoral Laws*.

system performance.[7] Usually phrased in terms of changes in party attachment or realignment and dealignment, a number of electoral researchers have pointed out that party systems undergo periodic changes as a result of the changing composition and political socialization of mass electorates.[8] According to this line of research, party systems change or remain the same because of changes (or lack thereof) in a country's social structure that produce changes in individuals' attachments to political parties.

Yet, due to differently structured political and electoral institutions and different electoral strategies, similar changes in social structure across two countries do not necessarily have similar consequences. While some countries' electoral institutions encourage the establishment of new political parties or the reorientation of old ones, others inhibit such responsiveness. As a consequence, political, and in particular electoral, institutions play a crucial role with regard to how social changes are translated into changes at the level of political parties.[9] Similarly, depending on how electoral rules condition the development of political alternatives, parties choose to target particular segments of the electoral market, thus mobilizing particular constituencies and neglecting others. Taken together, both the institutional and socio-structural approaches have shown quite convincingly that electoral rules produce different constellations of parties and party systems in the context of different societal and social structural constraints.[10]

This essay serves two tasks: first, it will examine the consequences electoral systems have for party and party system performance, as well as the relationships among party and party system performance. Second, it will also examine how institutions (such as electoral systems) and the performance they produce are related to how citizens evaluate the democratic performance of their particular polity.

A Model of Party System Performance and Democracy Satisfaction

Logically, the establishment of electoral procedures and institutions precedes the measurement of support for the system; this assumes a chain of causality running from institutions, party performance (e.g., voter mobilization), and party system performance (e.g., electoral volatility) on one hand to satisfaction with democracy on the other. Electoral rules frequently have been hypothesized to affect the levels of fragmentation as well as volatility of party systems.[11]

[7] S. M. Lipset, and S. Rokkan, *Party Systems and Voter Alignments* (New York, Free, 1967). R. Rose, and D. Urwin, 'Persistence and change in western party systems since 1945', *Political Studies*, 18 (1970), 287–319.

[8] R. J. Dalton, *Citizen Politics: Public Opinion and Political Parties in Advanced Industrial Democracies* (Chatham, NJ, Chatham House, 1996). R. Inglehart, *Modernization and Post-modernization* (Princeton, Princeton University Press, 1997).

[9] S. Bartolini, and P. Mair, *Identity, Competition, and Electoral Availability: the Stabilisation of European Electorates 1885–1985* (New York, Cambridge University Press, 1990).

[10] M. Duverger, *Political Parties*. A. Lijphart, *Electoral Systems and Party Systems: a Study of Twenty-Seven Democracies, 1945–1990* (New York, Oxford University Press, 1994). R. J. Dalton, S. Flanagan, and P. Beck, *Electoral Change in Advanced Industrial Societies: Realignment or Dealignment* (Princeton, Princeton University Press, 1984).

[11] M. Duverger, *Political Parties*. D. W. Rae, *Political Consequences of Electoral Laws*. A. Lijphart, *Electoral Systems and Party Systems*.

Based on this research, electoral rules thus should result in particular kinds of party and party system performance, which, in turn, should affect citizen satisfaction with democratic governance. The effect of electoral institutions on democracy satisfaction, however, should be indirect and hence mediated by political performance. We can express this model of how electoral rules, party system performance, and democracy satisfaction are related as follows:

Electoral system → Party/Party system performance → Satisfaction with democracy   (1)

According to this model, electoral system and party system performance indicators can be taken to be independent variables that affect the level of citizen satisfaction with democratic performance. They afford citizens greater or fewer choices; preferences are translated in a very proportional or not very proportional fashion; and they define the extent to which citizens can vote strategically. Taking a similar approach, Miller and Listhaug have argued, for example, that a smaller number of parties in a system (which, to some degree, may be a consequence of electoral laws) is correlated with popular dissatisfaction with democratic governance because there are fewer policy choices for citizens.[12] Put differently, because some electoral systems inhibit the emergence of new parties to take account of new demands, system support may be lower in the long run. Thus, countries with fewer parties also should have lower levels of citizen satisfaction with the system. In contrast to the research by Miller and Listhaug, however, Weil's cross-national study of system support in western democracies found that party system fragmentation – that is, a larger number of parties – was systematically associated with lower levels of democratic support.[13] However, to date few scholars have sought to systematically disentangle the fragmentation-citizen support linkage.

Some scholars have pointed to the changed role parties play in western democracies as an influence on system support. In terms of their representative role, established parties seem to have become less relevant and to be losing some of their key functions, while at the same time they seem more privileged than ever in public office and in terms of their linkage to the state.[14] This combination is probably one of the main factors associated with anti-party sentiment, electoral volatility, and the emergence of new and protest parties.[15] Following this line of argument, a greater number of parties also should be associated with lower levels of system support. Below, I will test whether party system fragmentation and volatility – that is, indicators of party system performance – indeed are systematically associated with levels of performance satisfaction in contemporary democracies.

Based on the notion that electoral institutions work in distinct and variable socio-structural as well as politically relevant strategic contexts, it is hypothesized that electoral systems also are related to party performance – that is, to parties' electoral and organizational strategies as well as to their effectiveness.

[12] A. H. Miller, and O. Listhaug, 'Political parties and confidence in government: A comparison of Norway, Sweden and the United States', *British Journal of Political Science*, 29 (1990), 357–86.
[13] F. Weil, 'The sources and structure of legitimation in western democracies: a consolidated model tested with time-series data in six countries since World War II', *American Sociological Review*, 54 (1989), 82–706.
[14] Katz and Mair, 'Changing models of party organizations'.
[15] S. Scarrow, and T. Poguntke, 'The politics of anti-party sentiment', *European Journal of Political Research*, 29,3 (1996): 57–262.

Specifically, in systems that have a more proportional translation of seats into votes – that is, systems in which the electoral market is more likely to be segmented – parties should rely more on mobilizing voters along traditional lines of social group ties and party membership. Such mobilization strategies are relatively effective and inexpensive because they are based on existing networks and social milieus as well as enduring formal and informal group ties. The extent to which parties in particular systems are able to do so can be considered an indicator of party performance.

Finally, party and party system performance can be expected to be related to each other as well. Party system fragmentation and volatility are expected to be lower in systems with parties that have strong social-group ties and high rates of organizational membership. Taken together, Model 1 can be modified to include a link between party and party system performance as well:

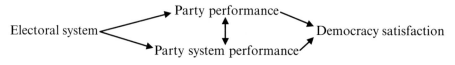

Whether citizens evaluate the functioning of their democracy based on the recent performance of their electoral institutions and organization or based on the more lasting institutions, such as electoral laws, holds importance for the broader scholarly debate about the design of democratic institutions. Specifically, political theorists have debated whether it is more important that the institutions produce superior outcomes or that the institutions are designed in a way that produces maximum process fairness to all participants.[16] Translated for the present study, this would mean asking whether party/party system performance or the type of electoral institutions have a stronger effect on democracy satisfaction.

Below, I test these models of the relationships among electoral systems, party system performance, and democracy satisfaction in greater detail. Based on systematic data collected in 19 European democracies, the analysis examines the following hypotheses:

Hypothesis 1: The more proportional the electoral system, the more fragmented the party system and the higher the level of electoral volatility.

Hypothesis 2: The more proportional the electoral system, the stronger the linkages between parties and voters.

Hypothesis 3: The stronger the linkages between parties and voters, the lower the level of party system fragmentation and volatility.

Hypothesis 4a: A greater number of parties in a system is correlated with higher levels of system support (Miller and Listhaug).

Hypothesis 4b: A greater number of parties in a system is correlated with lower levels of system support (Weil).

Hypothesis 5: Higher levels of electoral volatility are correlated with lower levels of system support.

Hypothesis 6: Closer links between citizens and political parties are correlated with higher levels of system support.

[16] A. Lijphart, *Democracies* (New Haven, Yale University Press, 1984). G. B. Powell, *Contemporary Democracies: Participation, Stability and Violence* (Cambridge MA, Harvard University Press, 1982).

The countries included in this study are 14 of the member states of the European Union (Austria, Belgium, Denmark, Finland, France, Germany, Greece, Ireland, Luxembourg, the Netherlands, Portugal, Spain, Sweden, and the United Kingdom),[17] as well as five new democracies of east central Europe (Bulgaria, Czech Republic, Hungary, Poland, and Slovakia). Because the rise of democratic systems among the countries of the former Soviet bloc is such a recent phenomenon, much of the theorizing and most of the empirical studies about electoral systems, party systems, and system support has been based on the experience of established democracies. The countries included here were chosen because they allow for the testing of theories of democracy both in established and newly established democratic systems; the new democracies included here also fulfil the criterion of having the most stable democratic systems of east central Europe.

Electoral Systems and Party System Performance

The model proposed above posits that the nature of a country's electoral system is related to party system performance. To compare electoral systems across the variety of democracies included in this study, I rely on an index of proportionality (or disproportionality) originally developed by Loosemore and Hanby.[18] The disproportionality index represents the total deviation from proportionality (% votes minus % seats). To calculate the index, the absolute values of all vote-share differences are added and divided by 2:[19]

$$D = \tfrac{1}{2}|v_i - s_i|$$

One can easily transform the index of disproportionality into an index of proportionality by subtracting its values from 100 ($P = 100 - D$); in this case, 100 would be equal to perfect proportionality.[20] This kind of index has the advantage of providing a representation of any electoral system, regardless of whether it is based on proportional representation, single-transferrable vote counts, or plurality rules.

To assess party system performance, I rely on indicators of fragmentation and volatility. For the fragmentation measure, I utilize the Laakso and Taagepera index measuring the effective number or parliamentary parties in a system.[21] The effective number of parties is calculated as follows:[22]

$$N = 1/\sum_{i=1}^{n} p_i$$

[17] Italy was left out of the analysis because it experienced significant electoral volatility, elections under a new electoral law, as well as the fundamental reformation of its party system during the period investigated here. Interested readers may obtain the empirical results with the Italian case included by contacting the author.

[18] J. Loosemore and V. Hanby, 'The theoretical limits of maximum distortion: some analytic expressions for electoral systems', *British Journal of Political Science*, 1 (1971), 467–77.

[19] A. Lijphart, *Electoral Systems and Party Systems*, p. 60.

[20] T. Mackie and R. Rose, *The International Almanac of Electoral History*. rev. 3rd ed. (Washington DC, Congressional Quarterly Press, 1991).

[21] M. Laakso and R. Taagepera, 'Effective number of parties: a measure with application to west Europe', *Comparative Political Studies*, 12 (1979), 3–27.

[22] Instead of using the more widely known Rae/Taylor index of party system fractionalization, I measure party system change by changes in the effective number of parliamentary and electoral

where p_i is the proportion of parliamentary seats for the I-th party.[23] This formula contains information about the number and relative size of the parties in the system. It thus helps to differentiate not only between two- and multi-party systems, but it is also a more subtle measure than simply counting the number of parties that gain representation or receive votes. The proposed measure takes the relative strength and parliamentary viability of parties into account. Or, as Taagepera and Shugart have put it:

> The advantage of using the effective, rather than the actual, number of parties is that it establishes a nonarbitrary way to distinguish 'significant' parties from less significant ones. The construction of the index is such that each party weights itself by being squared. Tiny parties contribute little to the index, while large parties contribute relatively more.[24]

Finally, to gauge electoral volatility, I utilize the volatility index devised by Pedersen,[25] measuring the net electoral shifts among political parties in a system. Volatility estimates the total change in electoral outcomes, irrespective of the direction of change. Thus, changes across parties, can be measured by the total net change from one election to the next:

$$V = \tfrac{1}{2}\sum |P_{i,t}|$$

where $P_{i,t}$ is the percentage of the vote obtained by party I at election t.

Table 1 shows the distribution of the countries along the proportionality index, as well as the level of party system fragmentation and electoral volatility. There is significant variation among the country cases included here on all three dimensions.

Table 2 reports the Pearson correlation coefficients for the association between the electoral system and party system performance indicators. Two correlation analyses were conducted: To see whether the inclusion of the new democracies of east central Europe affected the results, one included just the older democracies of Western Europe and one included all cases.

Confirming earlier work by Lijphart and others, the results indicate that the proportionality of the electoral system indeed is positively associated with party system fragmentation, here measured by the effective number of parliamentary parties. The association is of roughly equal strength regardless of whether we include the new democracies of East Central Europe, although it does not reach conventional levels of statistical significance: The more proportional the

parties in a system. Note, however, that the formula for the effective number of parties carries the same information as Rae's index of party system fractionalization, only expressed in a different metric. The reader can obtain Rae's fractionalization index (F) by substituting the value for the effective number of parties (N) in the following formula: $F = 1 - (1/N)$.

[23] A. Lijphart, *Democracies*, p. 120.

[24] R. Taagepera, and M. Shugart, *Seats and Votes* (New Haven, Yale University Press, 1993), p. 455.

[25] M. Pedersen, 'The dynamics of European party systems: changing patterns of electoral volatility', *European Journal of Political Research*, 7 (1979), 7–26. M. Pedersen, 'Changing patterns of electoral volatility in European party systems, 1948–1977: explorations in explanation', in H. Daalder and P. Mair (eds), *West European Party Systems: Continuity and Change* (London, Sage, 1983), pp. 29–66.

TABLE 1. Electoral Proportionality, Fragmentation, and Volatility in 19 Democracies

Country	Proportionality[a]	Eff. no. of parties[b]	Volatility[c]	Elections[a,c]
Austria	97.83	3.40	7.45	15
Belgium	94.02	7.95	7.10	16
Bulgaria	92.14	2.72	20.00	1
Czech Republic	95.90	4.85	19.90	1
Denmark	96.66	4.70	8.90	20
Finland	94.94	4.88	9.20	14
France	79.11	2.96	19.15	15
Germany	96.69	2.78	6.90	13
Greece	81.04	2.17	10.75	8
Hungary	85.00	2.89	25.00	2
Ireland	94.78	3.48	15.05	15
Luxembourg	95.22	3.90	5.10	11
Netherlands	97.04	5.38	19.55	15
Poland	79.85	3.85	27.60	2
Portugal	93.11	2.55	10.10	8
Slovakia	86.14	4.41	25.90	2
Spain	84.89	2.67	6.30	6
Sweden	97.45	3.51	11.25	15
United Kingdom	87.09	2.26	5.10	14

Sources:

[a]A. Lijphart, *Electoral Systems and Party Systems: a Study of Twenty-Seven Democracies* (New York, Oxford University Press, 1994), Appendix B; own calculations on the basis of data reported in *European Journal of Political Research* (various issues).

[b]L. LeDuc, R. Niemi, and P. Norris, *Comparing Democracies: Elections and Voting in Global Perspective* (London, Sage, 1996), Table 1.4. Most recent election only.

[c]P. Mair, Party System Change (Oxford, Clarendon Press, 1997), Table 8.1; own calculations on the basis of data reported in *European Journal of Political Research* (various issues).

TABLE 2. Pearson Correlations of Electoral System, Party System Fragmentation, and Electoral Volatility

	Western Europe Proportionality of electoral system	All cases Proportionality of electoral system
Effective no. of parl. parties	0.45	0.39
Volatility	−0.12	−0.39*
N:	14	19

*p < 0.10.

electoral system, the greater the fragmentation of the party system (Pearson correlation coefficient 0.4).[26]

Levels of electoral volatility, however, are largely unrelated to the proportionality of the electoral system when we consider the mature democracies alone. However, when all cases are included, electoral volatility appears to be negatively associated with the nature of the electoral system: more proportional systems are associated with lower levels of volatility.[27] Given that it also is the case that more proportional systems produce a greater number of parties, it appears that more proportional electoral institutions lead to stronger attachments to political parties; or, at the very least, it provides an aggregate indication of producing fewer incentives to switch parties from one election to the next.

Electoral Systems and Party Performance

While the relationship between electoral system type and party system performance appears to point in the direction that more proportional systems are associated with higher levels of party system fragmentation, and possibly lower levels of volatility, the evidence presented so far is not overwhelming when viewed from the perspective of total variance explained. To investigate whether the linkage between electoral system and party performance is any stronger than that between electoral system and performance of the party *system*, we require indicators of the linkage between voters and individual political parties. For this, I rely on two variables: One is the extent to which class voting takes place; that is, the strength of the bivariate association between indicators of social class and party choice in a system.[28] The other is political party membership in a country as a percentage of the electorate.[29] Table 3 displays these variables by country.

We again estimated correlation coefficients between electoral system (proportionality) and these party performance measures.

The results, shown in Table 4, are particularly strong with regard to the relationship of electoral system and party membership: countries with more proportional electoral systems also have significantly higher levels of party membership. Regardless of whether the east central European cases are included in the analysis, the relationship holds and displays statistically significant coefficients (Pearson's $r = 0.5$). The relationship between strength of class voting and electoral system type also points to stronger class voting in more proportional systems. (As an aside, it is noteworthy that class voting and party membership figures are positively correlated.[30]) Thus, the results suggest that electoral system type is strongly associated with party performance. Where there

---

[26] The somewhat lower levels of significance reported in some of the analyses may be due to the small number of cases analysed here. Thus, our interpretive strategy examines the direction and size of the correlation coefficient first, and its statistical significance second.

[27] The relationship between party system fragmentation and electoral volatility is virtually zero. Thus, it would be difficult to conclude that systems with a greater effective number of parties also display higher levels of electoral volatility.

[28] For details, see R. Dalton, *Citizen Politics: Public Opinion and Political Parties in Advanced Industrial Democracies.* 2nd ed. (Chatham, NJ, Chatham House, 1996).

[29] These data are taken from R. Katz, and P. Mair, *Party Organisations: a Data Handbook on Party Organisations in Western Democracies, 1960–1990* (London, Sage, 1992).

[30] The Pearson correlation coefficient is 0.33 (Western Europe) and 0.46 (all cases; $p < 0.1$).

TABLE 3. Strength of Class Voting and Party Membership in 19 Democracies

Country	Class voting[d]	Party membership[e]
Austria	0.20	21.80
Belgium	0.16	9.20
Bulgaria	NA	NA
Czech Republic	0.05	1.80
Denmark	0.21	6.50
Finland	0.16	12.90
France	0.15	1.70
Germany	0.13	4.20
Greece	NA	NA
Hungary	0.03	2.50
Ireland	0.14	5.30
Luxembourg	NA	NA
Netherlands	0.18	2.90
Poland	0.12	1.50
Portugal	0.11	4.90
Slovakia	0.04	3.10
Spain	0.15	4.00
Sweden	0.16	21.20
United Kingdom	0.18	3.30

Sources:

[d]P. Mair, *Party System Change* (Oxford, Clarendon Press, 1997), Table 8.2.
[e]R. Dalton, 'Political Cleavages, Issues, and Electoral Change', in L. LeDuc, R. Niemi and P. Norris (eds), *Comparing Democracies: Elections and Voting in Global Perspective* (London, Sage, 1996), Table 13.1; and G. Tóka, 'Parties and Electoral Choices in East-Central Europe', in G. Pridham and P. Lewis (eds), *Stabilising Fragile Democracies: Comparing New Party Systems in Southern and Eastern Europe* (London, Routledge, 1995), Table 4.4 and own calculations.

TABLE 4. Pearson Correlations of Electoral System, Party Membership, and Class Voting

	Western Europe Proportionality of electoral system	All cases Proportionality of electoral system
Party membership	0.53*	0.55**
Class voting	0.22	0.35
N:	12	16

*$p < 0.10$; **$p < 0.05$.

is a more proportional translation of votes into seats, I also find a closer link between parties and their voters. These results are consistent with those found for the relationship between electoral system and party system performance, indicating that proportional systems produce a greater number of parties, less electoral volatility, and stronger linkages between citizens and parties. What is not clear, however, is whether this is the case because parties in proportional systems are better able to target well-defined segments of the electoral market or because voters are more likely to find parties that are close to them ideologically (or both). In all likelihood, it is a combination of both, although these data do not allow us to address this question.

Party and Party System Performance: Is there a Link?

The theoretical models specified above hypothesized that there should also be a link between individual party performance and party system performance. Specifically, it postulated that party system volatility should be lower in systems that have strong organizational and mobilization linkages between individual parties and voters, whereas it is unclear what the relationship between fragmentation and party performance should be. Table 5 shows the associations between these conditions.

TABLE 5. Pearson Correlations of Party System Fragmentation, Electoral Volatility, Class Voting, and Party Membership

	Western Europe	All cases
	Effective no. of parl. parties	Effective no. of parl. parties
Class voting	0.29	0.10
Party membership	0.14	0.10
	Volatility	Volatility
Class voting	−0.37	−0.71***
Party membership	−0.30	−0.48*
N:	12	16

$*p < 0.10$; $**p < 0.05$; $***p < 0.01$.

The results indicate that there is a positive relationship between party system fragmentation (i.e., effective number of parties) and organizational linkages, and a negative one between electoral volatility and the organizational linkage variables. Thus, in systems that have higher levels of class voting and party membership, the party system also tends to have a greater number of parties. Conversely, electoral volatility tends to be lower in systems with high levels of class voting and party membership.

Overall, these relationships are very consistent. In particular the link between class voting and volatility (both indicators of the strength of the connection between voters and parties) turns out to be extremely strong, whereas the association between party membership and fragmentation is weaker, and possibly also less obvious from a theoretical perspective. Countries with parties that are able to mobilize core electorates along the traditional cleavage-lines thus experience less volatility.

Satisfaction with Democratic Governance: Measures and Data

To assess current levels of system support, I rely on comparative survey data from the Eurobarometer averaged over the period of 1993–95 in the member states of the European Union.[31] Moreover, for reasons of comparability I make use of the data collected as part of the Central and Eastern Eurobarometer (CEEB) in a number of the emerging democracies of east central Europe during the same time period. For 1993 and 1994 the (western) Eurobarometer includes random national samples for Belgium, Denmark, France, (West) Germany, Greece, Ireland, Luxembourg, the Netherlands, Portugal, Spain, and the United Kingdom. For 1995, it also includes the new member states Austria, Finland, and Sweden. The CEEB surveys include data from Bulgaria, the Czech Republic, Hungary, Poland, and Slovakia.

System support is defined in a straightforward manner as citizens' satisfaction with democracy. Appropriately, the question wording for the system support measures differs slightly in Western and east central Europe in order to account for different political realities in these environments. Thus, citizens in the member states of the European Union were asked: 'On the whole, are you very satisfied, fairly satisfied, not very satisfied or not at all satisfied with the way democracy works in (our country)?' In central and eastern Europe, respondents were asked: 'On the whole, are you very satisfied, fairly satisfied, not very satisfied or not at all satisfied with the way democracy is developing in (our country)?' System support is measured by the percentage of respondents in a country who indicate that they are very or fairly satisfied with democracy.[32]

Satisfaction with democracy measures system support at a low level of abstraction. It does not refer to democracy as a set of norms, but to the functioning of the democratic political system.[33] Thus, it gauges people's responses to the process of democratic governance[34]; that is, a country's 'constitution in operation'[35] or its 'constitutional reality'.[36, 37]

---

[31] I use averages here to smooth out any temporary fluctuations that may exist in the data. Note, however, that the substantive conclusions are unchanged when I employ year-by-year data.

[32] Studies that have employed the democracy satisfaction measure as a dependent variable include C. J. Anderson, and C. A. Guillory, 'Political institutions and satisfaction with democracy: a cross-national analysis of consensus and majoritarian systems', *American Political Science Review*, 91,1 (1997), 66–81. H. D. Clarke, N. Dutt, and A. Kornberg, 'The political economy of attitudes toward polity and society in western European countries', *Journal of Politics*, 55 (1993), 998–1021. R. Harmel, and J. Robertson, 'Government stability and regime support: a cross-national analysis', *Journal of Politics*, 48 (1986),1029–40.

[33] For analyses of support for democratic norms in Eastern Europe and the former Soviet Union, see J. L. Gibson, 'A mile wide but an inch deep (?): The structure of democratic commitments in the former USSR', *American Journal of Political Science*, 40,2 (1996), 396–420. G. Evans, and S. Whitefield, 'The politics and economics of democratic commitment: support for democracy in transition societies', *British Journal of Political Science*, 25,4 (1995), 485–514.

[34] See F. Weil, 'The sources and structure of legitimation in western democracies'.

[35] J.-E. Lane, and S. Ersson, *Politics and Society in Western Europe*, 2nd ed. (London, Sage, 1991) p. 194.

[36] D. Fuchs, G. Guidorossi, and P. Svensson, 'Support for the Democratic System', In H.-D. Klingemann and Dieter Fuchs (eds) *Citizens and the State* (New York, Oxford University Press, 1995). p. 328.

[37] H. D. Clarke, and A. Kornberg, 'Support for the Canadian Federal Progressive Conservative Party since 1988: the impact of economic evaluations and economic issues', *Canadian Journal of Political Science*, 25 (1992), p. 47, n. 24; and A. Kornberg, and H. D. Clarke, 'Beliefs about democracy and satisfaction with democratic government: the Canadian case', *Political Research Quarterly*, 47 (1994), 537–63, report on a variety of tests designed to establish construct validity of the satisfaction with democracy question as an indicator of system support. They find that satisfaction with democracy is clearly an indicator of actual system support and *not* coterminous with support for the incumbent government. Similarly, Fuchs (D. Fuchs, 'Trends of political support', in D. Berg-Schlosser and R. Rytlewski (eds), *Political Culture in Germany* (New York,

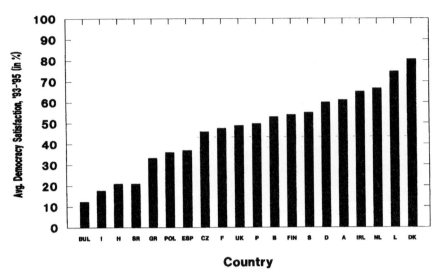

Figure 1. Democracy Satisfaction in Europe

This dependent variable is also useful for reasons of research design with regard to the number of cases that can be analysed. The Eurobarometer data used here are among the few available sources that permit an analysis of mass political support across a meaningful number of contemporary democracies. Moreover, they uniquely allow for comparative studies of attitudes that combine both established and emerging democracies. Figure 1 shows the distribution of responses across the countries included in this study, averaged over the 1993–95 period.

The graph shows clearly that democracy satisfaction in east central Europe is systematically lower than in the mature democracies of western and southern Europe. This holds true at both ends of the distribution. The highest levels of democracy satisfaction in western Europe can be found in countries such as Denmark, Luxembourg, and the Netherlands; they are about twice the level of the highest levels in central/eastern European states such as the Czech Republic and Poland. Conversely, the lowest levels of satisfaction in eastern Europe (e.g., Bulgaria) are roughly half that of the lowest levels in the west (e.g., Greece). Support ranges from 70–80% in the highest western nations to about 10–15% in the lowest eastern ones.

Attitudes toward democracy should differ somewhat across older and newer democratic systems because the emerging democratic systems have existed for only a fairly short period of time relative to the older democracies of the West. Given that they have not been able to develop deep reservoirs of diffuse system support, it should not be surprising that levels of satisfaction with democratic

St. Martin's), p. 242) examines the validity of the satisfaction with democracy indicator and finds that the results constitute 'a successful validation of the indicator as a measuring instrument for a generalized attitude towards the political system on the legitimacy dimension'. Weil ('Structure and Sources of Legitimation', pp.692–3) provides some indirect construct validity for the satisfaction with democracy indicator as well by reporting high positive correlations with political trust.

performance are consistently lower in central and eastern Europe than in the West.[38]

Electoral Institutions, Political Performance, and Democracy Satisfaction

Are electoral institutions, party performance, and party system performance related to levels of system support? That is, do different kinds of electoral institutions and political performance lead to systematically different levels of satisfaction with democratic performance, as hypothesized in Model 1? Moreover, do institutions – in the form of electoral laws – have a stronger impact than recent performance, or do they contribute equally to variation in democracy satisfaction across the democracies studied here?

These questions are of obvious relevance to our understanding of how democracies function. Most immediately, if there is only a weak link between how electoral institutions and organizations perform and how citizens evaluate the system as a whole, the central role of elections and parties in advanced democracies may be called into question. Conversely, if there is a link, policy makers and those who write the rules of the electoral game may want to know what the direction of these relationships are. After all, low levels of citizen support can pose serious problems for democratic systems because both the functioning and the maintenance of democratic polities are intimately linked with what and how citizens think about democratic governance.[39]

This is particularly the case for systems that are undergoing the transition to a more democratic political system. In contrast to the more stable democracies of western Europe, questions of popular support for the regime are particularly important for emerging democracies in Latin America and central and eastern Europe. In these systems citizen support for the political system is of practical and immediate relevance for the design and continued stability of democratic institutions.[40] Moreover, the relationships among electoral institutions, party system performance, and democracy satisfaction also will shed light on the question concerning the effects of institutions versus performance on citizen attitudes toward the political system. Put simply, can we explain cross-national differences in system support with the help of institutions, performance, or both?

To answer the question posed above, I again conducted correlation analyses between the institutional and performance variables on one hand, and levels of democracy satisfaction on the other. Table 6 shows the results.

The results indicate that the strongest correlations exist between proportionality (electoral system) and democracy satisfaction: the more proportional the electoral system, the higher the level of satisfaction. I also find that class voting is significantly and positively associated with democracy satisfaction: the higher the level of class voting, the higher the level of democracy satisfaction. This relationship is most significant when central/east European countries are

[38] G. Tóka, 'Political support in East-Central Europe', H.-D. Klingemann and D. Fuchs (eds), *Citizens and the State* (New York, Oxford University Press, 1995). For an overview, see A. H. Miller, V. L. Hesli, and W. M. Reisinger, 'Conceptions of democracy among mass and elite in post-soviet societies', *British Journal of Political Science*, 27 (1997), 157–90.

[39] S. M. Lipset, *Political Man: the Social Bases of Politics* (Garden City NY, Doubleday, 1959). G. B. Powell, *Contemporary Democracies*. G. B. Powell, 'Extremist parties and political turmoil: two puzzles', *American Journal of Political Science*, 30 (1986), 357–78.

[40] W. Mishler and R. Rose, 'Trust, distrust and skepticism: popular evaluations of civil and political institutions in post-communist societies', *Journal of Politics*, 59 (1997), 418–51.

TABLE 6. Pearson Correlations of Democracy Satisfaction with Electoral System and Party/Party System Performance

	Western Europe	All cases
Electoral system	0.74**	0.61***
	[N = 14]	[N = 19]
Effective no. of parties	0.38	0.31
	[N = 14]	[N = 19]
Volatility	−0.04	−0.56**
	[N = 14]	[N = 19]
Party membership	0.11	0.34
	[N = 12]	[N = 16]
Class voting	0.51*	0.79***
	[N = 12]	[N = 16]

$*p < 0.10$; $**p < 0.05$; $***p < 0.01$.

included in the analysis. Thus, both institutions and party performance appear to have strong effects on democracy satisfaction across the countries included in this study.

Regarding the associations of the other conditions with democracy satisfaction, the results suggest that levels of electoral volatility and democracy satisfaction are negatively related. However, this is only the case when the new democracies of east central Europe are included in the analysis. Levels of democracy satisfaction are thus lower when levels of electoral instability are particularly high; conversely, in those countries where election results are fairly stable over time, levels of satisfaction tend to be higher. However, these correlations are not nearly as strong as those found for electoral system and the party performance variables and should be treated with some caution.

Party system fragmentation (that is, *effective number of* parties) is positively related to democracy satisfaction. This suggests that levels of democracy satisfaction are marginally higher in systems that have parties which target segments of the electoral market. Thus, the results found here support Miller and Listhaug's view (and argue against Weil's) that a greater number of parties is, in fact, positively correlated with measures of system support. Thus, a greater probability for any one voter to find a political party that is fairly close to her/his true preferences is associated with higher levels of system support.

Finally, party membership levels are positively associated with levels of democracy satisfaction; a higher percentage of citizens is active in political parties in countries that display higher levels of democracy satisfaction. Despite recent disenchantment with political parties across a number of European democracies, these results indicate that closer linkages between citizens and individual political parties – the prime organizational vehicle for political representation in modern democracies – are associated with positive results in terms of citizen satisfaction with political performance.

Conclusions and Implications

This essay examines the interrelationships among electoral institutions, party and party system performance, and citizens' support for democratic governance from a cross-national perspective. Starting with the assumption that electoral institutions condition the development and dynamics of party systems as well as parties themselves, and the notion that party and party system performance affect how citizens evaluate democratic performance, the analysis tested these relationships with recent data collected in 19 democracies of western, southern, and east central Europe.

On the basis of directly comparable survey evidence and data on party system performance collected between 1993 and 1995, this article examined the determinants of cross-national differences in democratic support in both old and new democracies; that is, the 15 member states of the European Union as well as several of the emerging democracies of east central Europe. I investigated whether and to what extent electoral rules and party system performance help us understand differences in levels of satisfaction with the political system in both old and new democracies.

Regarding the relationship of electoral institutions and party/party system performance, the empirical analysis indicated that more proportional electoral systems are associated with higher levels of party system fragmentation and a closer link between parties and their voters. Furthermore, systems with a greater number of parties have higher levels of class voting and party membership, the party system also tends to have a greater number of parties. Conversely, in systems with high levels of class voting and party membership, electoral volatility tends to be lower.

The empirical analysis also demonstrated that electoral institutions affect democracy satisfaction more than either party or party system performance. Thus, institutional factors – such as electoral system types – are, in fact, better predictors of whether citizens are supportive of democratic governance than is current political performance of the party system. The results also showed that, among the performance measures, party performance (class voting) was the best indicator of differences in democracy satisfaction across contemporary democracies. Coupled with the negative relationship of electoral volatility on democracy satisfaction, we can thus conclude that systems where electoral dealignment has taken place or is taking place have lower levels of democracy satisfaction than those where voters' ties with political parties are relatively stable.

Overall, these results show that different attributes of democratic governance – electoral systems along with party and party system performance – move together in systematic and predictable ways. Moreover, these syndromes of democratic politics systematically affect how citizens perceive the functioning of democratic institutions. Perhaps most importantly, these relationships hold in both mature and emerging democracies, lending greater validity to our theories of how democracies function.

Finally, this essay extends an existing and developing research agenda that examines the relationships among political institutions and political/democratic performance on one hand, and citizens' attitudes about the political system on the other.[41] Building on work in political economy and the comparative study of

---

[41] C. J. Anderson, and C. A. Guillory, 'Political institutions and satisfaction with democracy'. P. Norris, 'Designing democracies: Institutional arrangements and system support', Paper presented at the JFK School of Government Workshop on Confidence in Democratic Institutions: America in Comparative Perspective, 25–27 August 1997, Washington D.C.

political institutions, this line of research has only recently begun to systematically investigate the interrelations of institutions, performance – both political and economic – and system support. This analysis has shown that electoral institutions in particular are an important factor to consider in this context. While the relationship between party system performance and democracy satisfaction was more ambiguous, this analysis should be taken to be more suggestive than definitive, and further research into this web of interrelations is clearly warranted in order to gain a more complete understanding of the functioning of modern democracies.

Appendix: Descriptive Statistics of the Variables Used in the Analysis

	Minimum	Maximum	Mean	Std. Dev.	N
Proportionality of electoral system[a]	79.11	97.83	91.00	6.47	19
Effective no. of parl. parties[b]	2.17	7.95	3.75	1.40	19
Volatility[c]	5.10	27.60	14.23	7.60	19
Party membership (as % of electorate)[d]	1.50	21.80	6.68	6.51	16
Class voting[e]	0.03	0.21	0.14	0.05	16
Democracy satisfaction[f]	12.33	80.40	48.57	18.32	19

Sources:

[a]A. Lijphart, *Electoral Systems and Party Systems: a Study of Twenty-Seven Democracies* (New York, Oxford University Press, 1994), Appendix B; own calculations on the basis of data reported in *European Journal of Political Research* (various issues).

[b]L. LeDuc, R. Niemi, and P. Norris, *Comparing Democracies: Elections and Voting in Global Perspective* (London, Sage, 1996), Table 1.4. Most recent election only.

[c]P. Mair, *Party System Change* (Oxford, Clarendon, 1997), Table 8.1; own calculations on the basis of data reported in *European Journal of Political Research* (various issues).

[d]P. Mair, *Party System Change* (Oxford, Clarendon, 1997), Table 8.2.

[e]Dalton (1996, Table 13.1) and G. Tóka, 'Parties and Electoral Choices in East-Central Europe', in G. Pridham and P. Lewis (eds), *Stabilising Fragile Democracies: Comparing New Party Systems in Southern and Eastern Europe* (London, Routledge, 1995), Table 4.4 and own calculations.

[f]Eurobarometers (39–44) and Central and Eastern Eurobarometers (4–6).

Party Appeals and Voter Loyalty in New Democracies

GÁBOR TÓKA*

Introduction

Some parties obviously have a more stable electoral basis than others. Is this so because of differences in the way they appeal to their voters? If such is the case, does it help explain why some countries have less volatility (that is, voters changing their vote or voting intention between two points in time) than others? Supposing that all these questions can be answered in the affirmative, why would the factors cementing the party loyalty of voters be relevant for empirical democratic theory? These are the questions confronted in this essay.

The first section discusses the theoretical and practical significance of electoral volatility. What is argued is not that political parties aim at low volatility, but that it may improve the quality of democracy if they nevertheless achieve that. The second section briefly indicates that the most frequently marshalled explanations (party allegiances inherited from a distant democratic past, instability of institutions, party fragmentation, the organizational style of parties) leave unexplained some of the noteworthy variations in electoral volatility between Poland, the Czech Republic, Hungary, and Slovakia. The balance of the paper investigates whether the way parties appeal to their voters may offer an explanation of volatility or its opposite, party loyalty.

The third section elaborates on this often heard but so far untested explanation, and I develop some related hypotheses. The fourth section presents an empirical test of some aspects of the theory. Following an innovative study by Oddbjørn Knutsen and Elinor Scarbrough, several alternative types of party-voter linkages are distinguished conceptually and empirically. The Knutsen-Scarbrough methodology is further developed to estimate the extent to which an individual is a 'cleavage', 'value' or 'structural' voter. Finally, panel data are utilized to assess which of these three voter types are most likely to be steadfast supporters of their parties.[1]

* I would like to thank the editor, Peter Mair, participants at a faculty seminar at the Central European University's Political Science Department, and the workshop on Issue Ownership convened by Hans Anker at the 25th Joint Session and Workshops of the ECPR and, above all, I thank Iván Csaba and Cees van der Eijk for their helpful comments on earlier drafts.

[1] The data used in this study, unless otherwise noted, come from a series of mass surveys conducted by the Central European University (CEU), *The Development of Party Systems and Electoral Alignments in East Central Europe*, Machine readable data files (Budapest, Department of Political Science, Central European University, 1992–96). The surveys have been carried out since Fall 1992 with the assistance of one of the major commercial political polling institutes in each country: CBOS in Poland, STEM in the Czech Republic and Slovakia, and Median in Hungary. The samples were representative for the non-institutionalised adult population of the respective countries. In Poland we used clustered random sampling, with sample sizes of 1149, 1188, 1468, 1209, 1162, 1173, and again 1173 in the successive waves. In the Czech Republic and Slovakia we

The Implications of High Electoral Volatility

Aggregate level or *net* volatility means half the sum of the absolute percentage differences between the votes received by each party in two consecutive elections. Suppose that there are three parties contesting the first of two elections. The first two receive 40% of the vote each, and the third gets 20%. If the last one goes out of business by the time of the next election, and the remaining two receive 60 and 40% of the vote, respectively, then the total volatility between the two elections was $(|60 - 40| + |40 - 40| + |20 - 0|)/2 = 20\%$. *Individual* level or *gross* volatility means the percentage of 'voters' (e.g. survey respondents who expressed a party preference) changing their voting preference from one point in time to another. Theoretically, individual level and aggregate volatility may vary independently: movements of voters into various directions may cancel out each other on the aggregate, and temporal changes in the composition of the active electorate may cause net shifts even in the absence of any gross change. However, a recent review of the available West European data and a computer simulation concluded that empirically they are closely related (their Pearson correlation is between 0.60 and 0.70).[2]

Volatility is an important dimension of party system stabilization and institutionalization.[3] The lower it is, the more likely that in the electoral arena the established party labels (brand names) have some value independent from the appeal of the parties' present leaders, issue positions, record, and scandals. Consequently, disgruntled political entrepreneurs and interest groups need to work through the established parties, whose elites are likely to have already developed some commitment to – and stakes in – the existing political system. In contrast, high electoral volatility cannot help suggesting to the elite that there is no positive payoff on sticking to a currently unpopular party label. The easy access to the media by parliamentarians and other notables, the skills of a well-paid campaign staff, the personal appeal of some new faces, anti-establishment rhetoric or the attraction of a well selected bundle of positions on some topical issues may all prove more important electoral assets than does an established trade mark.

Historical experience suggests a negative relationship between democratic consolidation and electoral volatility. In West European elections between 1885 and 1985, average aggregate volatility was 8.6%.[4] New or unstable democracies have usually had much higher volatility. In the first elections after authoritarian rule, postwar Germany, Italy, Greece, Portugal, and Spain experienced a 13–19% volatility.[5] In the elections in the Weimar Republic aggregate volatility was 32, 27, 10, 13, 22, 21, 6, and 11 (beware that the three lowest figures in the

---

started with clustered random sampling but switched to quota from 1993. The Czech sample sizes were 815, 939, 1117, 1562, 1515, 1291, 1569, 1443, and 1595, and in Slovakia the samples included 712, 920, 871, 845, 757, 1213, and 1027 respondents. In the Hungarian studies the Ns have been 1200 (1196 in June 1995), and the method of sampling clustered random route. The dates of the surveys are shown in the tables.

[2] Bartolini and Mair, *Identity, Competition, and Electoral Availability*, pp. 27–34.

[3] Here much of my reasoning follows P. Mair, 'What is different about post-communist party systems?', *Studies in Public Policy*, 259. (Glasgow, University of Strathclyde, Centre for the Study of Public Policy, 1996).

[4] Bartolini and Mair, *Identity, Competition, and Electoral Availability*, p. 69. Elections in Portugal, Greece and Spain are not included.

[5] P. Mair, 'What is different …'.

series are based on the comparisons of the two 1924, the two 1932, and the November 1932 and March 1933 elections respectively, each pair of which were separated only by a few months).[6] A similar pattern was observed in Latin America. In legislative elections between 1970 and 1990 the average aggregate volatility was below 20% in those countries that, by around 1990, had developed relatively stable democratic institutions, in contrast to a level above 30% in the more fragile democracies of Bolivia, Ecuador, Brazil and Peru.[7]

Precise data from contemporary Eastern Europe are hard to come by as the vote returns for the smaller parties are usually not available in accessible sources. But the few available estimates paint a rather dramatic picture. Estonia, with a 54% net volatility between 1992 and 1995, is in the same league with the Peru of the 1970s and 1980s. Poland, with 34.5% net volatility between 1991 and 1993, looks similar to Bolivia or Ecuador. Somewhat more stable are Hungary, with 28.3% net volatility between 1990 and 1994, the Czech Republic, at 22.0 and 31.4% 1990–92 and 1992–96 volatility, respectively, and Slovakia, with 23.1 and 23.8% 1990–92 and 1992–94. Nevertheless, all of these countries are, by the standards of consolidated democracies, simply off the mark.[8]

It has been powerfully argued that party institutionalization, and a consequently low electoral volatility, is a critical independent variable influencing the pace of democratic consolidation.[9] A recent paper on the Spanish, Portuguese and Greek transitions to democracy, as well as an analysis of the four Visegrad countries took issue with this view and suggested that democratic consolidation may be a cause of (and thus precede), rather than a consequence of (and therefore preceded by) party institutionalization.[10]

For reasons that were detailed elsewhere, I believe that volatility and democratic consolidation are not very closely related in east central Europe.[11] Indeed, a very low electoral volatility may signal polarization caused by an extreme emotional hostility between the main party camps, or a high frequency of elections – neither of which is normally associated with high political legitimacy. But it seems widely accepted that the accountability of elected office holders and their responsiveness to their constituents are strengthened by party institutionalization. The latter means some stabilization of the party alternatives and their respective shares of the electoral market. A very low electoral volatility and the virtual certainty that no new party can possibly expect success may

[6] Bartolini and Mair, *Identity, Competition, and Electoral Availability*, Appendix 2.
[7] S. Mainwaring and T. Scully, 'Introduction: Party Systems in Latin America', in S. Mainwaring and T. R. Scully (eds), *Building Democratic Institutions: Party Systems in Latin America* (Stanford CA, Stanford University Press, 1994), p. 8.
[8] On volatility in the four Visegrad countries see G. Tóka, 'Political parties and democratic consolidation in east central Europe', *Studies in Public Policy*, 279 (Glasgow, University of Strathclyde, forthcoming in February 1997). Note that from the herein reported Czech, Slovak and Polish volatility figures mere changes of party labels were discounted.
[9] Cf. Mair, 'What is different ...'; Mainwaring and Scully, 'Introduction: Party Systems in Latin America'.
[10] L. Morlino, 'Political Parties and Democratic Consolidation in Southern Europe', in R. Gunther, P. N. Diamandouros and H. Puhle (eds), *The Politics of Democratic Consolidation: Southern Europe in Comparative Perspective* (Baltimore MD, The Johns Hopkins University Press, 1995), pp. 315–388; Tóka, 'Political parties and democratic consolidation'. The two studies also agreed that the direction of the causal relationship may be contingent upon the initial legitimacy of the democratic regime and the international environment of democratisation.
[11] Cf. G. Tóka, 'Political parties and democratic consolidation'.

cause political *immobilisme*. A moderate amount of volatility, which is enough to cause shifts of governmental and legislative power, is clearly important for making party leaders responsive to their broader following. But new democracies appear to have much more volatility than that, and this excess can also undermine electoral accountability. For the ordinary voters, it is next to impossible to monitor (not to speak about anticipate) the voting record of individual legislators,[12] and independent-minded legislators are often uninterested in re-election anyway.[13] On these counts, new parties may be fairly similar to independent legislators. At the very least, they cannot be judged on the basis of their previous record. Consequently, the credibility of their promises is difficult to evaluate. The higher the underlying volatility is believed to be, the more new parties are likely to be started; the more votes are cast for new parties and independent candidates, the weaker the electoral accountability of incumbent office-holders.

New parties, however, do not necessarily bring in new faces. A low expected payoff from sticking to old labels may lead veteran politicians to undermine electoral accountability by constantly regrouping under ever-new flags. Furthermore, if volatility is exorbitant while party ideologies remain largely stable, politicians may lose whatever little faith they used to have in the electoral impact of their policy offerings. I know of no evidence that would suggest that a 10% electoral penalty for a financial or sex scandal would make politicians more risk averse than a 1% loss. It seems plausible that the more severe these penalties are, the less easy it is for politicians to appreciate the electoral impact of policy choices. Quite clearly, an extremely strong party loyalty in large parts of the electorate may make any alternation of government and opposition unlikely. But given the above cited evidence about electoral volatility in new democracies, this theoretical possibility is sufficiently remote that it need not interest us in the present context.

To conclude this section: High volatility may occasionally be an instrument of electoral control, and some scepticism is warranted regarding its alleged regime-destabilizing potential. Yet, a constant and predictable weakness of party loyalties may undermine the accountability and responsiveness of elected office-holders. Hence, parties and party systems can make an unintended contribution to the quality of democracy by so behaving that the expected electoral volatility is kept on a low level.[14]

Conventional Explanations of Volatility

This section summarizes briefly some findings on whether the age and organizational style of parties, the level of party fragmentation, and the stability of

---

[12] M. Fiorina, 'Party Government in the United States: Diagnosis and Prognosis', in R. Katz (ed.), *Party Government: European and American Experiences* (Berlin and New York, Walter de Gruyter, 1987), pp. 270–300.

[13] K. Prewitt, 'Political ambitions, volunteerism, and electoral accountability', *American Political Science Review*, 61 (1970), 5–17.

[14] That is, on the lowest possible level which still keeps the probability of an alternation of government and opposition on a level providing sufficient incentives for politicians to court the electorate.

electoral institutions can influence electoral volatility.[15] Before we can assess the importance of these variables, the cross-national differences in voters' party loyalty (that is, the dependent variable) have to be clarified. Given the differences in the electoral calendars of different countries, individual level data about gross volatility offer an arguably more reliable and detailed picture than do the aggregate net level election outcomes.

Table 1 shows survey data about the temporal stability of electoral preferences in east central Europe. Although these data somewhat overstate stability (see the notes to Table 1), the displayed figures are nevertheless much lower than those found in Western democracies.[16] In the way of intra-regional comparison, the table suggests a relatively clear ranking of the four countries. At least for most of the 1992–95 period, Czechs and Slovaks had more stable party loyalties than Hungarians, and Hungarians more stable ones than Poles (compare any two rows referring to surveys taken in different countries after similarly long times after elections).

How can we account for this ranking of the countries? Obviously, the age of the democratic system may go some way to explain, in general, why new democracies tend to have unusually high volatility. But the number of elections since the recent transition to democracy and the sheer passing of the time do not explain all the between-country variations apparent in Table 1. Note, for instance, that in June 1991, just a year after the first election, there was no more gross electoral volatility in the Czech Republic than in June 1995 in Hungary, a year after the second election.

A similarly plausible reason for the weakness of party loyalties in east central Europe could be the novelty of most parties. Mainwaring and Scully note that in the early 1990s, in all of the better institutionalized party systems in Latin America the percentage of lower chamber seats held by parties established before 1950 was between 56 and 98%, whereas in the more volatile party systems of Brazil, Bolivia, Peru and Ecuador such parties only controlled 0.6–40% of the seats.[17] The east central European countries appear to be closer to this latter group. Among the presently significant parties, only the Polish Peasant Party (PSL), the Communist Party of Bohemia and Moravia (KSCM), and the Christian democratic Czech People's Party (CSL) have maintained significant continuity of organization since the late forties. This factor alone was no guarantee of social entrenchment. The similarly 'historical' Czech Socialist Party (CSS) and the Polish Democratic Party (SD) retained just a minimal electorate and were soon discontinued after the transition to democracy.

Yet, columns two and three of Table 1 show that the constituencies of the historical parties showed greater party loyalty than other voters throughout the entire period covered by the CEU surveys. Since the three historical parties are, certainly not by chance, also the only real mass parties in the region (their membership figures are by far the highest), it is difficult to tell whether a party's historical continuity or the organizational encapsulation of its voters is more effective in stabilizing a (narrow) electoral basis. One or the other apparently

---

[15] This section is a heavily condensed and somewhat modified version of sections 3 to 6 of Tóka, 'Political parties and democratic consolidation'.

[16] See I. Crewe, and D. Denver (eds), *Electoral Change in Western Democracies: Patterns and Sources of Electoral Volatility* (Beckenham, Croom Helm, 1985).

[17] Mainwaring and Scully, 'Introduction: Party Systems in Latin America', p. 13.

TABLE 1. *Surveys of Party Loyalty in Four New Democracies

| Survey date | % Standpatters among voters of: | | | Months since election |
	All parties	New parties	Historical parties	
Czech Republic				
Dec. 90	70	67	82	6
June 91	69	67	74	12
Dec. 91	66	64	71	18
Sep. 92	78	75	90	3
Apr. 93	67	65	76	10
Nov. 93	65	64	70	17
Apr. 94	61	58	72	22
Nov. 94	60	56	72	29
June 95	61	56	81	36
Jan. 96	66	61	85	43
Apr. 96	61	59	68	46
May 96	58	54	70	47
Slovakia (All parties treated as 'new')				
Dec. 90	–	75	–	6
June 91	–	57	–	12
Dec. 91	–	63	–	18
Sep. 92	–	76	–	3
Apr. 93	–	65	–	10
Nov. 93	–	61	–	17
Apr. 94	–	60	–	22
July 95	–	79	–	10
Apr. 96	–	77	–	19
Poland				
Oct. 92	51	48	71	12
Jan. 93	60	53	93	15
Aug. 93	43	40	63	23
Apr. 94	76	71	88	8
Dec. 94	73	70	80	16
June 95	59	56	68	21
Dec. 95	49	51	42	27
Hungary (All parties treated as 'new')				
Sep. 92	–	50	–	29
Jan. 93	–	51	–	33
Dec. 93	–	47	–	44
Apr. 94	–	44	–	49
June 95	–	69	–	13

Note: Table entries in the first column from the left show the proportion of respondents who expressed a voting intention – 'if there were an election next weekend' – for the same party that they voted for in the last parliamentary election, in percentage of all voters in the last election. The third and second columns show the same figure for all historical and for the other (that is, the new) parties, respectively. The 'historical' parties are defined by the uninterrupted continuity of their grass-roots organization, and thus they are the Czech People's Party (CSL), the Czech Socialists Party (CSS), the the Communist Party of Bohemia and Moravia (KSCM), and the Polish Peasant Party (PSL). In Hungary and Slovakia there are no historical parties. The respondents who would have rather not voted, or did not know which party to support 'if there were an election next weekend' are excluded from the computation of the percentages. The same applies for respondents who did not tell or did not know which party they voted for in the last election. The data on participation and vote in the last election are based on the respondents' recall, and are thus likely to overstate the percentage of 'standpatters'. Those respondents who ('next weekend') would have voted for a (new) party (e.g., in Poland, Freedom Union, UW) which had absorbed the party (e.g. the Liberal Democratic Congress, KLD, the Democratic Union, UD) they had reportedly voted in the last election are counted as standpatters. Similarly, the Czech respondents who recalled voting for the Liberal Social Union (LSU) in 1992 and named the Agrarian Party (ZS) or CSS as their current preference, or recalled voting for the Left Bloc (LB) in 1992 and at the time of the survey preferred the KSCM were counted as standpats. In the 1990 and 1991 Czech data responses naming the Civic Forum (OF), Liberal Democratic Party (LDS), Club of Non-partisan Citizens (KAN), Civic Democratic Party (ODS), Civic Movement (OH), Civic Democratic Alliance (ODA), and Romani Civic Initiative (ROI) were collapsed; so were references to the Movement for a Democratic Slovakia (HZDS), Publice Against Violence (VPN), Independent Hungarian Initiative (FMK) and Civic Democratic Union (ODU) in the 1990-1991 Slovak data.
Source: The 1990–91 data come from surveys of clustered random sample of the adult population of Slovakia and the Czech Republic by the Prague-based STEM research institute. All other data come from the Central European University (CEU) surveys.

does the trick, and it is also clear that the communist regimes deprived virtually all parties of both. Equally clearly, these criteria cannot account either for Poland's relatively high volatility, or for the similarity between the Czech and Slovak volatility figures.

Using a multivariate framework, Bartolini and Mair's monumental study identified five factors as important determinants of the magnitude of electoral change:[18]

- institutional changes (that is, of the electoral system and franchise)
- significant changes in turnout
- the number of parties
- religious and ethnic heterogeneity and
- the membership of left-wing parties.

Taken together, these factors go a long way towards explaining the unusually high electoral volatility of east central Europe in general, and of Poland in particular. Among the four Visegrad countries left party membership is the highest in the Czech Republic, and Slovakia is the only one which has a noteworthy ethno-religious heterogeneity (with 11% Hungarian population). In contrast, while Poland can claim absolutely negligible ethno-religious heterogeneity or party membership figures, it has the most significant changes in election law and the highest fragmentation of parties in any of the four countries. Clearly, the greater the number of parties, the more likely that voters will find an ideologically proximate party for the sake of which they can abandon their previous partisanship (no matter how strong it was). In the 1991 and 1993 Polish elections, the fractionalization of the vote was excessive by any standards. Hungarian, Czech and Slovak elections did not differ a lot in this respect, they all produced a lesser fragmentation of the vote than the two Polish elections, but appreciably more than the post-war average in any West European democracy.[19]

However, the volatility-boosters identified by Bartolini and Mair fail to explain why Slovak parties had more loyal voters than did the Hungarian parties in the 1992–95 period. Even if we assume that the ethnic cleavage reduced the volatility of minority voters in Slovakia, their proportion in the total population and the impact of ethnic-heterogeneity on volatility – according to Bartolini and Mair's analysis[20] – are so small that this factor cannot possibly explain why Hungary had greater electoral instability than Slovakia, despite Hungary's arguably greater stability of electoral institutions,[21] similar party fractionalization, and much smaller change of turnout.[22] Similarly, the

---

[18] See Bartolini and Mair, *Identity, Competition, and Electoral Availability*, pp. 254–85.

[19] Cf. Tóka, 'Political parties and democratic consolidation'.

[20] Cf. Bartolini and Mair, *Identity, Competition, and Electoral Availability*, pp. 276 and 229 on the controlled effect and the bivariate relationship, respectively.

[21] The marginal changes in the electoral law were a little more significant in Slovakia than in Hungary. Furthermore, the emergence of entirely new parties and the total disappearance of others generated more movement of votes in Slovakia and in the Czech Republic than in Hungary (cf. Tables 2 and 4 of Tóka, 'Political parties and democratic consolidation'). Similarly, almost all the more significant Slovak parties that were founded or reborn in 1990–91 eventually split along a line dividing more radical nationalists and moderates, while the Hungarian six party system remained proverbially 'stable'.

[22] Turnout increased by 4% in Hungary between 1990 and 1994 and by 9% in Poland between the 1991 and 1993 elections, but decreased by 12% between 1990 and 1992 and by another 8–9% between 1992 and the third elections in both the Czech Republic and in Slovakia.

voter/member ratio may give a highly plausible explanation of the stronger loyalty of the voters of the Czech than of the Hungarian ex-communists. Yet, the propositions that have so far been put on the table hardly account for why the entirely new or discontinuous-historical Czech parties have more stable voters than do their Hungarian counterparts.

Cleavage and Value Voting

One of the most frequently heard assertions about electoral politics in east central Europe goes like this: '... [the Czech party system] is anchored neither in a social nor in an interest structure, and that is why the parties do not have regular voters ... This unanchored system of parties will for a long time not be a support, but rather a danger for democracy'.[23] This section addresses the proposition that the stronger (A) the mobilization of cleavages, and/or (B) value voting in a country, the less volatile are voting intentions.

At the heart of both propositions is the intuition that certain motives or causes of individual voting decisions are likely to cement party attachments more firmly than others. This intuition is clearly captured in the concept of 'cleavage', and this, indeed, may well be *the* reason why this obscure concept has become so popular among analysts of electoral behaviour and political parties. There is little agreement in the scholarly literature about precisely what 'cleavage' means,[24] but there is an apparent consensus on what its most important consequence in electoral politics can be. Simply by talking of 'cleavage' instead of the more ordinary alternatives like 'division' or 'opposition', most scholars seem to stress that there is something puzzling in the persistence and intensity of some political conflicts, which cannot be explained by reference solely to the instrumental rationality of the individual actors.

The persistence of social structures can be one source of this endurance of partisan attachment. Quite obviously, conflicts between rich and poor are likely reproduced over and over again, at least as long as income taxation is a major source of government revenues. But ever since the publication of Lipset and Rokkan's classic essay, 'cleavage' has meant more than merely the persistent reproduction of a conflict line through current issues over a long period of time. The much cited, though excessively enigmatic *freezing* hypothesis (that is, that the party systems of the 1970s reflected, 'with few, but significant exceptions' the party systems of the 1920s) was to stress exactly that the mobilization of cleavages made West European party systems resistant to sweeping social

---

[23] Brokl, Lubomír, 'Between November 1989 and democracy – antinomies of our politics', *Czechoslovak Sociological Review*, 28, Special Issue (1992), 33.

[24] As Meisel once noted, in their 1967 classic on cleavages, Lipset and Rokkan use 'cleavage' interchangeably with 'contrast', 'conflict', 'opposition' and 'strain'; see J. Meisel, *Cleavages, Parties and Values in Canada* (Beverly Hills, Sage, 1974), p. 6. Very often cleavage means any persistent issue dimension that divides the parties in a country and which keeps being reproduced (through different issues) over a longer period of time (see e.g. I. McAllister and S. White, 'Democracy, political parties and party formation in post-communist Russia', *Party Politics*, 1 1995, 49–72). Others equate cleavages with group-based political divisions – cf. those studies which try to explore the influence of cleavages on electoral behaviour by looking at the strength of association between various socio-demographic criteria and party choice (see e.g. M. N. Franklin, T. Mackie, H. Valen with C. Bean *et al.*, *Electoral Change: Responses to Evolving Social and Attitudinal Structures in Western Countries* (Cambridge, Cambridge University Press, 1992)).

changes, even though the latter 'have made the old established alternatives increasingly *irrelevant*'.[25]

What could make electoral alignments relatively immune to social change? To spare the concept from inflated use, both Bartolini and Mair and Knutsen and Scarbrough have recently advocated a more faithful following of what they believe Stein Rokkan's implicit definition of a *cleavage* to have been.[26] Both Bartolini and Mair, on the one hand, and Knutsen and Scarbrough, on the other, ended up with a three-dimensional definition which incorporates socio-structural, normative and organizational elements. In other words, they argue that it is only admissible to talk of a *cleavage* if an enduring organizational form is given to a politically mobilized opposition between such members of relatively closed social groups who have distinct values, beliefs and identity. The requirement of social closure implies that only a few quasi-demographic differences (class, ethno-religious or regional identity, urban-rural residence) can serve as the bases of cleavages.

A great advantage of this definition is that it immediately explains why cleavages could produce more electoral stability than what would be expected in their absence: the temporal stability of value preferences, organizational encapsulation, and the relative political homogeneity (in terms of party preferences) of the social environment may make some voters resistant to impulses that would otherwise be sufficient to bring them under different banners. Knutsen and Scarbrough stress, in particular, the role of value conflicts in the making of cleavages: and this helps one to understand persistence too, since the general value conflicts can be invoked daily, even also on issues where only a few voters are sufficiently strongly affected in terms of their immediate interests so as to make them alarmed.[27] Value references and invocation of group solidarity can thus help to keep a substantial part of the mass following in a more or less constant state of ideological mobilization along a given cleavage line.

The equally obvious disadvantage of these complex definitions stems from the problems they pose for measurement. Bartolini and Mair are forced to give up making any attempt at measuring the normative aspect of cleavage strength ('the cultural distinctiveness' of the values characterizing the consciousness and identity of any given group), and they do not manage to design an appropriate measure for the social (as opposed to the organizational) basis of the class cleavage. Since they work with survey data instead of long term trends in aggregate electoral statistics, Knutsen and Scarbrough can utilize supposedly appropriate data on both the social and the cultural–ideological (that is, value) homogeneity of the various parties' electorates. Furthermore, they reject the idea that the relationship between the three elements of cleavage could be additive. Bartolini and Mair allow for the possibility that 'the three elements

[25] S. M. Lipset and S. Rokkan, 'Cleavage Structures, Party Systems and Voter Alignments. Introduction', in S. M. Lipset and S. Rokkan (eds), *Party Systems and Voter Alignments. Cross-National Perspectives* (New York, Free, 1967), p. 54, emphasis added.

[26] Bartolini and Mair, *Identity, Competition, and Electoral Availability*; O. Knutsen and E. Scarbrough, 'Cleavage Politics', in J. van Deth and E. Scarbrough (eds), *The Impact of Values* (Oxford, Oxford University Press, 1995), pp. 492–523.

[27] Suffice here to refer to D. Sears, C. Hensler, and L. Speer's work on the symbolic aspects of political issues, see their 'Whites' opposition to "busing": self-interest or symbolic politics?', *American Political Science Review*, 73 (1979), 369–84.

[of cleavage] may vary quite autonomously in the cases of both existing and emerging cleavages. For example, it is possible that a cleavage may become enfeebled in terms of its social-structural basis without necessarily experiencing a similar decay at the ideological or organizational level.'[28]

Knutsen and Scarbrough counter that this 'set[s] no limits on how far any, or all, of the three elements may vary before a form of cleavage politics ceases to constitute cleavage politics and becomes some other form of politics'. They posit a multiplicative relationship between the three elements: 'cleavage politics entails that members of an identifiable social group adhere to the values associated with that group and vote for a party identified with that group and advocating those values'.[29] They submit that the structural bases of cleavage politics – that is, the impact of class and religion on voting preferences – have been declining in the process of social and technological modernization, and an individualistic 'value voting' has been on the rise. However, they add, what really declines is 'pure structural' voting – workers voting for left wing, Catholics voting for the Christian party, or middle-class voters opting for liberal or conservative parties, even if their values would not make that choice any more likely than others. Parallel to this, 'pure value' voting is rising, that is, party choice becomes more congruent with values even if neither are reinforced by membership in a relatively closed socio-demographic group in which their values and partisan preference are dominant. But as long as the normative (value), structural (demographic) and organizational (party) elements of a cleavage remain correlated, the two processes counterbalance each other and the strength of the old cleavages may remain practically unaffected.

From this, Knutsen and Scarbrough proceed to develop a novel measurement of 'cleavage', 'structural' and 'value' voting that will be utilized in the next section. Note at this point that their reasoning implies two explanations for a puzzle of east central European electoral politics – namely why comparatively high levels of aggregate electoral volatility and frequent complaints about the weak embeddedness of political parties in the system of societal conflicts go together with relatively strong correlations between a number of demographic variables and party choice.[30]

Firstly, Klingemann and Wattenberg argued that voters in the new east European democracies can much more easily collect and process credible, reliable and consistent information about the socio-cultural background of the elites of the various parties (e.g. in terms of their generational, religious, or professional background) than about their policy commitments, competence, etc. Thus, even though the latter may be the more salient information, its short supply makes people vote more congruently with their demographic background than with their broadly conceived policy preferences. As more, and more credible information about party policies becomes available at affordable prices, voters will change their loyalties accordingly. Thus voters may shift allegiance based on who candidates *are* to what policies candidates *stand for*. A high initial volatility of the vote can thus be the result of the same factor that

[28] Bartolini and Mair, *Identity, Competition, and Electoral Availability*, p. 210.

[29] O. Knutsen, and E. Scarbrough, 'Cleavage Politics and Value Conflicts'. Paper presented at the meeting of Group 4 of the 'Beliefs in Government' project of the European Science Foundation in Paris, 1993.

[30] See G. Tóka, 'Parties and Electoral Choices in East Central Europe', in P. Lewis and G. Pridham (eds) *Stabilising Fragile Democracies* (London, Routledge, 1996), pp. 115–7.

caused the relatively strong impact of demographic variables on party choice previously.[31]

The second explanation offered by the above conceptualization of cleavage is that only certain socio-demographic divisions can become the social basis of cleavages: religious denomination, ethnicity, social class, the urban-rural differentiation, and probably not much else. The argument is that religiosity (conventionally measured by church attendance), education, and age, for instance, lack that kind of social closure and/or temporal stability which are necessary preconditions for the functioning of the freezing effect. On this latter score, both Knutsen and Scarbrough and Bartolini and Mair fully agree. Incidentally, their examples (church attendance, age, education) are exactly those background variables that are the most likely to be important correlates of party choice in these early years of the democratic experiment in east central Europe.[32]

Thus, high electoral volatility and relatively strong correlations between some socio-demographic variables and party choice do not necessarily preclude each other. What about 'pure value voting'? While they do not address the question of volatility, Knutsen and Scarbrough's argument points to the proposition that cleavages do and 'pure value voting' probably does not turn voters into a captive audience. For instance, they stress that 'in our view, materialist-postmaterialist opposition is about value conflict unencumbered by the immo-bilities of cleavage politics. Whereas the cleavage model suggests a relatively robust structuring of mass politics, the "new politics" perspective points to the more fluid, volatile relationship between social groups, value orientations, and party preferences which might be expected of a politics unanchored in cleavages'.[33]

All in all, my reading of the cleavage literature suggests the following hypotheses:

(1) *Group Membership and Party Loyalty*: a probabilistic relationship between membership in a social group and party preference will lend above average endurance to the initial party preference of those individuals, whose party preference, at the beginning of the observed period, did not contradict but rather strengthened this probabilistic relationship between group membership and party choice (hypothesis 1). The rationale of this proposition is twofold. First, group conflicts have some persistence, and membership in a social class or church is more stable than say voters' positions on particular issues or their personal evaluations of the competence of various party leaders. Second, Bartolini and Mair argue that the closure of social relationships – that is, that individuals belonging to a given class, religion, and place of residence, are exposed to interaction with people who tend to have the same partisanship – cements party preferences beyond the degree that could be explained by the direct appeal of the parties to the individual voters. Indeed, previous American scholarship points to some environmental influences on the direction of the

---

[31] See H. Klingemann and M. Wattenberg, 'Decaying versus developing party systems: a comparison of party images in the United States and West Germany', *British Journal of Political Science*, 22 (1992), 131–49.

[32] Tóka, 'Parties and electoral choices'.

[33] Knutsen and Scarbrough, 'Cleavage Politics', p. 497.

vote.[34] What is not clear, however, is whether these environmental influences can also stabilize voting intentions over time. Also unclear is whether the political homogeneity of the immediate environment must reach a critical threshold before its effect starts to be felt, or whether just about any probabilistic relationship between membership in a macro-group (like class or church) and vote can generate such environmental influences. My counter-hypothesis is that, given the fragmentation of the east central European party systems alone, no large social group is likely to sustain the kind of environmental influence, that is, the political homogeneity of the social environment, that would make party loyalties enigmatically stable. Thus, 'pure structural' voters (as defined by Knutsen and Scarbrough) are just as volatile in their preferences as anybody else because they lack the reinforcement that comes from sustained interaction with like-minded people.

(2) *Value Homogeneity and Party Loyalty*: Bartolini and Mair further argue that value homogeneity – that is, 'pure value voting' – among the supporters of a party can also cement their party loyalties (hypothesis 2). They do not seem to be very clear about the psychological mechanism at work, but it seems plausible that for the voters themselves their own 'value voting' may appear richer in substantive and enduring political meaning. It is likely too that most voters prefer listening to such sources and communicating with such fellow citizens who appear to share their values, irrespectively of whether or not these also share their party preference and social background. Through these two mechanisms, value homogeneity may be more effective than social homogeneity in stabilizing a party's constituency. The counterargument would be that both the voters' value orientations and the parties' programmatic appeals are so fluid – at least in new democracies undergoing rapid and radical economic, cultural and political changes – that pure value voting will not lead to below average volatility of voting intentions. Voters may hold steadily to their value commitments, while seeking a compatible party among a shifting partisan landscape.

(3) *Cleavage Mobilization and Party Loyalty*: Knutsen and Scarbrough seem to suggest that cleavage mobilization – that is, a simultaneous appeal to group interests and identity on the one hand, and to the values that distinguish the targeted social group on the other – is more likely to cement party loyalties than are either 'pure structural' or 'pure value' voting. Why this kind of party appeal may be particularly effective in recruiting a captive audience can be best explained with the example of the Czech Liberal Social Union (LSU). Their case suggests that an appeal for 'pure structural' and 'pure value' voting can be combined with the opposite of what Knutsen and Scarbrough mean by cleavage mobilization. The LSU was the 1992 electoral coalition and short-lived parliamentary club comprised of the Czech Agrarian Party (ZS), the Czech Socialist Party (CSS), and the Greens (SZ). The coalition combined an appeal to post-materialist, culturally liberal values, and, in effect, to the young, urban, educated part of Czech society, on the one hand, with an appeal to the narrow economic interests and group identity of the farming population (which

---

[34] B. R. Berelson, P. F. Lazarsfeld, and W. N. McPhee, *Voting: a Study of Public Opinion Formation in a Presidential Campaign* (Chicago IL, The University of Chicago Press, 1954), p. 120; R. Huckfeldt and J. Sprague, 'Social Order and Political Chaos: the Structural Setting of Political Information', in J. A. Ferejohn and J. H. Kuklinski (eds), *Information and Democratic Processes* (Urbana IL, University of Illinois Press, 1991), pp. 33ff.

is usually not very post-materialist or culturally liberal), on the other. There-fore, if considered in isolation, neither the voters' values, nor their socio-demographic traits were strongly related to support for LSU. The noticeable impact of both on LSU vote becomes apparent only if they are considered simultaneously.

It is easy to conclude that it may be troublesome to lead a party like this to electoral success. Indeed, the LSU itself was soon disbanded, and its various successor organizations ended up in electoral oblivion in the 1996 election. And it seems plausible that few voters can display more than half-hearted commit-ment and stable support to such a party. Thus, 'cleavage voting' (to borrow Knutsen and Scarbrough's term) increases, while 'negative cleavage voting', which was apparent in the case of the LSU, undermines the supporters' party loyalty (hypothesis 3). The counterhypothesis is that the confusion in the appeal of parties like the LSU might depress the level of support for the party, but will not do anything to undermine the loyalty of its (probably few) voters, once their support was won. Since 'cleavage voting' does not have its own mechanism to cement party loyalties, but merely combines the mechanisms underlying struct-ural and value voting, its capacity to stabilize party preferences is intermediate between, and not greater than that of the two other types (hypothesis 3a).

(4) *Party Organization and Party Loyalty*: Bartolini and Mair make an obviously plausible point in suggesting that the organizational encapsulation of voters by their parties may also provide for an above average endurance of party loyalties (hypothesis 4). The apparent explanation is again that the political homogeneity of the everyday social environment makes the politically relevant stimuli received by the encapsulated voters extremely skewed towards those which are likely to reinforce their preferences.

Quite obviously, organizational encapsulation and 'cleavage', 'pure value' and 'pure structural voting' are likely to be promoted by different party strategies and different party appeals. If the argument of the second section of this essay about the relationship between the quality of democracy and volatility was correct, then the following section should offer some insight about which, if any, party appeal is likely to make the greatest contribution to democratic control via the reduction of the astronomic electoral volatility of some new democracies.

Empirical Analysis

The data considered in this section come from seven panel studies of electoral preferences. The analysis is carried out for each panel separately, which also means that we hold election laws, ethno-religious heterogeneity, left-party membership and party fragmentation constant, and concentrate on some of the variance in party loyalties that these factors leave unexplained. The final dependent variable is whether or not the party preference of a respondent changed between the two waves of the respective panel. In the April–May 1994 Hungarian, the May–June 1996 Czech, and the August–October 1993 Polish panel, the two interviews were only separated by three to seven weeks. In the 1992–93 Slovak and Czech, and the December 1993–May 1994 Hungarian panel, the two interviews were separated by several months, and in the September 1992–May 1994 Hungarian panel by 20 months. In the 1992–93 Czech and Slovak panels, the current voting preference in the second wave was compared to the current voting preference in the first. In all other panels, the voting preference revealed in the first interview was compared to the actual vote as reported one to three weeks after the next election.

The final dependent variable (*Stability*) has just two values: '2' if the voting preference remained unaltered between the two interviews and '1' otherwise. The respondents who, in the first interview, revealed no preference or named a very small party as their most likely choice are excluded from the final analysis. To increase the number of cases included in the analysis, some smaller parties were merged (see the Appendix).

The three independent variables (*Cleavage, Value* and *Structure*) of the final analysis were constructed solely on the basis of information available from the first wave interviews. They measure the extent to which the individual respondents, given their party preference, values and demographic traits seemed to be 'cleavage', 'value' or 'structural' voters. The testing of the hypotheses involved regressing *Stability* on *Cleavage, Value* and *Structure*. Since *Stability* is a dummy variable, logistic regression was employed.

Before assessing the results, we have to turn to the critical question of how *Cleavage, Value* and *Structure* were constructed via a discriminant analysis which, except for some inevitable differences in the independent variables, is identical to Knutsen and Scarbrough's model. In that model, the strength of cleavages is measured by the *indirect* effect of *selected* socio-demographic variables on party choice via *value orientations*. In technical terms, this requires separate runs of three models of party choice. The first uses only the socio-demographic variables, the second only value orientations, and the third all of these as independent variables. Beside those measures of religion and social class which were used by Knutsen and Scarbrough, here (perfectly in line with their argument) a variable referring to the urban-rural dimension is also included among the socio-demographic variables. Beside a scale measuring left vs. right wing socio-economic values, indicators of nationalist vs. cosmopolitan, secular vs. clerical, and anti- vs. pro-communist attitudes are included among the value orientations. The independent variables included in the various models are described in the Appendix. Note that to test hypothesis 4, the entire analysis was redone. This replication is called analysis B below. The only difference between analyses A and B was in the independent variables included in models 1, 2 and 3 of the discriminant analyses. Model A, to review a bit, includes church membership, urbanism, education, and occupation. Model B, in the interest of measuring a voter's engagement in organizational networks, adds to these four the frequency of church attendance and communist party membership prior to 1989.

The discriminant analyses utilized the observed statistical relationships between party preference and the independent variables to maximize our ability to 'postdict' correctly the party preferences of the respondents. The immediate results (not shown) were linear combinations of the independent variables (so called discriminant functions) that best explained the observed party preference of the respondents.[35]

[35] The Knutsen-Scarbrough analysis focused on the 'explanatory power' of the three different models, which they believed to warrant inferences about variations across samples (that is, time and countries) in the strength of 'value', 'structural' and 'cleavage' voting. However, a different path will be taken here as their measure of a model's explanatory power (that is, the Wilks' lambda statistics) can in no way be interpreted – as they did – analogously to the R-squared statistics familiar from

Each model gives a numerical estimate, for each respondent, of the probability of supporting each of the parties, given the respondent's value on the independent variables in the model and the observed relationship between these variables and party preference. The probability that an individual, given his or her set of demographic and/or value characteristics, would vote for party i, can be used to distinguish the three linkage (and voter) types sketched by Knutsen and Scarbrough. Recall that pure structural voting is exemplified by such working class voters who do not adhere to left-wing values in the socio economic domain, but nevertheless vote for a left wing working class party. Those middle class voters who vote for a bourgeois party without displaying right-wing socio-economic attitudes are another case in point. In contrast, a middle-class person who has socialist value orientations and also votes socialist would be an example of a 'pure value voter'. Finally, cleavage voting occurs if 'structural' and 'value' voting are simultaneously displayed by an individual. An example is an upper-class conservative voter who has right-wing views on economic issues.

In the spirit of Knutsen and Scarbrough's work a minor innovation was introduced to capture such differences between individual voters. For each party i, one variable was generated by the discriminant analyses for each model. Let T_i denote the probability that voters j will support party i given their value orientations and demographic traits on the one hand, and the observed linear relationship between these independent variables and support for the different parties in the sample, on the other. Similarly, let S_i denote the probability that voters j will support party i given their demographic traits only, and V_i denote the probability that voters j will support party i given their values only. If, for instance, values are totally unrelated to party preference, then all V_i variables will have the same (non-zero) value for all voters and all parties, and T_i will always be equal to S_i for each voter and party. Next, the T_i, V_i, and S_i variables (note that there are as many of each of them as parties in the analysis) were replaced with T, V, and S, respectively. The new variable T equaled T_j for all respondents who named party j as their voting preference in the first interview, S equaled S_j for all respondents who named party j as their voting preference in the first interview, and V equaled V_j for all respondents who named party j as their voting preference in the first interview. Consequently, T, S and V were undefined (that is, declared missing) for those individuals who had no party preference, or favoured one of the smaller parties excluded from our analysis. They were not included in the rest of the analysis.

regression analysis. Technically put, a nominal variable (such as party preference) has no variance – not to speak of a normal distribution – in the statistical sense of the word. On this and discriminant analysis in general, see W. Klecka, *Discriminant Analysis* (Beverly Hills CA, Sage, 1980). To clarify this point without recourse to statistical jargon, the problem can be highlighted with an example. Wilks' lambda (and analogous measures like canonical correlation) would suggest a deterministic relationship between party preference and an independent variable if that independent variable had a deterministic relationship with support for one, however small, party. A good example would be an ethnically divided polity where a party speaking for the interests of a small ethnic minority manages to get the vote of everybody belonging to that ethnic group, but obtains absolutely no votes from other ethnic groups. The three Hungarian parties – the Hungarian Christian Democratic Movement, the nationalist Co-existence and the liberal Hungarian Civic Party (MKM, ESWS and MOS, respectively) in Slovakia closely approximate this situation. Yet, if membership in the ethnic group in question does not discriminate between the supporters of the rest of the parties, then there is something obviously wrong in interpreting the data as if ethnicity 'perfectly' explained party choice.

Imagine a two-party system with strong class voting and an equally strong correspondence between conservative vs. socialist values and party choice. The middle class socialists voting for the left wing party will have a high V-value but a low S-value, while those upper-class voters of the right wing party who have conservative values will have a high score (that is, relatively close to 1) on both V and S. If class status and conservatism are correlated, then some of the apparent relationship between class and vote is, of course, spurious, and entirely due to their shared association with conservative values. But to obtain a measure of pure structural and pure value voting, we need just a little more algebra:

(1) *Structure* $= T - V$
(2) *Value* $= T - S$
(3) *Cleavage* $= T - Value - Structure$[36]

As a result, the three new variables show the net contribution of the three types of voting to our ability to explain the respondent's party choice. The rest of the analysis is really simple. According to hypothesis 1, *Structure* has a direct positive effect on *Stability*. According to hypothesis 2, *Value* has a direct positive effect on *Stability*. According to hypothesis 3, Cleavage's direct effect on *Stability* is positive and larger than the direct effects of *Value* and *Structure*. Hypothesis 3a contradicts Knutsen and Scarbrough as it posits that the direct effect of *Cleavage* is halfway between that of *Value* and *Structure*.

Finally, hypothesis 4 attributes a key role to organizational encapsulation in stabilizing party preference. If it is correct, then replacing church attendance and former communist party membership with direct measures of attitude in the construction of the *Value* variable must diminish the impact of the latter on *Stability*. Adding church attendance and former party membership to our set of demographic variables seems reasonable on the ground that organizational encapsulation and structural voting are expected to owe their stabilizing effect to identical socio-psychological mechanisms (see above). According to hypothesis 4, this step should increase the observed effect of *Structure* on *Stability*. Therefore, all analyses are done twice. In analysis A, church attendance and former communist party membership are treated as indicators of 'values', while in analysis B they turn into 'structural' variables (see the Appendix too).

Obviously, 'structural', 'value' and 'cleavage' voting do not exhaust the universe of all possible types of party-voter linkages. Evaluations of party leaders, economic conditions, and a host of other factors can just as well influence voting decisions as the voter's values. However, the present analysis does not distinguish among these other types. In effect, the influence of

---

[36] Although this will not be relevant here it has to be noted that the discriminant analyses assumed an equal prior probability of support for each party. Therefore, T_j, V_j and S_j had the same mean for each party in a given sample. This mean was equal to $1/n$ (plus-minus a minor computation error), where n is the number of categories (parties) distinguished on the dependent variable. One divided by n is the random chance of correct classification. This chance element (which is constant across respondents and parties) was automatically subtracted from the values of *Structure* and *Value* when they were defined as in (1) and (2) because T, V and S all incorporated the same chance element. However, since *Cleavage* is defined (theoretically) as in (4), the value of the *Cleavage* variable would not be reduced by the chance element in such an automatic way. Therefore, *Cleavage* was actually computed as:

(4) *Cleavage* $= T - V - S - 1/n$.

Cleavage, Structure and *Value* on the stability of voting intentions are assessed relative to the combined impact of all these 'other' factors together (see Table 2). If, for instance, *Structure* has a statistically significant positive effect on *Stability*, then structural voting is more, and if the observed effect is negative, then it is less likely to stabilize party preferences than all other possible reasons of party choice combined.

Let us consider analysis A first. Given the relatively small Ns in the analysis, it is not very surprising that many regression coefficients are insignificant. More important is whether an effect is consistently positive or negative in all the seven panel studies that we can analyse. Out of the seven logistic regression analyses (one for each panel survey), *Value* had a positive, statistically significant effect on *Stability* five times. The exceptions were the first Czech and the third

TABLE 2. The Impact of Cleavages, Structural, and Values Linkages between Voters and Parties on the Stability of Voting Intentions

Analysis A:

	Cleavage	Structure	Values	N
Poland, 1993	**8.66** (2.02)	**2.45** (0.50)	**2.62** (0.74)	640
Czech R., 1992–93	2.75 (2.09)	−0.03 (1.12)	0.71 (0.57)	344
Czech R., 1996	1.75 (1.76)	0.03 (1.86)	**1.81** (0.52)	505
Slovakia, 1992–93	0.81 (2.16)	−0.28 (1.36)	**2.65** (0.69)	367
Hungary, 1992–94	2.44 (2.47)	1.41 (1.23)	**3.85** (0.85)	372
Hungary, 1993–94	1.53 (2.35)	1.40 (1.35)	**2.63** (0.69)	356
Hungary, 1994	2.24 (2.12)	−1.48 (1.26)	0.74 (0.76)	349

Analysis B:

	Cleavage	Structure	Values	N
Poland, 1993	**7.69** (1.53)	**2.31** (0.43)	**3.85** (0.94)	640
Czech R., 1992–93	1.39 (1.05)	0.39 (0.59)	**1.58** (0.97)	344
Czech R., 1996	**2.43** (0.90)	**1.12** (0.63)	**2.07** (0.96)	505
Slovakia, 1992–93	**4.46** (1.31)	**1.63** (0.82)	**2.13** (0.81)	367
Hungary, 1992–94	**4.55** (1.87)	**2.48** (0.71)	1.00 (1.41)	372
Hungary, 1993–94	**5.91** (1.81)	**1.49** (0.73)	**1.84** (1.06)	356
Hungary, 1994	0.12 (1.56)	−0.58 (0.74)	**2.58** (1.02)	349

Note: The table entries are logistic regression coefficients (standard errors in parentheses). The dependent variable is *Stability* (coded 2 if the respondent revealed the same party preference in both waves of the panel in question, and 1 otherwise). Those respondents who revealed no party preference in either wave are excluded from the analysis. Significant effects (0.10 level) are printed in **bold**. The constant terms of the equations are omitted from the table. The independent variables measure the extent to which individual voters are 'structural', 'value', or 'cleavage' voters. On their construction see the main text. In creating *Cleavage, Structure* and *Value*, former communist party membership and the frequency of church attendance were considered indicators of value preferences in analysis A, and as indicators of organisational encapsulation (and thus, a possible cause of 'structural voting') in analysis B. For further details see the Appendix. Data set: seven different CEU panel-surveys, each having two waves of interviews.

Hungarian panel, but even there the effect was clearly positive. Thus, hypothesis 2, which suggests that stable party loyalty is a function of value homogeneity, receives support from the analysis.

In contrast, *Structure* and *Cleavage*'s direct effects on *Stability* were significant just once each (both in the Polish panel). While the effect of *Cleavage* was positive in all other panels, it never reached statistical significance. Hypothesis 1 can be clearly rejected, especially since *Structure* even records three negative, though insignificant, effects across the seven panels: structural voting does not seem to be an unusually strong stabilizer of party loyalties.

Hypothesis 3 suggests that the simultaneous mobilization of group interests and identity combined with values particular to a social group cement party loyalties. Thus, *Cleavage* should have a larger effect on *Stability* than either *Structure* or *Value*. This hypothesis receives no support. Comparing the coefficients in the three columns we can see that in analysis A this proposition was confirmed only in three out of seven surveys. *Cleavage*, on the whole, performs only a tiny bit better than *Structure*.

However, the robustness of these findings has to be checked against a possible criticism. Given the inclusion of membership in certain, politically relevant social networks among the indicators of value preferences in analysis A, one might speculate that it is probably not 'value voting', but the (informal) organizational encapsulation of some voters by the Christian and the post-communist political subcultures that is responsible for *Value*'s positive effect on *Stability*. In other words, hypothesis 2 is probably false and hypothesis 4 has to be supported instead.

Analysis B tests this possibility. This time, church attendance and former communist party membership were moved from among the value indicators among the structural (demographic) traits, and attitude-based indicators of clerical-secular and pro- vs. anti-communist values replace them among the value indicators (see the description of analysis B in the Appendix).

In analysis B, the effect of *Structure* on *Stability* was significant and positive five times, and negative (though insignificant) only once. Indeed, moving from analysis A to analysis B, the logistic regression coefficient measuring the net impact of *Structure* on *Stability* changed in the direction anticipated by hypothesis 4 in each of the seven panels. Thus, there is considerable support for hypothesis 4, holding that the organizational encapsulation of voters by their parties provides for strengthened party loyalties. Thus, we might expect that associating frequently with co-religionists or a history of communist party activism reinforces the effect of structural conditions on voters' partisan attachments.

However, *Value* still had a clearly significant impact on *Stability* in all but the 1992–94 Hungarian panel, and thus hypothesis 2 was still supported: value-based party preferences tend to be more lasting than party choices based on other considerations are on the average. But this time, hypothesis 3 received stronger support than in analysis A as the impact of *Cleavage* was appreciably stronger than that of either *Structure* or *Value* – in every survey (but only in those surveys) where *Structure* too had a significant positive effect on *Stability*. Since cleavage voting is a combination of structural and value voting, this restriction makes a very good sense. It seems, then, that the combined impact of these two voting types on the stability of party choice may indeed be bigger than the simple sum of their effects when they do not work in tandem. When they work in isolation, though, the stabilizing impact of value voting is probably stronger than that of structural voting (compare the respective coefficients in the two rightmost columns of Table 2), but we have no strong evidence of that.

Summary and Conclusions

In the new democracies of east central Europe, voters' willingness to stay with party preferences over time is a function of their 'value voting' along such dimensions as religious-secular, left-right, and nationalism-antinationalism. This effect of values on voter loyalty is largely independent of status or demographic circumstances. And, when it comes to sustaining commitment to particular parties, values are at least as effective as is the political mobilization of organizational networks. Values are definitely more effective in sustaining party loyalty than are the effects of socio-demographic traits unmediated by those value orientations. Rather than stick with parties whose followers or leaders 'look like them', voters are most likely to stick with the parties with whom they agree on major issue dimensions. If the argument of the opening section about the link between democratic accountability and volatility survives closer scrutiny, then this finding underlines the positive contribution that can be made by parties that differentiate themselves ideologically from one another in new (but probably also in old) democracies. The clarity and sharpness of value-based choices for the voters can help make the often astronomic electoral volatility of new democracies lower. Given the amount of praise that ideological moderation, pragmatism and centrism receive in discussions of democratization, this is not entirely trivial.

Furthermore, it was found that 'pure structural voting', on the basis of social class, religion, or place of residence, seldom makes a contribution to the stabilization of critical alignments. Except in Poland, no direct effect of structural voting, unmediated by value orientations, was evident on the stability of party. Several explanations are possible. One is that these countries have rather fractionalized party systems, and therefore very few sizeable groups become homogeneous enough in their party preferences so as to allow 'structural voting' to stabilize party attachments. Alternatively, one could allude to the oft-supposed weakness of group identities after decades of communist rules. In contrast, however, no one has shown that 'pure structural' voting would be particularly instrumental in stabilizing voters' party preferences even in more established democracies. Thus, the burden of proof is now on those who would still like to argue that the frequently demonstrated decline of class voting is leading to an increased (potential) volatility of the western electorates, or that the absence of class etc. voting destabilizes new party systems. Value preferences seem to provide for relatively more solid, stable basis for enduring partisan attachments, at least in these four relatively new democracies. Another factor that is apparently effective in sustaining such attachments is the organizational encapsulation of voters, which is a particularly powerful influence when it is combined with value voting among the supporters.

Much further work can and needs to be done to fill in gaps in the argument presented above. Clearly, it was assumed, but not demonstrated, that the incidence of various voting types in a polity is a function of the kind of appeals that parties use. At best, it is a plausible proposition that direct appeals to group interests and identities (through nakedly redistributive proposals presenting

politics as a zero sum game) induce 'structural' effects on voting, while ideological appeals (calling for improvements in the allocative efficiency and fairness
of public policies that, presumably, would make nearly every one better off)
invite 'value voting'. The implication of the present analysis is that the latter is
more likely to create stable party allegiances in new electorates.

Appendix: Variables, the Treatment of Missing Values, and Effective Ns in the Discriminant Analyses

I: Variables in the discriminant analyses

I.A: The **dependent variable** is current party preference as revealed in the first
wave of a panel survey by the responses to the question: 'Which party would you
vote for if there were a parliamentary election next weekend [in the elections this
May (June, September)]?' References to parties that merged later – as Democratic Union (UD) and the Liberal Democratic Congress (KLD) in Poland, the
Civic Democratic Party (ODS) and the small KDS in the Czech Republic, and
the Democratic Party (DS) and the Party of Conservative Democrats (SKD,
formerly Civic Democratic Union, ODU) in Slovakia – or that joined in an
electoral coalition (like the various constituent parts of the 1992 Czech LSU,
which, for all practical purposes, became extinct by the time of the 1996
election, or the three Hungarian parties, MKM, ESWS and MOS, in Slovakia)
were collapsed. However, the Slovak Green and Social Democratic parties,
though merged with each other, were kept separate from the post-communist
SDL (their electoral coalition partner in 1994). Respondents supporting parties/
coalitions represented by less than 20 supporters in the first wave of the
respective panel survey were excluded from the analysis. For the present analysis
party preferences were recoded as:

Poland: (1) Confederation for Independent Poland (KPN); (2) Partia X; (3)
   Christian-National Union (ZChN) or just 'Christian party''; (4) electoral list
   of the Solidarity Trade Union (NSZZ Solidarnosc); (5) the Non-Partisan
   Block for the Reforms (BBWR); (6) UD or KLD; (7) Union of Labour (UP);
   (8) Polish People's Party (PSL) or just 'peasant party'; (9) Alliance of the
   Democratic Left (SLD) or just 'left wing party';
Czech Republic: (1) Christian Democratic Union-Czech People's Party (KDU-
   CSL); (2) Civic Democratic Alliance (ODA); (3) ODS or KDS; (4)
   Republicans (SPR-RSC); (5) Civic Movement (OH, (only in the 1992–93
   panel) or Free Democrats-Liberal Social National Party (SD-LSNS, only in
   the 1996 panel); (6) Movement for Self-Governing Democracy-Association
   for Moravia and Silesia HSD-SMS (only in the 1992–93 panel); (7) Liberal
   Social Union (LSU) and its socialist, agrarian and green component parts
   (CSS, ZS, and SZ, respectively) (only in the 1992–93 panel); (8) Czech Social
   Democratic Party (CSSD); (9) the Communist Party of the Czech and
   Moravian Lands (KSCM) or the Left Block (LB) electoral alliance which
   included KSCM (but not the small SLB which happened to use the LB label
   in the 1996 election and was excluded from the present analysis);
Slovakia: (1) DS, SKD or ODU; (2) Christian Democratic Movement (KDH);
   (3) the three Hungarian parties (MKM, ESWS, MOS); (4) Slovak National
   Party (SNS); (5) Movement for a Democratic Slovakia (HZDS); (6) Slovak

Social Democratic Party (SDSS) or Slovak Green Party (SZS); (7) Party of the Democratic Left (SDL);

Hungary: (1) Alliance of Young Democrats (FIDESZ); (2) Independent Small Holders Party (FKGP); (3) Christian Democratic People's Party (KDNP); (4) Hungarian Democratic Forum (MDF); (5) Hungarian Socialist Party (MSZP); (6) Alliance of Free Democrats (SZDSZ).

I.B: Independent variables in Model 1: In analysis A they are church membership (yes or no); respondent's place of residence (population size coded on a four point scale where $1 = 1$ to 1.999, $2 = 2.000-19.999$, $3 = 20.000-99.999$, $4 = 100.000$ or more inhabitants); education (four point scale); occupation (five dichotomous variables measuring whether or not the respondent's present or last occupation was 1: farming; 2: professional or managerial job; 3: other non-manual work; 4: manual occupation (agriculture excluded); and 5: whether or not the respondent was self-employed. In analysis B, they are the same as in analysis A plus frequency of church attendance (six point scale running from $1 =$ never to $6 =$ more than once a week); and communist party membership before 1989 (yes or no).

Note:
The entire analysis reported in the paper was replicated by adding region (Moravia or not) to the demographic variables in the Czech, and ethnicity (ethnic Hungarian or not) in the Slovak data. Since the results of these replications only influenced the some findings concerning the Moravian regionalist and the Hungarian minority parties that are not dealt with in the paper, but left all conclusions regarding the theoretically relevant hypotheses unaltered, they are not reported here.

I.C: Independent variables in Model 2: In analysis A they were religious vs. secular orientation (measured by a six point frequency of church attendance scale running from $1 =$ never to $6 =$ more than once a week); left-right value orientation (a composite index summing the responses to the following items: 'It should be the government's responsibility to provide a job for everyone who wants one'; 'Giving the former state-owned companies into private property is going to help very much in solving the economic problems of our country'; 'Unprofitable factories and mines should be closed down immediately even if this leads to unemployment' on four point agree-disagree scales); nationalist-antinationalist value orientation (a composite index summing the responses to 'Nationalism is harmful for the development of our country'; 'In the case of a politician I prefer a strong patriot to an expert' on four point agree-disagree scales); and former communist party membership (yes or no) as an indicator of attitudes towards the *ancien régime*. In analysis B, they were the same as in analysis A, except that church attendance is replaced with a composite index summing the responses to 'A woman should be allowed to have an abortion in the early weeks of pregnancy, if she decides so', 'The Church has [in Hungary: the churches have] too much influence in our country' and 'Politicians who do not believe in God should not perform public functions' on four point agree-disagree questions); and former communist party membership was replaced with the personal importance rating of 'removing former communists from positions of influence' (9 point scale) as an indicator of attitudes towards the *ancien régime*.

I.D: Independent variables in Model 3: All the variables featuring in models 1 and 2 together.

II. Missing values and Ns
Missing values were substituted by the variable mean on all attitude-items as well as on the education, place of residence, and frequency of church attendance variables. The discriminant analyses only used information from the first wave of the respective panel studies. Respondents were included in the discriminant analyses irrespectively of whether or not they were re-interviewed in the second wave of the panel. As noted above, respondents supporting parties/coalitions represented by less than 20 supporters in the first wave of the respective panel survey were excluded from the analysis. The number of respondents was identical in all discriminant analyses of the same data set, namely 802 in the August 1993 Polish data, 628 in the September 1992 Czech data, 1288 in the May 1996 Czech data, 564 in the September 1992 Slovak data, 713 in the September 1992, 670 in the December 1993, and 619 in the April 1994 Hungarian data set.

Effects of Party Organization on Performance during the 'Golden Age' of Parties

KENNETH JANDA AND TYLER COLMAN

Introduction

The study of parties and party systems has always been central to the study of politics, but the study of party organization *per se* has had its ups and downs. Party organization as a field owes much to the foundations laid by Ostogorski and Michels early in this century.[1] Nevertheless, contemporary scholars hold that the 'dearth' of recent empirical studies of party organization has formed 'lacunae' in modern party research.[2] Much contemporary research focuses on the party system level, notably on questions of change and stability overtime.[3] Other recent studies examine the sociological bases of party support.[4] Currently, there is renewed interest in the study of party organization – most impressively demonstrated with the publication by Katz and Mair of a 'data handbook' on party organization in twelve countries from 1960 to 1990.[5] Indeed, after a long period only occasionally punctuated by the study of party structure, the 1980s and 1990s produced a spate of works that range from models of party organization, to the study of comparative organization in

[1] M. I. Ostrogorski published *Democracy and the Organization of Political Parties* (London, Macmillan) in 1902; R. Michels' work was originally published in 1911 as *Zur Soziologie des Partieiwesens in der modernen Demokratie*, but is more readily available as *Political Parties: a Sociological Study of the Oligarchical Tendencies of Modern Democracies* (New York, Free, 1962).

[2] Neglect of party organization is discussed in K. Janda, 'Cross-national measures of party organizations and organizational theory', *European Journal of Political Research*, 11,3 (1983), p. 319; and P. Mair, 'Party Organizations from Civil Society to the State', in R. S. Katz and P. Mair (eds), *How Parties Organize: Change and Adaptation in Party Organizations in Western Democracies* (London, Sage, 1994), p. 1.

[3] S.M. Lipset and S. Rokkan, 'Cleavage Structures, Party Systems, and Voter Alignments', in S.M. Lipset and S. Rokkan (eds), *Party Systems and Voter Alignments* (New York, Free, 1967), pp. 1–64; H. Daalder and P. Mair (eds), *West European Party Systems: Continuity and Change* (London, Sage, 1983); and P. Mair and G. Smith (eds), *Understanding Party System Change in Western Europe* (London, Frank Cass, 1989).

[4] M. Maguire, 'Is There Still Persistence? Electoral Change in Western Europe, 1948–1979', in Daalder and Mair, *West European Party Systems*, pp. 67–94; M. N. Pedersen, 'Changing Patterns of Electoral Volatility in European Party Systems, 1948–1977: Explorations in Explanation', in Daalder and Mair, pp. 29–66; and R. J. Dalton, S. C. Flanagan and P. A. Beck (eds), *Electoral Change in Advanced Industrial Democracies: Realignment or Dealignment?* (Princeton, New Jersey, Princeton University Press, 1984).

[5] R. S. Katz and P. Mair (eds), *Party Organizations: a Data Handbook on Party Organizations in Western Democracies, 1960–1990* (London, Sage, 1992).

advanced industrial democracies, and even to organization in emergent party systems, such as Eastern Europe.[6]

Mair contends that thinking about party organization 'remains caught' within concepts 'established almost a generation ago'.[7] He mainly meant Duverger's distinction between 'old' *cadre* parties, based on informal groupings of a few political notables, and 'modern' *mass* parties, that recruit large numbers of formal members.[8] This distinction still figures prominently in a recent, comprehensive text on comparative political parties.[9] According to Mair, the mass party model defines party organizations with reference to their relationships with civil society; party organizational strength is measured primarily with reference to the size of the membership and the capacity of the party to close off (often predefined) sectors of the electorate; and party structures are understood and assessed primarily in terms of modes of internal representation and accountability.[10] If any of these elements are attenuated, it 'involves also the attenuation, and decline, of party *per se*'.

In the first two decades after World War II, European politics was shaped by mass membership parties. But from the 1960s to the 1980s, all but two of eleven European countries experienced a decline in party membership as measured by the percent of the electorate.[11] Mair says, 'the period of the mass party can therefore be seen to coincide with the "golden age" of parties, and since then everything has been downhill'.[12] The shift away from the mass party has led to hypotheses of party 'decline' or even party 'failure'.[13] However, other models of party that de-emphasize relations with civil society have emerged to replace the mass-party model and to underscore the continued importance of vitality of parties in general terms.[14] They have led to a more explicit focus on the study of

[6] Party models are discussed in A. Panebianco, *Political Parties: Organization and Power* (Cambridge, Cambridge University Press, 1998); and R. S. Katz and P. Mair 'Changing models of party organization and party democracy: the emergence of the Cartel Party', *Party Politics*, 1, (1995), 5–28. Comparative studies of party organization are in A. Appleton and D. S. Ward, 'Party transformation in France and the United States: the hierarchical effects of system change in comparative perspective', *Comparative Politics*, 26,1 (1993), 69–98; and Katz and Mair, *How Parties Organize: Change and Adaptation in Party Organizations in Western Democracies*. Development of party organizations in emerging democracies in former communist nations is studied in R. W. Orttung, 'The Russian right and the dilemmas of party organization', *Soviet Studies*, 44,3 (1992), 445–78; and P. Kopecky, 'Developing party organizations in east-central Europe: what type of party is likely to emerge?', *Party Politics*, 1,4 (1995), 515–34.

[7] Mair, 'Party Organizations: from Civil Society to the State', p. 2.

[8] M. Duverger, *Political Parties: their Organization and Activity in the Modern State* (London, Methuen, 1959), pp. 62–79.

[9] A. Ware, *Political Parties and Party Systems* (Oxford, Oxford University Press, 1996), pp. 65–66.

[10] Mair, 'Party Organizations: from Civil Society to the State', p. 2.

[11] Mair, 'Party Organizations: from Civil Society to the State', p. 5.

[12] Mair, p. 2. Students of US parties tend to reserve 'golden age' to describe party politics in the late 1800s, e.g., Paul Allen Beck, *Party Politics in America* (New York, Longman, 1996), pp. 24–5.

[13] K. Lawson and P. Merkl (eds), *When Parties Fail* (Princeton, New Jersey, Princeton University Press, 1988).

[14] For example, see Katz and Mair, 'Changing Models of Party Organization and Party Democracy'. In the United States, where popular opinion holds that parties have declined greatly, scholars see their resurgence. See L.S. Maisel (ed.), *The Parties Respond: Changes in American Parties and Campaigns*, 2nd ed. (Boulder CO, Westview, 1994); and J. C. Green and D. M. Shea (eds), *The State of the Parties: the Changing Role of Contemporary American Parties*, 2nd ed. (Lanham MD, Rowman and Littlefield, 1996).

party organization to determine the extent and nature of party change and whether such change can be interpreted as party decline.

As it has become acceptable to study party organization for organization's sake, recent studies have examined specific aspects of organization, such as changes in the size and role of membership.[15] In this article, we study party organization to assess its effect on party performance. Although some other studies have focused on party organization and party performance, this literature is relatively sparse and its findings often inconclusive.[16] Moreover, virtually all previous research on organizational effects on party performance has been micro-analytical, using data from local electoral districts. This is perhaps the first macro-analytical study that uses national-level data to assess party performance.

The data for this analysis come from the International Comparative Political Parties Project data.[17] The ICPP Project collected data on 158 parties operating in 53 randomly selected countries from 1950 to 1962. Parties were scored on approximately 100 variables – separately for the first half of the period (1950–1956) and the second half (1957–62). We selected a small set of variables from that dataset and studied only the subset of 95 parties operating in 28 'democratic' countries that held free (or mostly free) elections during 1957–62. The counties and the parties are reported in Table 1.

We readily admit that the data are dated, involving parties – and in some cases, even countries – that no longer exist. However troubling this may be, this study is valuable for several reasons. First, because structuring of current party systems and the organization of current parties depends on paths taken in their past, the history of causal relationships among a random sample of the world's parties during their 'golden age' is relevant to understanding party politics today. In the words of Panebianco, 'a party's organizational characteristics depend more on its history, i.e. on how the organization originated and how it consolidated, than on any other factor'.[18] Second, we unite two literatures which have grown independently of one another but have much to share. Work on various aspects of party performance such as electoral fortunes and legislative

---

[15] P. Selle and L. Svåsand, 'Membership in party organizations and the problem of the decline of parties', *Comparative Political Studies*, 23 (1991), 459–77; L.Bille, 'Denmark, the Decline of the Membership Party? How Parties Organize', in Katz and Mair, *Party Organizations*, pp. 134–57; K. Heidar, 'The polymorphic nature of party membership', *European Journal of Political Research*, 25, 1 (1994), 61–86.

[16] One of the few scholars who studied the effect of party organization on the vote says, 'The lack of attention given to this particular problem area represents an anomaly in a generally abundant literature on political parties', W. J. Crotty, 'Party effort and its impact on the vote', *American Political Science Review*, 65,2 (1971), p. 439. See also E. S. Wellhofer, 'The electoral effectiveness of party organization, Norway, 1945–77', *Scandinavian Political Studies*, 8,3 (1985), 171–96; G. M. Pomper, 'Party organization and electoral success', *Polity*, 23,2 (1990), 187–206; for an assessment of such research, see K. Janda, 'Comparative political parties: research and theory', in Ada W. Finifter (ed.), *Political Science: the State of the Discipline II* (Washington DC, American Political Science Association, 1993), p. 178.

[17] The project was supported by grants GS-1418 and GS-2533 from the US National Science Foundation. The code book for the original raw data file is available as K. Janda, *Comparative Political Parties Data, 1950–1962* (Ann Arbor, Michigan, Inter-university Consortium for Political and Social Research, 1979). The data are distributed by the ICPSR as Study 7534. For methodological discussions, summary statistics, and how specific parties were coded, see K. Janda, *Political Parties: a Cross-National Survey* (New York, Macmillan and Free, 1980).

[18] Panebianco, *Political Parties*, p. 50.

TABLE 1. List of 28 Countries and 95 Parties in the Analysis*

Country	Parties
United States	Democratic, Republican
Britain	Labour, Conservative
Australia	Labor, Liberal, Country
New Zealand	National, Labor
Canada	Progressive Conservative, Liberal, NDP, Social Credit
Ireland	Fianna Fail, Fine Gael, Labour
India	Congress, Communist
Austria	Peoples, Socialist, VDU-FPO
France	MRP, Radical Socialist, SFIO, Gaullist, Communist
West Germany	CDU, SPD, FDP
Greece	Liberal, EPEK, ERE, EDA
Denmark	Social Democrat, Venstre, Conservative, Radical Venstre
Iceland	Independence, Progressive, Peoples Alliance, Social Democrat
Sweden	Social Democrat, Center, Liberal, Conservative
Netherlands	Catholic Peoples, Labor, Liberal, ARP, CHU, Communist
Luxembourg	Christian Social, Socialist Labor, Democratic, Communist
Ecuador	Velasquistas, Conservative, Radical Liberal, Socialist, CFP
Peru	Ordiistas, Christian Democrat, APRA, Popular Action, MDP
Uruguay	Colorados, Blancos
Venezuela	URD, COPEI, AD
Guatemala	MDN, Christian Democrat, Revolutionary, PRDN
Burma	Stable AFPFL, Clean SFPFL, NUF
Malaya	UMNO, MCA, MIC, PMIC
Lebanon	Progressive Socialist, Constitutionalist, Phalanges, National Bloc
Turkey	Republican, Democratic
Dahomey	PRD-PND, UDD, RDD
Kenya	African National Union, African Democratic Union
Uganda	Peoples Congress, Democratic, Kabaka Yekka

*During 1957–62, only these 28 countries from the larger set of 53 countries in the ICPP Project demonstrated some degree of democracy. Whether a country was 'democratic' was first determined by consulting Ted Gurr's Polity Persistence and Change data, ICPSR Study 5010. Polities neither clearly democratic nor autocratic by those data were included only if they held at least one competitive election during 1957–62. Two subversive parties in Guatemala and Malaya in the full data set were also omitted from this set of 95 parties, which is the same set used in R. Harmel and K. Janda, *Parties and Their Environments: Limits to Reform?* (New York, Longman, 1982).

success has been overly separated from work on party organizational variables such as organization and financing.[19] Finally, this study is important now because it will serve as precursor to a subsequent study with an updated data set.

[19] For studies that have integrated aspects of party organization to performance, see G. Evans and S. Whitefield, 'Economic ideology and political success: communist successor parties in the Czech Republic, Slovakia and Hungary compared', *Party Politics*, 1,3 (1995), 565–78.

This article analyses the effects of party organization on party performance. It is organized along the following lines: first, we present variables that measure three aspects of party performance; second, we introduce the variables on party organization; third, we assess organizational effects on each aspect of performance; fourth, we assess organizational effects on all three aspects taken together; finally, we conclude with a general discussion.

Measuring Party Performance

Unfortunately, the literature on party organization is rarely linked to that on organizational theory, which is based mostly on business firms.[20] Barney and Hesterly recently reviewed studies in organizational theory that ask, 'Why do some organizations out perform others?'[21] One approach, called the resource-based view of the firm, builds on two assumptions: '(1) that resources and capabilities can vary significantly across firms (the assumption of firm heterogeneity), and (2) that these differences can be stable (the assumption of resource immobility)'.[22] Our present study reflects that approach; we assume that parties differ in their organizational features (resources and capabilities) and that these differences, while not immutable, are relatively stable over adjacent elections.

> Although firms and parties are both organizations, do they both operate in a marketplace? Schlesinger says yes: elections are a type of political market, in which parties offer their candidates and their policies in exchange for the votes needed to gain office. In this market, parties gain what is surely their key resource, control of public office ... And, just as the economic market sends clear and unambiguous messages to the business firms concerning the success or failure of its product, the political market evaluates openly, automatically, externally, and with exquisite numerical precision the output of the political party.[23]

Political and economic markets are not identical; e.g., 'the political market operates much more discontinuously in accord with the electoral cycle'.[24] Competitive parties get their 'revenue reports' from periodic elections. Of course, parties use polls to estimate their status in the marketplace, but only votes define how parties fare against their competition in elections.

Most businesses focus on 'making profit' as the main criterion of success, and most parties focus on 'winning elections'. Party research, in the United States and in Europe, typically assesses electoral performance by votes won.[25] But

[20] For a review of this lack of linkages, see K. Janda, 'Cross-National Measures of Party Organization and Organizational Theory'. For a recent but rare attempt to utilize organizational theory in parties research, see T. A. Koelble, 'Economic theories of organization and the politics of institutional design in political parties', *Party Politics*, 2,2 (1996), 251–63.
[21] J. B. Barney and W. Hesterly, 'Organizational Economics, Understanding the Relationship between Organizations and Economic Analysis', in Stewart R. Clegg, Cynthia Hardy and Walter R. Nord (eds), *Handbook of Organizational Studies* (London, Sage, 1996), pp. 115–47.
[22] Barney and Hesterly, 'Organizational Economcs', p. 133.
[23] J. A. Schlesinger, 'On the theory of party organization', *Journal of Politics*, 46 (1984), p. 381.
[24] Schlesinger, 'On the theory of party organization', p. 381.
[25] C. Cotter J. Gibson, J.F. Bibby and R.J. Huckshorn, *Party Organizations in American Politics* (New York, Praeger, 1989); Pomper, 'Party Organization and Electoral Success'; N. Aylott, 'Back to the future; the 1994 Swedish election', *Party Politics*, 1,3 (1995), 419–29; R. J. Johnston and

seats won in parliament and winning control of government are other possible measures of electoral success. Moreover, parties have goals other than winning elections, so different criteria of party performance deserve consideration.[26] Among these are the party's success in shaping governmental policy, its ability to command cohesive behaviour from MPs, and the extent and breadth of the party's activities in promoting its message and attending to the needs of its members. All these conceptions of performance present their difficulties in measurement. Even more difficult is the party's success in shaping public policy, which, although crucial, is too complex to conceptualize and study in this essay.[27] The other aspects mentioned, however, are feasible to study with the ICPP data. Our research will therefore focus on assessing the party's electoral *success*, the *breadth* of its activities, and its *cohesion*. Party performance along each dimension will be assessed with our data set. To illustrate how parties were scored, we will cite scores assigned to the major parties in the United States and the United Kingdom for 1957–62.

Electoral Success

Electoral success can be measured in several ways – in terms of votes won, seats won, and governments formed. We have data on each indicator, but for this analysis we use only 'Electoral Strength', which is the average proportion of votes won in elections to the national legislature or parliament.[28] For the 95 parties in 28 'democratic' countries that held free or fairly free elections, the typical competitive party won 27% of the votes in elections held from 1957 to 1962.[29] We illustrate our scoring of electoral strength, with reference to parties in the US and UK. The Democrats and and Republicans respectively won 54% and 45% of the votes cast in House elections from 1957 to 1962, while the British Conservative and Labour parties won 49% and 44% of votes in parliamentary elections during the same period.

C. J. Pattie, 'The impact of spending on party constituency campaigns at recent British general elections', *Party Politics*, 1,2 (1995), 261–73; J. A. Schlesinger and M. S. Schlesinger, 'French parties and the legislative elections of 1993', *Party Politics*, 1,3 (1995), 369–80.

[26] R. Harmel and K. Janda, 'An integrated theory of party goals and party change', *Journal of Theoretical Politics*, 6,3 (1994), 259–87.

[27] For a recent cross-national study of how parties affect government policy, see H. Klingemann, R. I. Hofferbert, and I. Budge, *Parties, Policies, and Democracy* (Boulder, Westview, 1994).

[28] The data also contain indicators of 'Government Leadership' and 'Legislative Strength'. The conceptual discussions, operational definitions, and summary statistics for all variables and all parties in the ICPP dataset are given in K. Janda, *Political Parties*. These three variables are discussed on pp. 33–8. Note that 1957–1962 corresponds to the subfile 'Second' in the tables published in *Political Parties*.

[29] The average party in our study also held one-quarter of the seats annually, and led the government nearly 30% of the time. Parties demonstrated more variation in governmental leadership than in electoral and legislative strength. Of course, votes won is a major cause of legislative seats won. In parliamentary systems (i.e., 21 countries and 71 parties in the study), the number of seats won directly affects the party's chances for heading the government. If the causal path were truly electoral strength→legislative strength→government leadership, the correlation between electoral strength and government leadership would equal the product of the intervening correlations, or $0.81 \times 0.81 = 0.66$. This is nearly identical to the observed correlation, 0.64. The causal chain presumably runs: votes→seats→leadership, which is consistent with the observed correlations: $r = 0.81$ for votes with seats, $r = 0.81$ for seats with leadership and $r = 0.64$ for votes with leadership.

Unfortunately, party success cannot be directly measured by electoral strength, which is affected strongly and negatively by the number of parties in the system: the more parties, the harder it is to be 'successful' competing for vote shares. Because electoral success is relative to the party system, we adjust for system differences by recomputing the parties' votes as *deviations* from the mean values for all parties in that system. For example, the more successful parties – e.g., Democrats in the US and Conservatives in the UK – obtained positive deviations while Republicans and Labour received negative scores. In essence, we are measuring electoral success *relative* to other parties in the system.

Breadth of Activities

Parties engage in activities that have functions for society. *Activities* are what parties actually do while *functions* are what scholars see as the social consequences of those activities.[30] Presumably, the more activities in which parties engage, the more multi-functional they are. At a point, activities and functions become blurred, as in the list of about a dozen functions attributed to American parties.[31] The 'breadth of activities' concept focuses on what parties actually do rather than on imputed consequences of their actions. It is measured by the sum of party scores on two distinct factor-analytic dimensions: (a) propagandizing ideas and programs and (b) providing for members' welfare.

The 'propagandizing' factor contained four indicators: (1) passing resolutions and platforms; (2) publishing position papers; (3) operating party schools; and (4) operating mass communications media. The 'welfare' factor contained five: (1) providing food, clothing, and shelter to members from *party* resources; (2) running employment services; (3) interceding with government on members' behalf; (4) providing basic education in addition to political education; and (5) providing recreational facilities or services.[32] Thus the breadth of activities scale is based on nine different indicators.

Due to missing data on the 'welfare' indicators, only 50 parties were scored on breadth of activities. The mean for all parties was 0.11. The US parties, which did few of these nine things, scored low on the scale (Democrats −0.47 and Republicans −0.67). The British parties scored somewhat higher (−0.24 for both Conservatives and Labour).

Cohesion

In a 'proper' party, party members are expected to carry out party policy, especially in voting on issues in the legislature, where a perfectly cohesive party would vote unanimously. Blondel even cites 'unity' as one of the four requirements of an ideal party, and Özbudun contends, 'the more cohesive a party is,

---

[30] H. A. Scarrow, 'The function of political parties: a critique of the literature and the approach', *Journal of Politics*, 29 (1967), 770–90.

[31] R. K. Scott and R. J. Hrebenar, *Parties in Crisis* (New York, Wiley, 1979), provide a list of eleven functions, p. 2; Wattenberg, *the Decline of American Parties 1952–1994*, cites twelve, pp. 1–2; and Beck subsumes most of these functions under three party activities (acting as electors, propagandizers, and governors) and the 'indirect' consequences of these activities, pp. 14–16.

[32] These two dimensions, which were strongly related ($r = 0.51$), and their indicators are described in Janda, *Political Parties*, pp. 84–89 and 150–151.

the greater is its role as a policy-making agent'.[33] The concept of Legislative Cohesion was operationalized by computing (or estimating) the Rice Index of Cohesion for samples of party votes on issues before the legislature.[34] It proved difficult to obtain the data for computing the index of legislative cohesion, and the index often was estimated from impressionistic judgments of the party's cohesiveness. Even so, we were only able to score 70 parties on their legislative cohesion, so there is considerable random measurement error in this measure of party performance.

The mean level of legislative cohesion for 70 parties was 0.85. The Democrats and Republicans averaged 0.63 and 0.65 respectively on voting in the House of Representatives during this period, while the Conservatives and Labour parties displayed virtually complete cohesion (1.0).

Measuring Party Organization

The conceptual framework of the ICPP Project proposed ten major concepts for comparing political parties. We focus on only four dealing specifically with organization: complexity, centralization, involvement, and coherence (re-conceptualized for our purposes as 'factionalism').

Complexity

This concept taps the complexity of regularized procedures for coordinating the efforts of party supporters in executing the party's strategy and tactics.[35] We measured Complexity of Organization with six indicators: Structural Articulation; Intensiveness of Organization; Extensiveness of Organization; Frequency of Local Meetings; Maintaining Records; and Pervasiveness of Organization. Each of these items was measured on a multi-point continuum. Factor analysis of the items for all 158 parties in the original data set showed that a single factor accounted for 52% of the variance among the six items, which formed a scale with reliability of 0.82.[36] The mean level of complexity for our parties was −0.09. The Democrats at 0.14 and the Republicans at 0.01 were slightly above average on complexity of organization, but they were substantially below the more highly organized British parties (Conservatives scored 0.51 and Labour 0.42).

Centralization

The location and distribution of effective decision making authority within the party are the components of 'Centralization of Power'.[37] A centralized party is one that concentrates effective decision-making authority in the national party

[33] J. Blondel, *Political Parties* (London, Wildwood House, 1978), p. 138; and E. Özbudun, *Party Cohesion in Western Democracies: A Causal Analysis* (Beverly Hills, Sage Professional Papers in Comparative Politics, 1970), p. 303.

[34] The Rice Index of Cohesion and the process of coding parties on legislative cohesion are described in Janda, *Political Parties*, pp. 118–19.

[35] Janda, *Political Parties*, pp. 98–107.

[36] Janda, *Political Parties*, p. 152. All reliability coefficients reported are Cronbach's alpha. All scales were formed after the items were standardization into z-scores and summed.

[37] Janda, *Political Parties*, pp. 108–17.

organs. We tapped the locus of power within a party with eight indicators: Nationalization of Structure; Selecting the National Leader; Selecting Parliamentary Candidates; Allocating Funds; Formulating Policy; Controlling Communications; Administering Discipline; and Leadership Concentration. These items were also scored on a multi-point continuum, factor analysed, and combined into a composite scale with reliability of 0.83.[38] The mean centralization score was −0.14. The Democrats and Republicans were among the least centralized parties in the world, scoring −1.48 and −1.41 respectively – far below the British parties (Conservatives scored 0.41 and Labour 0.21).[39]

Involvement

'Involvement' assesses the extent to which party activists or militants are psychologically committed to the party and work to further the party's objectives.[40] This concept was indicated with five items – Membership Requirements; Membership Participation; Material Incentives; Purposive Incentives; and Doctrinism. These items were also factor analysed and subjected to the same procedures for scale construction, resulting in an Involvement scale with a reliability of 0.78.[41] The mean was −0.04 for all parties. As expected, activists in both the Democratic and Republican parties had low levels of involvement in furthering party objectives, each rating only −0.77. Participation in the Conservative and Labour parties, featured higher levels of involvement (−0.20 and 0.20), with greater involvement shown within the Labour party.

Factionalism

The 'Factionalism' concept captures four sources of intraparty disputes: Ideology, Issues, Leadership, and Strategies or Tactics. Each type of factionalism was scored on a 7-point continuum ranging from 0 (the basis of division was not subject to debate or disagreement among party leaders) to 6 (the matter created a 'large' faction within the party with some formal organization of its own or provoked a split after the beginning of the period). Factionalism of one type tends to spill over into another type, and these four items formed a scale with reliability of 0.71.[42] In the US, suffice it to say that the Democrats were scored higher for ideological and issue factionalism, while Republicans were more factionalized on leadership and strategy. In the UK, the Labour Party was rated as more factionalized than the Conservative Party on every indicator.

Factionalism is certainly an aspect of party organization, but it differs from the other concepts – complexity, centralization, and involvement. Given a particular political environment and their unique goals, parties presumably determine their appropriate levels of complexity, centralization, and involvement. They do not ordinarily settle upon an 'appropriate' amount of factionalism, which occurs in spite of organizational intentions rather than because of

[38] Janda, *Political Parties*, p. 153.

[39] Note that complexity and centralization are quite different concepts, and the two scales are virtually unrelated ($r = -0.10$) for our set of parties.

[40] Janda, *Political Parties*, pp. 126–32.

[41] Janda, *Political Parties*, p. 154.

[42] See Janda, *Political Parties*, pp. 109–23, for a discussion of these indicators. Note that this four-item factionalism scale differs from the five-item coherence scale discussed on page 154.

them. Because factionalism is not a matter of choice, the variable will be employed only when it helps explain performance.

Organizational Effects on Each Aspect of Performance

In theorizing about the relationship of party organization and performance, we must be clear on our assumption of causality. For example, do we assume that high complexity, low centralization, and low involvement *cause* electoral success? *Or*, do successful parties develop more complex organizations, become more decentralized through expansion, and sacrifice the psychological involvement of their members? Clearly, there is feedback in the relationship, but like most scholars we assume that organization causes performance, not the other way around.[43] Inquiring further into the direction of causality is the task for another study with a different design. Recall also that we are dealing with party organization and performance at national, not sub-national, units. Up to now, there has been no firm evidence that organizational traits and party performance are significantly related at the national level.

Assessing Effects on Electoral Success

Any theoretically complete explanation of party success in winning votes must involve such critical factors as the parties' positions on issues, the voters' attitudes toward party policies, the state of the economy, and the parties' traditional bases of social support. Our analysis includes *none* of these factors, so our explanatory model will certainly be incomplete.[44] Seeking *the* causally correct model of political phenomena is, like pursuing the Holy Grail, inherently elusive. Causal models improve by a process of correcting theoretical errors and omissions through continuing research. Our goal is not to provide a complete explanation of electoral success but to determine whether organizational factors *alone* have significant effects – and whether their apparent empirical effects make theoretical sense. Later, however, we will include institutional factors to tease out additional effects of organization.

The theory that guides our inquiry comes from several sources. The effect of complexity on electoral success is treated in the empirical research literature cited above. Studies of party organizational activity to mobilize voters were concerned closely with what we have called 'organizational complexity'. This yields our first proposition:

H1: *The greater the complexity, the greater the electoral success.*

There is no scholarly consensus about the effect of the next concept, centralization of power, on electoral success. Some major non-quantitative studies theorize that centralized parties are also more successful in mobilizing voters. Certainly this figured in Duverger's explanation of the superiority of 'modern' mass-membership organizations, adopted by leftist parties, over the loose

---

[43] As Pomper says, 'organization must be regarded as the independent variable and electoral success as the dependent variable', in 'Party Organization and Electoral Success', p. 190.

[44] In more formal terms, our explanatory model of electoral success is incompletely specified. See M. S. Lewis-Beck, *Applied Regression: an Introduction* (Beverly Hills, Sage Quantitative Applications in the Social Sciences, No. 22, 1980), pp. 26–7, for a brief, straightforward explanation of specification error.

caucus-type organizations of older, more conservative parties.[45] In contrast, Epstein argued that modern technology favored rightist parties that could afford to campaign via television. The counter-organizational tendencies he saw in the 'new' modern party rejected only the *complexity* or mass-membership aspect of leftist organization, not centralization of power. Indeed, Epstein believed that the small membership and less complex parties 'made it easier to impose a central and an efficient direction of campaigns by professionals'.[46]

On the other hand, some scholars have stressed campaign advantages from the *decentralization* of power, which enables parties to capitalize on local environmental conditions.[47] This argument appeared in Agranoff's early analysis of the 'new style' in election campaigns and is echoed in some modern explanations of the 'decline of parties'.[48] Reflecting this more recent argument, our second proposition is:

H2: *The less the centralization, the greater the electoral success.*

Conventional parties' wisdom says that 'pragmatic' parties are more successful in elections than 'doctrinaire' parties, which are reluctant to bend principles to win votes.[49] In 1964, many Republicans worried that nominating the right-wing candidate, Barry Goldwater, would cost the presidential election. In 1972, many Democrats opposed nominating the left-wing favorite, George McGovern, for the same reason. For both groups, the folklore was vindicated. Kirchheimer saw a tendency to abandon doctrinaire involvement in favor of electoral rewards in the 'catch-all' party, which collected votes from socially diverse groups by adopting policies to fit their interests.[50] In our terminology, the relevant proposition becomes:

H3: *The less the involvement, the greater the electoral success.*

The data in Table 2 support the argument that variations in party organization do indeed affect electoral success. About 20% of the variance (R square) in relative electoral strength can be attributed simply to differences in complexity, centralization, and involvement – without taking into account the state of the economy, political personalities, or other important electoral factors. If we assume that these organizational variables pertain mainly to 'the party on ground' that helps mobilize the electorate, we would expect such results.[51] However, the organizational effects are not entirely as hypothesized. While

[45] Duverger, *Political Parties*, p. 25.

[46] L. D. Epstein, *Political Parties in Western Democracies* (New York, Praeger, 1967), p. 258.

[47] R. J. Huckshorn, *Party Leadership in the States* (Cambridge, University of Massachusetts Press, 1976), p. 265.

[48] Agranoff, *The New Style in Election Campaigns*, 2nd ed. (Boston, Holbrook, 1976); A. R. Gitelson, M. M. Conway, and F. B. Feigert, *American Political Parties: Stability and Change* (Boston, Houghton Mifflin, 1984); S. E. Frantzich, *Political Parties in the Technological Age* (White Plains, New York, Longman, 1989); and M. P. Wattenberg, *The Decline of American Political Parties 1952–1994* (Cambridge MA, Harvard University Press, 1996).

[49] But for a different argument, see A. A. Etzioni, *A Comparative Analysis of Complex Organizations* (New York, Free, 1975), pp. 8–9.

[50] O. Kirchheimer, 'The Transformation of the Western European Party System', in J. Lapolombara and M. Weiner (eds), *Political Parties and Political Development* (Princeton, New Jersey, Princeton University Press, 1966), p. 190.

[51] R.S. Katz and P. Mair, 'The Evolution of Party Organizations in Europe: Three Faces of Party Organization', in W. J. Crotty (ed.), *Political Parties in a Changing Age*, special issue of the *American Review of Politics*, 14 (1994), 593–617.

TABLE 2. Effects of Organization on Electoral Success

Variables	Intercorrelation matrix			Regression equation			
	Elec. St.	Complexity	Centralization	B	Std. err. B	Beta	T*
Elect. Strength							
Complexity	0.15			0.07	0.02	0.42	0.000
Centralization	0.13	−0.10		0.04	0.02	0.20	0.037
Involvement	−0.28	0.50	0.06	−0.09	0.02	−0.50	0.000
			(Constant)	0.01	0.01		0.492

N of parties = 92.
Adjusted $R^2 = 0.20$.
*Two-tailed significance test.

complexity increases electoral success and involvement decreases it as predicted, contrary to expectation centralization also increases success. This finding supports Duverger-style arguments for party centralization over later arguments for decentralization in campaigning. But it may only hold for the 1957–62 period, which predates the impact of television on elections in most of the nations covered. In sum, the manner in which parties are organized does relate to party performance at the polls. Involvement of party members in the broader purposes of the party has a significant negative effect on electoral success, meaning that pragmatic parties do indeed win more votes. Well-organized (i.e., more complex and more centralized) parties also do better in elections. The beta coefficients in the regression analysis demonstrate that, when the other two factors were controlled, each organizational variable had a stronger effect on electoral strength than suggested by their simple correlations.

These findings shed no light on questions about alternative forms of party performance. For example, do parties with greater involvement of their members do better on other aspects of performance? Do they spend their members' energies in activities *beyond* electioneering? We turn to the concept of 'Breadth of Activities' for a partial answer.

Assessing Effects on Breadth of Activities

To construct a 'complete' explanation of party efforts in propagandizing their ideas and programs and providing for members' welfare, one might cite the type and intensity of the party ideology, the economic condition of the party's supporters, the nature of the competition the party faced from other parties, and the social welfare role assumed by the government itself. In attempting to explain parties' reliance on propaganda and welfare activities using only organizational characteristics, we again rely on only a few factors theoretically important. As before, we seek only to determine what proportion of the variance in breadth of party activities can be attributed to organizational characteristics in theoretically sensible ways.

The basic theory underlying this analysis was expressed in different terms by several scholars during or soon after the 'golden age' of parties. Duverger wrote of variations in the 'nature' of participation within parties, some of which were 'communities' or even 'orders' instead of mere 'associations'.[52] Neumann distinguished between the parties of 'individual representation' and those of 'social integration', which take over a good part of their members' social existence.[53] Blondel contrasted 'representative' and 'mobilizing' parties.[54] All these authors separated parties which were exclusively vehicles for electing candidates to government office from those which did not confine their activities to election campaigns but conducted continuous campaigns of political education and attended to the social needs of their supporters. The general argument was that the broader the scope of party activities, the greater the need for 'strong' party organization and the more involved members are in party life. Limitations on organizational complexity, centralization, and involvement constituted limits to party activities. Translated into concepts in the ICPP Project, the proposition to be tested is

H4: *The greater the complexity, centralization, and involvement, the broader the scope of party activities.*

The data in Table 3 generally support the proposition. Complexity, centralization, and involvement all display simple correlations with breadth of activities from 0.42 to 0.58. Moreover, the multiple regression analysis explains 44% of the variance, with all of the Betas in the predicted direction (0.41, 0.31, and 0.15, respectively). However, only complexity and centralization have significant effects at the customary 0.05 level.

TABLE 3. Effects of Organization on Breadth of Activities

Variables	Intercorrelation Matrix			Regression Equation			
	Breadth of Activities	Complexity	Centralization	B	Std. Error	Sig.	T*
Breadth of Activities							
Complexity	0.58			0.48	0.12	0.47	0.000
Centralization	0.42	0.10		0.32	0.12	0.31	0.009
Involvement	0.49	0.48	0.36	0.18		0.14	0.243
			(Constant)	0.10	0.08		0.212

N of Parties = 50.
Adjusted $R^2 = 0.44$.
*Two-tailed significance test.

Assessing Effects on Legislative Cohesion

Özbudun carefully studied the factors in party organization thought to be important for explaining the voting cohesion of parties in parliament. He cites 'strong party organization' (our 'complexity'), 'central control' of discipline and nominations (our centralization), and the party's 'social integrationist

[52] Duverger, *Political Parties*, p. 124.
[53] S. Neumann, 'Towards a Comparative Study of Political Parties', in S. Neumann (ed.), *Modern Political Parties* (Chicago, University of Chicago Press, 1966), pp. 404–5.
[54] Blondel, *Political Parties*, p. 22.

character' (our 'involvement').[55] Other studies of voting behaviour in the US Congress and in other countries have also cited high factionalism.[56] These considerations lead to the hypothesis:

> H5: *Legislative cohesion is increased by complexity, centralization, and involvement – but decreased by factionalism.*

To test H5, legislative cohesion was regressed on all four organizational characteristics. The results (not shown here) are unsatisfying. For all 70 parties scored on this variable, the adjusted R-square is only 0.19, and complexity and factionalism are the only significant variables. This is the time when other conditions need to be included in the model for the organizational variables to produce substantial effects.

There are several possible system-level causes of cohesion in parliamentary voting. Kornberg's comparison of party cohesion in the US and Canada also attributes fundamental importance to the legislative structure, confirming Özbudun's contention that parliamentary systems elicit more cohesive behavior than presidential systems.[57] Accordingly, the parliamentary status of the party system will be included as an institutional variable, supplementing our organizational factors. Moreover, trying to explain legislative cohesion makes sense only in countries that have effective legislatures, and 7 of our 28 countries did not have effective legislatures during the period of the data.[58] The revised model holds that party cohesion in *effective* legislatures is a positive function of one environmental variable, *parliamentarism*, and three organizational variables: *complexity, centralization,* and *involvement*. Only *factionalism* is expected to predict negatively to cohesion:

> H6: *Legislative cohesion in effective legislatures is increased by parliamentarism, complexity, centralization, and involvement – but decreased by factionalism.*

The data reported in Table 4 demonstrate the effects of organizational characteristics after features of the parliamentary system are taken into account. Eliminating systems lacking an effective legislature reduces the sample size from 70 to only 53 parties. However, the adjusted R-square is 0.39 and all of the variables are significant at the 0.05 level using a one-tailed test. As hypothesized, party cohesion in legislative voting is positively related to parliamentary government, organizational complexity, and centralization – and negatively

---

[55] Özbudun, *Party Cohesion in Western Democracies: a Causal Analysis*, pp. 325, 339 and 340.

[56] D. MacRae, Jr., *Parliament, Parties, and Society in France, 1946–1958* (New York, St. Martin's Press, 1967), pp. 41–55; F. P. Belloni, 'Factionalism, the Party System, and Italian Politics', in F. P. Belloni and D. C. Beller (eds), *Faction Politics* (Santa Barbara, California, ABC-Clio, 1978), pp. 101–3; and M.J. Aronoff, 'Fission and Fusion: the Politics of Factionalism in the Israel Labor Parties', in Belloni and Beller, *Faction Politics*, p. 136.

[57] A. Kornberg, 'Caucus and cohesion in Canadian parliamentary parties', *American Political Science Review*, 60 (1966), 83–92; Özbudun, *Party Cohesion in Western Democracies: a Causal Analysis*, p. 380.

[58] A.F. Banks and R.B. Textor, *A Cross-Polity Survey* (Cambridge, MIT Press, 1963) defined a 'fully effective legislature' as one that 'performs normal legislative function as reasonably "co-equal" branch of national government', p. 110. Their list of legislatures that did not qualify included Greece, Ecuador, Venezuela, Guatemala, Burma, Lebanon, Turkey, Dahomey, Kenya, and Uganda, p. 174. See R. Harmel and K. Janda, *Parties and Their Environments: Limits to Reform?* (New York, Longman, 1982), footnote 10, p. 94, for more explanation.

TABLE 4. Effects of Organization on Legislative Cohesion in Effective Legislatures

Variables	Intercorrelation matrix					Regression equation			
	Cohes.	Complx.	Central.	Involv.	Faction.	B	Std. Error	Beta	Sig. T*
Legislat. Cohesion									
Complexity	0.22					0.14	0.04	0.44	0.001
Centraliz.	0.36	−0.11				0.09	0.05	0.28	0.049
Involvement	0.08	0.33	0.40			−0.08	0.04	−0.26	0.053
Fact'ism	−0.43	0.17	−0.25	−0.00		−0.10	0.03	−0.38	0.002
Parliament**	0.38	−0.12	0.51	0.28	−0.20	0.19	0.08	0.29	0.028
(Constant)						0.69	0.08		0.000

N of parties = 53; Adj. R-square = 0.39.

*Two-tailed significance test; given a one-tailed test, involvement is significant < 0.05.

**Scored 1 if the parties operated in a parliamentary system; scored 0 otherwise.

related to factionalism. But, contrary to theory, cohesion is negatively related to 'involvement'.

Involvement has an insignificant, but positive, simple correlation with cohesion (0.08). Yet its effect is significant and *negative* once the other conditions are taken into account. Controlling for the parliamentary system, complexity, centralization, and factionalism, the analysis shows that high citizen involvement in the party actually decreases cohesion. *Ex post facto* explanations are suspect, of course, but parties with high levels of member involvement in party purposes may be more apt to have legislators who deviate from the majority on matters of principle in voting. In contrast, going along with the majority may be easy for legislators when there is little involvement by party activists.

Organizational Effects on Overall Party Performance

Up to now, we have been concerned with explaining variations in three different aspects of party performance. Can we provide a more comprehensive explanation which simultaneously involves all three? If so, it would approximate scholars' efforts to 'type' parties according to similar organizational and behavioural traits. Wright, for example, distinguishes between the 'rational-efficient' and 'party democracy' models of behaviour according to their functions, structural characteristics, party processes, and evaluative criteria.[59] For Wright, rational efficient parties focus on their electoral function, engage in limited activities, are motivated by material incentives, employ organization suited to situational requirements, lack formal membership, neglect the policy role of the party, and evaluate effectiveness solely by electoral success. In contrast, those fitting his party democracy mold pursue ideological and governing functions, engage in activities beyond campaigning, stress purposive incentives, feature extensive and integrated structures, require formal party membership, emphasize policy making, and judge their effectiveness in terms of policy results. If we can somehow relate variations in all four organizational variables (complexity, centralization, involvement, and factionalism) simultaneously to all three aspects of performance (electoral success, breadth of activities, and legislative cohesion), we can give empirical content to such trait configurations, which we will call 'party syndromes'.

Canonical analysis provides a method for relating two such sets of variables on each side of an equation. It weights the variables on each side to produce two sets of composite scores and then calculates one or more canonical correlations, which are equivalent to product-moment correlations between the sets of weighted variables. The number of canonical correlations computed is equal to the number of variables in the smaller set. R_{can1} can be interpreted as the maximum correlation that can be obtained through the best linear combinations of both sets of variables. R_{can2} is the next best linear combination of the variables, under the constraint that this pair of composite scores is uncorrelated

---

[59] W. E. Wright (ed.), *A Comparative Study of Party Organization* (Columbus OH, Charles E. Merrill, 1971), pp. 31–54. See also E. S. Wellhofer and T. Hennessey, 'Models of political party organization and strategy: some analytical approaches to oligarchy, *British Political Sociology Yearbook*, 1 (1974), pp. 279–316. Wright's original distinction is still employed in analysing party organizations, witness B. D. Graham, *Representation and Party Politics: a Comparative Perspective* (Oxford, Blackwell, 1993), pp. 57–62.

with the first pair – and so on. Whether the first or any of the subsequent correlations are significant, of course, depends on the relationships within the data.[60] In essence, the number of significant canonical regressions indicates the number of clusters of relationships in the set of elements analysed. Since we have posited two sets, more or less equivalent to the 'rational-efficient' versus 'party democracy' distinction, we expect two groupings from the canonical analysis.

Our canonical analysis of organizational characteristics and party perform-ance is guided by the theory discussed above. To simplify the interpretation of the results, we dropped the two environmental variables, a parliamentary system and an effective legislature. The need for complete data for all variables on all cases reduced the number of parties to 44. Most of the findings discussed above reappear in the canonical results in Table 5. Of the three canonical correlations produced from the analysis, only the first two, $R^2_{can1} = 0.61$ and $R^2_{can2} = 0.32$, were significant at the 0.05 level.

Canonical correlations are essentially product-moment correlations between sets of weighted scores. So the squared canonicals in Table 5 express the variance in one set of variables explained by the other. Each correlation represents a different, unrelated solution to the relationship among the observa-tions. The analyst's task is to interpret these solutions by referring mainly to two sets of values on the computer output.[61] One set is the standardized canonical variate coefficients, which are akin to the beta-coefficients in an ordinary regression equation. These coefficient can be compared for the relative effect of each variable in one set to the composite score constructed from the other set of variables.

The other and perhaps more useful indicators are the simple correlations between the canonical scores and their composite variables. These correlations are called canonical 'loadings' – like variable loadings in factor analysis. Based on the variables' standardized variate coefficients and their loadings on both canonical scores, we interpret the two canonical correlations reported in Table 5 as reflecting different syndromes of party performance. They correspond to Wright's 'party-democracy' and 'rational-efficient' party models, but we prefer to label them the 'doctrinaire' and the 'mobilizing' party syndromes. Whereas 'model' implies categorization, 'syndrome' suggests a measurable pattern of traits that are common to all parties but are exaggerated by some.

Doctrinaire Parties

The first canonical solution is called the 'doctrinaire' party syndrome due to the configuration of canonical variate coefficients on the performance side in Table 5: high values for legislative cohesion and breadth of activities and a negative value for electoral strength. The simple correlations on the far right show that cohesion and breadth of activities correlated 0.81 and 0.76 with the composite score, while electoral strength barely had any correlation (0.12). The canonical correlation squared reveals that 61% of the variance in the

[60] For a lucid discussion of canonical analysis, see M. S. Levine, *Canonical Analysis and Factor Comparison* (Beverly Hills, Sage University Paper series on Quantitative Applications in the Social Sciences, 07-001, 1977).

[61] This analysis was conducted using the 'cancorr macro' for SPSS 6.1. See M.J. Norusis, *SPSS Advanced Statistics 6.1* (Chicago, SPSS, 1995), Appendix A. The terminology comes from that source.

TABLE 5. Squared Canonical Correlations between Organizational Traits and Party Performance*

Correlations with composite Scores[a]	Four Organizational Variables	Canonical Variate Coefficients[b]		Canonical Variate Coefficients	Three Aspects of Party Performance	Correlations with Composite Scores
First Canonical Analysis: the *Doctrinaire* party syndrome						
0.38	Complexity	0.14		−0.16	Electoral Strength	0.12
→0.88	Centralization	0.70	$R^{2}_{can1} = 0.61$	0.64	Breadth Activities	0.76←
→0.70	Involvement	0.41		0.66	Legis. Cohesion	0.81←
−0.28	Factionalism	−0.13				
Second Canonical Analysis: the *Mobilizing* party syndrome						
→0.84	Complexity	1.16		0.73	Electoral Strength	0.79←
−0.12	Centralization	0.03	$R^{2}_{can2} = 0.32$	0.46	Breadth Activities	0.53
−0.02	Involvement	−0.67		−0.54	Legis. Cohesion	−0.33
−0.18	Factionalism	0.07				

*This canonical analysis is based on 44 parties that had valid data on all seven measures.

[a] The simple product-moment correlations between the variable and the composite scores computed in the canonical analysis.

[b] The standardized coefficient of the variable used in computing the canonical variate that generated the composite scores.

→ indicates high loadings that define the two unrelated party syndromes.

performance composite can be linked to the composite score of the organizational variables, for which centralization and involvement are the most important. In fact, centralization by itself correlates 0.88 with the organizational composite. Of little importance in the analysis is complexity, a condition that figured in most of the regression analyses above.

Although involvement has a negative effect on cohesion alone (Table 5), it makes a positive contribute to the doctrinaire party syndrome (0.70), which is somewhat puzzling. The effect of involvement on party performance appears to vary considerably, depending on the control of other variables and the mix of performance indicators. It deserves closer scrutiny at a later time. A succinct verbal summary of the first canonical analysis might be that *highly centralized parties with highly involved activists, moderate complexity, and little factionalism tend to be very cohesive, engage in many activities, but are not particularly successful.*

This analysis is illustrated in Figure 1, which identifies and plots the composite organization and performance scores from the first canonical analysis for 44 parties. Note that the most doctrinaire parties, located in the upper right corner of the figure, *according to their performance in 1957–62*, were the West German SPD, the French and Indian Communists, and Peru's APRA. At the other extreme, the least doctrinaire – in the sense of pursuing electoral success at the cost of legislative cohesion marked by very low centralization and considerable factionalism – were both US parties and the Dutch CHU.

Mobilizing Parties

The second canonical correlation (Table 5) corresponds to the 'mobilizing' party syndrome – so named for the dominant influence of electoral strength, which by itself correlates 0.79 with the composite score, followed by breadth of activities at 0.53. The mobilizing syndrome reflects a second attempt to maximize the correlation between the two sets of variables, under the constraint that the second solution be uncorrelated with the first. The squared canonical correlation for the mobilizing syndrome explains only 32% of the trait variation – much less than that for the doctrinaire syndrome. Nevertheless, its theoretical linkage is clear. Mobilizing performance is related mainly to high complexity (0.04) and very low involvement (−0.02). Centralization and factionalism have virtually no effect. A brief summary of these results might be that *very successful parties that engage in a moderate range of activities – but have little legislative cohesion – tend to be distinguished by high organizational complexity and little else in the way of party organization.*

The plot for all 44 parties in Figure 2 illustrates the second analysis of party performance in 1957–62. The highest performers on the mobilizing syndrome were the Uruguayan Blancos, the German Christian Democrats, and the Swedish Social Democrats. The lowest performers were the Mayalan MIC and the Australian Country party. The Democrats placed in the upper group, while the Republicans placed in the center followed by the British Conservatives and British Labour.

Summary and Conclusion

We believe that our cross-national study offers two main contributions to the parties literature. First, we demonstrate that party organization features do

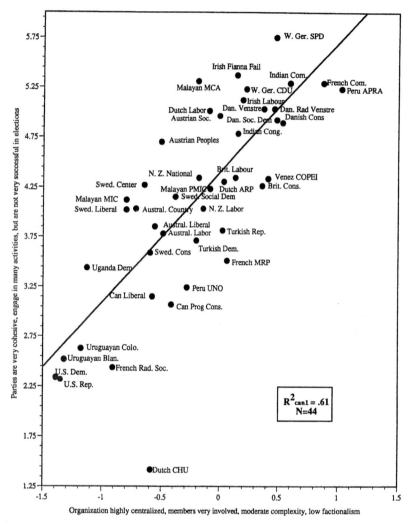

Figure 1. 'Doctorinaire' Party Syndrome: Plot of Composite Scores from the First Canonical Analysis

correlate significantly with indicators of performance, even in a macro analysis at the national level. Most of our six hypotheses were supported in their broad outlines.[62] Concerning the concept of 'party performance', we argue for looking at more than electoral success, and our empirical findings substantiate the case for measuring different aspects of performance. In fact, electoral success was less well explained by organizational conditions than were legislative cohesion and breadth of activities, two other aspects of performance. While this may strike some observers as disappointing, the predominant finding in the scarce literature on sub-national electoral districts is that organization variables

---

[62] Except that centralization significantly increased, rather than decreased, electoral performance.

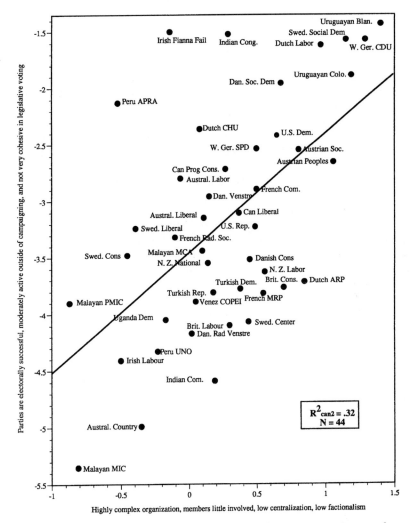

Figure 2. 'Mobilizing' Party Syndrome: Plot of Composite Scores from the Second Canonical Analysis

provide only weak explanations of electoral success.[63] Recall also that we omitted all variables usually thought to explain why parties win votes, e.g., the state of the economy, civil unrest, political scandals, politicians' popularity, and so on. In retrospect, our findings that complexity, centralization, and involvement are better explanations of a party's legislative cohesion and breadth of activities than its electoral success, seem intuitively reasonable.

Second, our use of canonical analysis introduces an empirical method for identifying party syndromes, clusters of interrelated organizational and behavioural traits. Scholars often loosely characterize parties as packages of

---

[63] Pomper, 'Party Organization and Electoral Success', reviews studies that fail to demonstrate much relationship between measures of organization and measures of electoral success, pp. 190–1.

attributes. Duverger excelled in this, and more recently Epstein described 'responsible parties' as 'organized, centralized, and cohesive' – using precisely our language.[64] We demonstrate that parties we call 'doctrinaire' experienced high degrees of centralization and involvement with low levels of complexity and factionalism in their organizations and fared poorly at the polls while maintaining strong cohesion in the legislature and engaging in many activities. On the other hand, parties that we call 'mobilizing' tend to do well in elections while engaging in several non-campaign activities although showing little legislative cohesion. Organizationally, mobilizing parties tend to be highly complex but not very centralized, and they have little factionalism and low levels of membership involvement.

These findings on party organization and performance reflect arguments in Duverger's *Political Parties*. This is with good reason since the data come from the 'Golden Age' of political parties – the time of his writing. But what Duverger theorized, we can support empirically.[65] Whether or not such findings would hold today is questionable. Presumably if parties have moved more toward 'electoral professional' or 'cartel party' models, the more society-oriented variables of involvement and breadth of activities would diminish in significance while complexity and electoral success might increase. As this study has supported Duverger's thinking for his time period, we hope to test contemporary theories of party with more current data in a future cross-national study.

---

[64] Epstein, *Political Parties in Western Democracies*, p. 7.

[65] See also K. Janda and D. King, 'Formalizing and testing Duverger's theories on political parties', *Comparative Political Studies*, 18,2 (1985), pp. 139–69.

Party Families and Democratic Performance: Extraparliamentary vs. Parliamentary Group Power

RACHEL GIBSON AND ROBERT HARMEL*

Introduction: Alternative Dimensions of Party Performance

If to 'perform' is to 'produce' or 'achieve'[1] some intended result, then it is reasonable to assume that most competitive parties would gauge at least part of their performance in votes and seats. Hence, for many students of parties, performance has come to mean electoral performance.

However, some participants in party politics may have other than electoral intentions, and hence may employ other (or at least, additional) yardsticks in measuring results. Indeed, it has become commonplace to assign to parties not only electoral but also governmental and policy goals (or strategies), each with its related means of measuring success: votes/seats, cabinet participation, and legislative achievements.[2] Presumably, a given party actor would consider one or more of those dimensions in assessing the party's performance. It is a premise of this essay that for some parties, or at least for some party actors, there is a fourth dimension of performance that is considered to be as (or even more) important: democracy, and specifically internal party democracy.

In his classic *Political Parties: a Sociological Study of the Oligarchical Tendencies of Modern Democracy*,[3] first published in 1911, Robert Michels focused attention upon this dimension. Its continued relevance was vividly demonstrated in the formation of the German Greens in the early 1980s, when much

* We wish to thank those who have contributed so importantly to this study. We are especially indebted to participants in a workshop on parliamentary party groups at the 1996 ECPR joint sessions in Oslo – and particularly to Petr Kopecky, Knut Heider, and Ruud Koole, who provided much constructive criticism. We know that the paper has been strengthened by our efforts to address their very legitimate concerns; where our efforts have fallen short, the weaknesses that remain are our responsibility alone. We are also grateful to the National Science Foundation, which supported much of this research through joint grants to Robert Harmel and Kenneth Janda, Grants SES-9112491 and SES-9112357.

[1] See, for instance, *Roget's Thesaurus of Words and Phrases*, rev. ed. (New York, Grosset and Dunlap, 1971); *Webster's New World Dictionary of the American Language* (William Collins and World Publishing, 1978).

[2] For example, see Kaare Strom, 'A behavioral theory of competitive political parties', *American Journal of Political Science*, 34 (1990), 565–98; Michael Laver and Norman Schofield, *Multiparty Government: the Politics of Coalition in Europe* (Oxford, Oxford University Press, 1990; Ian Budge and Hans Keman, *Parties and Democracy: Coalition Formation and Government Functioning in Twenty States* (Oxford, Oxford University Press, 1990); Joseph A. Schlesinger, *Political Parties and the Winning of Office* (Ann Arbor, University of Michigan Press, 1991).

[3] Robert Michels, *Political Parties: a Sociological Study of the Oligarchical Tendencies of Modern Democracy* (New York, Free, 1962; originally published in German in 1911).

attention and effort were paid to developing structure that would assure adherence to grass roots democracy. (For more discussion of 'democracy' as a party goal, see Harmel and Janda.)[4]

Though it is beyond the scope of our study and of available data to measure and explain democratic performance writ large, a much more modest objective is within reach. In this study we present and analyse some new (albeit quite limited) empirical evidence concerning parties' varying propensities to structure themselves – particularly with regard to the distinction between parliamentary group and extraparliamentary organization – for enabling (or inhibiting) grass roots control.

Internal Party Democracy

Taking as given that democracy means 'rule by the people', and that it is party decision making and behaviour that would be governed by the people in the case of internal party democracy, there is still the question of which people constitute 'the party'. The range of possibilities is suggested by Duverger,[5] who distinguished among several 'concentric circles' of participants: militants, members, supporters, and electors (i.e. voters). In mass parties, 'membership is taken as the basis of representation', while in 'cadre parties the counting of electors provides the only possible measure of the party community'.[6]

But in either of those cases, it would be the more central and more active participants – members (including militants) in mass parties; militants in cadre parties – who would 'animate and guide' the others, and:

> In so far as the first are representative of the second – that is to say where there is coincidence of general orientation – the system can be called democratic; otherwise this series of concentric circles is to be defined as an oligarchy.[7]

For Duverger, then, the degree of democracy would be determined by the extent to which the party's voters were adequately represented by its members and/or militants. For Michels, whose main focus was upon mass socialist parties, the operative distinction was between 'members' and 'electors'. For him, the members *were* the party; the electors merely voted for its candidates. It was the party's members, then, who should rule it. The degree of internal party democracy would be determined as the ability of the members (not the voters) to control their party leaders and their representatives in governmental offices.

Obviously, Duverger's and Michels' conceptions of internal party democracy[8] – both of which seem quite reasonable – are significantly different from one another, consistent with their very different concerns over democratic performance. Duverger was primarily concerned with what might be called

[4] Robert Harmel and Kenneth Janda, 'An integrated theory of party goals and party change', *Journal of Theoretical Politics*, 6 (1994), 259–87.

[5] Maurice Duverger, *Political Parties: their Organization and Activity in the Modern State* (London, Methuen, 1964; originally published in 1951 by Armond Colin, Paris).

[6] Duverger, Political Parties: *Organization and Activity*, p. 91.

[7] Duverger, *Political Parties: Organization and Activity*, p. 91.

[8] Or as Duverger refers to it, 'the democratic character of the organization' (Duverger, *Political Parties: Organization and Activity*, p. 91)!

'external democracy', meaning democracy for a broader context than just the party itself, narrowly defined:

> [D]emocracy requires that parliamentary representatives should take precedence over party leaders and the members of the electorate over the members of the party, since the electors constitute a larger group than party members, who are moreover included in it. In practice the opposite often takes place: in many parties there can be seen a tendency of party leaders to give orders to the parliamentary representatives in the name of the militant members. This domination of the party over its elected representatives constitutes a form of oligarchy that might be termed 'external' by comparison with the oligarchic nature of leaders within the community of party members.[9]

Michels, on the other hand, was concerned primarily (at least in immediate terms) with precisely that oligarchic nature of leaders *within the community of party members*. Michels' lament was not that voter-elected parliamentary representatives would be controlled by the militant members through their leaders, but rather that the mass membership of the party could control neither their leaders nor, particularly, their elected representatives. Much to his chagrin:

> In a party, and above all in a fighting party, democracy is not for home consumption, but is rather an article made for export.[10]

Because Duverger's ultimate concern was more with external democracy, while Michels' was clearly with internal party democracy, per se, we will adopt Michels' version of internal party democracy and will label Duverger's concept 'external party democracy'. For us, performance on 'internal party democracy' will mean the extent to which party members (or, in the absence of membership, party militants or activists) are able to govern the decisions of their party and the behaviour of their party leaders and their representatives in governmental offices.

Parliamentary vs. Extraparliamentary Power and Internal Democracy

Though the concept of party democracy clearly entails more than just the relationship of party members to extraparliamentary organization leaders and through them, to the parliamentary party group, that triangular relationship was obviously of major concern to both Michels and Duverger, and it will be our main focus here.

Though Michels was concerned generally over the willingness of the masses – even in parties of democratic beginnings and ambitions – to make themselves subservient to party leaders, he clearly believed that it was even less likely that they could control their parliamentary representatives than the leaders of the extraparliamentary organization. While a leader of the extraparliamentary organization – at least in mass parties – owed his/her office to the members, the representative in parliament 'largely escape[d] the supervision of the rank and file of the party, and even the control of its executive committee', since he/she was beholden not to the party's members but to the 'electoral masses'.[11] In turn, Michels' preference for the extraparliamentary

---

[9] Duverger, *Political Parties: Organization and Activity*, pp. 182–3.
[10] Michels, *Political Parties: Oligarchical Tendencies*, p. 79.
[11] Michels, *Political Parties: Oligarchical Tendencies*, p. 153.

organization over the parliamentary group was driven by this perception of party members being attached to the extraparliamentary party while the parliamentary representatives were the instruments of the voters.

Hence, for Michels, the power relationship between the parliamentary and extraparliamentary wings of the party was inextricably linked to the propensity (indeed, 'law') for all parties – even those of a social democratic ilk – to eventually become oligarchies. Even the parties founded by the masses of workers were electoral animals, with seats in parliament (and eventually control of government) as the immediate objective. But with development of a parliamentary group would inevitably come the superiority of that group – with its advantage in skills and information – over the extraparliamentary party. This would come at a high price for democratic performance. The party's militants, after forming the party in the first place, would now lose control to parliamentarians more concerned with pleasing voters than with pursuing the interests and (sometimes more revolutionary) strategies of the party members. The only hope for internal party democracy rested with members controlling their extraparliamentary organization, which in turn would control the parliamentary party group on behalf of the members. Much to his chagrin, Michels arrived at the conclusion that all parties would eventually and inevitably arrive where the bourgeois parties had begun, with deputies and their electors dominating over party leaders and members.

Writing four decades later and driven by his very different concern, Duverger[12] arrived at a somewhat different conclusion, which nevertheless would have offered little comfort to Michels. For Duverger, the history of party development could be visualized in three distinct 'phases', each identified with a particular type of party.[13] In the first phase, parties born in parliaments naturally put the parliamentary groups in charge over the extraparliamentary organs they had spawned. In the second phase – beginning roughly at the end of the nineteenth century – mass-based parties would develop large, hierarchical organizations with potential for challenging the dominance of parliamentary representatives. The degree to which the extraparliamentary wing could actually control the deputies, though, would depend on several factors including the size of the organization and the degree of party alliance with trade unions. The greater prestige and ability of the deputies would continue to work to their advantage and, in the end 'it would not be correct to speak either of domination of the party over parliamentary representatives or of the parliamentary representatives over the party; rather is there a separation of powers between the internal leadership and the parliamentary leadership, and a permanent rivalry between them'.[14] Such would be the case for most socialist parties and at least some Christian Democratic parties. In the third phase, Communist and fascist parties – due more to their 'general structure' and 'general orientation' than to any particular technical devices – would succeed in placing their representatives in government under the clear domination of the party outside government.

Concerned more with what we have called *external party democracy* (i.e. the relationship of voters to their representatives) than with members' control of their party, Duverger could take heart from that fact that for parties other than

[12] Duverger, *Political Parties: Organization and Activity*.
[13] Duverger, *Political Parties: Organization and Activity*, pp. 182–202.
[14] Duverger, *Political Parties: Organization and Activity*, p. 190.

communist and fascist, the parliamentary parties would likely remain dominant or at least become co-equal to their extraparliamentary counterparts. Even for the mass parties with a propensity to place greater power in the hands of extraparliamentary organs, the ageing process itself would eventually strengthen the parliamentary wing. This would occur as the party matured in parliamentary representation, but would be accelerated if and when the party participated in controlling government.[15]

Whereas Michels concluded that historical differences between bourgeois and mass parties would eventually disappear in favour of parliamentary group domination in all parties, and Duverger felt the parliamentary group would become at least coequal (and hence largely independent) in all such parties,[16] von Beyme is led to a very different conclusion. While sharing the view that different origins initially set bourgeois and socialist parties apart on this dimension, von Beyme highlights different trends:

> First, as parties become more established and take over more new functions the parliamentary party is overstrained and the central party organization becomes more important. The greater sophistication of political planning is also tending to strengthen the party apparatus rather than the parliamentary parties. State financial aid to parties also benefits the party outside parliament; in very few countries do the funds flow mainly to the parliamentary party. Further, greater democracy within the parties combined with renewed and more intense discussion on the party programme is also strengthening the party congress rather than the parliamentary party discussions... Elites have become more professional, and this is a further factor which is strengthening the party outside parliament... The growth in the power of heads of government under the modern system of Prime Ministers has also strengthened the party over the parliamentary party.[17]

As a result: 'the balance of power between the central party organizations and the parliamentary party has shifted to the *disadvantage* of the latter in almost all the Western democracies'[18] to the extent that 'the party outside parliament generally prove[s] strongest when conflict flares up'.[19]

So while Michels argued and Duverger observed that socialist parties were moving toward their bourgeois counterparts in placing more power in the parliamentary wing, von Beyme sees bourgeois parties edging closer to extraparliamentary-dominated socialist parties. We can at least speculate on a possible cause for this divergence in the literature.[20] The three authors were writing at very different times. Michels' work was first published in 1911, as

---

[15] Duverger, *Political Parties: Organization and Activity*, p. 97.

[16] Here we exclude from 'mass parties' the Communist and Fascist parties. Duverger notes that while the latter might be better designated as 'devotee' parties, they may still be classified 'as mass parties so long as we remember their rather particular character'. We prefer to treat them as a separate category.

[17] Klaus von Beyme, *Political Parties in Western Democracies* (Aldershot, Gower, 1985), pp. 320–2.

[18] Von Beyme, *Parties in Western Democracies*, p. 320.

[19] Von Beyme, *Parties in Western Democracies*, p. 322.

[20] We should note that von Beyme himself does not recognize this disagreement between Duverger's scenario and his own. He interprets Duverger – incorrectly, in our view – as assuming that 'in every system there would be a gradual transition of power from the parliamentary party to the party organization outside parliament' (von Beyme, *Parties in Western Democracies*, p. 315).

some socialist parties were still struggling to maintain control by the members; his 'iron law of oligarchy' was developed as prediction as much as established fact. By the time Duverger's book was published (first in 1951), he could draw upon four more decades of party development; for him, the critical 'second phase' could be addressed in the past tense. And by the time von Beyme was penning his observations, three more decades had passed. Certainly some of the factors to which von Beyme attributes the shift to the extraparliamentary side had not yet occurred by the time of Duverger's writing. Regardless of the reason for the disagreement, though, it poses empirical questions sufficiently important to warrant more systematic research. Indeed, it is a point of agreement among the three authors that power distribution between parliamentary and extra-parliamentary wings is very important to the functioning of the parties, and especially to issues of internal and external-party democracy.[21]

In that vein, the empirical analysis which follows is driven by two related questions stemming from this literature. First: *do substantial differences remain among competitive parties on the matter of parliamentary vs. extraparliamentary party power?* While recognizing that such differences existed historically, Michels predicted and von Beyme observed a convergence over time, though the authors disagreed on which side would/did ultimately prevail. Second: *to the extent that differences do continue to exist, do they conform to the purported historical pattern of the socialist parties showing more concern for member control (through their extraparliamentary party) over the parliamentary group?*

Before addressing those questions, though, we must introduce our measures for the relevant variables.

Indicators of Parliamentary vs. Extraparliamentary Party Power

In order to address questions involving parliamentary vs. extraparliamentary party power in a systematic, empirical way, it was necessary to develop new indicators and cross-nationally comparable data. As part of Harmel and Janda's NSF-supported Party Change Project, we have produced judgmental data for a number of relevant indicators for nineteen parties in Denmark (9), Germany (4), the United Kingdom (4) and the United States (2).

The seven indicators, which collectively were designed to tap 'the extent to which the parliamentary group personnel and their actions may be controlled by the extraparliamentary party',[22] are, in question form:

(1) To what extent is *parliamentary candidate selection* controlled by the extraparliamentary party?

(2) To what extent is the extraparliamentary party directly involved in the *selection of the official parliamentary group leader* of the party?

(3) Is there a requirement that the party's *MPs rotate out of office* after a particular period of time, and if so, is it taken seriously?

---

[21] This point is made explicitly in Michels, *Political Parties: Oligarchical Tendencies*, and Duverger, *Political Parties: Organization and Activity*, and at least implicitly in von Beyme, *Parties in Western Democracies*.

[22] It should be stressed that the grass-roots constituency of the extraparliamentary party is assumed to be the party members, while the primary constituency of the parliamentary representa-tives (and hence, of the parliamentary party) is the electorate (or 'supporters'). The quotation is from the Coding Scheme, 9/94 Revised Version.

(4) Who, if anyone, is responsible for *disciplining parliamentary representatives* who deviate from the extraparliamentary party's policy positions?

(5) To what extent is the parliamentary group required to *conform to the extraparliamentary organization's policy positions?*

(6) To what extent is the extraparliamentary party (as opposed to the parliamentary group) responsible for formulating the party's *public positions on policy?*

(7) Who is the *primary leader of the party*, officially and in fact, the parliamentary or the extraparliamentary leader?

The first three relate to controlling the parliamentary group personnel, including aspects of both selection (1 and 2) and maintenance of 'amateur status' (3). The last two (including 7 since the party's 'primary leader' is normally the party's primary policy spokesperson) deal with the two wings' roles in formulating and communicating party policy positions. Those in the middle (4 and 5) deal with the extent of the parliamentary personnel's independence from extraparliamentary direction in acting upon policy.

Following judgmental coding techniques developed for Kenneth Janda's ICPP Project in the 1960s, a principal investigator developed multi-value coding schemes for each of the seven variables,[23] and the coder then chose the appropriate codes for each party after reviewing relevant information from multiple secondary and reference sources.[24] Though data were coded for each year from 1950 through 1990, we limit our analyses here to the cross-section of data for the most recent time point, 1990.[25] Tables 1–7 summarize the coding schemes and data.

Candidate Selection

The primary distinction in the power over *candidate selection* is between selection by the party's 'voters' or 'supporters' and selection by the party's extraparliamentary 'organization' (including its *members*). As is evident from Table 1,[26] nearly four fifths of the parties have no or very little

[23] Throughout the process, the intent was to develop 'abstractly interval' coding schemes. In other words, to the extent possible, Harmel developed coding categories with equidistant gaps between adjacent categories. Though these are not strictly interval measures, they may be considered approximations to interval scales. Researchers using the data must determine for themselves whether interval or ordinal statistics are appropriate. We have opted for the former on grounds that any violations of assumptions should not be of sufficient magnitude to jeopardize correct inferences.

[24] The coding procedure consisted of reading all available English-language literature on the relevant topic for the party being coded, writing a summary statement of paragraph-length, and choosing the appropriate value from the coding scheme for that variable. The parties included in the data set are: Denmark's Centre Democrats, Christian People's Party, Conservative People's Party, Left Socialists, Liberals (Venstre), Progress, Social Liberals (aka Radical Liberals), Social Democrats, and Socialist People's Party; (West) Germany's Christian Democratic Union, Free Democrats, Greens, and Social Democrats; Britain's Conservatives, Labour Party, Liberals, and Social Democrats; and America's Democrats and Republicans. Gibson was chiefly responsible for coding these data.

[25] The British Liberal and Social Democratic parties had left the scene as separate parties before 1990, and hence 1988 data are used for those two cases.

[26] In Tables 1, 4, 5, and 7, the reader will observe that provision was made in the relevant coding schemes for differences of a technical and less substantial nature by using alphabetized subcategories of a given numerical value (as in '1a' and '1b'). For most purposes – including ours in this paper – only the numerical codes will actually be used in analysis (e.g., with '1a' and '1b' both treated as '1').

TABLE 1. Candidate Selection: Coding Values and Frequencies

Value	Coding category	Frequency	(%)
1	Party 'supporters' nominate; no pre-selection or post-ratification by organization	2	11.1
2a	Party membership nominates from local committee list; post-rat. not required	9	50.0
2b	As in 2a, but list can be adjusted by the national organization	3	16.7
3b	Party members nominate; must be ratified by some national organ	1	5.6
4	Constituency organization nominates; must be ratified by national organization	3	16.7
5	National committee or congress/convention nominates	0	0.0

Note: Coding category descriptions are abbreviated for the table. The original coding scheme contains values of 3a and 3c, which were not assigned to any of the parties in this analysis. Missing: 1 (Left Socialist Party in Denmark, for which no information was available).

TABLE 2. Parliamentary Leadership Selection: Coding Values and Frequencies

Value	Coding category	Frequency	(%)
1	Selection is by parliamentary group alone	16	84.2
2	Both EPO and PPG involved, with PPG more than 50% responsible for decision	0	0.0
3	Both EPO and PPG involved, with PPG 50% or less responsible for decision	1	5.3
4	Selection completely or nearly so by the extraparliamentary party organization	2	10.5

Note: Coding category descriptions are abbreviated for the table. 1988 data for British Liberal Party; 1990 data for all other parties.

extraparliamentary control. Overall, there is more between-country than within-country variance on this variable, with all the parties within Germany utilizing the same candidate selection mechanism (2a); likewise, both American parties are assigned the same code (1). Internal country variance does exist, however, in the UK and in Denmark.

Parliamentary Leadership Selection

The measure of *parliamentary party leadership* is designed to establish how extensive a role the extraparliamentary party organization plays in selecting the parliamentary group's official leader, operationalized as the party's leader of the lower legislative body. As Table 2 reveals, the parties display little variance in this regard. Only two parties receive codes other than '1' (for reliance on the parliamentary group alone for selecting the parliamentary leader).

TABLE 3. Rotation Requirement: Coding Values and Frequencies

Value	Coding category	Frequency	(%)
1	No rotation requirement or term limitation at all	17	89.5
2	Party rules provide term limitation; not closely followed	0	0.0
3	Party rules provide for rotation after period of time, even if before next election; not foll. closely	0	0.0
4	Party rules provide for term limitation, which is closely followed	1	5.3
5	Party rules provide for rotation between elections, which is closely followed	1	5.3

Note: Coding category descriptions are abbreviated for the table. 1988 data for British Liberal Party and Social Democratic Parties; 1990 data for all other parties. The coding scheme also provides a missing value for cases where public law provides a term limitation for the lower house; this code was not assigned to any of these cases.

Originally we included a third alternative means for controlling deputies' tenure: the requirement of reselection of candidates between elections. After further consideration, we have determined that reselection is not as likely as the rotation or tenure limitations to have been motivated by the party's desire to maintain the amateur status of its representatives. Since the latter is the primary concern of this variable, we have dropped values associated with reselection and have recoded all data for *Rotation* accordingly for this study.

Member Rotation

Michels,[27] in particular, was concerned that professionalization of deputies would increase their influence within the party and make them more difficult for the extraparliamentary party to control. Some parties have tried at times to prevent Michels' concerns from becoming reality by restricting the likelihood of professionalization, even requiring rotation to assure that representatives would remain 'amateurs'. A less harsh alternative is to limit the number of consecutive terms a deputy can hold before stepping aside. Only two parties of the nineteen in the sample provided for rotation or term limitation in 1990. (See Table 3.) The German Greens, who had put in place a stringent rotation requirement once they had gained parliamentary representation in 1983, dropped that requirement in 1987 in favour of a 4-year term limit. The only party to follow the rotation principle, as of 1990, was the Left Socialist Party of Denmark.

Discipline

The *discipline* measure indicates which party wing, if either, can sanction parliamentary representatives for deviating from the extraparliamentary party's policy positions. A slight majority of parties make the parliamentary group responsible for disciplining its members (i.e., 1a). (See Table 4.) Three parties, though, have no discernible techniques for disciplining their representatives and two parties leave major disciplinary action to the extraparliamentary organization.

[27] Michels, *Political Parties: Oligarchical Tendencies*.

TABLE 4. Discipline of Parliamentary Representatives: Coding Values and Frequencies*

Value	Coding category	Frequency	(%)
1a	Parliamentary party group itself administers major disciplinary techniques	10	52.6
1b	Parliamentary party group itself formulates party's public policy positions**	4	21.1
2	No discernible techniques in party rules for disciplining parliamentary representatives	3	15.8
3	Extraparliamentary organization administers major disciplinary techniques	2	10.5

Notes:
*Coding category descriptions are abbreviated for the table. 1988 data for British Liberal Party and Social Democratic Parties; 1990 data for all other parties.
**The fact that 'conformation to extraparliamentary party position', whether applied to individual representatives, as in this measure of *discipline* or to the whole parliamentary party group (PPG), as in the measure of *conformity* (Table 5), is irrelevant when all policy formulation is in the hands of the PPG itself may lead some to treat '1b' as a missing value for both *discipline* and *conformity*. Indeed, we are somewhat inclined in that direction ourselves, and probably would do so for other purposes. However, treating '1b' as missing for *discipline* and *conformity* would effectively eliminate four of the nineteen parties (i.e., the four in which policy is determined completely by the PPG) from the factor analyses which follow. And because our composite *extraparliamentary* scores depend on nearly complete data for each case, most other analyses would be affected as well. Hence, since there is no solution without cost, the more appropriate decision rule is to select the alternative with less cost. Though lack of separate policy formulation by the extraparliamentary organization (EPO) may render moot the question of conformation to such policies, it is also clear, and hardly irrelevant, that this situation cannot put the EPO in the policy driving seat. And that is the issue, after all, with which *discipline* and *conformity* are most concerned. Hence, we concluded that less harm would be done by treating '1b' as a valid '1' than as missing data.

Policy Conformity

Table 5 reveals a considerable degree of variance on the extent to which parliamentary groups must conform to the extraparliamentary organization's public policy positions. While nearly 60% of the parties neither provide for nor necessarily expect conformation to extraparliamentary positions, approximately 20% have rules requiring conformity to the extraparliamentary party's positions, and a like percentage lack such rules but have a 'clear and strong expectation' of conformance.

Extraparliamentary Policy Influence

While *policy conformity* indicates whether the parliamentary group must conform to positions of the extraparliamentary party, *policy influence* measures the degree of responsibility (and hence control) that the extraparliamentary organization actually has over the formulation of the party's public positions on

TABLE 5. Conformation to Extraparliamentary Positions: Coding Values and Frequencies*

Value	Coding category	Frequency	(%)
1a	No requirement that EPO's positions be followed by parliamentary group	7	36.8
1b	Party rules say party policy positions to be formulated by PPG itself**	4	21.1
2a	Party rules require PPG to conform to EPO's public positions; largely ignored	1	5.3
2b	No rule; but strong expectation is that PPG should conform to EPO's positions	4	21.1
3	Party rules require PPG to conform to EPO's public positions; largely effective	3	15.8

Notes:
*Coding category descriptions are abbreviated for the table. 1988 data for British Liberal Party and Social Democratic Parties; 1990 data for all other parties.
**See Table 4, second footnote.

TABLE 6. Responsibility for Public Policy Formation: Coding Values and Frequencies*

Value	Coding category**	Frequency	(%)
1	All responsibility for formulating national policy rests with PPG itself	4	21.1
2	2/3 or more of responsibility rests with PPG; the rest with EPO	2	10.5
3	Between 1/3 and 2/3 of responsibility rests with the parliamentry group	3	15.8
4	Some, but 1/3 or less, of responsibility rests with parliamentary group	8	42.1
5	None of responsibility for making national policy rests with PPG	2	10.5

Notes:
*Coding category descriptions are abbreviated for the table. 1988 data for British Liberal and Social Democratic Parties; 1990 data for all other parties.
**The operational codes for *Policy* assume that policy is made by (a) the PPG and/or by (b) the EPO. No special allowance is made for a major role being played by party supporters (that is, voters). Coders were instructed that if the latter proved to be the case in some instance, one of the standard codes should be used, but the role played by supporters was to be noted in the description accompanying the numeric code.

policy. As is evident from Table 6, the parties display a significant amount of variance on this variable. Nearly a third give the dominant policy-formulating role to the parliamentary group, but just over half make the extraparliamentary party the more dominant partner.

TABLE 7. Primary Leader of the Party: Coding Values and Frequencies*

Value	Coding category	Frequency	(%)
1	Parliamentary party leader officially and in fact the primary leader of the party	2	11.1
2	Parliamentary leader is not officially, but is in fact, primary leader of the party	6	33.3
3a	Power is evenly split between parliamentary and EPO leader, officially and in fact	1	5.6
3b	EPO chair is official leader; & in fact except when country's chief exec. is from party	2	11.1
4	EPO leader not officially, but in fact, the primary party leader	1	5.6
5	EPO leader is recognized in party rules as primary leader, and is so in fact	6	33.3

Note:
*Coding category descriptions are abbreviated for the table. 1988 data for British Liberal and Social Democratic Parties; 1990 data for all other parties. Missing: 1 (British Social Democratic Party).

Primary Leadership

The measure of *primary leadership* is designed to indicate whether the ultimate leadership of the party rests with the parliamentary group or the extraparliamentary organization. Extreme codes are given to cases where one leadership position is both officially and effectively the ultimate position of leadership for the party. As is evident from Table 7, the distribution on *primary leadership* is decidedly bimodal with few parties providing for a sharing of ultimate party leadership between the leaders of the two wings. Nearly half of the parties place ultimate leadership in the hands of the parliamentary leader.

Composite Measure of Parliamentary vs. Extraparliamentary Power

Before combining the indicators for a composite measure of *parliamentary versus extraparliamentary power*, we subjected the 1990 cross-section of data to exploratory factor analysis to verify the unidimensionality of this set of indicators. Principal components factor analysis with varimax rotation produced three factors with Eigenvalues greater than 1.0 (as shown in Table 8). However, because Factors 2 and 3 lack much substantive meaning, we concentrated further attention on just Factor 1. Following standard procedures, we eliminated variables whose factor loadings were very small (with magnitude under 0.30) and repeated the factor analysis, producing a solution on which all remaining variables have substantial factor loadings (above the standard 0.40). That result is presented in Table 9.

Then a single composite score *extraparliamentary power* was developed, consisting of factor scores based on the four indicators. We interpret *extraparliamentary power* as measuring the extent to which the extraparliamentary party (as opposed to the parliamentary group) *controls party policy*, and

TABLE 8. Rotated Factor Matrix for Seven Indicators of Parliamentary versus Extraparliamentary Party Control*

Variable	Factor 1	Factor 2	Factor 3
Candidate selection	0.20	0.17	−0.87
Leadership selection	−0.10	0.78	−0.04
Rotation	0.85	−0.03	0.07
Discipline	0.56	0.66	0.23
Conformity	0.87	−0.28	−0.03
Policy	0.36	0.05	0.80
Primary leader	0.27	−0.71	0.21

Note:
*Mean value substituted for one missing value for each of *candidate selection* and *primary leader*. N = 19.

TABLE 9. Final Factor Matrix for Four indicators of Parliamentary versus Extraparliamentary Party Control*

Variable	Factor loading
Rotation	0.82
Discipline	0.65
Conformity	0.78
Policy	0.61

Note:
*N = 19. Because only one factor was extracted, the solution could not be rotated.

relatedly, the extent to which the parliamentary party group's policy behaviour is not independent of the extraparliamentary organization.[28]

Empirical Tests

Michels noted that, unlike bourgeois parties, socialist parties originated with the intention of keeping power in the hands of the members, and hence with their extraparliamentary organization. Similarly, Duverger argued that it was the mass-based parties on the left, and not the bourgeois parties of 'internal origins', that had the party structure necessary to challenge dominance by the parliamentary group. Michels concluded, though, that all parties would eventually (and presumably by now) deposit the greater amount of power in

---

[28] Though the measure of *rotation* is intended more as an indicator of control over parliamentary personnel, it should be noted that among the nineteen parties, only Denmark's Left Socialists and Germany's Greens had any rotation or term limit requirement as of 1990. Hence, the data for this variable – as applied to our limited sample – actually reflect *any* dimension on which that pair of parties (i.e., the Left Socialists and the Greens) differ from the other parties in the sample. Given the special emphasis that both parties place upon maintaining clear policy profiles, it is likely that *rotation* is at least partially tapping that emphasis.

the hands of the parliamentary group, and Duverger believed that the socialist parties would draw closer to their bourgeois counterparts on this dimension, though likely stopping at the point of parliamentary party group independence (rather than dominance). Von Beyme, while agreeing with the other two on the initial effects of the different party origins, concluded that all parties would eventually be dominated by their extraparliamentary organizations.

With both Michels and von Beyme predicting invariance – though on opposite ends of the continuum – the first order of business must be to test that assertion. Because factor scores are not easily interpretable, Table 10 reports frequencies of averages over the four indicators identified in Table 9. Though not spread evenly, scores do cover almost the entire available range, with at least one party scoring at or near each end of the scale. There clearly is, still, some variance across this sample of parties. With Michels forecasting that all parties would eventually place dominance in the hands of the parliamentary party group and von Beyme suggesting the opposite, it is evident that neither was entirely correct. Of the two, though, Michels' position clearly gains more support from Table 10. With the distribution of scores skewed in that direction, one fifth of the parties actually attained the minimum possible mean score, indicating minimal extraparliamentary organization power relative to the parliamentary party group. Several more parties score in the middle range, perhaps indicating some of the co-equality foreseen by Duverger for mass parties.

Having established that some variance does exist, the second order of business – testing for association with party family – remains relevant. Though both Michels and von Beyme expected the initial differences to disappear with the passage of time, the finding of continued variance leads us to ask whether the original patterns continue also. Duverger joined the latter authors in the belief that socialist parties started with more commitment to extraparliamentary control than had been the case for bourgeois parties, and he also observed that

TABLE 10. Frequency Distribution of Mean of Four Indicators of Extraparliamentary versus Parliamentary Power

Description	Mean	Frequency	(%)
Minimum possible mean	1.00	4	21.1
(strong parliamentary party control)	1.25		
	1.50	3	15.8
	1.75	5	26.3
	2.00	1	5.3
	2.25	3	15.8
	2.50	1	5.3
	2.75		
	3.00	1	5.3
	3.25		
	3.50		
	3.75	1	5.3
Maximum possible mean	4.00		
(strong extraparliamentary party control)			

Mean 1.86; standard deviation $= 0.71$.

among 'the factors determining the influence of parliamentary representatives on a party the origin of the party remains a fundamental one'.

> [In parties of parliamentary origins,] preponderance of the elected representatives is easily explained by the mechanism of the party's development in which the greatest part was played by the members of parliament. On the other hand parties of extra-parliamentary origin were set up without their intervention, so it is easy to understand that their influence is always less there. In fact in such parties there is a certain more or less open mistrust of the parliamentary group, and a more or less definite desire to subject it to the authority of an independent controlling committee.[29]

In Duverger's thinking, the mistrust of the parliamentary party group happened 'in all Socialist parties, whether of parliamentary origin ... or of extra-parliamentary origin', but origins would still have an independent effect. Hence, we are led to two related hypotheses:

> H1: *Socialist parties place more power in the hands of extraparliamentary groups than do non-socialist parties.*
> H2: *Parties of origins outside the legislature place more power in the hands of the extraparliamentary organization than do parties of 'internal' origins.*

(With regard to H1: because our sample does not include any Communist or fascist parties, we need not concern ourselves here with any implications of Duverger's caveat on parties of the 'third phase'.)

For H1, we analysed the data in two ways. First, we treated the independent variable – ideological orientation (or merely *ideology*) – as a continuous variable, with measurement based on another composite of indicators from the Harmel/Janda Party Change Project. Among the issue variables for which that project produced judgmental data from party manifestos are four variables clearly related to the left-right continuum: social services, state ownership of the means of production, regulation of the private sector, and taxes. For each variable, a party was assigned the appropriate integer code from -5 (most left position) to $+5$ (most right position). For our purposes, the four issue codes were then averaged to produce a single *ideology* score for left-right tendency, such that a negative composite score places a party to the left of centre, and a positive score places the party to the right.[30]

Given the polarity of the parliamentary versus extraparliamentary dimensions, a significant negative correlation with *ideology* would be supportive of the hypothesis. And, indeed, for our nineteen cases, the Pearson correlation coefficient is -0.530 (with two-tailed probability of 0.019). Hence, this

---

[29] Duverger, *Political Parties: Organization and Activity*, p. xxxv; see also p. 185.

[30] The Harmel/Janda project lacks issue data for three of our cases: Britain's Social Democrats and Denmark's Centre Democrats and Left Socialists. For those cases, substitute values for *ideology* were produced using regression techniques and expert judgement data from Francis G. Castles and Peter Mair, 'Left-right political scales: some "Expert" Judgments', *European Journal of Political Research*, 12 (1984), 73–88. Ideology scores for the other sixteen cases for 1990 were regressed on the Castles and Mair data for the early 1980s, with a resulting r-squared of 0.65. The regression equation was then used on Castles and Mair data for the three parties to produce estimated values for ideology in 1990. The estimated value for the Left Socialists, -5.48, fell outside the range of *ideology* and was truncated to -5.00. In all three cases, the estimates appear consistent with the authors' own impressions of the parties' ideological positions. Those values are included in the analyses reported in this paper.

correlation analysis – albeit based on a very limited sample – is supportive of Michels' original assumption of relationship, though not of his expectation that such relationship would be lost over time. That is, the left tilts more toward extraparliamentary power, and this pattern tends to hold even in contemporary contexts, suggesting a continued relationship since the time of Michels' observations (although, to be sure, he did not report correlation coefficients).

Given that Michels' assumption was actually based on observed differences between two groups of parties (socialists versus the rest), a comparison of mean scores for the two groups might provide an even more appropriate test than does Pearson correlation analysis (which is based on assumption of a linear relationship over the range of *ideology* scores). Given the polarity of the *extraparliamentary versus parliamentary* measures, a significantly higher mean for the socialist group would be supportive of hypothesis H1. With the 'socialist' parties in our sample consisting of the British Labour Party, the German SPD, and Denmark's Social Democrats, Socialist People's Party, and Left Socialists, Table 11 presents the results of the difference-of-means analysis for socialist versus other parties. The difference is not only in the expected direction, but is also significant at the 0.05 level, thereby giving additional empirical support to H1.

TABLE 11. Comparison of Socialist and Non-socialist Means on Extraparliamentary Party Control

Group	N	Mean	Standard deviation
Socialist parties	5	0.84	1.27
Non-socialist parties	14	−0.30	0.72

Difference of means = 1.14; t value = −2.49; 2-tail probability = 0.02.

In order to test H2 regarding the relevance of party origins, we first categorized the parties according to whether they were formed by governmental personnel or by individuals or groups outside of government.[31] A significantly higher mean for parties of 'outside' origins would be supportive of hypothesis H2. Though the mean for the group with outside origins is slightly higher, the difference fails of significance. (See Table 12.) Hence, we do not find support for Duverger's hypothesis concerning the influence of origins.[32]

[31] For parties that had been included in Janda's ICPP project (Kenneth Janda, *Political Parties: a Cross-National Survey*, New York, Free, 1980), we based our categorization on his data for his variable 2.07, 'Outside Origins'. Parties with values of 1 through 5 were categorized as 'inside'; those with higher values were coded as having 'outside' origins. For the few parties that were not included in Janda's data, we relied on our own coding from information in Vincent E. McHale, *Political Parties of Europe*, Vol. 1 (Westport, Greenwood, 1983), and Francis Jacobs, *Western European Political Parties: A Comprehensive Guide* (Harlow, Longman, 1989).

[32] Since Duverger noted a relationship between a party's being mass-based and outside origins, it should be noted that two of the five socialist parties in our sample (Denmark's Left Socialists and Socialist People's Party) were actually formed by splits of legislators or former legislators from existing parties. However, Duverger himself noted that some socialist parties (e.g. in France) had parliamentary origins, and that such parties would not be as mistrustful of the parliamentary party group as other socialist parties. Yet he still concluded that all socialist parties would be more mistrustful than would their non-socialist counterparts. See Duverger, *Political Parties: Organization and Activity*, p. xxxv.

TABLE 12. Comparison of Outside and Inside Origin Means on Extraparliamentary Party Control

Group	N	Mean	Standard deviation
Outside origins	9	0.08	0.81
Inside origins	10	−0.07	1.18

Difference of means = 0.153; t value = −0.32; 2-tail probability = 0.75.

Summary and Conclusions

We began this essay by noting Michels' and others' concerns over parties' performance on the dimension of 'internal party democracy'. Drawing from the works of Michels and other students of parties, we chose to highlight for empirical study the extent to which parties structure power between extra-parliamentary and parliamentary wings, on the premise that members' only hope for controlling the party's most important business rested with the former's having control over the latter. In particular, we focused upon the proposition that different party families began with different levels of concern for internal democracy, and we set out to investigate whether that pattern is evident today – despite Michels' and others' expectations to the contrary.

Though our data analyses are admittedly based on a small and less than representative sample of parties, the results are nonetheless intriguing. The strong bivariate relationship between left ideology and extraparliamentary power supports a conclusion that socialist parties do tend to place more power outside parliamentary parties than do parties of the centre and right. While this supports the historical premises of Michels' and Duverger's works, it does not support Michels' prognostication that all parties would conform in placing power in the hands of parliamentary groups. Nor does it support von Beyme's position that all parties would develop dominance by the extraparliamentary parties. In fact, our data reveal that there is still substantial variance over the full range of possibilities.[33]

While the data stop short of indicating universality of strong parliamentary parties, they provide no evidence at all for von Beyme's assertion that in all parties the parliamentary group is subservient to the extraparliamentary party. To the extent that parties of the left still provide for more control of their extraparliamentary wings over their parliamentary groups, Michels would presumably be pleased with the continuing possibility for rule-by-the-members, while Duverger – concerned more with external than internal party demo-cracy – would presumably be less pleased to learn that the voters still fall short of total control over their representatives.

We must not end before noting some very important caveats. First, we have dealt here with only two components of party structure; a more complete (albeit

[33] In separate analyses, we examined whether the distribution of 'average' parliamentary versus extraparliamentary scores (with component variable scores standardized by dividing each score (minus 1) by the range for that variable) was substantially different between the years 1950 and 1990, using just the twelve parties that were in existence at both time points. In fact, there was very little change in either the mean or variance between the two time points. This, of course, says nothing about change which might well have taken place in many parties prior to 1950.

much more complex) analysis would account also for possible implications of the party-in-government. Nor have we addressed the possibility that an extra-parliamentary organization may not be controlled by its members, which – according to Michels himself – is a very likely scenario. Indeed, a small group of party officials – perhaps including government ministers – could (and in some cases have) run an organization in oligarchical fashion.

Our data and findings relate to the parties' rules and overt behaviour, and suggest at least that there are patterned differences in the extents to which parties present images consistent with extraparliamentary dominance or parliamentary independence. To the extent that parliamentary parties depend on (or are subservient to) the outside organization is at least *one essential condition* for member control, our findings are relevant to that one essential condition. If party rank-and-file member control were indeed conditional upon mechanisms for extraparliamentary party organizational control over the parliamentary party group, then – from Michels' perspective – at least some level of hope continues to exist for internal democracy in some parties.

Institutional Arrangements and the Success of New Parties in Old Democracies

JOSEPH WILLEY

Introduction

This essay presents a multi-country analysis of the extent to which new political parties' electoral success and parliamentary representation is a function of institutional conditions. One of the most well developed fields of research in political science is the analysis of electoral systems and their effects on party system size. The statements known as *Duverger's Hypothesis*, 'the simple-majority system with second ballot and proportional representation favors multi-partyism',[1] and *Duverger's Law*, 'the simple-majority single ballot electoral system favors a two-party system',[2] are perhaps the most often repeated in political science. Researchers have refined these two assertions, making great strides in predicting the number of significant parties in a system.[3] Yet, there is little information connected with which parties are being counted. In a system that typically has two significant parties, there may nevertheless be a great turn-over in which two parties are actually present. Conversely a multi-party system may see little turn-over of which parties are significant; thus the multi-party system could be more stable than the two-party system. The question that remains to be asked is: Do the electoral institutions that affect the size of a party system also affect the entry of successful new parties?

This article examines how the electoral structure of a system affects the stability of a party system. More specifically, it tests the effect of the institutions that shape the electoral process on the success of new political parties. I have assembled a dataset containing all of the new political parties receiving national election votes in each of eighteen post-World War II democracies. The article explores the theoretical link between electoral structure and party system size. I derive hypotheses exploring the relationship between electoral systems and the success of new parties. Regression analysis is used to predict the success of new parties in winning votes and seats. The results demonstrate the relevance for new parties of the number of legislators per district – district magnitude. The more legislators per district, the smoother the road for new parties.

[1] M. Duverger, *Les Partis Politiques* (Paris, Librairie Armand Colin, 1951), p. 269.
[2] Duverger, *Les Partis Politiques*, p. 247.
[3] See especially A. Lijphart, *Electoral Systems and Party Systems* (New York, Oxford University Press, 1994). D. Rae, *The Political Consequences of Electoral Laws*, 2nd ed. (New Haven, Yale University Press, 1971). W. Riker, 'The two-party system and Duverger's Law: An essay on the history of political science', *American Political Science Review*, 76 (1982), 753–66. R. Taagepera and M. Shugart, *Seats and Votes* (New Haven, Yale University Press, 1989).

Prior Research

During the late 1960s and throughout most of the 1970s, party systems in established democracies seemed to conform to Lipset and Rokkan's 1967 'freezing hypothesis'.[4] That is, with the completion of the industrial revolution, the political systems of the West had reached an equilibrium that, among other things, fairly well blocked entry of new organized political competitors. However, by the close of the 1970s several new political parties, representing new political issues, had actually achieved significant levels of popular support in several national elections. The most thoroughly studied among these new parties has been the family of environmental parties. Inglehart's research on *post-materialism* presents one of the most important findings in this literature.[5]

The concept of *post-materialism* has been fruitful in explaining the rise of Green and New Left parties in Europe.[6] However, Inglehart's work omits the possibility of using post-materialist values to explain the rise of the New Right in Europe. Support for New Right parties, such as the French National Front and the German Republikaner, comes from a highly diversified group of voters, as does the support for New Left parties.[7] Kitschelt has extended the idea of post-materialism beyond Inglehart's unipolar analysis, creating a full pro- and anti- dimension of post-materialist values.[8] At one pole is the libertarian-Left, anchored by the Green parties, on the other is the authoritarian-Right, anchored by the New Right parties.[9] Kitschelt's work on New Left and Radical Right parties examines individual poles of the dimension and the corresponding parts of the 'Old Politics' dimension. Although he has examined both poles of the New Politics dimension, his work has not analysed both ends simultaneously. While important, Kitschelt's work represents only one revision to Inglehart's path-breaking research.

Other scholars have expanded Inglehart's concept to a more generalized paradigm for analysis of new political demands in established polities and the subsequent realignments caused by these new demands. The focus of that research has revolved mainly around the socioeconomic origins of new demands. The new parties are seen as important only in that they represent the willingness of voters' holding new issue preferences to express those preferences by voting for a new party. The research examining the dynamic links between the

[4] S. M. Lipset and S. Rokkan, *Party Systems and Voter Alignments: Cross-National Perspectives* (New York, Free, 1967).

[5] R. Inglehart, *The Silent Revolution* (Princeton, Princeton University Press, 1977). *Culture Shift in Advanced Industrial Society* (Princeton, Princeton University Press, 1990).

[6] See for example H. Kitschelt, *The Transformation of European Social Democracy* (New York, Cambridge University Press, 1994). R. Rohrschneider, 'New party versus old left realignments: environmental attitudes, party policies, and partisan affiliations in four West European countries', *The Journal of Politics*, 55 (1993), 682–701.

[7] H.-G. Betz, 'Political conflict in the post-modern age: radical right-wing populist parties in Europe', *Current Politics and Economics of Europe*, 1 (1990), 11–27.

[8] H. Kitschelt, *The Radical Right in Western Europe* (Ann Arbor, University of Michigan Press,1995).

[9] The libertarian-left are the New Left and ecology parties. Their programmes are typified by their 'libertarian commitments to individual autonomy and popular participation, with a leftist concern for equality' H. Kitschelt, 'Left-libertarian parties: explaining innovation in competitive party systems', *World Politics*, 40 (1988), p. 195. The New Radical Right 'advocates rightist free market economics and 'authoritarian' hierarchical arrangements in politics, together with a limitation of diversity and individual autonomy in cultural expressions', H. Kitschelt, *The Radical Right in Western Europe*, p. 2.

potential voters for a new party and the ability of the new parties to achieve any level of success is limited.[10]

Other studies that examine the role of electoral competition in new party success have focused mainly on the reactions of established parties to the formation of new parties. To capture the opportunities available to and constraints placed upon new parties of the 'libertarian-left', Kitschelt has developed the idea of 'opportunity structure'.[11] He notes that rational activists choose to express issue demands through the establishment of new interest groups or new parties only when established organizations do not respond to their demands. Thus a new party will be successful only where, '*the unresponsiveness* of existing political institutions coincides with favorable *opportunities* to displace existing parties'.[12]

These opportunities consist of socio-economic conditions that predispose people to be receptive to the new group's issues. For example, the presence of an extensive welfare state is found to be more favorable to a non-socialist libertarian-left party than is the presence of a small, limited welfare state.[13] The opportunity for new parties is further affected (and diminished) by the ability of the old parties to coopt the issues around which the new party formed. To continue the previous example, where socialists have participated in government, they are more likely to be viewed as being unable to answer demands of dissatisfied customers of the welfare state.[14] Thus it will not be easy for the Socialists to coopt successfully the issue of welfare reform. A New Right party, however, is vulnerable to the extent that the established center-right is poised to take up the welfare reform issue.

Where Kitschelt forcefully de-emphasizes the potential role of electoral structures in the formation and success of new parties, Rohrschneider suggests that the forces of party competition strongly affect the outcome of New Left demands in political systems. He agrees with Kitschelt that, in order to be successful, new parties need the established parties to be unresponsive to new political demands. However, Rohrschneider's findings imply that where the electoral system shields major established parties from minor party competition it is unlikely that new parties will succeed. While Rohrschneider's article emphasizes the role of electoral laws in the success of new parties, it also illustrates the lack of generalizable research on the role of institutions in the life-cycle of new parties.

Among the few articles to test directly the effect of system level institutional properties on new parties, are pieces by Hauss and Rayside and by Harmel and Robertson.[15] Hauss and Rayside note that, traditionally, the formation and success of new parties has been explained away as occurring only when there is

[10] See R. Rohrschneider, 'New party versus old left realignments', pp. 683–4.
[11] This concept was extended to parties of the Extreme Right by Kitschelt in *The Radical Right in Western Europe*.
[12] H. Kitschelt, *The Transformation of European Social Democracy*, p. 19.
[13] H. Kitschelt, *The Transformation of European Social Democracy*, pp. 19–21.
[14] H. Kitschelt, *The Transformation of European Social Democracy*, pp. 23–4.
[15] R. Harmel and J. D. Robertson, 'Formation and success of new parties: a cross-national analysis', *International Political Science Review*, 6 (1985), 501–523. C. Hauss and D. Rayside, 'The Development of New Parties in Western Democracies Since 1945', in L. Maisel and J. Cooper (eds), *Political Parties: Development and Decay* (Beverley Hills, Sage, 1978), pp. 31–58. The timing of these two essays is of interest. They preceded the explosion of interest in new parties that was largely instigated by the Green party successes in the mid-1980s.

'something wrong' with the system, with little theoretical explanation given. They argue that this 'something wrong' need not be the result of such major societal transformations or revolutions as those envisioned by Lipset and Rokkan. Rather, new parties can also emerge from a changing cleavage, a sudden issue or a 'strain' on the party system. A combination of institutional factors (such as electoral laws) and political factors (the reaction of existing parties) create a barrier to entry into the party system. Where a strain is strong enough relative to the barrier, a new party will arise.[16] Using the same general model, Harmel and Robertson elaborate on Hauss and Rayside's hypotheses by examining socio-cultural circumstances.

While each of these articles analyses the relevance of institutions to the frequency of new party formation and success, neither Hauss and Rayside nor Harmel and Robertson provide much theoretical guidance for linking institutions to the emergence and success of new parties. The former summarize that they expect parliamentary and federal structures to be more hospitable to new parties than are presidential and unitary systems. However, they find that institutional factors have no measurable effect on the number of new parties born.[17]

Harmel and Robertson also include structural variables in the analysis of new party formation, cautioning, however, that, while 'these structural factors may indeed be related to new party success, there is no reason to assume that low prospects for success will inhibit new party *formation*'.[18] While positing the relationship between institutions and the success of new parties, they provide no explanation for their hypothesis. Of the structural variables included in the analysis only the electoral system is found to be related to either new party formation or new party success. Both new party formation and new party success are predicted to be higher in proportional representation electoral systems than in plurality electoral systems. The analysis shows that new party *success* is indeed greater in proportional representation systems than in plurality systems. However, new party *formation* is more common in plurality than in PR systems.[19] Harmel and Robertson suggest that the countries that use single-member districts tend to be larger and more diverse than the countries that use some form of proportional representation. The heterogeneous populations of nations with single-member district systems is claimed to override the effect of the electoral system; and that heterogeneity is the true cause of the unexpected relationship between district magnitude and new party formation.

Theory

Duverger's *mechanical effect* and *psychological effect* are at the core of comparative electoral theory. The mechanical effect refers to the deviations from proportionality caused by the electoral system in the translation of votes into seats. In a purely proportional system, every party contesting an election receives the same percentage of seats as it receives of the vote. The lower the

[16] C. Hauss and D. Rayside, 'The Development of New Parties in Western Democracies Since 1945', p. 36–7.

[17] Hauss and Rayside, 'The Development of New Parties in Western Democracies Since 1945', p. 54.

[18] Harmel and Robertson, 'Formation and success of new parties', p. 507.

[19] Harmel and Robertson, 'Formation and success of new parties', p. 514.

district magnitude (the number of legislators elected from any given district, with the lower limit being, of course, *one*) the more the distribution of seats will differ from the distribution of the vote.[20] With small district magnitudes, small parties are 'punished' by not receiving seats that are equivalent to their vote totals and large parties are 'rewarded' with extra seats beyond what they would seem to deserve according to their vote totals.

Duverger's psychological effect assumes that the voters are aware of the workings of the mechanical effect. Potential voters for minor parties under small magnitude electoral laws are aware that minor parties are unlikely to win any seats. A vote for a minor party would therefore be wasted. With the goal of influencing the outcome of the election, the voter is likely to abandon the minor party and vote for one of the major parties, perhaps as a lesser of evils. While the debate over the strength and impact of strategic voting continues, it is acknowledged that at least some individuals do switch votes so as to improve the chances of casting a significant ballot.[21] This rational choice approach to institutions and voting has also been extended to political elites. A new vein of research has emerged that analyses the calculations of political elites. This research analyses the rationality and knowledge of the political elite and finds support for the hypothesis that the elites rationally calculate the effects of the institutional context in making decisions.[22] This would imply that political entrepreneurs who start new parties are influenced by institutional settings.

Institutions and New Parties

Investigations of new parties requires a theoretical framework that begins with the formation of those parties. The focus of new party formation is by necessity on the political entrepreneurs who are deciding whether to enter the electoral market with a new product. As noted by Kitschelt, in the situation of unresponsive existing political institutions there is a group of dissatisfied voters. If actors with the necessary resources and abilities to begin a new party exist amongst these voters, then they may be faced with the choice of either working for change within the existing parties and interest groups or forming a new party or interest group. These choices are weighted by the polity's structure.

The structure of a polity affects all parties' chances for success, depending on their size and status, through the competition structure. The competition structure represents the sum of institutions that contain the governmental bodies where policy is formed. Potential party formers are most likely to establish new parties where the competition structure is open – where they perceive the greatest chance of winning enough elective offices to achieve the goal of affecting

[20] R. Taagepera and M. Laakso, 'Proportionality profiles of West European electoral systems', *European Journal of Political Research*, 8 (1980), 423–46. Taagepera and Shugart, *Seats and Votes*, chs 7 and 10.

[21] J. H. Black, 'The multicandidate calculus of voting: application to Canadian federal elections', *American Journal of Political Science*, 22 (1978), 609–38. A. Blais and R. K. Carty, 'The psychological impact of electoral laws: measuring Duverger's elusive factor', *British Journal of Political Science*, 21 (1991), 79–93. B. Cain, 'Strategic voting in Britain', *American Journal of Political Science*, 22 (1978), 639–655. I. McAllister and D. Studlar, 'Bandwagon, underdog, or projection? Opinion polls and electoral choice in Britain, 1979–1987', *Journal of Politics*, 53 (1991), 720–740.

[22] R. Gunther, 'Electoral laws, party systems, and elites: the case of Spain', *American Political Science Review*, 83 (1989), 837–58. S. R. Reed, 'Structure and behavior: extending Duverger's Law to the Japanese case', *British Journal of Political Science*, 20 (1990), 335–56.

public policy. When the probability of achieving success seems low, potential party formers will most likely turn to the second option of forming interest groups and pressuring existing parties. As with new party success, this choice can be placed in the context of the research linking the institutions shaping the competition structure to the number of parties in a system. Where institutions work to limit the number of parties with substantial representation, they limit the probability of success for new entrants into the party system. Therefore, they also limit the likelihood that political entrepreneurs will decide to form new parties.

Electoral systems, degree of centralization of government, and legislative-executive relationships associated with a low number of parties all affect the number of parties by under-rewarding small parties and over-rewarding big parties in the translation of votes into seats. It is therefore more difficult to win office, and the opportunity structure is relatively closed. Systems that are unitary and/or presidential, by having limited numbers of locations in government where policy can be influenced, also thereby diminish the chances of new parties gaining influence. Due to the smaller size of the voting population in the sub-national centers of power in federal systems, it is less expensive to earn seats in legislatures. Also, the established parties tend to focus on the national legislature. New parties, with lower expectations, can afford to focus on just a small number of seats in the sub-national legislatures. Beyond the restricting force of their method of election, presidential systems lower the power of legislatures over policy, thereby raising the costs of attaining sufficient representation for new parties to be effective in parliament. Compared to parties in parliamentary systems, parties in a presidential system must have more seats to have the same influence over the outflow of policy.

Institutions affect the success of new parties in two ways. Through the psychological effect, institutions affect the number of votes a party will receive. Additionally, through the mechanical effect, institutions determine the proportionality of the translation of votes into seats. A new party offers no supporting evidence with which to convince voters, especially in electoral systems with small disrict magnitudes, that it has a chance of winning the election.[23] Where the voters have no information as to the efficacy of voting for the new party, it seems likely that they would vote strategically, rejecting the new party in favor of the major parties that have a better chance to win.

The workings of the mechanical effect in the translation of votes into seats does not discriminate between old and new parties. The deviations between the percentage of votes for parties in a system and the percentage of seats that they respectively receive is well documented.[24] The size of the deviation and the degree of under-representation of small parties is a direct result of district magnitude.

---

[23] In the study of new parties in Britain and elsewhere, evidence has been found to support the hypothesis that new parties consciously attempt to use by-elections as a springboard to prove their electoral viability in up-coming general elections H. Berrington, 'New parties in Britain: why some live and most die', *International Political Science Review*, 6 (1985), 441–61. Personal communication from A. Day.

[24] R. Taagepera and M. Shugart, *Seats and Votes*, ch. 10.

Data and Operationalization

A reasonably complete cross-national dataset covering the formation and death of all political parties over any long period of time is not readily available.[25] As with any dataset, it was first necessary to create a coding process and decision rules for the inclusion or exclusion of particular new parties.

Any operational definition of a political party is bound to be controversial. The definitions range from '... [an organization's] self-definition as a political party'[26] to '... organization(s) that pursue a goal of placing their avowed representatives in government positions'.[27] Most researchers avoid the problem of definition by following Janda's lead and establishing some minimum percentage of the national vote that a party must get in order to be included in their research. However, this is not a satisfactory method for the study at hand. It is likely that a recently formed party will receive only a minuscule portion of a national vote, but in the future it may receive some significant percentage of the vote. Therefore, I used a definition of party that is relatively strict. A political party is defined as any group, identified as a party, that campaigns and receives votes in a national legislative election.

The definition of the 'newness' of parties is also problematic. Some view new parties as those that address new issues. Others scholars consider new parties as 'all those that have been added to a country's original party system, however the latter might be defined'.[28] Practically, the beginning of my time frame is World War II. In those countries whose democratic political systems were able to continue uninterrupted through the war, any party competing in its first election after 1945 is considered as new. In the countries that experienced a discontinuity in their democratic experience due to the war, any party formed after the first free election is coded as new.[29] Based on these coding criteria and definitions, 365 parties in 18 democracies are included in the dataset.

The main source of information on elections and the parties that received votes in them is Mackie and Rose's *International Almanac of Electoral History*.[30] Their work provides the broad outline of electoral results. However, they do not include the universe of parties. Parties that receive few of votes are combined under an 'other' category. Additional records, such as newspaper accounts, were consulted in order to break the 'other' category into its constituent

---

[25] Janda's set of parties around the world consists only of those parties that have surpassed 5% of the vote. It contains only 14 new parties in 16 western countries from 1950 to 1978. K. Janda, *Political Parties* (New York, Free, 1980). Hauss and Rayside, 'The development of new parties in Western democracies since 1945' examine only 23 parties in 8 countries from 1945 to 1978. Harmel and Robertson, 'Formation and success of new parties' explicitly include parties that are non-electoral.

[26] A. Day and H. W. Degenhardt, *Political Parties of the World*, 3rd ed. (Detroit, Gale Research Company, 1988), p. xi.

[27] K. Janda, *Political Parties* (New York, Free, 1980), p. 5.

[28] R. Harmel, 'On the study of new parties', *International Political Science Review*, 6 (1985), 405–6.

[29] Presumably, there are different circumstances between new parties as I have coded them and parties formed previous to the first election in these nations. Those parties formed previous to the first election resembled in many ways those parties present before the war that were reborn after the war. Both types of parties, in many cases, designed the resulting political institutions that set the political table for everyone else. Their decisions, made in a relative political void, affected those facing the potential of forming new parties in the newly created political environment.

[30] T. Mackie and R. Rose, *The International Almanac of Electoral History*, 3rd ed. (New York, Facts on File, 1990).

TABLE 1. Countries, Number of Elections, and Number of Parties

Country	Number of elections	Number of new parties
Australia	19	17
Austria	13	30
Belgium	14	24
Canada	14	27
Denmark	19	17
Finland	11	11
France	11	17
Germany	11	28
Iceland	14	11
Ireland	14	24
Italy	9	69
Netherlands	13	16
New Zealand	16	8
Norway	11	14
Sweden	14	9
Switzerland	12	14
United Kingdom	12	28
United States	23	41
N = 18	250	365

parts.[31] Other sources included official publications of national statistical services and secondary sources such as election analyses.

The life-cycle of any political party contains electoral ups and downs. The measures of new party success are the maximum vote percentage and the maximum percentage of seats won. 110 of the 365 new parties entered their respective national legislatures. In 14 cases where the vote and seat measures occurred in different elections, the numbers for maximum percentage of seats is used, based on the number of seats won in the election with the highest vote percentage.[32]

Institutions

Three features of the electoral arena are included in the analysis: district magnitude, federalism, and legislative-executive relations. *District magnitude* is defined as the number of legislators elected from each electoral district. *Federalism* is the presence of sub-national elected offices that exercise a significant amount of political power. Legislative-executive relations, or *presidentialism*, is measured as the presence of a powerful president (0 = no; 1 = yes).

---

[31] A full listing of these is available from the author upon request.

[32] The only exception to this rule is the Australian Democrats. Their highest level of vote occurred in 1977 when they did not win a seat. However, in 1984 they won a seat with a lower vote proportion. The latter is used in the dataset.

District Magnitude

H1. *New party success is positively affected by district magnitude*

'It is by now agreed in the comparative elections literature that *the* critical institutional variable influencing the formation and maintenance of parties is district magnitude.'[33] The major effect of magnitude is in how it determines the minimum percentage of the vote that is necessary to win a seat. Rae was among the first to identify district magnitude explicitly as the prime force behind Duverger's mechanical effect.[34] Rae's simple definition was 'the number of seats assigned by the electoral law to any district'.[35] However, district magnitude is rarely homogenous. The number of seats per district often varies widely. Furthermore, many nations have adjustment seats or a national level distribution of seats in addition to the distribution of seats within electoral districts. Rae's original measure of average magnitude (the number of seats divided by the number of districts) captures neither the effect of heterogeneous districts nor national tier seat distributions.

Ordeshook and Shvetsova use the example of the German electoral system to illustrate this problem.[36] In 1990 German voters elected 662 deputies to the Bundestag. Half of these were selected from single-member districts (SMD); the other half were selected in a nationwide district. For Germany, Rae's average magnitude would equal two (2). However, the German electoral law is more forgiving than it seems. A party could win representation to the Bundestag if it received more than 5 percent of the vote in either the old West Germany or the old East Germany, or if it won more than 3 SMD seats. If it received less than 5 percent, or failed to win 3 SMD seats, its votes were not calculated in the distribution of the national level seats. Thus the true magnitude of the German election system is greater than what Rae's measure would allow. An indicator of the true strategic imperatives of an electoral system requires capturing such legal thresholds.

Lijphart and Taagepera and Shugart have created measures of district magnitude that capture the effect of legal thresholds, adjustment seats, and other particularities of various electoral systems that can change the strategic implications of those systems.[37] Taagepera and Shugart begin with the idea of a simple average district magnitude and then consider the implication of the other electoral laws. The procedure most often used in their calculation of 'effective magnitude' is the interpretation of legal thresholds. They develop a mathematically based interpretation of legal thresholds that equates effective magnitude to $(50\%)/(\text{vote threshold } \%)$.[38]

---

[33] P. Ordeshook and O. Shvetsova, 'Ethnic heterogeneity, district magnitude, and the number of parties', *American Journal of Political Science*, 38 (1994), p. 105.

[34] While noting the number of legislators per district in passing, Duverger focused more on the way in which those seats were allocated. Rae, *The Political Consequences of Electoral Laws*, p. 19.

[35] Rae, *The Political Consequences of Electoral Laws*, p. 19.

[36] Ordesshook and Shvetsova, 'Ethnic heterogeneity, district magnitude, and the number of parties' p. 105.

[37] A. Lijphart, *Electoral Systems and Party Systems*, ch. 2. Taagepera and Shugart, *Seats and Votes*, ch. 12.

[38] Taagepera and Shugart, *Seats and Votes*, pp. 274–7.

Lijphart's measure is based on similar reasoning. However, he quantifies not magnitude, but what he labels 'effective threshold'.[39] The effective threshold is defined as the mean of the threshold of inclusion, the minimum vote percentage needed for parliamentary representation, and threshold of exclusion, the highest vote percentage at which a party is not guaranteed a seat. It is determined through either legal means or by the average magnitude. Lijphart notes that the threshold of exclusion in his measurement is quite similar to the less restrictive Taagepera and Shugart measure.[40] The two measures differ mostly in how they quantify SMD systems. For effective magnitude the assigned value is 1. Lijphart approximates that the effective threshold is 35 for these systems. This would translate into an effective magnitude of 1.43 when returned through the Taagapera and Shugart formula applied above. Both measures were analysed for this article. While the measures are similar, effective magnitude provided better results.

Federalism

H2. *New party success is greater in federal polities than in unitary polities*

Both Riker and Rae used the presence of a federal system as a contributing factor in explaining the Canadian SMD counter-example to Duverger's Law. Riker argues that Canada's multiparty system at the national level is the result of aggregating different two-party provincial systems. The decentralized nature of Canadian politics means that controlling a provincial government is sufficient incentive to maintain even a marginal national party.[41]

The same logic can provide a link between federalism and new party success. It takes a lower level of resources to gain control of, or win seats in, sub-national legislatures than it does to achieve entry into national legislatures. Where a party has a chance to build a regional base, it should be less affected by the workings of the psychological effect than where the structure of competition is not as open for new parties to build regional strongholds. Voters may resist abandoning a party that might have little chance of winning an election nationally if that party has a good track record in local or regional elections, than they are to abandon a party that lacks a track record.

Federalism is a concept that is difficult to measure accurately because of its many possible dimensions. My focus is on the political facet of federalism. Hence, I use a coding scheme based around the concept of *political federalism* developed by Huber, Ragin and Stephens.[42] They use a single indicator where countries are coded as zero (0) for unitary polities, one (1) for federal polities and two (2) for confederal, or extremely decentralized, polities. I have replaced their indicator with two dichotomous indicators. The first differentiates between

[39] A. Lijphart, *Electoral Systems and Party Systems*, p. 12.
[40] A. Lijphart, *Electoral Systems and Party Systems*, p. 25–7.
[41] W. Riker, 'The two-party system and Duverger's Law', p. 760.
[42] E. Huber, C. Ragin, and J. D. Stephens, 'Social democracy, christian democracy, constitutional structure, and the welfare state', *American Journal of Sociology*, 99 (1993), 711–49. Their coding scheme is as follows: 0 = no federalism, 1 = weak federalism, 2 = strong federalism. I have changed some of their original scores that seemed to be incorrect. Where they have Australia scored as 1, I changed it to 2. Also, they have Germany as a strong federal country where I would say its system is more characterized by weak federalism. Unfortunately, there is no satisfactory and completely objective way to score the degree of federalism.

federal states, those with powerful sub-national elected legislatures which are coded as (1), and *unitary* states, those without powerful sub-national elected legislatures which are coded as zero (0). This score merges federal and confederal states into a single category. Secondly, I merge unitary and federal, thus distinguishing them from confederal systems.[43]

Presidentialism

H3. *New party success will be greater in parliamentary systems than in presidential systems*

The basis for the effect of the structure of executive-legislative relations is largely the work of Shugart and Carey.[44] Any presidential office is almost by definition a nation-wide single-member district.[45] This single-member district is seen to restrict the number of effective parties in the same manner as for the legislative elections. The psychological effect occurs with more force in presidential systems than in parliamentary systems. The single person office serves to reinforce the effect where the legislature is elected in single member districts, and serves to introduce the effect where the legislature is elected in multi-member districts. As well, the nature of electing a single office-holder places a higher electoral barrier in front of parties to affect policy in presidential as compared to parliamentary systems. In parliamentary systems political activity is completely monopolized through the district magnitude used to elect the legislature. In presidential systems political activity is shared between the legislature, selected under whatever district magnitude, and the president, selected by an election from a single member national district.

Shugart and Carey do a thorough job of analysing the nuances of executive-legislative power distribution in presidential, semi-presidential, and pure parliamentary systems throughout the world. They find that most of the presidential systems are limited to the unstable democracies of the Americas. In the established democracies covered in my dataset there are not enough cases of presidential systems to reasonably utilize the full range of Shugart and Carey's scheme. Of the eighteen countries in the dataset, only six countries – Austria, Finland, France, Iceland, Ireland and the United States – have directly elected presidents. Of these, only the Finnish, French and American presidents have substantial powers. If the psychological effect is triggered by the mere presence of a presidential election then all six countries should see lower levels of new party success than is found in the purely parliamentary systems. However, if the psychological effect revolves more around the policy powers then lower levels of

---

[43] The reason for splitting the single trichotomous indicator into two dichotomous indicators is largely statistical. The trichotomous indicator assumes complete linearity in the relationship between federalism and new party success. Any difference in the relationship between the steps from unitary systems to federal systems and from federal systems to confederal system is hidden. If the relationship is curvilinear in any way, analysis using the trichotomous indicator may present either a false positive or a false negative to the significance of the relationship. The two dichotomous indicators allow the analysis to look at each step independent of the other as well as the overall difference.

[44] M. Shugart and J. M. Carey, *Presidents and Assemblies: Constitutional Design and Electoral Dynamics* (New York, Cornell University Press, 1992).

[45] The three exceptions to this being the short-lived collegial executives in Uruguay and Cyprus, and the Swiss Federal Council. See Shugart and Carey, *Presidents and Assemblies*, ch. 5.

success for new parties should be found only in Finland and France. Since these do not provide enough cases to fully apply Shugart and Carey's measures of presidentialism, the indicator for presidentialism is operationalized by including dummy variables for each of these nations in the analysis.

The Models

This analysis is not meant to be a complete explanation for the success of new parties. A full analysis of the determinants of for new party success would certainly require data on the resources available to new parties as well as the characteristics of the issue niche in which new parties locate themselves. Rather, the focus here is on the question of whether the structure of the electoral arena has an independent impact on the success of new parties. It is openly acknowledged that there are many theoretically grounded indicators that should be included if complete understanding were the goal. However, each party or would-be party must face the institutions that shape its electoral imperatives.

Lacking an indicator of the number of people who may have a new party as their first preference, it is impossible to determine exactly how strongly the force of the psychological effect occurs under various electoral arrangements. I must assume that, other things equal, no particular country is more predisposed to new parties than any other. Further, I assume that the overall difference in new party success is independent of time throughout the period contained in the dataset.

$$\text{Proportion Vote} = a + \beta_1 M_{\text{eff}} + \beta_2 \text{ Fed1} + \beta_3 \text{ Fed2} + \beta_{4-9} \text{ Presdums}$$

Where:

Proportion Vote: The highest proportion of the national vote attained by a new party

M_{eff}: The district magnitude as measured by Taagepera and Shugart's effective magnitude

Fed1: Dummy variable scored as zero (0) for unitary countries and one (1) for federal and confederal countries

Fed2: Dummy variable scored as zero (0) for unitary and federal countries and one (1) for confederal countries

Presdums: Dummy variables for each of the six presidential systems.

This equation is most similar to the ones that appear in the literature on the size of party systems.[46] It gives the basic outlines of the circumstances where new parties tend to receive the most votes. If the institutional environment by itself can stimulate the psychological effect, then there should be statistically significant relationships between the indicators of the electoral arena and the maximum electoral success achieved by new political parties.

---

[46] Based on Sartori's logic [G. Sartori, 'The Influence of Electoral Systems: Faulty Law or Faulty Method?', in B. Grofman and A. Lijphart (eds), *Electoral Laws and their Political Consequences* (New York, Agathon, 1986)], Ordeshook and Shvetsova, 'Ethnic heterogeneity, district magnitude, and the number of parties', pp. 106–7, conceive of district magnitude having a curvilinear effect, operationalized by taking the natural log of magnitude. In regressions unreported here the linear functional form was found to perform much better.

However, the proportion of the vote alone does not completely explain how much a new party is able to attain the goal of influencing policy. For that, it is necessary to see how the institutions affect the ability to win a significant proportion of the seats in a national legislature. I start with the basic conception of institutional influence.

Model 1s: Proportion Seats $= a + \beta_1 M_{eff} + \beta_2$ Fed1 $+ \beta_3$ Fed2
$$+ \beta_{4-9} \text{ Presdums}$$

This equation measures the psychological effect through both its direct and indirect impact on party success. The direct impact of the psychological effect on the success of new parties is captured in the first model where the dependent variable is the proportion of the vote received. Voters are able to observe the structure of electoral competition captured by the indicators included in the model and are dissuaded to varying degrees from voting for the party of first preference. Using the maximum proportion of seats received captures the interaction between the voter driven psychological effect and the rule driven mechanical effect, in addition to the basic workings of the psychological effect alone.

In the previous model the mechanical effect, the translation of votes to seats, is captured through its interaction with the psychological effect and the error term. I isolate the full effect of the psychological effect by including the vote proportion received by a party as an independent variable. Using the vote proportion as an independent variable controls for the mechanical effect, allowing the relationship between the institutional variables and the dependent variable to capture both the independent force of the psychological effect and the impact of the psychological effect in its interaction with the mechanical effect.

Model 2s: Proportion Seats $= a + \beta_1 M_{eff} + \beta_2$ Fed1 $+ \beta_3$ Fed2
$$+ \beta_{4-9} \text{ Presdums} + \beta_{10} \text{ Proportion Vote}$$

It is not reasonable to expect that district magnitude affects only the intercept of the vote-seat translation. The difference between the translation of a five percent national vote share into seats and the translation of a ten percent national vote share into seats is bound to be radically different between a very proportional system such as the Netherlands with one national district for seat calculation and any of the single-member district systems. The true slope of the translation must thus be modeled as an interactive relationship.

Model 3s: Proportion Seats $= a + \beta_1 M_{eff} + \beta_2$ Fed1 $+ \beta_3$ Fed2
$$+ \beta_{4-9} \text{ Presdums} + \beta_{10} \text{ Proportion Vote}$$
$$+ \beta_{11} M^*_{eff} \text{ Proportion Vote}$$

Results

Table 2 presents the relationship between institutions and the proportion of votes that new parties receive. The explanatory power of the model is obviously not great. Considering that there are important variables that are explicitly

TABLE 2. Institutional Effects on Percent Vote for New Parties

Variable	
Intercept	0.014* (0.004)
Fed1	−0.012 (0.006)
Fed2	0.017 (0.007)
Effective Magnitude	0.0004* (0.0001)
France Dummy	0.049* (0.011)

Note: Standard Error in parentheses. Adjusted $R^2 = .08965$, $F = 9.9622$, $N = 365$, $* - p < 0.05$

excluded, this is not truly a cause of concern. The model itself is significant, as are three of the four institutional variables. Of the presidential systems a significant relationship was found only for new party success in France. Including all of the presidential indicators does not significantly change the results. Therefore, for simplification, only the results with France are presented.[47] District magnitude (M_{eff}) is significant in the expected direction ($b = 0.004$), while the France dummy variable is significant in the unexpected direction ($b = 0.05$).[48] The second federal dummy variable, indicating confederal systems, has a coefficient that is significant in the expected direction ($b = 0.017$). The first federal dummy variable, indicating a federal system, has an unexpected negative coefficient ($b = -0.012$) that falls just short of significance at the 0.05 level ($p < 0.056$).

Contrary to expectations, vote proportions for new parties tend to be lowest in federal systems, while they are higher in unitary systems and confederal systems. New parties are slightly more successful in confederal systems then in unitary systems, but the difference is not truly significant.

The strongly significant coefficient for *effective district magnitude* indicates that new parties are more successful where the number of seats selected from any one district is greater. This signifies that the psychological effect decreases in importance as the electoral system becomes more open to new parties. The coefficient would likely be stronger if some measure of new party resources were available. In low district magnitude systems, political entrepreneurs would seem to be less likely to form a new party at any given level of resources and public support than they would be in high district magnitude systems. Thus, the average level of resources of new parties in low district magnitude systems are probably much higher than they are in high district magnitude systems. In this situation the true impact of the psychological effect is much stronger than it appears to be from my analysis.

Interpreting the causes of the results of the unitary – confederal indicators is more difficult. Under decentralized systems, it is hypothesized that the presence

---

[47] In addition to the model with a dichotomous variable for each presidential system, an analysis was done using a single dichotomous indicator for the presence of a presidential system. It was not significantly related to new party success of any type, nor were the parameters of any of the other variables significantly different.

[48] Models including the dummy variables of the other countries with directly elected presidents were analysed. However, only the French variable was significant in any of the models for either of the dependent variables.

of some local stronghold or a minority that is a local majority should lead to higher new party success than in unitary systems. However, the results show that in federal systems, the middle category, new parties are substantially less successful then they are in unitary or confederal systems.

Examining the party systems of the four federal countries – Austria, Belgium (since 1981), Germany, and the United States – provides some explanation for the unanticipated negative coefficient. The three long-term federal systems share the characteristic of having among the most stable configurations of parties in power, even beyond the lack of success for new parties. The United States – the only genuine two-party system – has not seen a new party with substantial legislative presence since beginning of the Civil War in 1860. There are two electoral factors in the United States which restrict the openness of the political opportunity structure beyond the typical force of an SMD and presidential system. First, the open primary system for candidate nomination allows for the input of novel unmet issue demands into the political arena. The parties themselves are more open to new issue demands and dissatisfaction than they are in systems where influence in shaping election programmes is limited to members of party caucuses and party conventions. Second, the two main American parties, through their legislators at the state level, control ballot access laws. Because of their monopoly of power in the states, the old parties have been able to create some of the toughest ballot access laws in the world.

Germany and Austria have configurations of parties in power that are relatively similar to each other, but they have different reasons for the lack of success for new parties. Both countries have been dominated by two main parties since World War II (the Christian Democratic Union and the Socialist Party in Germany and the Peoples' Party and the Social Democrats in Austria), with significant third parties (the Free Democrats in Germany and the Freedom Party in Austria) that could provide the balance of power. New party success in Germany has been limited not only by the five percent electoral exclusion rule, but also by Article 21 of the Basic Law of West Germany. Article 21 guaranteed the legitimacy of political parties, but only those that accepted the principles of democratic governance. Initially intended to block parties of the extreme right from returning to power, Article 21 has also been used to ban the Communist Party (1956–1969). It thereby limits the possible range of party competition on both sides of the traditional Left–Right dimension of competition. This limits the opportunities of new parties, especially original new parties, to compete. They are either relinquished to a small limited electoral niche or forced to compete directly against the large established parties.

As in Germany, Austria's two top parties have consistently garnered over 85% of the national vote, often (6 out of 12 elections) combining for more than 90% of expressed ballots. Although, it is harder to find an obvious institutional reason for the lack of success for new parties in Austria than in Germany, there may be structural explanation. At the start of the Second Republic, following World War II, the Social Democrats and the Peoples' Party, being the descendants of the dominant pre-War parties, were the primary political forces. They cemented their control over the country by installing the 'party state'.[49] In Austria, party control over political and economic appointments reached a level in the Second Republic seen in no other advanced democracy. The

[49] A. Pelinka, *The Austrian Party System* (Boulder CO, Westview, 1989), p. 23.

nationalization of the economy, education, even real estate, and the control over these by the two main parties made voting against them too expensive for the citizens. Party control over much of Austrian life outweighed the effect of a multi-member electoral system and the potential aid to new party success of a federal system.

Explaining the contrary results for the French dummy variable is more difficult. One reason for the unexpected French result may be incomplete data. French electoral data as presented in election reports or in *Le Monde* include vague categories such as 'extreme left', 'diverse right', or 'regionalist', that make it very difficult to determine the true extent of party formation and success. This has the probable effect of under-counting small, especially new, parties in France.

The other possible explanation for the unexpected direction of the coefficient for the French dummy variable is the peculiar nature of the French party system. French parties tend to be umbrella organizations of relatively auto-nomous political factions more than they are unitary organizations. This is especially true for the three main parties [the Giscardiens (UDF), the Gaullists (RPR), and the Socialists (PS)]. The factions within parties are jealous of their own prerogatives and are resistant to orders from the parent parties. The factions, most often those at the fringes, commonly bolt the umbrella parties and play the political game on their own.

In the dataset, France is coded as having 17 new parties that were added to the original post World War II party system. Of these, only five were original and twelve were the result of either a split or a merger (8 splits and 4 mergers). The party factions that split off from the large parties tend to be quite large. For example, the Independent Republicans (FNRI), which split from the Giscardien National Center of Independents and Peasants (CNIP) before the 1962 election, garnered more than 1.8 million votes (8.4%) in the 1968 legislative elections. All told, 6 of the 8 party splits won at least one percent of the national vote in a legislative election. While the new parties resulting from mergers will naturally be larger, the size of the new parties resulting from splits gives new parties in France higher levels of success than seen elsewhere.[50]

Under what is officially a mixed parliamentary-presidential system, but is in fact a highly presidential system, I would normally expect that even highly factionalized parties would stay together for the sake of maintaining the highest possible presidential vote. In France the tendency towards fragmentation means that parties must coalesce to some degree around the time of a presidential election. In most cases where they do not formally merge, the various factional parties can agree on a common candidate for president from their domain in the ideological spectrum. The presidency in France may itself be the cause of the high frequency of new party formations in France. The need for a majority to win artificially forces the otherwise fractious party system to create alliances that are bound to fail at some point after the election.

Table 3 presents the results for the three models run in the analysis of the proportion of seats. The first model tests only the independent effects of the

---

[50] Whether the overall level of votes for parties involved in splits and mergers is affected is entirely a different matter. For the effect of mergers on the combined vote levels of the parties beforehand, and the effects of split on the overall level of vote received by a party before, and the new parties combined with the source party after the split, see Mair (1990).

TABLE 3. Institutional Effects on Percent Seats for New Parties

Variable	Model 1	Model 2	Model 3
Intercept	0.005 (0.004)	−0.007 (0.001)	−0.005* (0.002)
Percent		0.822* (0.027)	0.749* (0.032)
Fed1	−0.005 (0.006)	0.005 (0.003)	−0.004 (0.003)
Fed2	0.001 (0.007)	−0.003 (0.004)	−0.003 (0.003)
Effective magnitude	0.0006* (0.0001)	0.0002* (0.00008)	−0.00004 (0.00009)
Effective magnitude *Percent			0.004* (0.001)
France dummy	0.051* (0.008)	0.0004 (0.006)	0.003 (0.006)
Adjusted R^2	0.07	0.74	0.75
F-stat	7.64	202.86	179.75

Note: Standard error in parenthesis, N = 365, * = $p < 0.05$

institutional variables. It is a slightly less robust predictor of maximum seats (7% of the variation explained) than the similar equation analysing the proportion of votes. What is striking is the relative similarity of the coefficients and standard errors within each model between the two equations. The second model in Table 2 analyses the independent effects of institutions with the control of percentage vote. The increase in explanatory power (74%) is not surprising. For the first time, the dummy variable for France is not significant. This was expected. The presence of a presidential office has no expected role on the translation of votes into seats.

The third model tests for an independent role of district magnitude while controlling for vote proportion and the interactive effect between the two. The interactive effect shows that the slope of the conversion process of votes into seats is dependent upon district magnitude (b = 0.004). What is most surprising about the model is the nonsignificant coefficient for the independent effect of district magnitude. The controlling factor behind the negative sign is the strong positive contribution of the interactive term (executive independence X percent vote) to the slope of the votes-seats relationship.

Conclusion

The results of the analysis of new party success indicate that electoral systems have an independent effect on the success of new parties. Although my previous findings show no significant impact of district magnitude on new party formation, the findings here provide strong evidence that the stability of a party system (that is, the absence of new parties) is a function of district magnitude.[51] The new parties that do form under small district magnitude are less likely to be successful than new parties that form under large district magnitudes. The engineering of electoral systems by creating systems with small district magnitudes promises greater stability of identity in the actors, major and minor, of the party system.

Federalism and the mode of legislative-executive relations were not found to play the expected role in new party success. In all but the last model, the

[51] J. Willey, 'Institutional Effects on New Party Formation in Western Democracies', manuscript.

federalism variables were somewhat close to significance. A more precisely crafted indicator than the simple ones used here might reveal a significant role. All but the French presidential dummy variables were found to be insignificant, and it was the reverse of my expectations. As others have often found a relationship between presidentialism and the number of parties, it might be the case that moving beyond the set of established democracies analysed here and the inclusion of more cases (including, perhaps, newer democracies) that have presidential systems is necessary to see if the relationship exists in new party success.

Finally, as can be seen from the poor overall fit of the first models, there needs to be some inclusion of the resources available to new parties as a predictor of new party success. Measures such as the number of candidates, the restrictiveness of ballot access laws, and access to media during a campaign would help flesh out not only the strength of discrimination against new parties posed by the electoral system, but also such added considerations might also provide a sharper insight into the true strength of the psychological effect.

Contributors

CHRISTOPHER J. ANDERSON is Assistant Professor of Political Science at the State University of New York at Binghamton. Author of *Blaming the Government: Citizens and the Economy in Five European Democracies* (1995), he is currently engaged in research projects dealing with democracy satisfaction, economic perceptions, and the relationship between public opinion and policy outcomes in democracies. His most recent publication is 'The political economy of election outcomes in Japan' which appeared in the *British Journal of Political Science* (1997).

ALI ÇARKOGLU is Assistant Professor in the Department of Political Science and International Relations at Bogazici University in Istanbul, Turkey. His research includes cross-national investigation of the political business cycle, as well as work on Turkish political parties and development.

TYLER COLMAN has studied at the London School of Economics and is currently a doctoral candidate at Northwestern University. His main interests are in European politics and in the comparative analysis of political parties and elections.

RACHEL GIBSON is lecturer in Politics at the University of Salford. She has published articles on the New Right in Scandinavia and has forthcoming publications on British political parties and the Internet.

GRIGORII V. GOLOSOV is a Lecturer in Comparative Politics in the Sociology and Political Science Department of the European University at St. Petersburg. He has written extensively on the development of political parties and political institutions in post-communist Russia.

ROBERT HARMEL is Professor of Political Science at Texas A&M University. He has published books and many articles on political parties. His most recent research has focused on the topics of new political parties and party change.

RICHARD I. HOFFERBERT is Distinguished Professor at the State University of New York at Binghamton, as well as Recurring Visiting Research Professor at the Science Center, Berlin. He has published widely in policy analysis and political parties. His most recent book, co-authored with Ian Budge and Hans-Dieter Klingemann, is *Parties, Policies, and Democracy*, 1997, a study of the linkages between party election programmes and policy in ten democracies over the post-war period.

KENNETH JANDA is Payson S. Wild Professor of Political Science at Northwestern University. His most recent book is *The Challenge of Democracy: Government in America* (1997, with Jeffrey Berry and Jerry Goldman), but most of his published research is on comparative political parties. He is also co-editor of the international journal *Political Parties* (with David Farrell and Ian Holliday).

MICHAL KLIMA is Associate Professor of Political Science at the University of Economics in Prague. He specialises in the fields of Comparative Government and European Integration. He has published books on Elections and Political Parties in Modern Democracies.

ALGIS KRUPAVICIUS is Associate Professor of Politics at the Kaunas University of Technology and Vytautas Magnus University. He has published *Political Parties in Lithuania*, as well as many articles on problems of democratization, consolidation of democratic institutions, and party systems in the Baltics.

DAVID M. OLSON is Professor of Political Science and the Director of the Parliamentary Documents Center for Central Europe at the University of North Carolina at Greensboro. He has published on parliaments and on political parties and elections in the United States, western Europe and central Europe. His most recent book, *The New Parliaments of Central and Eastern Europe*, reviews parliaments and elections in post-communist Europe.

GABOR TÓKA is Assistant Professor at the Political Science Department of the Central European University, Budapest, Hungary. He is editor of *The 1990 Hungarian Elections to the National Assembly* (1995), and he has published articles on electoral behaviour, political parties, and democratic consolidation.

JOSEPH WILLEY is a doctoral candidate in the Department of Political Science at the State University of New York at Binghamton. He has conducted research on the linkage between electoral systems and political parties. His current research is a cross-national study of the conditions facilitating entry of new political parties in established democracies.

Parties and Democracy

Index